HALF-LIVES AND HALF-TRUTHS

School for Advanced Research
Resident Scholar Series

James F. Brooks
General Editor

HALF-LIVES AND HALF-TRUTHS

Holly M. Barker
Scientific Advisor, Embassy of the Republic of the Marshall Islands, Washington, DC

Marie I. Boutté
Department of Anthropology, University of Nevada, Reno

Susan E. Dawson
Department of Sociology, Social Work, and Anthropology, Utah State University, Logan

Paula Garb
Departments of Anthropology and International Studies, University of California, Irvine

Hugh Gusterson
Cultural Studies Program, George Mason University

Barbara Rose Johnston
Center for Political Ecology, Santa Cruz, California

Joshua Levin
Department of Anthropology, Community College of Southern Nevada

Edward Liebow
Battelle Centers for Public Health Research and Evaluation

Gary E. Madsen
Department of Sociology, Social Work, and Anthropology, Utah State University, Logan

Laura Nader
Department of Anthropology, University of California, Berkeley

David H. Price
Department of Anthropology, St. Martin's College

Kathleen Purvis-Roberts
Department of Chemistry, Claremont Colleges

Theresa Satterfield
Associate Professor of Culture, Risk, and the Environment, University of British Columbia

Edith Turner
Emerita, Department of Anthropology, University of Virginia

Cynthia Werner
Department of Anthropology, Texas A & M University

HALF-LIVES AND HALF-TRUTHS

Confronting the Radioactive Legacies
of the Cold War

Edited by Barbara Rose Johnston

WITHDRAWN

A School for Advanced Research Resident Scholar Book

Santa Fe, New Mexico

School for Advanced Research Press
Post Office Box 2188
Santa Fe, New Mexico 87504-2188
www.sarpress.sarweb.org

Co-Director and Executive Editor: Catherine Cocks
Copy Editor: Margaret J. Goldstein
Design and Production Manager: Cynthia Dyer
Proofreader: Sarah Soliz
Indexer: Catherine Fox
Printer: Edwards Brothers, Inc.

Library of Congress Cataloging-in-Publication Data:
Half-lives and half-truths : confronting the radioactive legacies of the cold war / edited by
Barbara Rose Johnston. — 1st ed.
       p. ; cm. — (Resident scholar series)
   "A School for Advanced Research resident scholar book."
   Includes bibliographical references and index.
   ISBN-13: 978-1-930618-82-4 (pbk. : alk. paper)
   ISBN-10: 1-930618-82-4 (pbk. : alk. paper)
1. Medical policy—Soviet Union. 2. Medical policy—United States. 3. Radioactivity—Soviet Union.
4. Radioactivity—United States. 5. Cold War. 6 Nuclear Warfare—Soviet Union. 7. Nuclear Warfare—United States.
I. Johnston, Barbara Rose. II. School for Advanced Research (Santa Fe, N.M.) III Series.
   [DNLM: 1. Nuclear Warfare—USSR. 2. Nuclear Warfare—United States. 3. Accidents, Radiation—USSR.
4. Accidents, Radiation—United States. 5. Environmental Exposure—adverse effects—USSR. 6. Environmental
Exposure—adverse effects—United States. 7. Politics—USSR. 8. Politics—United States. 9. Radiation Injuries—
USSR. 10. Radiation Injuries—United States. WN 610 H169 2007]
   RA393.H3468 2007
   363.17'99--dc22   2006102477

Chapter 4 originally appeared in *Anthropology and Humanism* 22 (1):95–109, 1997, and is reprinted here
by permission.

Front Cover illustration: Adapted by Cynthia Dyer from image XX-81, Operation Hardtack I, thermonuclear
detonation during the Pacific tests in 1958, photo courtesy of National Nuclear Security Administration/Nevada
Site Office, and GS053033, Goodshot Photos. © 2007 School for Advanced Research. Back Cover: Civil Defense
poster, circa 1955. Image source: Civil Defense Museum, www.civildefensemuseum.org.

Contents

Figures

Maps

Tables

o n e
Half-Lives, Half-Truths, and Other Radioactive Legacies of the Cold War

Barbara Rose Johnston

Half-Lives and Half-Truths: Confronting the Radioactive Legacies of the Cold War examines some of the events and consequences of what many call the first nuclear age—the age when uranium was exploited, refined, enriched, and used to end a world war and fight a cold war. It is a book written by anthropologists who study the culture and history of science, document the environmental health problems that are the legacy of the Cold War–era nuclear war machine, and assist communities in their struggles to secure information, accountability, and meaningful remedy. In essays addressing the US and former Soviet nuclear war machines, contributors outline some of the human and environmental impacts of preparing for nuclear war and the related problems created by the heavy hand of the security state. Contributors also explore the dynamic tensions that structure human response to such problematic radioactive realities: How do people come to terms with their past, and the current and future risks from this past, and find ways to carry on? What strategies are employed to cope? What efforts are taken to secure meaningful remedy? What actions do people—survivors, families, communities, scientists, advocates, organizations, and governments—take to ensure never again?

The essays and case studies explore the biases and political constraints intrinsic to atomic energy research on behalf of the security state, and the radioactive legacy of the Cold War in the United States and its former territories of Alaska and the Marshall

Islands, and in the former Soviet Union. While these historical and ethnographic analyses of human response to the radioactive legacies of the Cold War–nuclear war machine reflect specific contexts within time and space, collectively they support a number of generalized observations that are relevant to current events.

First, and foremost, for the communities that hosted the nuclear war machine—uranium mines, mills, and enrichment plants; weapons production facilities; military "proving" grounds; battlefields; and nuclear waste dumps—the "cold" war was truly hot, generating acute and lasting radiogenic assaults on the environment and human health.

Second, actions taken in the name of national security have profoundly shaped both the biophysical nature and sociocultural identity of host communities, creating what might be best termed radiogenic communities. A radiogenic community is produced by the process of radioactive decay: its members are people whose lives have been profoundly affected and altered by a hazardous, invisible threat, where the fear of nuclear contamination and the personal health and intergenerational effects from exposure color all aspects of social, cultural, economic, and psychological well-being. Some radiogenic communities are the end result of a geographic location (downwind from or adjacent to mines, mills, nuclear weapons tests, battlefields, or military training grounds). Others are formed by occupational exposure as a soldier, scientist, miner, or other worker. For far too many people whose identities have been shaped by radiogenic community membership, the "half-life" nature of radioactive decay has resulted in compromised "half-lives," where people struggle with the degenerative conditions associated with their exposure. They struggle with the pain and suffering associated with miscarriages and the birth of congenitally deformed children, the difficulties of raising physically disabled children and caring for increasingly feeble elderly, the fear of and anxiety over additional exposures, the fear of and anxiety over intergenerational and other unknown effects of radiation, and the psychosocial humiliation, marginalization, and stigmatization experienced by the population as a whole as a result of nuclear victimization.

Third, the ability of radiogenic communities to understand, confront, and address environmental health problems is strongly linked to and constrained by their relative status in society. This inequity, in turn, influences access to information and relative power in decision-making processes. Given this sociocultural dynamic, when governments are forced to confront and remedy the messes they have made, their institutionalized responses (for example, biomedical research, biomedical and social welfare entitlement programs) reflect the biases, power struggles, and schisms in society (cf. Liebow, this volume; Petryna 2002).

And finally, the heavy hand of the Cold War security state demanded—through cultural and political means—control over systems that produced and disseminated information. Control over science and the dissemination of scientific findings allowed the systematic use of half-truths to pacify public concerns while expanding the nuclear war machine.

One of those half-truths is the popular misconception that the Cold War enter-

Figure 1.1. Office of Civil Defense Mobilization exhibit at a civil defense fair, circa 1960. The Executive Office of the President established the Office of Civil Defense Mobilization (1958–61), which became the Office of Civil Defense (1961–72) under the Department of the Army. Civil defense programs were largely meant to pacify public concerns over nuclear weapons tests. Officials used fallout shelter displays at county fairs, posters, and other materials to promote products and actions that citizens might take to "protect yourself from radioactive fallout." Credit: National Archives. ARC identifier: 542102

few of the indigenous, ethnic, and other minority groups who have hosted the nuclear war machine. The disproportionate burden borne by these groups is no accident. Their selective victimization occurs because they live in relatively isolated lands and occupy the bottom strata of society. Their social status is rationalized and reinforced by cultural notions as well as political and economic relationships and histories (Johnston 1994:11–12).

The security state and its control over science represented the primary mechanism used to shape and deliver the calculated half-truths that sustained Cold War nuclear militarism. For those who worked to build and expand the nuclear war machine, scientific agendas were shaped according to military needs and findings directed toward the classified, rather than broader scientific, community. Controlling information meant the government was able to convince the public of the relatively minimal threat posed by atmospheric tests.

In the United States, a key mechanism used to shape public knowledge and opinion was the formal inclusion of a public relations plan as a component of the technical plan for every weapons test. As noted by Lawrence Livermore Laboratory historian Barton Hacker:

> AEC [Atomic Energy Commission] officials in general, headquarters staff members in particular, mostly preferred to reassure rather than inform. Convinced that trying to explain risks so small would simply confuse people and might cause panic, they feared jeopardizing the testing vital to American security. Their policy prevailed. A formal public relations plan became as much a part of every test as the technical operations plan. Carefully crafted press releases never to my knowledge lied, though they sometimes erred. Yet, by the same token, they rarely if ever revealed all. Choices about which truths to tell, which to omit, could routinely veil the larger implications of a situation. (Hacker 1994:69)

A comment by AEC director Willard Libby, in a 1956 *US News and World Report* article exploring whether fallout from atmospheric weapons tests represented a significant public health threat, illustrates Hacker's observation. Libby comments, "The world is radioactive. It always has been and always will be. Its natural radioactivities evidently are not dangerous and we can conclude from this fact that contamination from atomic bombs small in magnitude or even of the same order of magnitude as these natural radiations is not likely to be at all dangerous" (Miller 1986:199). While Libby's platitudes in this popular-press article articulate the informed opinions of a scientist who was not particularly alarmed by increased levels of strontium-90 in the atmosphere, Libby's classified opinions reflect deep and serious concern. In 1953, under contract to the AEC and the air force, the Rand Corporation convened a review of Project Gabriel, first initiated in 1949 to determine the impact of nuclear weapons on local populations (Rand Corporation 1953). Libby directed this study, and the "resulting report concluded that strontium 90 (Sr-90) was the most dangerous long-term, global radioactive product of bomb testing and that a global study of strontium 90 fallout was needed" (ACHRE 1995:637). A subsequent study (Project Sunshine) tested for strontium-90 levels in the human body using bone samples and teeth harvested from stillborn babies and deceased people between the ages of one and thirty. Samples were harvested from bodies throughout the world (see the ACHRE discussion of "body snatching," 1995:640). Findings from these studies eventually led to the ban on the atmospheric testing of nuclear weapons adopted by the United Nations in 1963.

The tensions between the political agenda of Cold War nuclear militarism and the scientific study of its devastating effects on humans and their environment not only resulted in overt efforts to keep information from the public (and therefore to deceive and lie to the public), but also generated biases that skewed scientific research from inception to conclusions. The AEC essentially funded a program of research supporting preconceived conclusions: a ban on atomic weapons tests is not needed because such tests pose no danger to humanity; humans evolved in a world where radiation from the sun and naturally occurring elements was present, and radiation at some levels is natural and beneficial; radiation exposure from weapons use has no significant mutagenic, intergenerational effect; any adverse heath effect of radiation exposure is the occasional and accidental result of high levels of exposure; and any resulting adverse heath effect from radiation exposure is limited to the individual, not his or her offspring. When scientists produced data that differed from the official government stance on radiation effects, studies were often censored, researchers were discredited, and research funding was withdrawn (cf. Chomsky et al. 1997; Deepe Keever 2004; Hacker 1994; Hefner and Gourley 1995; Price, this volume).

With the fall of the Soviet Union, the dismantling of the Cold War–era nuclear war machine, and the 1990s change in political administrations in the United States, a brief window of government transparency was opened. From declassified studies on uranium miners we have learned that there is a linear relationship between uranium miners' cumulative exposure levels and lung cancer. Cancer-causing radon gases, released as uranium decays, are more efficient at causing cancer at lower exposure levels than at higher exposure levels. And there is a significant latency period: some twenty years may pass between initial exposure and the health outcome. Exposure can also generate or exacerbate nonmalignant respiratory problems, including pneumoconiosis, tuberculosis, emphysema, chronic obstructive respiratory disease, chronic renal disease, heart disease, miscarriage, cleft palate, and other birth defects (cf. Archer et al. 2004; Gilliland et al. 2000; Johnston, Dawson, and Madsen, this volume; Samet 1991; Shields et al. 1992).

Declassified studies of the Marshallese and their acute exposure to Bravo fallout in 1954 documented an array of immediate effects including beta burns, loss of hair, depressed red cell and leukocyte counts, flulike symptoms, nausea, fingernail discoloration, radioactivity in the urine, and changes at the cellular level in blood and bone marrow (Cronkite et al. 1954). Long-term studies documented immune-deficiency diseases, metabolic disorders (diabetes), growth impairment in children, cancers, leukemia, premature aging (dental decay, cataracts, degenerative osteoarthritis), and a host of reproductive problems including miscarriages, congenital birth defects, and sterility. The long-term studies also confirmed what other classified research suggested: that radioiodine-131 adheres to and accumulates in the thyroid, stimulating the production of benign and cancerous nodules and interfering with the production of hormones, leaving children and pregnant women especially vulnerable. Thyroid cancer and other radiogenic changes occur not only in people exposed to an acute level of ionizing radiation but also in those who were born or moved into contaminated areas long after the initial blast and fallout had occurred (Barker, this volume; Conard 1975; Goldman et al. 2004; Sutow et al. 1965).

The controversial contention that exposure to even the smallest dose of low-level ionizing radiation can produce health risks (Gofman 1990) was explored by the National Academy of Sciences' Board on Radiation Effects ResearchBiological Effects of Ionizing Radiation (BEIR) VII Committee. The BEIR VII Committee concluded that there is no threshold of exposure below which low levels of ionizing radiation can be demonstrated to be harmless (National Academy of Sciences 2005). Health risks, as defined by the development of solid cancers in organs, rise proportionately with exposure to ionizing radiation: as overall life exposure increases, so does the risk. While the risk of inducing solid cancers from low-dose exposures is thought to be small, other degenerative health effects have been demonstrated. And there is a differential risk for women compared to men, and a differential risk for children. Thus radiation in the first year of life for boys produces three to four times the cancer risk as does exposure between the ages of twenty and fifty, and female infants have almost double the risk of male infants (National Academy of Sciences 2005; Simon et al. 2006). Furthermore, findings from a recent study of childhood cancers and strontium-90 in baby teeth demonstrate that the greatest per-dose risks for the very young are at the lowest doses (Mangano 2006). And there is compelling evidence of mutagenic damage from exposure to fallout emerging from intergenerational research in the former Soviet Union. For example, a study of three generations of families living near the test site in Kazakhstan demonstrated genetic mutation in the germline (the sequence of cells with genetic material that can be passed along to children). Exposed people had eight times the risk of mutation in the inherited genes than did rural families outside the fallout zone. Their children had five times the risk (Dubrova et al. 2002).

What have we done with this knowledge? In the United States significant effort was taken in the 1990s to evaluate the extent of radiogenic contamination associated with Manhattan Project research and nuclear weapons development and testing. Evaluations were part of a broader effort to implement remedial programs, such as the US Department of Energy's Long-term Stewardship Program. Assessment studies guided efforts to clean up the environment by removing stored radioactive waste, soils, metal, construction debris, and other contaminated materials, and by binding materials to contain and inhibit the movement of radioisotopes through the environment and the food chain. Significant effort was also taken to assess historic and current exposures and related health risks experienced by Manhattan Project and Cold War nuclear facility workers and residents (Liebow, this volume; Probst and McGovern 1998; Satterfield and Levin, this volume). And Congress passed legislation designed to compensate downwinders, workers, and veterans for health problems resulting from Cold War radiation exposure (see Barker, Boutté, and Dawson and Madsen, all this volume).

At the same time, while some scientists were occupied with assessment of the environmental health threats of Cold War nuclear weapons production and testing sites, and were developing plans and approaches to clean up the environment, reduce public health risks, and provide some sort of remedy for those who developed cancers from prior exposures, others were involved in actions that created new nuclear hot spots. A new generation of radiogenic weapons—depleted-uranium-tipped missiles, bullets, and shielding—has found its way into the battlefield. Depleted uranium (DU) weaponry was used in the 1991 Gulf War, the 1994–95 war in Bosnia, the 1999 war in Kosovo, the 2002 invasion of Afghanistan, and the war in Iraq that began in 2003. DU is also being introduced into the soil, watershed, and food chain in sites around the world by war games and other training exercises conducted by the United States and by the twenty-nine countries that have purchased DU weaponry from the United States. Depleted uranium is a human-made radioactive heavy metal derived from uranium ore; it is a by-product of enrichment. Recent calculations suggest that it has 75 percent of the radioactivity found in natural uranium and a half-life measured in billions of years. The rationale for widespread use of DU relies heavily upon the controversial belief that low-level exposure produces no significant harm to humans or their offspring. However, recent reviews of animal studies and human epidemiological data support the contention that DU is a teratogen: parental exposure can result in offspring with birth defects (Hindin et al. 2005. See also Baverstock 2005; United Nations Environment Program 2003; World Health Organization 2001; WISE 2006a).

In the first years of the twenty-first century, the meaning of security has been redefined from the previous focus on human security as implemented via the human rights framework to the current focus on political and economic security as imposed and reinforced by a military framework. The many calls for a reduction of warheads and a comprehensive ban on all nuclear weapons, so common in the 1990s, have largely been silenced, and some nations again threaten to adopt policies of nuclear preemptive strikes. In March 2005, the United States revised *The Doctrine for Joint Nuclear Operations*, stating its intent to use nuclear weapons against an adversary "using or intending to use WMD against the United States" (Joint Chiefs of Staff 2005:III–2).

Economic priorities have also shifted as larger portions of the world's national budgets are now earmarked to cover military research, weapons development, expansion of armed forces, the costs of engagement, and the costs of developing new sources of energy. One measure of the economic impact of these shifts can be seen in the changing value of uranium oxide, which sold in December 2000 for US$7 per pound and six years later sells for US$60 per pound and is expected to continue its rise, prompting exploration and new mining worldwide. While half of the world's production in 2005 came from Canada and Australia, the escalating value of uranium ore has prompted expansion or recommissioning of existing mining and contracts for new ventures in the United States, Guatemala, Argentina, India, Armenia, the Czech Republic, Slovakia, Finland, Russia, Kazakhstan, Kyrgyzstan, Mongolia, Uzbekistan, Pakistan, Saudi Arabia, Niger, Namibia, Malawi, Zambia, and South Africa (WISE 2006b). (See map 1.2.) Uranium mining has become big business, providing the fuel for a new generation of nuclear power plants and a reinvigorated weapons industry.

These political and economic shifts reflect fundamental transformations in the social meaning of government and the prioritization of its actions. Where the state once served as the institutional mechanism that secured the fundamental rights of its citizens to life and livelihood, it now functions to protect the individual right to power and profit.

For many of us who lived through the Cold War years, there is a strong sense of déjà vu—that we have stepped back in time to a world where governmental policies and actions prioritize "security interests" over the fundamental rights of people and

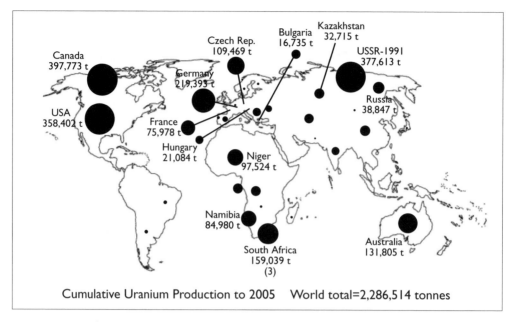

Map 1.2. Cumulative uranium production around the world up to 2005. Credit: World Information Service on Energy (WISE), uranium maps, http://wise-uranium.org/umaps.html. Map adapted by School for Advanced Research Press.

their environment. Thus a collective sense of urgency has fueled efforts to produce this book. Military concerns and the prioritization of funding again dominate the scientific agenda. Nations are seeking more and newer nuclear weapons. And radiogenic elements are increasingly dispersed through military testing and battlefield engagements around the world. The nuclear war machine has shifted into higher gear, and those of us who have spent much of our lives studying the political forces and human consequences of Cold War nuclear militarism fear that the lessons of the past are no longer recognized or considered relevant. It is in this climate, in these dangerous times, that we offer this collection of essays and their varied cautionary tales.

Confronting the Radioactive Legacies of the Cold War

Understanding and utilizing the lessons of the past requires free access to information and transparent decision-making processes. The window of transparency opened by declassification orders in the 1990s allowed public access to documents that confirmed the worst fears about how a government takes evil action to ensure a political good. A flood of documents from the Soviet Union and the United States provided material evidence of how the Cold War was fought: with military and economic actions that involved horrific abuses of fundamental human rights. Declassification and public scrutiny of historic injustices provided an opportunity to come to terms with the past, and in doing so to take honest and significant effort toward making amends. The

United States acknowledged culpability for some of the consequential damages of Cold War actions, issuing apologies to human radiation subjects (ACHRE 1995), as well as to nations whose governments had been destabilized and toppled through covert US action, as in President Clinton's apology to Guatemala (Gibney and Warner 2000). In 2001 the Russian Duma adopted a law with social guarantees for citizens affected by radiation from nuclear weapons tests within Russia, as well as outside it (BBC Monitoring Service 2001).

At the most fundamental of levels, the struggle to address the radioactive legacy of the Cold War has been a struggle over who has the right and power to shape, access, and use information. People seek access to information that depicts "the whole truth" about the nuclear war machine and its human health effects. And governments seek to control or remove from public access such information. They do so because this information demonstrates past harm and present or future risk, and thus demonstrates liability and supports demands for accountability. As detailed in the following chapters, the struggle to address the radioactive legacy of the Cold War calls into question the nature of science, the ethical dimensions of scientific research, and the political use of science. In so doing, the struggle has at times produced social movements that threaten to transform the balance of power in society.

Chapter 2, "'more like us than mice': Radiation Experiments with Indigenous Peoples," gives a historical overview of Cold War science that specifically conducted research with discrete biological populations, especially indigenous and other place-based peoples, to understand radiation, manage exposure, and reduce risks. Beginning in the late 1940s, the United States funded research that tracked fallout in the environment, food chain, and people. Beginning in the early 1950s, it funded studies that attempted to identify the human effects of exposure to naturally occurring sources of radiation and studies that documented the immediate and long-term effect of exposure to "environmental sources"—classified code for radioactive fallout from atmospheric weapons tests. Early genetic studies using fruit flies, corn, and mice were followed by human population studies involving groups who had experienced acute radiation exposure during nuclear weapons tests. Both the United States and the Soviet Union conducted such research, though the chapter presented here focuses on the US research experience. Research discussed here includes the targeted and opportunistic use of indigenous peoples in the Marshall Islands, Arctic, and Andes, whose participation typically occurred without meaningful informed consent. These people were selected as human subjects because they were heavily exposed to fallout, lived in areas with high levels of naturally occurring radiation, or were considered to be unexposed and thus could serve as a control group. Selected study populations all lived on traditional lands, depended upon the local environs for food, and lived in tightly defined social groups. The science was designed to produce findings in support of the military and its capacity to fight and win a nuclear war.

Cold War scientific research was, of course, conducted by an array of people, with an array of motivations and sensibilities, altruistic and otherwise. In chapter 3, "Earle

Reynolds: Scientist, Citizen, and Cold War Dissident," David Price examines the experience of an Atomic Bomb Casualty Commission (ABCC) scientist whose research findings demonstrated the harmful effects of fallout on Japanese atomic bomb survivors. Because these findings ran counter to US public policy, his work was censored. Using archival documents and records released by the Department of Energy, the Federal Bureau of Investigation, and the Central Intelligence Agency under the Freedom of Information Act, Price depicts Earle Reynolds's transition from physical anthropologist working with children who survived the bombing of Hiroshima and Nagasaki to devoted activist risking his life opposing US development of the hydrogen bomb. Reynolds's research, and the censorship of his research findings, changed his political orientation and led him to protest the development of weapons of mass destruction. As Reynolds obstructed nuclear weapons tests and spoke out in public settings on the dangers of these weapons, the FBI and other intelligence agencies increased their surveillance of him and actively hindered his work. While many elements of Reynolds's life were extraordinary, Price makes the point that the basic problems Earle Reynolds faced in trying to reconcile the interests of his employer and those of the population he studied were similar to many essential dilemmas faced by academics and scientists working in today's national security state.

A very different story of scientific research and political advocacy is presented in chapter 4, "There Are No Peripheries to Humanity: Northern Alaska Nuclear Dumping and the Iñupiat's Search for Redress," by Edith Turner. This reprint of a 1997 journal article explores the meaning of anthropological fieldwork and the evolving role of the author as she worked with a northern Alaskan Iñupiat community whose water, soil, and food were contaminated by radioactive soils imported from Nevada by the AEC. The consequential damages of unwittingly hosting a nuclear dump site are detailed, as is the anthropologist's efforts to facilitate and support the Iñupiat in their struggle for meaningful remedy. The article is reprinted here, juxtaposed with the Earle Reynolds story, for a number of reasons. Turner's work with the Iñupiat began in 1987, some three decades after Reynolds did his research in Japan, and this essay paints the picture of life in very different political times. Turner's ability to document health conditions, communicate findings from her work, challenge the federal government to acknowledge culpability, and see an eventual acknowledgment of harm and efforts to make amends stands in sharp contrast to Earle Reynolds's experience. It is important to note that her work illustrates some of the many ways in which anthropology changed in the years following World War II, the Korean War, and the Vietnam War. As an ABCC scientist, Earle Reynolds studied human subjects. The implied power relationship between scientist and subject, as well as the unquestioned support of a military research program, was not unusual for the time. Edith Turner, on the other hand, saw her role in the community evolve from that of the traditional anthropologist conducting fieldwork, with the goal of producing new intellectual insights on human behavior, to that of a proactive scholar–adviser–advocate who works for and with her host community.

In chapter 5, "Uranium Mining and Milling: Navajo Experiences in the American Southwest," by Barbara Rose Johnston, Susan Dawson, and Gary Madsen, we move the focus of this book back to the nuclear war machine, examining the context and times in which uranium was mined and processed to fuel the early Cold War buildup of nuclear weapons in the United States. This chapter places specific focus on the impact of uranium mining as experienced by the primary host community: the Navajo Nation. We examine the role of the AEC in structuring the uranium mining industry, noting its complete disregard for the occupational health and safety of Navajo miners, millworkers, and the broader residential community. We explore some of the consequential damages of this environmental racism for worker and community health. We argue that the US federal government fundamentally abused its trustee responsibilities to exploit uranium resources. And we describe recent Navajo Nation efforts to identify and remediate environmental health hazards.

The consequential damages of mining and processing uranium are explored in greater detail in chapter 6, "Uranium Mine Workers, Atomic Downwinders, and the Radiation Exposure Compensation Act (RECA): The Nuclear Legacy," by Susan Dawson and Gary Madsen. This chapter presents the broader history of uranium production and atmospheric testing in the United States and their devastating environmental and health impacts on workers and communities in the American Southwest, with a critical look at government efforts to protect the health of workers and residential communities. Reviewing findings from fifteen years of fieldwork, the authors demonstrate that a significant time lag occurred between government studies confirming significant health risks in 1951 and the implementation of basic occupational health and safety regulations in 1971. Workers developed lung cancer and other radiogenic illnesses—and these problems were predicted and studied by government scientists—yet for many years, workers were not informed of their illnesses or treated. The authors also summarize some of the actions taken by community residents to mobilize and seek redress. And they critically explore the federal response: the Radiation Exposure Compensation Act, passed in 1990 and amended in 2000. Dawson and Madsen conclude with a cautionary discussion of US government attempts to expand the nuclear industry and resume nuclear testing—actions that require renewed mining and milling of uranium and may result in the recurrence of problems that impacted Colorado Plateau residents in the past.

Moving from uranium mining and milling to an examination of community legacy issues associated with nuclear weapons production, Edward Liebow, in chapter 7, "Hanford, Tribal Risks, and Public Health in an Era of Forced Federalism," considers some of the problems associated with uranium enrichment facilities. Attention in this chapter is placed on the Native tribes who live around and downstream from the Hanford enrichment facility in southeastern Washington—that segment of the surrounding community that is most closely tied to the land and the local food chain and thus receives a greater degree of exposure to radioactive contamination. Liebow reviews the history of medical research meant to address questions posed by residents:

To what extent were the Native peoples of the Columbia Plateau exposed to different doses of Hanford radiation than their non-Indian counterparts in the general population? And which of the public health problems evident in Indian Country today can be attributed to Hanford's radiation releases? To ask these questions, and to participate in the various studies and political processes initiated by the federal government, Liebow notes that Hanford's tribal neighbors had to organize, develop technical capacities, and compete with states for scarce federal public health resources. Critically assessing flaws in the resulting scientific studies, and situating the science within the broader sociopolitical context, Liebow allows the reader to see the institutional landscape of tribal involvement in Hanford health studies, the roles of several anthropologists, and the problematic aspects of state-tribal relations. The chapter concludes by raising serious questions concerning prospects for public health, pointing toward the need to develop studies and environmental health policies that treat actual conditions rather than look for illusive proof of direct causality.

A parallel study of the efficacy and inhibiting factors in federal response to contamination and the health risks posed by uranium enrichment facilities is presented by Theresa Satterfield and Joshua Levin in chapter 8, "From Cold War Complex to Nature Preserve: Diagnosing the Breakdown of a Multi-Stakeholder Decision Process and Its Consequences for Rocky Flats." Satterfield and Levin take a focused look at the processes of risk communication and public involvement in decisions about contamination cleanup at the Rocky Flats Environment Technology Site, where the detonating devices for hydrogen bombs were produced from 1952 to 1989. They report on a political process that incorporated "best practice" public participation models that are increasingly used to define and shape environmental remediation. In this case, risk and science communication efforts at Rocky Flats were successful to the extent that much of the "involved" public achieved an impressive level of technical sophistication. However, this scientific literacy did not lead to a reduction of conflict about the risks posed by residual contaminants at the site. Instead, improved public understanding of the risk estimates and the attributes of radiation hazards occurred in a context of increased conflict: participants, with a greater knowledge of the technical issues, were unable to manage the tradeoffs underpinning core cleanup decisions, and this situation led to a crisis in public confidence in the environmental remediation process. The authors argue that the processes that bring about informed public involvement in decision making are laudable, but in the long run, they will likely fail if the overriding goal of regulators is to simply educate and convince the public that already-made decisions are in their best interest. Satterfield and Levin conclude with a "lessons learned" discussion, proposing an alternative model to explain the dynamics of risk communication and public involvement in the cleanup of contaminated sites.

Chapter 9, "Health Assessment Downwind: Past Abuses Shadow Future Indicators," by Marie Boutté, presents findings from a community health assessment pilot project that gathered baseline health data in rural Nevada during 2000–01 as part of the state's oversight of the proposed permanent, national repository for high level nuclear waste at Yucca Mountain. The community selected was on a likely transportation route for high-level nuclear waste and was also downwind from the Nevada test site. For years, this community was exposed to nuclear radiation from both atmospheric and underground weapons tests. Boutté outlines the history of exposure and community perceptions of injustice and describes how this history and sense of injustice led community members to challenge the federal government to define and assess their health. Cultural notions of identity, governance, and personal versus governmental responsibilities are identified as key variables influencing community perception of environmental risk, awareness of the relationships between exposure and health, and interest in or ability to pursue compensatory claims under RECA.

In chapter 10, our focus moves from downwinders in Nevada to the acutely and chronically exposed communities in and downwind from the US Pacific proving grounds. In "From Analysis to Action: Efforts to Address the Nuclear Legacy in the Marshall Islands," Holly Barker explores health effects from radiation exposure, noting that Marshallese women suffer from a multitude of birth anomalies and that linguistic evidence demonstrates that these health problems did not occur prior to nuclear weapons testing. Barker's use of participatory ethnography has helped refine Marshallese people's firsthand understanding of the devastating health and environmental impacts of the testing program and has allowed them to identify their own meaningful strategies and priorities in adjusting to the sociocultural upheaval caused by exile from a contaminated homeland. Thus, as with many of the case studies in this volume, Barker explores radioactive legacy issues from a community perspective. In describing how she works with affected communities, she demonstrates the role of the engaged anthropologist as adviser and advocate—that is, empowering people to address problems in meaningful and locally appropriate ways.

Very different issues, actions, and observations are offered by Paula Garb, who writes about her work with ethnic Russian, Bashkir, and Tatar communities exposed to radiation from nuclear weapons facilities in the Chelyabinsk region of Russia. In chapter 11, "Russia's Radiation Victims of Cold War Weapons Production Surviving in a Culture of Secrecy and Denial," Garb outlines the divergent perceptions of ordinary citizens living near the former Soviet Union's largest uranium enrichment facilities: how their health and lifestyles were affected by the exposure, who they blame, and what strategies they have devised to ameliorate the problems and to preserve their cultures in contaminated environments. Material presented in this chapter is derived from a multiyear study involving in-depth interviews of the victims, survey data on the local population, and newspaper articles.

Chapter 12, "Unraveling the Secrets of the Past: Contested Versions of Nuclear Testing in the Soviet Republic of Kazakhstan," by Cynthia Werner and Kathleen Purvis-Roberts, provides an overview of Soviet nuclear weapons testing in Kazakhstan, focusing on resident populations and the consequential damages of Cold War secrecy associated with the test site. Emphasis is placed on Kazakhstani citizens' descriptions of their experiences—that is, what people were and were not told about the "military tests"; how some individuals were forced to stay behind during evacuations; how those who tried to challenge the government were silenced; how radiation-related illnesses were systematically underreported; and how doctors prevented parents from seeing stillborn children. Content is based on an interdisciplinary multiyear study employing a variety of methods to determine how different groups (villagers-victims, doctors, and nuclear scientists) understand the risk and health impacts of radiation. The methods included risk-perception surveys, focus group interviews, ethnographic interviews, and textual analysis of newspaper accounts, in addition to an analysis of environmental data and health statistics.

The conclusion to this collection, Laura Nader and Hugh Gusterson's "Nuclear Legacies: Arrogance, Secrecy, Ignorance, Lies, Silence, Suffering, Action," offers critical commentary on these essays and case studies. Nader and Gusterson note that anthropologists, like other scientists, have a mixed history with regard to their role in Cold War militarism. This history includes failure to demand a public accounting of the true costs of nuclear weapons testing, as well as occasional overt involvement in research that sustained nuclear militarism. Observing the transformations in anthropology and other sciences, from "passive inhalation of the official point of view to a more muscular interrogation of received wisdom," Nader and Gusterson consider the contributions in this book to be evidence of a growing trend to resituate science within civil society. Given the strength of the military-industrial-academic complex, this is by no means an easy task. Nader and Gusterson note that today, once again, "science is saturated with politics"; "the atomic energy cover-up continues, and victims and their families have had to work hard to get accurate information about what was done to them and even harder to get any kind of remedy." They suggest that one of the collective lessons emerging from this book is that accountability is intrinsically linked to transparency—both in terms of access to information and the broader structure of government. Demands and struggles to secure accountability require a reshaping of the values and priorities of government, and it is only through such processes that opportunities for truly democratic form and practice emerge.

At one level, these essays offer a sampling of Cold War radioactive legacy issues, with snapshot descriptions of people, events, problems, and responses from the varied perspective of the anthropologist as participant, observer, analyst, or advocate. Yet while chapters vary in their focus on people, place, and time, all essays demonstrate the complex nature of the problems and the politics involving radiogenic contamination. They illustrate how actions taken in the name of national security have profoundly shaped sociocultural identity and fundamentally transformed the biophysical nature of communities.

I end this introductory chapter with a final note to the reader. As you read the following pages, do so with this thought in mind: In this world, where conflict and violence are increasingly the norm, now more than ever we need to listen to and learn from the experiences of those who understand what it is to host the nuclear war machine and survive nuclear war.

References

ACHRE. *See* Advisory Committee on Human Radiation Experiments

Advisory Committee on Human Radiation Experiments
1995   Final Report of the Advisory Committee on Human Radiation Experiments. Washington, DC: US Government Printing Office.

Archer, Victor E., Teresa Coons, Geno Saccomanno, and Dae-Yong Hong
2004   Latency and the Lung Cancer Epidemic among United States Uranium Miners. Health Physics 87(5):480–89.

Argonne National Laboratory
2005   Human Health Fact Sheet, August 2005, Strontium. Electronic document, http://www.ead.anl.gov/pub/doc/strontium.pdf, accessed July 18, 2006.

Baverstock, Keith
2005   Science, Politics and Ethics in the Low Dose Debate. Medicine, Conflict and Survival 21:88–100.

BBC Monitoring Service
2001   Russian Duma Passes Law on Allowances for Nuclear Tests Victims. Electronic document, http://www.downwinders.org/!duma_article.html, accessed November 9, 2006.

Beck, Harold J., and Burton G. Bennett
2002   Overview of Atmospheric Nuclear Weapons Testing and Estimates of Fallout in the United States. Health Physics: The Radiation Safety Journal 82(5):591–608.

Bennett, B. B., L. E. de Geer, and A. Doury
2000   Nuclear Weapons Test Programmes of the Different Countries. *In* Nuclear Test Explosions: Environmental and Human Impacts. Sir F. Warner and R. J. C. Kirchman, eds. Pp. 15–32. New York: Wiley and Sons.

Center for Nonproliferation Studies
2002   Resources on China: China's Nuclear Tests: Dates, Yields, Types, Methods and Comments. Electronic document, http://cns.miis.edu/research/china/coxrep/testlist.htm, accessed July 14, 2006.

Chomsky, Noam, Ira Latznelson, R. C. Lewontin, David Montgomery, Laura Nader, Richard Ohmann, Ray Siever, Immanuel Wallerstein, and Howard Zinn
1997   The Cold War and the University: Toward an Intellectual History of the Postwar Years. New York: New Press.

CNS. *See* Center for Nonproliferation Studies

Conant, James B., A. H. Compton, and H. C. Urey
1943   Memorandum to: Brigadier General L. R. Groves From: Drs. Conant, Compton, and Urey, War Department, United States Engineer Office, Manhattan District, Oak Ridge Tennessee, October 30, 1943. Electronic document, http://www.mindfully.org/Nucs/Groves-Memo-Manhattan30oct43a.htm, accessed October 26, 2006.

Conard, Robert A.

1975   A Twenty-Year Review of Medical Findings in a Marshallese Population Acciden-
        tally Exposed to Radioactive Fallout. Upton, NY: Brookhaven National Laboratory.

Cronkite, E. P., V. P. Bond, L. E. Browning, W. H. Chapman, S. H. Cohn,
R. A. Conard, C. L. Dunham, R. S. Farr, W. S. Hall, R. Sharp, and S. Shipman

1954   Report to the Scientific Director, Operation Castle—Final Report Project 4.1.
        Study of Response of Human Beings Accidentally Exposed to Significant Fallout
        Radiation. Department of Energy, Marshall Islands Historical Documents Archive.
        Electronic document, http://worf.eh.doe.gov/data/ihp2/2776_.pdf, accessed October
        25, 2006.

Deepe Keever, Beverly Ann

2004   News Zero: *The New York Times* and the Bomb. Monroe, ME: Common Courage
        Press.

Department of Health and Human Services

2005   Report on the Feasibility of a Study of the Health Consequences to the American
        Population from Nuclear Weapons Tests Conducted by the United States and Other
        Nations. Electronic document, http://www.cdc.gov/nceh/radiation/fallout/
        default.htm, accessed July 18, 2006.

DHHS. *See* Department of Health and Human Services

Dubrova, Y. E., R. I. Bersimbaev, L. B. Djansugurova, M. K. Tankimanova,
Z. Z. Mamyrbaeva, R. Mustonen, C. Lindholm, M. Hulten, and S. Salomaa

2002   Nuclear Weapons Tests and Human Germline Mutation Rate. Science 295:1037.

Federation of American Scientists

2002   FAS Weapons of Mass Destruction, WMD around the World, Pakistan Nuclear
        Weapons. Electronic document, http://www.fas.org/nuke/guide/pakistan/nuke/
        index.html, accessed July 14, 2006.

Gibney, Mark, and David Warner

2000   What Does It Mean to Say I'm Sorry? President Clinton's Apology to Guatemala
        and Its Significance for International and Domestic Law. Denver Journal of
        International Law and Policy 28(2):223–33.

Gilliland, F. D., W. C. Hunt, M. Pardilla, and C. R. Key

2000   Uranium Mining and Lung Cancer among Navajo Men in New Mexico and Arizona,
        1969 to 1993. Journal of Occupational Environmental Medicine 42(3):278–83.

Göes, Eva, Birger Schlaug, Ragnhild Pohanka, Per Lager, Elisa Abascal Reye

1997   Global Justice—Indigenous Peoples and Uranium Mining. Electronic document,
        http://www.wise-uranium.org/uip412.html, accessed July 18, 2006.

Gofman, John W.

1990   Radiation-Induced Cancer from Low-Dose Exposure: An Independent Analysis. San
        Francisco: Committee for Nuclear Responsibility.

Goldman, Lynn, Henry Falk, Philip J. Landrigan, Sophie J. Balk, J. Routt Reigart, and Ruth A. Etzel
2004   Environmental Pediatrics and Its Impact on Government Health Policy. Pediatrics 13(4):1146–57.

Hacker, Barton C.
1994   Elements of Controversy: The Atomic Energy Commission and Radiation Safety in Nuclear Weapons Tests, 1947–74. Berkeley: University of California Press.

Hefner, Loretta, and Karoline Gourley
1995   Human Radiation Studies: Remembering the Early Years. Oral History of Dr. John W. Gofman, M.D., Ph.D. Electronic document, http://www.eh.doe.gov/ohre/roadmap/histories/0457/0457toc.html, accessed October 25, 2006.

Hindin, Rita, Doug Brugge, and Bindu Panikkar
2005   Teratogenicity of Depleted Uranium Aerosols: A Review from an Epidemiological Perspective. Environmental Health 4:4–17.

International Physicians for the Prevention of Nuclear War—Institute for Energy and Environmental Research
1991   Radioactive Heaven and Earth: The Health and Environmental Effects of Nuclear Weapons Testing in, on, and above the Earth. New York: Apex Press.

IPPNW-IEER. *See* International Physicians for the Prevention of Nuclear War—Institute for Energy and Environmental Research

Johnston, Barbara Rose
1994   Environmental Degradation and Human Rights Abuse. *In* Who Pays the Price? The Sociocultural Context of Environmental Crisis. Barbara Rose Johnston, ed. Pp. 7–16. Washington DC: Island Press.

Joint Chiefs of Staff
2005   Doctrine for Joint Nuclear Operations, Final Coordination (2), 15 March 2005. Electronic document, http://www.globalsecurity.org/wmd/library/policy/dod/jp3_12fc2.pdf, accessed March 1, 2006.

Makhijani, Arjun, Howard Hu, and Katherine Yih, eds.
1995   Nuclear Wastelands: Nuclear Weapons Production Worldwide and Its Environmental and Health Effects. Cambridge, MA: MIT Press.

Mangano, Joseph
2006   A Short Latency between Radiation Exposure from Nuclear Plants and Cancer in Young Children. International Journal of Health Services 36(1):113–35.

Miller, Richard L.
1986   Under the Cloud: The Decades of Nuclear Testing. New York: Free Press.

National Academy of Sciences
2005   BEIR VII: Health Risks from Exposures to Low Levels of Ionizing Radiation. Washington, DC: National Academy Press.

Nuclear Weapons Archive

2006   The Nuclear Weapon Archive: A Guide to Nuclear Weapons. Electronic document, http://nuclearweaponarchive.org/, accessed July 16, 2006.

Petryna, Adriana

2002   Life Exposed: Biological Citizens after Cherobyl. Princeton, NJ: Princeton University Press.

Preston, Diana

2006   Before the Fallout: From Marie Curie to Hiroshima. New York: Berkeley Books.

Probst, Kathryn, and M. H. McGovern

1998   Long-Term Stewardship and the Nuclear Weapons Complex: The Challenge Ahead. Electronic document, http://www.rff.org/reports/PDF_files/stewardship, accessed July 18, 2006.

Rand Corporation

1953   Worldwide Effects of Atomic Weapons: Project Sunshine: AECU-3488. Oak Ridge, TN: Atomic Energy Commission, Technical Information Service Extension.

Samet, J. M.

1991   Diseases of Uranium Miners and Other Underground Miners Exposed to Radon. Occupational Medicine 6(4):629–39.

Shields, L. M., W. H. Wiese, B. J. Skipper, B. Charley, and L. Banally

1992   Navajo Birth Outcomes in the Shiprock Uranium Mining Area. Health Physics 63(5):542–51.

Simon, Steven L., André Bouville, and Charles E. Land

2006   Fallout from Nuclear Weapons Tests and Cancer Risks: Exposures 50 Years Ago Still Have Health Implications Today and Will Continue into the Future. American Scientist 94:48–57.

Smith, D. K., D. L. Finnegan, and S. M. Bowen

2003   An Inventory of Long-Lived Radionuclides Residual from Underground Nuclear Testing at the Nevada Test Site, 1951–1992. Journal of Environmental Radioactivity 67:35–51.

Speer, Albert

1971   Inside the Third Reich. New York: Avon Books.

Sutow, W. W., R. A. Conard, and K. M. Griffith

1965   Growth Status of Children Exposed to Fallout Radiation on Marshall Islands. Pediatrics 36(5):721–31.

United Nations Environment Program

2003   Depleted Uranium in Bosnia and Herzegovina: Post-Conflict Assessment. Electronic document, http://postconflict.unep.ch/publications/BiH_DU_report.pdf, accessed October 25, 2006.

Warner, Sir Frederik, and René J. C. Kirchmann

2000   Nuclear Test Explosions: Environmental and Human Impacts. Scope 59. Scientific Committee on the Problems of the Environment. New York: Wiley and Sons.

WISE. *See* World Information Service on Energy

World Health Organization

2001   Depleted Uranium: Sources, Exposure and Health Effects. Geneva: World Health Organization, United Nations, Ionizing Radiation Unit.

World Information Service on Energy

2006a   Bibliography: Military Use of Depleted Uranium. Electronic document, http://www.wise-uranium.org/dlit.html, accessed February 5, 2006.

2006b   Uranium Mining News. Electronic document, http://www.wise-uranium.org/new.html, accessed July 14, 2006.

two
"more like us than mice"
Radiation Experiments with Indigenous Peoples

Barbara Rose Johnston

We think that one very intriguing study can be made and plans are on the way
to implement this—"Uterik" Atoll is the atoll furtherest from the March 1
shot where people were exposed got initially about 15 roentgens and then they
were evacuated and they returned.

They had been living on that Island; now that Island is safe to live on but
is by far the most contaminated place in the world and it will be very interesting to go back and get good environmental data, how many per square mile;
what isotopes are involved and a sample of food changes in many humans
through their urines, so as to get a measure of the human uptake when people
live in a contaminated environment.

Now, data of this type has never been available. While it is true that these
people do not live, I would say, the way Westerners do, civilized people, it is
nevertheless also true that these people are more like us than mice. So that is
something which will be done this winter. (ACBM 1956a:232)

—*Merril Eisenbud*

The above quotation is drawn from the transcript of a 1956 meeting of the Atomic
Energy Commission (AEC) Advisory Committee on Biology and Medicine. In the
meeting, Merril Eisenbud, then director of the AEC Health and Safety Laboratory, discussed radiation research plans for the Marshall Islands. The remark "these people are
more like us than mice" reflects the state of radiation-effects research at the time:

largely based on studies of corn, fruit flies, and animals such as mice. The remark, however, also suggests a hierarchical view of humanity and the presumed relative subordinate status of indigenous peoples. This view—that human groups are more or less evolved, with primitive "natives" being biologically inferior to Western "civilized people"—was a common and useful notion. Such ideas helped dampen any moral qualms about the planned use of a Marshallese population in human radiation experiments.

To understand the public risks posed by nuclear weapons testing and the military risks associated with atomic warfare, beginning in the late 1940s, the United States funded research that tracked fallout in the environment, food chain, and people, as well as studies that attempted to identify the human genetic effects of exposure to naturally occurring radiation. Some of this research required groups of human subjects who depended upon the local environs for food, lived on traditional lands in tightly defined social groups, and lived in areas with high levels of naturally occurring radiation. This chapter describes examples of the targeted and opportunistic use of indigenous peoples in the Marshall Islands, Arctic, Andes, and Amazon and calls for a more detailed examination of this history and its consequences.[1]

Point of Entry

The original impetus for this chapter was derived from research exploring the relationship between nuclear militarism, environmental degradation, and human rights abuse in the Marshall Islands (Johnston 1994) and subsequent research conducted for the Republic of the Marshall Islands Nuclear Claims Tribunal, Office of the Public Advocate, on behalf of claimants in the Rongelap Land Claims case (Johnston and Barker 1999, 2001). In the Rongelap Land Claims case, ethnographic research was contextualized and substantiated with evidence found in a review of declassified documents released by the Department of Defense, Department of Energy (DOE; formerly the Atomic Energy Commission or AEC), and other agencies as a result of President Clinton's 1993 executive order establishing the Advisory Committee on Human Radiation Experiments (ACHRE). In 1994 ACHRE assessed the available record of nuclear weapons testing and related human-subject research, concluding that the Marshallese had served as research subjects in several experiments involving radioisotopes but finding no conclusive evidence that their long-term service as subjects in a radiation-effects research program was an example of human radiation experimentation. Following publication of ACHRE's findings, the declassified database was scanned, and in 1996 it was placed on a word-searchable Human Radiation Experiments (HREX) website. After ACHRE released its final report, additional human radiation experiment documents were located by the Department of Defense, Central Intelligence Agency, Department of Energy, and other agencies, and up through December 1999, new materials were placed in HREX. Materials declassified by the DOE pertaining to the Marshall Islands were also scanned and placed as historical documents on the DOE's Marshall Islands website.[2]

ACHRE and DOE declassified-document archives were used in the Rongelap claim to investigate, contextualize, and substantiate informant complaints. These archives not only contain documents associated with the nuclear weapons testing program and its contamination of natural resources, they also contain detailed evidence of human-subject experiments exploring the biophysical consequences of exposure to fallout and the long-term degenerative effects of living in a radioactive environment. AEC-funded research in the Marshall Islands monitored the movement of radioactive elements through the food chain and the human body, documented the biophysical changes associated with radiation exposure, and predicted the degenerative and genetic effects of radiation exposure. Data was often presented and conclusions contextualized with reference to the broader body of classified research, including similar work conducted with indigenous populations in the Arctic, Amazon, and Andes. Preparation of the expert witness report for the Nuclear Claims Tribunal involved, to some degree, consideration of this broader record of classified Cold War science.

My research into the history of research on radiation effects in human populations was further influenced by the publication of Patrick Tierney's *Darkness in El Dorado: How Scientists and Journalists Devastated the Amazon* (2000); the subsequent American Anthropological Association (AAA) inquiry into ethical issues surrounding anthropological and human population studies in the Amazon; the fierce controversies that arose over the depictions of science, scientists, research motivations, and relationships; and the consequential damages of conducting scientific research with isolated, indigenous subjects. Tierney's book includes a chapter titled "Atomic Indians" that describes, among other things, AEC-funded interdisciplinary research, designed and directed by geneticist James V. Neel, involving the Yanomami of the Amazon. AAA facilitated my efforts to review the James V. Neel collection at the National Academy of Sciences archives. These records largely reflect Neel's work developing the Atomic Bomb Casualty Commission (ABCC) protocol and coordinating research on the effects of radiation as experienced by Japanese survivors of atomic bombs. They also include references to his research in the Amazon, Africa, and the Marshall Islands. The driving questions in this review were: Why was AEC funding Neel's work with the Yanomami? How did AEC use, or hope to use, the resulting research products? What, if any, were the relationships between the Yanomami research described by Tierney and previous work by Neel with Japanese and Marshallese populations? In considering the broader record of human population research conducted by Neel, are there recognizable patterns in his approach to human-subject work, especially with regard to informed consent and treatment priorities? What were the conditions and human-subject consent parameters associated with reported injections of radioactive isotopes among the Yanomami? What were the legal norms of the time with regard to human-subject research and the use of radioisotopes? My review of the declassified records found much to support the contention that Cold War–era research was conducted in the Amazon to support a US Cold War military agenda, with little or minimal concern for the health and welfare needs of study subjects and without their meaningful informed consent (see Johnston 2002).

Many researchers and organizations conducted investigations into the allegations raised by Patrick Tierney, and some of these investigations specifically addressed the above questions (cf. AAA 2002; ASHG 2002; IGES 2001). An investigation conducted by the American Society of Human Genetics (ASHG), of which James Neel was a founding member, noted:

> In the late 1950s and early 1960s, the AEC funded approximately half of all federally supported genetic research in the United States.... Approximately 20% of active members of the Genetics Society of America performed AEC-sponsored research.... The AEC's support of Neel's work with the Yanomami was therefore not exceptional. Because it was already known that ionizing radiation could induce genetic mutations, any kind of genetic investigation that might have some bearing on atomic research and the aftereffects of atomic bombing was encouraged by the AEC. Full understanding of the genetic effects of radiation required investigations in lower organisms as well as in human populations. Conclusions regarding possible mutational damage in humans required elucidation of the various forces that affected the genetic structure of human populations. None of this was remarkable either then or now. It is noteworthy that the Department of Energy (the successor agency to the AEC) has recently been a major force in the initiation and execution of the Human Genome Project—an undertaking of great interest to medicine and human biology in general. (ASHG 2002:5)

This statement, originally voiced by D. B. Paul and J. Beatty in a Society for Latin American Anthropology newsletter article, was used in the ASHG report to support the arguments that AEC funding was not, in itself, a rationale for ethically compromised research and that allegations of ethical impropriety by Neel were baseless given the record of his actions and the norms of the time.

Rather than answering the research praxis questions raised by Tierney, this statement prompted for me a renewed drive to review the broader record of human population research funded by the AEC, especially work involving "biologically discrete" human populations. If half the federally supported genetic research conducted in the 1950s and 1960s was funded by the AEC to better understand the mutagenic effects of radiation, the AEC obviously wielded incredible power in shaping scientific agendas. How were these studies structured? What populations were involved? What methods (and radioisotopes) were used? Under what conditions and contexts? How were these studies related to the Marshallese history of service as human subjects? What were the social impacts of serving as a research subject? Whose interests were served, and who paid the price?

To explore these questions, in 2004–05, with a research and writing grant from the John T. and Catherine D. MacArthur Foundation, I reviewed ABCC and other files at the University of Texas Medical School Historical Library, population research records in the Pacific trust territory archives at the University of Hawaii, Nuclear Claims Tribunal personal injury files in the Marshall Islands, and human radiation experimentation and biochemical warfare records at the National Security Archives at George Washington University. I also conducted an online review of AEC documents archived by the DOE, including radiation-effects and population research and related declassified contracts, protocols, human-subject consent procedures and forms, reports, letters, memos, and resulting publications. And I reviewed declassified documents authored by James V. Neel provided by the DOE through a Freedom of Information Act request. Given the immense amount of data amassed during these various research forays, analytical work continues. Thus, this chapter represents a preliminary overview of the research record. I begin with a summary of the human radiation research agenda defined and shaped by US militarism and then outline the application of this research agenda in studies involving the indigenous peoples of the Arctic, Amazon, and Andes and the Marshall Islands.

Early Atomic Detonations and Key Questions Shaping Human Radiation Research

On August 11, 1945, two days after the bombing of Nagasaki, Major General Leslie R. Groves ordered a medical survey team to Japan to determine whether radiation levels were safe enough for American troops to enter and occupy the area, and to secure all possible information concerning the effects of the bombs, especially radioactive effects, on people and property. The September 1945 investigation reported widespread casualties from the initial flash and subsequent firestorm, with many survivors suffering and dying from burns, and reported that radiation injuries were modest, accounting for only 5 to 7 percent of casualties. A second, more detailed survey by navy, army, and Manhattan Project scientists documented to a much greater degree the lingering effects of radiation and the human health consequences of radiation exposure. This second set of reports was classified and included data on some fourteen thousand Japanese exposed to radiation and data from studies conducted on US soldiers of the occupying army. Report findings noted significant health problems associated with radiation exposure, and recommendations included the establishment of a long-term study of Japanese atomic bomb casualties (Weisgall 1994:208–10).

It was in this context—where public and congressional debate over the future of atomic weapons testing was influenced by the nonclassified version of the initial biomedical reports from Nagasaki and Hiroshima, which suggested that atomic weapons produced immense immediate effect but no obvious long-term effect—that Operation Crossroads was planned. The exercise was meant to determine the relevance of a naval fleet when atomic weapons could simply be dropped by air. In addition to demonstrating the tactical uses of the atomic bomb and its effect on naval forces, the exercise was meant to send a signal to the Soviet Union that "the dropping of the atomic bombs

Figure 2.1. Atomic cloud during Baker Day blast at Bikini, July 25, 1946. Credit: Department of the Navy. National Archives Record Collection, ARC identifier 520714

was not so much the last military act of the second world war, as the first major operation of the cold diplomatic war with Russia," according to Gar Alperovitz (Weisgall 1994:61).

On July 1 and July 25, 1946, two atomic bombs, code-named Able and Baker, were detonated over and in Bikini Lagoon, where ninety-five target vessels were anchored. The exercise not only resulted in loss of the target fleet—twelve vessels sunk; the rest were scuttled due to overwhelming contamination—but radioactive contamination brought about the eventual loss of much of the targeted Pacific Fleet. The underwater detonation of Baker produced a huge cloud of radioactive mist that did not disperse and that blanketed the lagoon and atoll with a heavy deposition of radiotoxins, briefly enshrouding the naval fleet, which had briefly reentered the lagoon shortly after the test. Radioactivity was dangerously high even a week after the blast when the fleet returned. Decontamination was next to impossible, as radioactivity adhered to all exposed organic materials, including rope, canvas, wood, clothing, food, and people. Efforts to communicate risk or enforce safety procedures were complicated by the fact that radiation was not visible and could not be smelled or tasted, and even the instruments used to measure its presence were inadequate and faulty (DOD 1946).

The exercise demonstrated the extreme threat produced by fallout, prompting a reconceptualization of the atomic bomb—from a weapon that explodes and incinerates to a new tool in the chemical weapons arsenal. This reconceptualization was articulated in the December 1946 *Radiological Warfare* report by Joseph Hamilton, a scientist deeply involved in World War II–era human experiments with plutonium and an early proponent of radiological warfare. Submitting his report soon after his return from Operation Crossroads, he noted that "fission products can not only be used to impair or destroy civilian and military personnel, they can be used to contaminate soils and food chains and thus impair or destroy food production systems." Hamilton recommended both an offensive and defensive approach to a radiological warfare program, writing, "I strongly believe that the best protection that this nation can secure against the possibilities of radioactive agents being employed as a military tool by some foreign power is a thorough evaluation and understanding of the full potentiality of such an agent…such studies must be made by means of large scale experimentation, as well as laboratory research, it will be essential that there be available in some isolated region an extensive proving ground. Here a large variety of field trials could be conducted" (Hamilton 1946a).

In addition to its impact on military strategies, Operation Crossroads deeply affected the priorities and research questions that drove biomedical research in the early years of the Cold War, and it initiated a host of projects and studies examining the nature and multifaceted power of radioactive debris. Joseph Hamilton's Project 48, research exploring the human health impact of plutonium, received expanded funding. New studies included human-subject experimentation to explore the metabolic impact of fission products and transuranic elements, Operation Crossroads decontamination studies, tracer studies, radio autographic studies, radiochemistry, and human experiments to investigate possible methods to treat plutonium poisoning (DOD 1947; Hamilton 1946b). Similar projects were funded or reinstated at other AEC-sponsored facilities affiliated with the universities of Rochester, California, and Chicago and at Oakridge National Laboratory (ACHRE 1995:257–64; Warren 1947; Welsome 1999:120–62).

By 1949 the main questions driving this research, as articulated by an ad hoc committee charged with planning biological aspects of future atomic bomb tests, were: What will happen to humans when exposed at infrequent times to relatively high doses of radiation? What is the nature and persistence of fission by-products? How do they accumulate in the environment, the food chain, and the human body and to what biophysical effect? What are the potential late effects of the atomic bomb upon the germplasm of the exposed population? And, related questions: What is the naturally occurring mutation rate in humans, and what is the mutagenic rate from added radioactivity? (AEC 1949; see also Neel 1949). To address these questions, Project Gabriel was initiated later that year, with the mandate of exploring and predicting how the use of nuclear weapons in warfare might adversely affect local populations.

Project Gabriel documented fallout effects and the potential hazards of human ingestion of plutonium, strontium-90, and yttrium-90 particles in bomb debris; tracked where fallout accumulated locally and around the world; and determined the biomedical impact on the lungs and metabolism of humans who inhaled radioactive particles. In addition to lab experiments, weapons tests were conducted to study particle size and fallout patterns, and environmental surveillance sites were established around the world to monitor Soviet and Chinese weapons tests and to track radioactive fallout (AEC Division of Biology and Medicine 1954b).

Project Gabriel led to the creation of subsidiary programs. Operation Teapot collected human urine, animal milk, and tissue samples under the guise of a nutritional study (Walter Reed Army Institute of Research 1955). Operation Sunshine grew to be the "largest of fifty-nine tissue-analysis studies conducted by atomic scientists during the Cold War. Operation Body Snatch, a Sunshine program, collected approximately 9000 samples of human bones and nearly 600 fetuses from around the world" (General Accounting Office 1995:3). By 1956 human bone collection stations had been established in Brazil, Chile, China, Colombia, Denmark, Ecuador, England, France, Germany, India, Iran, Italy, Japan, Liberia, Puerto Rico, South Africa, Switzerland, Canada, Venezuela, and the United States (Kulp 1956). A number of Sunshine studies were conducted with collaborative assistance from the World Health Organization and its regional bodies and included collection and analysis of samples of soil, vegetation, food, and water to assess the accumulation of fallout isotopes such as strontium-90 (Sr-90) and iodine-131 (I-131) (AEC Health and Safety Laboratory 1958; Kulp 1956). To allow global studies to flourish, scientists from nations around the world came to the United States for training in the use of radioisotopes. AEC also provided materials and technical assistance for setting up radioisotope-generating facilities and subsequently supported collaborative research in scientists' home countries. This effort to develop a global network of scientists tracking fallout and conducting biomedical research with radioisotopes began in 1947 at Clinton Laboratories (renamed Oakridge National Laboratory in 1948). The work was greatly expanded under the Atoms for Peace program established in December 1953 (DOE 1995:ch. 2).

Cold War biomedical research activity within and outside the United States produced an increased demand for human subjects. In 1949, when the Ad Hoc Committee for Biologic Aspects for Future Atomic Bomb Tests met and defined the research agenda for "future proof tests of atomic weapons at Enewetak," a high priority was placed on research studying the human effects of radiation (AEC 1949). In 1950, anticipating the use of the nuclear bomb as a tactical weapon in the Korean War, General James Cooney proposed total-body irradiation experiments on a population of two hundred healthy civilian and military subjects to address battlefield questions—establishing the threshold of unsafe exposure, where soldiers might become sick or incapacitated, being the greatest concern (ACBM 1950:12). Although this and other proposals for human-subject experiments involving large groups of healthy people prompted debate in various military-civilian advisory committees, as outlined below, projects were eventually authorized. Approval for human-subject research involving the use of radioactive materials on human subjects was easily secured when subjects were civilian "volunteers" or were procured by collaborating civilian scientists, or when a foreign government granted blanket research approval, thus negating the need to secure permission from the secretary of the navy or another top official as mandated by military regulations.[3]

Atomic Agendas and Indigenous Population Research in the Arctic

Human-subject research was conducted in the Arctic for two major reasons. First, the area contained groups of people who had lived in a cold climate for thousands of years. Efforts to understand how the human body functions in cold settings would provide information of use to a military that relied on airplanes for surveillance and for carrying nuclear weapons and that shared the Arctic Circle with a Cold War enemy. Secondly, the area received a great deal of environmental contamination from the atmospheric detonation of nuclear weapons. The Arctic was not only contaminated by deposition from US tests in the Pacific. In 1955 the Soviet testing program at Novaya Zemlya began, and over the next thirty-five years, these arctic islands were the sites of approximately 132 nuclear tests, including more than ninety atmospheric detonations between 1955 and 1962. High-yield atmospheric tests conducted by the Soviets beginning in 1958 added to the fallout reaching Alaska and northern Canada. In the 1960s and early 1970s, the United States conducted three underground tests at Amchitka in the Aleutian Islands (Kohlhoff 2002:44). Biologically discrete populations, living in traditional communities and with a heavy reliance on locally harvested foods, provided the opportunity to track the movement of radioactive elements through the food chain and the human body.

In 1947 the US Air Force established the Arctic Aeromedical Lab at Ladd Air Force Base. Field stations were also established at Anaktuvik Pass and Cleary Pass to allow short-term studies with Natives or with military personnel serving as subjects in "basic and applied research in the medical and related sciences which will help solve problems affecting the health and efficiency of Air Force personnel in arctic climates" (US Air Force 1957a). Initial research was conducted under a 1948 contract with the University of Washington, which provided a physiologist, biochemist, psychologist, anthropologist, and zoologist-botanist to conduct research out of the Ladd Field facility in Alaska (DOD 1948). The research goals of the Arctic Aeromedical Lab addressed "problems concerning medical defense against atomic, biological, and chemical warfare agents in the arctic." Studies included investigation of the incidence of cardiovascular disease among Alaska Natives, peripheral vascular response to cold (and the differences between Eskimo, Caucasian, and Negroid response), comparative sweat activity in Eskimo and Caucasian populations, and tularemia antibody studies. In 1952 the lab began basal metabolic rhythm (BMR) studies, analyzing blood samples collected at monthly intervals to track changes and determine human response to seasonal cycles, explore seasonal variation in skin temperature, and document basal metabolic changes (US Air Force 1957b). By 1954 human-subject research had taken place at twenty-five different research sites throughout Alaska (DOD 1967).

In 1955 "tracer doses up to 65 microcuries of I-131 were used to determine thyroid uptake, urinary and salivary elimination, total plasma and protein-mobile I-131." This study involved clinical evaluation, estimates of dietary iodine uptake, and biological monitoring following environmental exposure. Subjects included coastal and inland Eskimos, two groups of Athabascan Indians of Fort Yukon and Arctic Village, and white controls including army and air force personnel. In forty-six cases, the I-131 uptake procedure was repeated in the same subjects in different seasons of the year. Between 1955 and 1957, "a total of 200 tracer experiments was made in 19 whites, 84 Eskimos and 17 Indians" (Rodahl and Bang 1956a, 1956b, 1957; see also ACHRE 1995:598–603).

In 1957 research findings from Sunshine program work conducted in Scandinavia and Canada documented high levels of Sr-90 and cesium-137 (Cs-137) in lichen, caribou, and reindeer (US Congress, Atomic Energy Committee 1957). Radiation ecology studies of the northern Alaskan ecosystem, begun in 1959 as part of the Project Chariot bioenvironmental program, confirmed high levels of fallout radionuclides in plants, birds, and small mammals. Follow-up research in the arctic regions of Scandinavia, reported in 1961, reconfirmed findings of Sr-90 and Cs-137 in animals and humans. A subsequent annual study demonstrated high levels of Cs-137 in Laplanders and their food (Miettinen 1977; Miettinen et al. 1964). Beginning in 1962, Alaska Natives at Anaktuvak Pass were surveyed to determine body burdens of Cs-137 and I-131, resulting in the publication of "Contamination of Soft Tissues of Infants and Children with Radioactive Fallout" and findings of I-131 in children's thyroids (Hanson 1967, 1968, 1971, 1982).

In December 1967, a thyroid research proposal, part of a Naval Arctic Research Laboratory study of circumpolar populations, was presented to and approved by Eskimo residents of Wainwright and Point Barrow as part of a study on the effects of cold and exercise on thyroid function under different environmental conditions. A single dose of radioactive iodine was to be administered (National Research Council 1996).[4] In proposing the study, the village council noted that "the people would not allow nude photographs of themselves as were taken by the Air Force sponsored studies of cardiology by the team from University of Oregon Medical School in 1958. The people wanted positive feedback from the examining physicians relating to their health. The people did not want to be treated as 'guinea pigs'" (DOD 1967).

In May 1993, the Arctic Aeromedical Lab's thyroid-function study was discussed at the Arctic Contamination Conference in Anchorage, Alaska (Hanson 1994). Public outcry over this study prompted Senator Frank Murkowski to spearhead a congressional request to the National Research Council (NRC) to investigate (1) whether the thyroid-function study violated ethical guidelines and (2) whether the I-131 doses posed a health threat to the human participants. The committee collected accessible documents, held public hearings, and interviewed available scientists and subject participants. In 1996 the NRC issued a report finding that nontherapeutic research had been conducted and that no effort had been made to interpret medical procedures (what was being done and why) or obtain consent. The committee observed the inability of scientists to speak the language and their failure to provide translators, concluding that language and cultural barriers played a significant role in preventing meaningful informed consent. The committee also acknowledged that additional experimentation involving the use of radioisotopes may have occurred, in this and other communities, as reported by Alaska Natives, but it was unable to locate supporting documentation; no Arctic Aeromedical Laboratory documents prior to 1958 could be located at the time of the review (National Research Council 1996:21, 24).

ACHRE (1995:598–604) also reviewed the Arctic Aeromedical Laboratory thyroid-function study and determined that a wrong had been committed. Per ACHRE recommendations, in October 2000 US Air Force secretary F. Whitten Peters presented a formal apology to Alaskan subjects and their families. The apology was accompanied by the announcement of an award settlement of $7 million, including payments of $67,000 to each study participant or his or her descendents as compensation for perceptions of health risk associated with an oral dose of I-131, especially the anxiety and stress caused by learning of the radioactive dosage. The North Slope Borough also received $1.36 million for damages relating to the community experience of hosting a medical survey team whose presence implied health care treatment rather than research objectives (Bishop 2000).

Atomic Agendas and Indigenous Population Research in the Andes and Amazon

In the early years of the Cold War, primary research concerns were associated with developing military capacity to fight a nuclear war: how to survive long flights at high altitude; understanding the human effects of radioisotopes in order to treat radiation injury; and understanding the nature of radioactive fallout on food production and human populations in order to develop offensive and defensive strategies. At the same time, the US military had lost most of its force through decommissioning and came to rely upon collaborative science—where funds, equipment, and technical assistance were provided by the United States in exchange for research that directly contributed to US Cold War interests.

The ability to conduct international collaborative work required US investment in facilities and expertise. In return, research supporting US military objectives could be conducted in field laboratories with acclimated subjects procured by project collaborators. Thus, in Peru in 1947, the Morococha Lab was built on land provided by the Cerro de Pasco Copper Company, with funds from the AEC, the Rockefeller Foundation, the US Public Health Service, and the US Air Force. At 4,500 meters, this was the highest research facility in the world. Indigenous employees of the nearby copper mine were used in the following years as "volunteer" subjects in a range of experiments exploring the effects of high altitude on the human body (Lawrence et al. 1952; Siri et al. 1954).

Examples of collaborative human-subject research in South America can be found as early as 1950, when Donner Lab scientists John Lawrence, William Siri, and others traveled to Peru to collaborate with Alberto Hurtado in studying high-altitude physiology and polycythemia using radioisotopes of iron, phosphorus, and carbon-14 in experiments with Native Peruvians of the high Andes (Lawrence 1950). In 1952 Donner Lab scientists returned to examine the effects of altitude on body water and red cell life. Findings were compared with data obtained from Hurtado, including data from subjects involved in Hurtado's long-term research program (Donner Laboratory 1952a, 1952b).

On some occasions high-altitude research in Peru was conducted under direct contract for the Department of Defense. For example, Alberto Hurtado was contracted to conduct radioisotope research on people living at high altitude to help address the problem of hypoxia experienced by pilots at high altitude (US Air Force 1954). US funds were also funneled through Hurtado's lab to support US scientists. In March 1955, the Department of Defense Research Council approved a proposal by Hurtado to hire a scientist on sabbatical from Bryn Mawr to test theories of how acclimated subjects are susceptible to bacterial infection and resistant to certain viral infections by studying metabolic changes (DOD 1955).

In 1957 Donner Lab scientists returned to South America, this time collaborating with Dr. M. Escobar on research in the mountains near La Paz, Bolivia. They studied red blood cell formation at high altitude and anemia using Fe-59 (radioactive iron), phosphorus-32, and tritium in an experiment involving four medical students and four Indian miners (Donner Laboratory 1966; Siri and Webster 1957). And AEC representatives visited Chile, Argentina, Peru, and Brazil to enlist local scientists in efforts to collect food samples as part of the Project Sunshine studies on Sr-90 and I-131 fallout and accumulation in the food chain, and to obtain samples of food that represented the primary sources of calcium intake for "primitive populations in areas with very low calcium content" (who might therefore exhibit a higher rate of Sr-90 and I-131 uptake). In a report describing findings from these collections, it was noted:

> The maximum level that has been found in this laboratory for a group of people was from the jungle of Ecuador. The people of one Indian village were consuming a major calcium source that carried 40 to 40 pC of Sr90 per gram of CA when the US diet was about 7pC of Sr90 per gram of Ca (late 1957). It is unlikely that people in such an environment exceed 0.0001% of the world population. Since this occurred in an area of 200 inches of mean annual rainfall, the concentration of Sr90 in this diet should drop very rapidly with depletion of the stratospheric reservoir. (Kulp 1961)

In the Amazon, Venezuelan scientist Marcel Roche and others used an array of radioisotopes to explore their effects on the thyroid, track uptake rates in indigenous lowland populations, and, in later years, compare uptake rates with data from Andean populations. Roche and others also explored hookworm anemia and related intestinal blood loss. Funding for these studies included support from the World Health Organization and its regional bodies, whose radioisotope research was organized at the request of AEC. While research titles suggest an emphasis on local health issues (surveying for the presence or absence of goiters, hookworm, and related anemia), the research findings contributed to broader biomedical concerns of radiation exposure. Studies of the biology of anemia and red blood cell production, as well as studies examining the variation in thyroid function in relation to different human populations, different exposures to radiation, varying altitude, and varying responses to I-131 exposure, allowed the US military to better treat acute radiation exposure. Human subjects used in these studies included the Maquiritare and Guaharibo Indians from the Venezuelan Amazon. A 1959 study involved some ninety-five subjects receiving I-131, and a February 1960 expedition involved I-131 uptake tests with eighteen Indians of the Maquiritare tribe, nine of whom had received radioiodine in February 1959. Findings were compared with values from studies conducted by other scientists at three sites in the "highly endemic Andean regions" of Venezuela and control studies in Caracas. In 1962 and 1968, Marcel Roche and others conducted a large-scale population study of thyroid uptake in the Yanomami Indians of the Venezuelan Amazon and indigenous groups living in the Venezuelan Andes, finding that at very high altitudes there was a uniformly higher thyroid radioiodine (I-131) uptake (De Venanzi et al. 1958; Rivière et al. 1968; Roche 1959a, 1959b; Roche and de Venanzi et al. 1957; Roche and Layrisse 1956; Roche and Perez-Gimenez 1959; Roche and Perez-Gimenez et al. 1957).

In addition to the above studies that contributed to an understanding of red blood cell production and thyroid function, the AEC also sponsored human population research in the Brazilian Amazon. In 1958 the AEC commissioned a feasibility study of a radioepidemiology project and developed an interdisciplinary experiment exploring background radiation and its relationship to disease, with the recommendation that the AEC fund a preliminary study involving a geneticist, anthropologist, epidemiologist, clinician, pathologist, demographer, and specialist in background radiation (Dunham 1958). In 1962 geneticist James Neel conducted AEC-financed research with a Chavante (now known as the Xavante) village on the Río das Mortes in the Mato Grosso region of Brazil, with an interdisciplinary team including a serologist, two human geneticists, a cultural anthropologist, and a physical anthropologist. In addition to consanguinity data, the team collected blood and saliva specimens and physical measurements (Neel 1962). In 1966 the AEC conducted a study of natural radioactivity in Brazil, finding soils with high radium content—twenty times average world levels. A report was later published on "the possible dose-effect relationship of populations subjected to chronic, low level ionizing radiation" in the Guarapari region of the Brazilian Amazon (De Gonzales et al. 1966). In 1967–68, with AEC funding, Neel returned to the Brazilian Amazon, where a new interdisciplinary team visited the Yanomami and collected similar blood and saliva samples, physical measurements, and family histories (Turner and Stevens 2001). Marcel Roche accompanied Neel's team, studying iodine deficiencies among the Yanomami with the use of I-131. Roche's work was evidently funded by the French Atomic Energy Commission (ASHG 2002; Rivière et al. 1968).

In the ACHRE archives, references to James V. Neel include his genetic research with the Japanese and Marshallese populations exposed to radioactive fallout, and his Yanomami data were used as a control to interpret findings (Neel et al. 1976). From the AEC point of view, Neel was "collecting blood samples from these rather isolated groups and storing the sera for the purpose of genetic identification of blood factors that possibly might give some clue to the factors which resulted in rejection of tissue transplants…important in that our one effective treatment for radiation sickness was marrow transplants" (Goldstein 1970) and "establishing long-range genetic trends in the relatively primitive Yanomama Indians of South America, a civilization unexposed to modern-day pollutants, and the Japanese survivors of the Hiroshima and Nagasaki bombings. These on-going projects will provide a basis of comparison for data developed on mutation rates in the United States" (ERDA 1976).

In 2000 some of this Amazonian research history was detailed, and consequential damages were suggested in *Darkness in El Dorado* by Patrick Tierney. Controversy over the account produced a number of investigations by universities, professional organizations, and individuals in the United States, Brazil, Venezuela, and elsewhere. Evidence emerging from these investigations suggests that Brazilian authorities granted consent for medical research expeditions among the Yanomami in the 1970s. However, no meaningful informed consent occurred with regard to the human subjects themselves (cf. Borofsky 2005).

While much of the research summarized in this section was brought to public light as a result of a Clinton administration declassification order and ACHRE review, human radiation experiments in Andean and Amazonian populations contracted by US agencies were not included in the deliberations of ACHRE, nor in its final report.

Atomic Agendas and Indigenous Population Research in the Marshall Islands

From 1946 to 1958, the US government conducted sixty-seven atmospheric atomic and thermonuclear tests in the Marshall Islands. Biomedical research in the Marshall Islands began in the summer of 1948, when the medical crew aboard the USS *Whidbey* conducted physical exams in an effort to examine every inhabitant of the Pacific trust territories. In the Marshall Islands, some 60 percent of the inhabitants were reportedly surveyed on two separate trips. In addition to physical exams conducted in the other trust territories, blood samples were also taken from the Marshallese (Hetzel 1959).

In 1951 AEC funded its first human population study to explore the genetic effects of radiation. It issued a series of three research contracts to geneticist James V. Neel to work with a Marshall Islands population, examining "natural occurring mutations in a human population." Described in AEC committee minutes and press releases as the crucial first step to understanding the human genetic effects of radiation, this research was expected to "yield data of considerable value in our thinking about the genetic effects of irradiation in man" (AEC Scientific Advisory Committee 1951). Neel, in a letter to his colleague Max Zelle, wrote that he expected to find "that the spontaneous rate of mutation in human genes is going to be relatively high, a fact which of course would make their apparent sensitivity to irradiation of less relative importance in the overall picture of man's decline" (Neel 1951). The letter further outlines his research plans, including the introduction of a naturally occurring agent, possibly a viral vaccine, to document mutagenic response in blood proteins.[5]

In 1953 the General Advisory Committee to the AEC recommended establishing a team of scientists to serve for a three-year period to respond to event exposures and collect urine and blood samples in support of ongoing Project Gabriel research, including research on "the carcinogenic action of ingested or inhaled radioactive materials" (AEC General Advisory Committee 1953).

On March 1, 1954, the people of Rongelap, Ailinginae, and Rongerik atolls, downwind from Bikini Atoll, were exposed to radioactive fallout from the Bravo test, a 15-megaton thermonuclear weapon detonated as part of Operation Castle. Three days after detonation, the Rongelapese were evacuated from their atoll and enrolled in medical studies documenting the long-term effects of radiation on a human population. After three years, the Rongelapese were returned to their atoll to live in what was then known to US scientists to be a heavily contaminated environment. Medical survey teams visited the atoll each year, and the Rongelapese were subjects in a series of studies documenting how human beings absorb radiation from a contaminated environment. Medical survey visits prioritized documentation and further experimentation, not treatment. The Rongelapese were not informed of the dangers of living in a radioactive setting until 1982, when EPA scientists attending an annual DOE–Republic of the Marshall Islands (RMI) meeting made suggestive comments (Johnston and Barker 2001).

Over the three months following their evacuation in 1954, 64 residents of Rongelap, 18 residents of Ailinginae, 157 residents of Utrik, and 28 Americans from Rongerik—together with control groups of 117 Marshallese living in Majuro and 105 US service personnel—provided biological samples in a variety of studies exploring the effects of radiation exposure on human beings (AEC Division of Biology and Medicine 1954a; Cronkite et al. 1954; Shipman 1954). Project 4.1—the Study of Response of Human Beings Exposed to Significant Beta and Gamma Radiation Due to Fallout from High Yield Weapons—"represented the first observations by Americans on human beings exposed to excessive doses of radiation from fallout" and documented significant burns, hair loss, depressed blood cell and leukocyte counts, flulike symptoms, fingernail discoloration, nausea, and radioisotope activity in the urine as a result of acute external exposure. Concerning the health and future of the people of Rongelap, Project 4.1 recommendations included the warning that they "should be exposed to no further radiation, external or internal with the exception of essential diagnostic and therapeutic x-rays for at least 12 years. If allowance is made for unknown effects of surface dose and internal deposition there probably should be no exposure for [the] rest of [their] natural lives" (Cronkite et al. 1954).

Data and findings from Project 4.1 were discussed by the AEC Division of Biology and Medicine in the July 1954 Conference on Long Term Surveys and Studies of Marshall Islands and were used to shape an integrated long-term human environmental research program to document the bioaccumulation of fallout and the human effects of this exposure. Two years later, the atolls were still contaminated; a series of nuclear weapons tests were planned for 1958, possibly recontaminating the area; and returning people to this setting presented a known hazard. Nevertheless, as the quote that opens this chapter illustrates, the exposed people presented unique opportunities to conduct research. A formal decision was made to return the people to Rongelap with the caveat: "[I]t is the opinion of the ACBM that if it should become necessary to re-evacuate because of further tests there would result world opinion unfavorable to the continuation of weapons testing" (ACBM 1956a:9–10). This resolution was unanimously passed. In a subsequent discussion of plans to return the people of Ronglelap to their home atoll, the value of Rongelapese service in planned long-term studies was again articulated: "[H]ere was a very small population exposed to a very high dose of radiation…this is an ideal situation to make your genetic study. It is far more significant than anything you could ever get out of Hiroshima and Nagasaki" (ACBM 1956b:21). The Rongelap community would serve as a study population, and the people of Utrik would serve as the controls for that study.

The nonevacuation policy meant that the people of Rongelap had to contend with contamination from the Bravo event; pre-1954 tests; tests that had occurred during their absence, such as the 1956 Redwing series; and later military operations. For example, the 1958 Operation Hardtack series generated additional fallout on Rongelap, producing elevated levels of plutonium noted in subsequent medical and environmental surveys (Conard et al. 1958). The testing of nuclear devices in 1961–62 resulted in increased concentrations of radioactive iron (Fe-55) in goatfish liver, documented by University of Washington scientists, and subsequent increases in average Rongelapese body burdens of Fe-55, documented by medical survey scientists (Beasley et al. 1970).

In addition to new exposures to radiation from subsequent nuclear weapons tests, the people of Rongelap were likely exposed to fallout from biological weapons tests. In the summer of 1968, the Deseret Test Center conducted a series of tests known as DTC 68-50 from the *USS Granville S. Hall*, anchored off Enewetak Atoll. This test series involved the atmospheric dissemination of "PG"—staphylococcal enterotoxin B—a toxin that causes incapacitating food poisoning and flulike symptoms that can

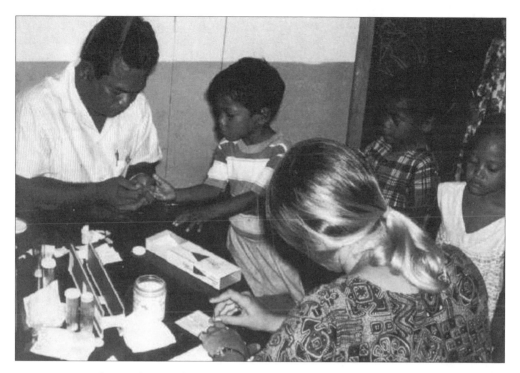

Figure 2.2. Working with control subjects: schoolchildren on Majuro, Marshall Islands. Credit: Pacific Trust Territory Photo Archive

be fatal to the very young, the elderly, and people weakened by long-term illness. Staphylococcal enterotoxin B was disseminated over a 40- to 50-kilometer downwind grid, and according to the final report, a single weapon was calculated to have covered 2,400 square kilometers, an area equal to 926.5 square miles (Regis 1999:204–06). The medical survey for 1967, 1968, and 1969 reports in the summary of health conditions that "[a] rather serious outbreak of Hong Kong influenza occurred among the Rongelap people in 1968 and may have been responsible for the deaths of a 58-year old exposed woman and of an unexposed boy who died of meningitis complicating the influenza." However, the same report gives findings from viral antibody tests demonstrating no antibodies in the Rongelap population to the "Asian influenzas" (Conard et al. 1969:3), suggesting that the deaths were a result of testing biological weapons.

Between 1954 and 1998, when responsibility for a long-term study conducted by Brookhaven National Lab was transferred to the Pacific Health Research Institute (PHRI) in Honolulu, Hawaii, the people of Rongelap hosted seventy-three biomedical research visits. Over the decades, biomedical research also involved control subjects from Utrik, Likiep, Bikini, and other atolls. Majuro and the village of Rita hosted at least eighteen research visits, and study participants were part of childhood development and aging studies. Over the years, control children were examined, had blood and other tissue samples (including bone marrow) extracted, and participated in some radioisotope studies (Barker, this volume; Johnston and Barker 2001).

To allow long-term monitoring of the degenerative effects of radiation, regular interval examinations were conducted. They consisted of physical examinations and interval histories; hematological studies such as hematocrit, white blood cell counts, differential counts, platelet enumeration, and bone marrow studies; full-body skin exams documented in color and black-and-white photographs, with skin biopsies if indicated; ophthalmological studies of the lens, including a photographic record of the anterior portion of the lens; growth studies of children, including studies of the development of teeth, skeletal measurements, bone marrow sampling, and full photographic documentation, especially as children entered puberty; monitoring of the progress of pregnancies and the status of newborn infants; quantitative studies of internally deposited radioisotopes by means of urinary excretion measurements, external radiological measurements and localization, and other radiography; and periodic radiation surveys of the affected islands and atolls and food and marine life. Interval examinations were recognized as opportunities to collect samples of interest to a wide range of ongoing studies. These projects included selection of extracted teeth to support ongoing studies on the radiation effects on growing teeth; extraction of teeth during autopsies, including those done on people who had died from other causes; bone marrow aspirations to support hematological studies; the use of radioisotopes in tagging procedures to measure red blood cell formation rates; interval X-rays of long bones to track roentgenographic changes and study radio element deposition; and the harvesting of various samples in postmortem autopsies (Johnston and Barker 2001:27–29).

In addition to radiation exposures that occurred while living in a radioactive laboratory, the Rongelap community incurred additional exposure to radioisotopes through medical experiments. The Brookhaven National Laboratory medical survey report for 1957 noted that "chromium tagging studies on red blood cells" were conducted. Chromium (Cr-51) tagging was also reported for the study of red blood cell function and anemia in the medical survey reports for 1961, 1962, 1963, 1964, 1965, 1967, 1968, 1969, and possibly 1974. Experiments involving tritiated water to establish the relationship of blood volume to lean body mass were reported in the medical survey reports for 1964, 1967, 1968, and 1969. In 1965 thyroid uptake studies were conducted, and I-132 was administered. In the twenty-year evaluation of the program, it was noted that nontherapeutic "studies of uptake have also included tests of radioiodine uptake and excretion on several occasions. In the field, I-132 was used.... In a number of cases a small amount of I-131 was administered prior to surgery.... One 48-year old man briefly developed acute thyroiditis after THS administration" (Brookhaven National Laboratory 1969:3). Hospital records appended to this report indicate that I-123 was used in lab work prior to thyroid surgery, and I-131 was given before surgery to allow radiographic studies of removed tissue. In 1971 samples of blood, food, soil, and the lagoon were taken to determine the movement of Fe-59 (an iron isotope) through soil, plants, fish, and people. In 1972, I-132 was again administered as part of the thyroid uptake study, and due to increased thyroid cancer, a decision was made to

Figure 2.3. Following the explosion of Bravo at the Bikini test site, islanders acutely exposed to radioactive fallout were enrolled in a long-term research program conducted by Brookhaven National Laboratory with funding from the Atomic Energy Commission. In this photograph, Dr. Robert Conard examines a Marshall Islander for thyroid abnormalities. Credit: Photograph courtesy of Brookhaven National Laboratory

conduct hematological surveys every six months. In the spring of 1973, I-129 was administered as part of an ongoing iodoprotein study. In the spring of 1974, I-129 was repeatedly administered (with plasma collection at two and four days) to support a study of the excretion rate of iodine in children. Six months later, thyroid uptake and iodoprotein studies were repeated, involving additional doses of I-129.

The ACHRE review of the Marshallese experience reflected the declassified documents available at the time (more were released after ACHRE completed its work). ACHRE concluded that the long-term research program was an example of opportunistic science, where nontherapeutic research was conducted in addition to studies that were plausibly related to the Rongelap community's acute exposure to fallout from the Bravo test. It noted failure to find evidence of informed consent. And it recognized that in at least three cases, subjects were used in radioisotope experiments that served no medical purpose (ACHRE 1995:583–98). In 1996 the DOE identified eleven of those subjects and issued letters of apology.

In the fall of 2001 (October 31–November 2), the Nuclear Claims Tribunal in the Marshall Islands received an expert witness report and testimony from the people of

Rongelap on the consequential damage of the nuclear weapons testing program and related human-subject experimentation (Johnston and Barker 2001). Noting that the DOE had already acknowledged three experiments involving Cr-51 and tritiated water, advocates for the Rongelap claim presented evidence in the form of research protocols, laboratory analysis reports, and published articles demonstrating use of a broader array of radioisotopes, including radioactive iodine, iron, zinc, and carbon-14, in a greater number of experiments than was acknowledged by DOE. In addition to isotope studies, the human-subject experimentation included radiation exposure–food chain studies involving systemic exposures to low-level radiation from varied radioisotopes as a result of diet and lifestyle in a known contaminated setting. The people of Rongelap requested that the Nuclear Claims Tribunal recognize the human-subject experimentation as a harm related to the nuclear weapons testing program and therefore deserving judicial remedy. They also asked judges to consider the communitywide experience associated with long-term studies on the effects of acute and systemic exposures to radiation. As of this writing, the Marshall Islands Nuclear Claims Tribunal has yet to issue findings or judgments in the case.

Conclusion

The atomic agendas that sustained the scientific research machine of the late 1940s and early 1950s moved the biological unit of radiation-effects research from the individual patient under the care of a doctor (who assumed responsibility for consent) to larger groups of soldiers, inmates, students, and, in the cases noted above, "biologically discrete" human populations under the care of the state. Assessments of the human-subject experimentation record by ACHRE, the National Academy of Sciences, and various scholars demonstrate that radiation experiments were conducted with large numbers of healthy people beginning in the 1950s. These studies tracked the nature, presence, and effect of radioactive fallout in the environment, food chain, and people. They identified the human genetic effects of exposure to naturally occurring sources of radiation. And they documented the long-term consequences of exposure to high levels of radioactivity, which required groups of defined and controllable human subjects, including communities that depended upon the local environs for food, lived on traditional lands in tightly defined social groups, and lived in areas with high levels of naturally occurring radiation.

In the past few years, critical scrutiny of Cold War–era biomedical history has produced a number of publications detailing US government use of its citizens and soldiers as human subjects in experiments that allowed the development of nuclear, biological, and chemical warfare capability (ACHRE 1995; Moreno 2001; National Research Council 1996; Regis 1999; Welsome 1999). This literature, however, largely focuses on the human-subject experiences of US citizens brought to light in declassified materials documenting radiation research conducted by or contracted by US government agencies and made public as a result of ACHRE. Where an effort has been made to describe US-funded research involving indigenous groups in other regions of the world, biases and flaws in depicting the chain of events resulted in a general public dismissal of the work, even those elements based on declassified documentation (Tierney 2000). As a result, the public discussion of US human radiation experiments has largely centered on the use of various individuals or groups (inmates, soldiers, hospital patients, schoolchildren) and the ethical and moral questions associated with the violation of individual rights.

This chapter briefly touches on the events and driving questions that gave rise to human radiation experiments and suggests the need for a more detailed look at those cases where indigenous populations were used as human subjects to refine scientific understandings of the biological effects of radiation and to enhance US military capability to fight a nuclear war. Indigenous groups and inhabitants of trust territories are "protected peoples," whose status and conditions are protected by UN covenants, including the Geneva Conventions of 1949, which describe medical experiments on protected persons as a grave breach and crime against humanity. In the case of the Marshall Islands, an occupied territory of the United States beginning in 1944 and a formal trust territory of the United States established by the United Nations in 1948, it is argued that the Marshallese were used in biomedical research to meet the national security interests of the United States in fighting its Cold War. Similar arguments can made with regard to research involving indigenous groups in the Arctic, Amazon, and Andes.

Coda

Dear Dr. Conard,

I'm sorry I was not at home when you visited my island. Instead, I have spent the past few months traveling to Japan and Fiji learning about the treatment of atomic bomb victims and about attempts to end the nuclear threat in the Pacific.

Since leaving Rongelap on the peace ship Fri, I have learned a great deal and am writing to you to clarify some of my feelings regarding your continued use of us as research subjects.

I realize now that your entire career is based on our illness. We are far more valuable to you than you are to us. You have never really cared about us as people—only as a group of guinea pigs for your government's bomb research effort. For me and the people on Rongelap, it is life which matters most. For you it is facts and figures. There is no question about your technical competence, but we often wonder about your humanity. We don't need you and your technical machinery. We want our life and our health. We want to be free....

As a result of my trip I've made some decisions that I want you to know about. The main decision is that we do not want to see you again. We want medical care from doctors who care about us, not about collecting information for the US government's war makers. (Anjain 1975)

Notes

1. This paper was prepared with the financial support of the John T. and Catherine D. MacArthur Foundation through a research and writing grant to the Center for Political Ecology (2004–05) entitled "Considering the Consequential Damages of Nuclear War Legacies." Earlier research into the record of human radiation experimentation sponsored by the United States and conducted in the Marshall Islands was supported in part by scientific research grants from the Office of the Public Advocate, Republic of the Marshall Islands Nuclear Claims Tribunal (1999–2001).

2. Many of the declassified documents cited here were made public following the ACHRE review and were archived on the DOE website (http://hrex.dis.anl.gov/). HREX documents listed in this paper were accessed by title and document number between 1999 and October 2003, when the Bush administration removed HREX documents from Web access. As of July 2006, the HREX website archive is still inaccessible. However, hard copies of HREX documents reviewed by ACHRE are accessible at the National Security Archive, George Washington University; the Republic of the Marshall Islands Embassy (Washington, DC); and the Nuclear Claims Tribunal (Majuro, RMI). Many HREX documents can also be accessed on the DOE's Marshall Islands Historical Documents site, http://worf.eh.doe.gov/index.html.

3. ACHRE, citing Advisory Committee on Biology and Medicine meeting transcripts of November 10, 1950, concluded that "on paper, the debate was decided in Shields Warren's favor. Following Warren's and the Division of Biology and Medicine's opposition, General Cooney and the military agreed that 'human experimentation' on healthy volunteers would not be approved" (ACHRE 1995:39). It is unclear whether ACHRE consulted transcripts from the DOD Research and Development Board Committee on Medical Science meeting of November 28–29, 1950, where Cooney's proposal and the ACBM decisions were discussed. Noting the politics of requesting human-subject approval, the DOD Research and Development Board concluded that it was legal to conduct research with human subjects without approval so long as the subjects were not naval personnel (DOD 1950).

4. The National Research Council inquiry could not determine if the research had actually been conducted (National Research Council 1996:21).

5. Note that while this research was the first contract for human-subject work involving the Marshallese, my efforts to locate the formal research protocol, field journals, trip reports, or other data relating to this project have been, to date, fruitless. It could be that biological samples were collected for him as part of the Whidbey survey. Several years later, in 1957, Neel requested additional data collection from Marshallese subjects in support of his genetics research (reported on September 25, 1957, by Dr. Robert Conard). Conard's report of the 1958 survey indicates that samples were obtained (Conard et al. 1958). James Neel, Robert Ferrell, and Robert Conard eventually collaborated on a formal publication (Neel et al. 1976).

References

AAA. *See* American Anthropological Association

ACBM. *See* Advisory Committee on Biology and Medicine

ACHRE. *See* Advisory Committee on Human Radiation Experiments

Advisory Committee on Biology and Medicine
1950   Meeting minutes. November 10–11, 1950. US Atomic Energy Commission. ACHRE Archive, HREX document 0711806.
1956a   Meeting minutes. January 13–14, 1956. US Atomic Energy Commission. ACHRE Archive, HREX document d9275.
1956b   Meeting minutes. May 26–27, 1956. US Atomic Energy Commission. HREX document 1749_f.

Advisory Committee on Human Radiation Experiments
1995   Final Report of the Advisory Committee on Human Radiation Experiments. Washington, DC: US Government Printing Office.

AEC. *See* Atomic Energy Commission

AEC Division of Biology and Medicine
1954a   Conference on Long Term Surveys and Studies of the Marshall Islands. Department of Energy, Marshall Islands Historical Documents Archive. Electronic document, http://worf.eh.doe.gov/ihp/chron/A30.PDF, accessed July 29, 2006.
1954b   Report on Project Gabriel. Washington, DC: Atomic Energy Commission.
1956   Minutes, 58th Meeting of A.E.C. Advisory Committee on Biology and Medicine. Department of Energy, Marshall Islands Historical Documents Archive. Electronic document, http://worf.eh.doe.gov/data/ihp1d/1751_f.pdf, accessed October 25, 2006.

AEC General Advisory Committee
1953   Minutes, Thirty-sixth Meeting of the General Advisory Committee to the US Atomic Energy Commission. Department of Energy, Marshall Islands Historical Documents Archive. Electronic document, http://worf.eh.doe./gov/data/ihp1d/881e.pdf, accessed October 25, 2006.

AEC Health and Safety Laboratory
1958   Environmental Contamination from Weapon Tests. New York: Atomic Energy Commission.

AEC Scientific Advisory Committee
1951   Monthly status and progress report. February 1951. ACHRE Archive, HREX document 18956001.

American Anthropological Association
2002   Final Report of the AAA El Dorado Task Force. Electronic document, http://www.aaanet.org/edtf/, accessed July 28, 2006.

American Society of Human Genetics
2002   Response to Allegations against James V. Neel in *Darkness in El Dorado*, by Patrick Tierney. American Journal of Medical Genetics 70:1–10.

Anjain, Nelson

1975 Letter to Robert Conard from Nelson Anjain, April 9, 1975. Department of Energy, Marshall Islands Historical Documents Archive. Electronic document, http://worf.eh.doe.gov/data/ihp2/1976_.pdf, accessed July 30, 2006.

ASHG. *See* **American Society of Human Genetics**

Atomic Energy Commission

1949 Letter to Shields Warren from W. D. Armstrong, S. L. Clark, D. B. Dill, R. H. Draeger. J. Furth, L. O. Jacobson, W. J. Langham, F. K. Sparrow, R.E. Zirkle, G. V. Leroy. Department of Energy, Marshall Islands Historical Documents Archive. Electronic document, http://worf.eh.doe.gov/data/ihp1b/5668_.pdf, accessed August 27, 2006.

Beasley, T. M., E. E. Held, and R. M. Conard

1970 Iron-55 in Rongelap People, Fish and Soils. Department of Energy, Marshall Islands Historical Documents Archive. Electronic document, http://worf.eh.doe.gov/data/ihp1c/0181_.PDF, accessed July 29, 2006.

Bishop, Sam

2000 Feds, Natives Settle over '50s Iodine Experiments. Fairbanks Daily News-Miner, October 26: 1.

Borofsky, Robert, with Bruce Albert, Raymond Hames, Kim Hill, Leda Leitao Martins, John Peters, and Terence Turner

2005 Yanomami: The Fierce Controversy and What We Can Learn from It. Berkeley: University of California Press.

Brookhaven National Laboratory

1969 Medical Survey of the People of Rongelap and Utrik Islands Thirteen, Fourteen, and Fifteen Years After Exposure to Fallout Radiation (March 1967, March 1968, and March 1969). Department of Energy, Marshall Islands Historical Documents Archive. Electronic document, http://worf.eh.doe.gov/data/ihp1b/3549_.pdf, accessed July 29, 2006.

Conard, Robert A., James S. Robertson, Leo M. Meyer, Waturo W. Sutow, William Wolins, Austin Lowrey, and Harold Urschel

1959 Medical Survey of Rongelap People, March 1958, Four Years after Exposure to Fallout. Washington, DC: Department of Commerce, Office of Technical Services.

Cronkite, E. P., V. P. Bond, L. E. Browning, W. H. Chapman, S. H. Cohn, R. A. Conard, C. L. Dunham, R. S. Farr, W. S. Hall, R. Sharp, and S. Shipman

1954 Report to the Scientific Director, Operation Castle—Final Report Project 4.1. Study of Response of Human Beings Accidentally Exposed to Significant Fallout Radiation. Department of Energy, Marshall Islands Historical Documents Archive. Electronic document, http://worf.eh.doe.gov/data/ihp2/2776_.pdf, accessed October 25, 2006.

De Gonzales, C., C. Costa Ribeiro, H. Mosse, T. L. Cullen, W. C. Pfeiffer, E. Penna Franca, and M. J. T. Soares

1966 Temporary Body Burdens in Dose-Effect Studies of the Brazilian Areas of High

Natural Radioactivity. ACHRE Archive, HREX document 27840075.

De Venanzi, F., M. Roche, and K. Gaede
1958   Studies in Endemic Goiter with Radioactive Iodine. Proceedings of the Second
        International Congress for the Peaceful Uses of Atomic Energy. Geneva: United
        Nations.

Department of Defense
1946   Operation Crossroads 1946, United States Nuclear Weapons Test Personnel Review.
        ACHRE Archive, HREX document e1581.
1947   Project Organizational List, 12/1/47. ACHRE Archive, HREX document 0715322.
1948   Contract with the University of Washington for Arctic Aeromedical Research.
        ACHRE Archive, HREX document d8457.
1950   Meeting transcript. Research and Development Board Committee on Medical
        Science. November 28–29, 1950. ACHRE Archive, HREX document 5426.
1955   Minutes, research council meetings, March 17, 1955. ACHRE Archive, HREX doc-
        ument d4880.
1967   Report of the Working Party Conference for the IBP/HA Study of Circumpolar
        Populations: Held at the Naval Arctic Research Laboratory, Pt. Barrow, Alaska
        17–22 November 1967. ACHRE Archive, HREX document e1231.

Department of Energy
1995   Human Radiation Experiments: The Department of Energy Roadmap to the Story
        and the Records. Electronic document, http://www.eh.doe.gov/ohre/roadmap/
        roadmap/part2.html, accessed August 27, 2006.

DOD. *See* **Department of Defense**

DOE. *See* **Department of Energy**

Donner Laboratory
1952a   Medical and Health Physics Quarterly Report for Jul–Sept 1952, Contract No. W-
        7405-ENG-48 (redacted). ACHRE Archive, HREX document 0724969.
1952b   Memo to Armstrong, Subject: Peruvian Work. ACHRE Archive, HREX document
        0715360.
1966   Semiannual Report—Biology and Medicine. Electronic document, http://ntrs.nasa.
        gov/archive/nasa/casi.ntrs.nasa.gov/19670006612_1967006612.pdf, accessed July
        29, 2006.

Dunham, C. L.
1958   Memorandum to Paul F. Foster, General Manager. From C. L. Dunham, Director,
        Division of Biology and Medicine. Subject: Report of status of review of feasibility
        of radioepidemiology project. November 5, 1958. Atomic Energy Commission.
        ACHRE archive, HREX document, on file at the Embassy of the Republic of the
        Marshall Islands.

Energy Research and Development Administration
1976   ERDA to Fund Mutation Monitoring Program. ERDA press release. February 16,
        1976. ACHRE Archive, HREX document 0703038.

ERDA. *See* Energy Research and Development Administration

General Accounting Office
1995   Fact Sheet for Congressional Requestors: Information on DOE's # Human Tissue Analysis Work. Gaithersburg, MD: General Accounting Office.

Goldstein, J. D.
1970   Letter to Dr. S. G. English from J. D. Goldstein, M.D., January 20, 1970. ACHRE Archive, HREX document 0718613.

Hamilton, Joseph G.
1946a   Joseph G. Hamilton to Colonel K. D. Nichols, Subject: Radioactive Warfare. Forwarding of report on aspects that were related to the military applications of fission products, project 48-A. December 31, 1946. Department of Defense. ACHRE Archive, HREX document 7793.
1946b   Confidential. Project 48A, Project 48B, Project 48C. ACHRE Archive, HREX document 0715324.

Hanson, W. C.
1967   Cesium 137 in Alaska Lichens, Caribou and Eskimos. Health Physics 13:383–89.
1968   Contamination of Soft Tissues of Infants and Children with Radioactive Fallout as Exemplified by 137 Cesium and 131 Iodine. Pediatrics 41:240–56.
1971   I-37Cs: Seasonal Patterns in Native Residents of Three Contrasting Alaskan Villages. Health Physics 22:39–42.
1982   I-37Cs Concentrations in Northern Alaska Eskimos, 1962–79: Effects of Ecological, Cultural and Political Factors. Health Physics 42:433–47.
1994   Radioactive Contamination in Arctic Tundra Ecosystems. Paper prepared for the Workshop on Arctic Contamination, Anchorage, Alaska, May 2–7.

Hetzel, A. M.
1959   Health Survey of the Trust Territory of the Pacific Islands. US Armed Forces Medical Journal 10(10):1199–1222.

IGES. *See* International Genetic Epidemiology Society

International Genetic Epidemiology Society
2001   Commentary on *Darkness in El Dorado*, by Patrick Tierney. Genetic Epidemiology 21:81–104.

Johnston, Barbara Rose
1994   Experimenting on Human Subjects: Nuclear Weapons Testing and Human Rights Abuses. *In* Who Pays the Price? The Sociocultural Context of Environmental Crises. Barbara Rose Johnston, ed. Pp. 131–41. Washington, DC: Island Press.
2002   Elements of the Professional Life of James V. Neel as Reflected in the Declassified Literature on Human Radiation Experimentation. Electronic document, http://members.aol.com/archaeodog/darkness_in_el_dorado/documents/0109.htm, accessed October 26, 2006.

Johnston, Barbara Rose, and Holly M. Barker

1999   The Rongelap Property Damage Claims Study: Efforts to Seek Redress for Nuclear Contamination and Loss of a Way of Life. Majuro, RMI: Nuclear Claims Tribunal, Office of the Public Advocate.

2001   Hardships Endured by the People of Rongelap as a Result of the US Nuclear Weapons Testing Program and Related Biomedical Research. Majuro, RMI: Nuclear Claims Tribunal.

Kohlhoff, Dean W.

2002   Amchitka and the Bomb: Nuclear Testing in Alaska. Seattle: University of Washington Press.

Kulp, J. Laurence

1956   Project Sunshine: Annual Report, Period March 31, 1955–April 1, 1956. Geochemistry Laboratory, Lamont Observatory, Columbia University. ACHRE Archive, HREX document 0710270.

1961   Radionuclides in Man from Nuclear Tests. Journal of Agricultural and Food Chemistry 9:122–26.

Lawrence, John

1950   Letter to A. Hurtado, Subject: Sincere Gratitude for the Hospitality Shown during Visit to Peru. ACHRE Archive, HREX document 0715349.

Lawrence, J. H., R. L. Huff, W. Siri, L. R. Wasserman, and T. G. Hennessy

1952   A Physiological Study in the Peruvian Andes Using Iron-59. Acta Medica Scandinavica 142(2):11733.

Miettinen, Jorma K.

1977   Radioactive Foodchains in the Subarctic Environment. Progress report prepared for the US Atomic Energy Research and Development Administration. August 15, 1976–November 14, 1977. ACHRE Archive, HREX document 0706397.

Miettinen, J. K., A. Jokelainen, P. Roine, K. Lidén, and Y. Naversten

1964   Cesium-137 and Potassium in Finish Lapps and Their Diet. Radiological Health Data 5:83–97.

Moreno, Jonathan D.

2001   Undue Risk: Secret State Experiments on Humans. New York: Routledge.

National Research Council

1996   National Research Council Committee on Evaluation of 1950s Air Force Human Health Testing in Alaska Using Radioactive Iodine 131. Washington, DC: National Academy Press.

Neel, James V.

1949   Preliminary Report of Genetics Section, July 1949. National Academy of Science Archives, Atomic Bomb Casualty Commission, box 19, genetics folder (3B), 1949–1955.

1951   Letter from Dr. James V. Neel to Dr. Max Zelle, Biology Branch, Division of
        Biology and Medicine, Atomic Energy Commission. February 20, 1951. National
        Academy of Sciences Archives, Atomic Bomb Casualty Commission, box 19, genet-
        ics folder (3B), 1949–1955.
1962   Letter to Richard Caldecott. August 13, 1962. National Academy of Sciences
        Archives, Atomic Bomb Casualty Commission, box 120, James V. Neel file,
        1960–1962.

Neel, J. V., R. E. Ferrell, and R. A. Conard
1976   The Frequency of "Rare" Protein Variants in Marshall Islanders and Other
        Micronesians. American Journal of Human Genetics 28(3):262–69.

Regis, Ed
1999   The Biology of Doom: The History of America's Secret Germ Warfare Project. New
        York: Henry Holt and Company.

Rivière, R., D. Comar, M. Colonomos, J. Desenne, and M. Roche
1968   Iodine Deficiency without Goiter in Isolated Yanomama Indians: A Preliminary
        Note. In Biomedical Challenges Presented by the American Indian. Pp. 120–23.
        Washington, DC: Pan American Health Organization and World Health
        Organization.

Roche, M.
1959a   Elevated Thyroidal I131 Uptake in the Absence of Goiter in Isolated Venezuelan
        Indians. Journal of Clinical Endocrinology and Metabolism 19:1440–45.
1959b   Studies on the Pathophysiology of Hookworm Anemia Utilizing Radioisotopes.
        Washington, DC: Atomic Energy Commission.

**Roche, M., F. De Venanzi, J. Vera, E. Coll, M. Spinetti-Berti, J. Mendez-Martenez,
A. Gerardi, and J. Forero**
1957   Endemic Goiter in Venezuela with I131. Journal of Clinical Endocrinology and
        Metabolism 17:99–110.

Roche, M., and M. Layrisse
1956   Effect of Cobalt on Thyroid Uptake of I131. Journal of Clinical Endocrinology and
        Metabolism 16:831–33.

Roche, M., and M. E. Perez-Gimenez
1959   Intestinal Loss and Reabsorption of Iron in Hookworm Infection. Journal of
        Laboratory and Clinical Medicine 54:49–52.

Roche, M., M. E. Perez-Gimenez, M. Layrisse, and E. Di Prisco
1957   Study of Urinary and Fecal Excretion of Radioactive Chromium Cr51 in Man: Its
        Use in the Measurement of Intestinal Blood Loss Associated with Hookworm
        Infection. Journal of Clinical Investigation 36:1183–92.

Rodahl, K., and G. Bang
1956a   Endemic Goiter in Alaska. Technical Report AAL-TN-56-9. Ladd Air Force Base,
        AK: Arctic Aeromedical Laboratory.

1956b Endemic Goiter in Alaska. Proceedings of Seventh Alaskan Science Conference. Washington, DC: American Association for the Advancement of Science, Alaska Division.

1957 Thyroid Activity in Men Exposed to Cold. Technical Report 57-36. Ladd Air Force Base, AK: Arctic Aeromedical Laboratory.

Shipman, Thomas

1954 Telex from Thomas Shipman, director, Health Division, Los Alamos Laboratory, to John Bugher, director, Division of Biology and Medicine, Atomic Energy Commission, March 10. Department of Energy, Marshall Islands Historical Documents Archive. Electronic document, http://worf.eh.doe.gov/data/ihp2/40045_pdf, accessed October 25, 2006.

Siri, W. E., C. Reynafarje, N. I. Berlin, and J. H. Lawrence

1954 Body Water at Sea Level and at Altitude. Journal of Applied Physiology 7(3):333–34.

Siri, W. E., and C. Webster

1957 Report on Studies Conducted in Bolivia by Donner Laboratory. Berkeley, CA: Lawrence Berkeley National Laboratory.

Tierney, Patrick

2000 Darkness in El Dorado: How Scientists and Journalists Devastated the Amazon. New York: Norton.

Turner, Terence, and John Stevens

2001 Annotated Index of Selected Documents and Correspondence from the Collection of James V. Neel Papers in the Archive of the American Philosophical Society. Electronic document, http://www.umich.edu/~idpah/SEP/sep_tn.html, accessed July 29, 2006.

US Air Force

1954 Minutes. Research Council meeting. University of Virginia. May 13, 1954. ACHRE Archive, HREX document d1245.

1957a History of the United States Air Force Medical Service (1947–1957). ACHRE Archive, HREX document e1048.

1957b History of the Arctic Aeromedical Laboratory, July 1957–31 December 1957. Alaskan Air Command, Elmendorf Air Force Base, Anchorage, Alaska. ACHRE Archive, HREX document, National Security Archives.

US Congress. Joint Committee on Atomic Energy. Subcommittee on Radiation

1957 Hearings on the nature of radioactive fallout and its effects in man. 85th Cong. 1st sess. May 27, 28, 29; June 3.

Walter Reed Army Institute of Research

1955 Recovery of Radioactive Iodine and Strontium from Human Urine—Operation Teapot. November 1955. ACHRE Archive, HREX document e0883.

Warren, Stafford L.

1947   Report of the 23–24 January 1947 Meeting of the Interim Medical Committee, US Atomic Energy Commission. Electronic document, http://www.gwu.edu/~nsarchiv/radiation/dir/mstreet/commeet/meet3/brief3.gfr/tab_f/br3f1h.txt, accessed July 29, 2006.

Weisgall, Jonathan

1994   Operation Crossroads: The Atomic Tests at Bikini Atoll. Annapolis, MD: Naval Institute Press.

Welsome, Eileen

1999   The Plutonium Files: America's Secret Medical Experiments in the Cold War. New York: Dial Press.

t h r e e
Earle Reynolds
Scientist, Citizen, and Cold War Dissident

David H. Price

The Cold War expanded opportunities for anthropologists working inside and outside the academy. It brought a wealth of funds to study foreign languages and cultures of interest to the national security state and to work on problem-oriented, military-derived research projects. Those who could learn to see the world in ways aligned with the dominant agencies of the era found many opportunities at places like Rand, the Central Intelligence Agency, the Nuclear Regulatory Commission, the Defense Advanced Research Projects Agency, the Office of Naval Intelligence, and the Pentagon. Although a good number of anthropologists found meaningful work in these institutions, others found the experience of doing anthropology for the military transformative. Some of the latter began to apply their anthropology in opposition to America's Cold War policies.

One such anthropologist was Earle Reynolds, whose work on the Atomic Bomb Casualty Commission (ABCC) in postwar Hiroshima left him with a deep sense of duty and responsibility—not to his employers but to those he studied, and more significantly, to those people who would be affected by the future deployment of atomic weapons.

True to his interdisciplinary anthropological training, Reynolds did not compartmentalize his knowledge of the individuals he studied. In the people he studied and the institution he worked for, he saw larger disturbing patterns in the US medical-military establishment's accommodation of plans for the repeated use of nuclear weapons, and he recognized the dangers facing all peoples of all cultures. As a result, he chose to sound the alarm about the consequences of nuclear weapons deployment. There were personal and professional consequences for these decisions, and while Reynolds was comfortable with a career at the periphery of mainstream academia, his marginalization served as a warning to other scholars who also had misgivings about the uses of their research in the nuclear age. Though Reynolds left his employment as a scientist at ABCC and became an antinuclear activist, he did not stop being a scientist. Instead, he applied his skills and used his knowledge to impact public opinion and public policy.

This paper draws upon Reynolds's autobiographical writing, correspondence, and more than seven hundred pages of Federal Bureau of Investigation, Department of Energy (DOE), State Department, and CIA documents released under the Freedom of Information Act to chronicle how Reynolds's applied anthropological perspective led him to undertake a series of acts of radical activism.[1] The travails of Earle Reynolds illustrate how the Cold War enforced narrow limits of political interpretation for scientists working on nuclear issues in ways that rewarded scientists whose political views accommodated US nuclear policies, while leaving those whose science informed political views opposing US policies to fend for themselves. The FBI's records on Reynolds clarify some of the ways Cold War government policies and programs constricted applied anthropology. As the case of Reynolds shows, career consequences for those who opposed the dominant policy developments of the Cold War could be severe. The professional marginalization of Earle Reynolds demonstrates how political pressures routinely limited the abilities of scientists to freely study and question government claims about the effects of atomic weapons and weapons testing.

Most significantly, Reynolds's story maps out the course of a path seldom taken by other Cold War scientists. Thus Reynolds's biographic narrative both sheds important light on the abilities of a determined anthropologist to effect change and raise public awareness of nuclear policies and clarifies how the penalties of undertaking campaigns so directly opposed to the dominant military-industrial complex included a life of surveillance, peripheral underemployment, and feelings among his professional cohort that his strong views about the misapplication of scientific policy might indicate some sort of political instability. In a world ignoring the risks of nuclear weapons and weapons testing, those sounding alarms proclaiming these policies as madness are culturally represented as dangerous if not mad themselves.

Preactivist Reynolds

Reynolds was born Earle Schoene in 1910 to German parents who had come to the United States to perform as trapeze artists in the Ringling Brothers Circus. He later took the surname Reynolds from his stepfather. As a young man, he studied cultural and physical anthropology at the University of Chicago (MA 1943) and the University of Wisconsin (PhD 1944).[2] In 1951 Reynolds and his family moved to Hiroshima, where he worked as a biostatistician for ABCC's Pediatrics Department, studying survivors of the atomic bomb the United States dropped on the city in 1945. Initially, he seems to have enjoyed his work and his colleagues. DOE records released under the Freedom of Information Act portray him as a bright and enthusiastic staff member. In a letter of August 17, 1951, Grant Taylor, director of ABCC, described him as "an eager, enthusiastic, competent worker who gets along well with the Japanese and American staff. He has adjusted himself quickly. In short, he is a bright, constructive addition to our staff" (DOE 1951). Personnel records establish that Reynolds worked well with teams of military personnel, medical doctors, biologists, statisticians, and other research scientists, including James Neel, Grant Taylor, Newton Morton, Carl Harris, Lowell Woodbury, and others.

Reynolds's anthropological research with nuclear bombing victims transformed him. He documented the devastation that survivors and their offspring suffered—physiological horrors that most of us would rather never confront. He got to know people whose families had been incinerated, people whose bodies had been broken and deformed by the blast and radioactive fallout, and people who were dying of leukemia and other cancers. The tragedies he studied and documented on a daily basis deeply affected Reynolds and his politics (BAAA 1954; Reynolds 1951, 1952, 1960, 1961). For him, human research subjects were not just data points on biostatistical charts; he saw them as his equals—people whose suffering he believed to be the future of humankind unless the nuclear arms race was stopped.

Why did Reynolds, unlike other scientists working for ABCC, turn from government work to antinuclear activism? Although Reynolds was steeped in the culture of science, his anthropological-humanistic background set him apart from the scholarly experience of many of the scientists studying the impact of America's atomic bomb on the people of Hiroshima. The pervading culture of science at ABCC allowed many researchers to distance themselves from the bomb victims. The language and concerns of ABCC scientists tended to be antiseptic and indifferent to the human pain that nuclear weapons threatened. Reynolds could not be indifferent; his work with bombing victims was traumatic. While studying thousands of irradiated children (Reynolds 1954a, 1954b), he had difficulty treating the pain of the research subjects as epiphenomena, as ABCC's laboratory culture encouraged scientists to do. A memo from James Neel to Reynolds typifies the scientific selfishness that Reynolds found increasingly difficult to tolerate:

> The proportion of people in the population exposed to the bomb is decreasing, especially among [those] exposed closer to the hypocenter so that the feasibility of continuing the program after the 5 year period is open to question. The main reason for continuing the program is to double the amount of data so that the size of the error will be decreased. However, if the birth rate is decreasing, the decrease in error will be affected. The Law of diminishing Returns has already started so that the decrease in error may be reduced to 20% instead of the expected 30%. The cost of continuing the program will be

Figure 3.1. The Reynolds family and crew set sail from Hiroshima in 1954 for their voyage around the world. Source: Atomic Bomb Casualty Commission

> about $1,500,000. Some data may be obtained from certain secondary sources of information there are about 49 reference points. (ABCC 1952)

Neel's antiseptic tone and limited concern reveal that he primarily regretted these victims' deaths only because they confounded the ABCC's research aims.

While Neel and others at ABCC cultivated a mental and physical distance from Hiroshima's humanity, Reynolds was drawn into it. As he worked on his detailed "Analysis of Body Measurements and Observations Taken in 1952 on 4,200 Hiroshima Children," his dissatisfaction with this work grew. The lives of these young victims took their toll on him, and Reynolds came to see his work as contributing to a bureaucratic approach that calculated acceptable levels of death and disfigurement for future nuclear wars that could be fought and won. Reynolds resigned from ABCC in the summer of 1954. With a small crew, including his wife Barbara and two children, he set out in September to sail around the world on a year-and-a-half journey aboard his 50-foot ketch, the *Phoenix of Hiroshima* (see Reynolds and Reynolds 1962). The freedom of the sea and an open itinerary of exploration and adventure helped remove Reynolds and his family from the heavy consequences of his work with bomb victims. But it was toward the end of the around-the-world journey that Reynolds moved beyond his own mental protestations against the development of nuclear weapons to acts of physical protest that changed the nature of his life's work.

Bikini Tests

In June 1958, after circumnavigating the globe, Reynolds and his family arrived in Honolulu on the *Phoenix*. There, they learned that the US Coast Guard had just arrested George Bigelow, captain of the ship *Golden Rule*, on charges of conspiring to violate an injunction prohibiting vessels from entering the area of the Enewetak Proving Grounds in the Marshall Islands. The US Atomic Energy Commission (AEC) was testing a new generation of nuclear weapons in the islands. These events captivated Reynolds.

In the week following Bigelow's arrest, and after much discussion as a family, Reynolds, his wife and two children, and a Japanese crew member left Honolulu to enter the test area. Reynolds realized that this action not only placed his and his family's lives in jeopardy but also had serious career consequences. As he wrote later, "[I]f we do this thing, even though we win the legal fight, my formal scientific career is ended" (Reynolds 1961:36). DOE drew up plans to arrest the Reynolds family and the crew member even as the *Phoenix* set sail on June 11 (DOE 1952).

On June 30, a US Coast Guard vessel notified *Phoenix* that it was within the 100-mile "off-limits" area encircling the nuclear testing site. Reynolds declared his intention to enter the test area, indicating that "he understood that by so sailing he was endangering his crew and his vessel" (DOE 1958). CIA documents record navy personnel glibly noting that their

> proposal [to intercept and arrest Reynolds] has the advantage of preventing a
> recurrence of the original phoenix incident in which the fabled bird phoenix
> was consumed by fire and rose again from the ashes. Dr. Reynolds may perhaps
> fancy himself as a 20th Century Phoenix capable of duplicating both portions
> of the fable. Despite [the navy's] natural curiosity as to the outcome we must
> deny him the opportunity. (NRC 1958)

The navy and coast guard orders prevented allowing the ship's crew to become martyrs.

That night, the *Phoenix* was intercepted by a coast guard ship that recklessly overtook them in absolute darkness. Reynolds later wrote that this was "the closest call we have had in four years and fifty thousand miles at sea" (Reynolds 1961:58). The coast guard pulled alongside the *Phoenix* just before it crossed into the test zone and warned crew members that they would be breaking the law if they crossed into the zone. Reynolds stated his position that there were no laws that could prevent his ship from passing through the high seas. But the following morning, two members of the coast guard boarded the *Phoenix* and arrested Reynolds. He was allowed to sail back to Hawaii with two coast guard escorts. Early the next morning, before sunrise, a huge flash lit up the sky to the west as an atomic bomb was detonated as part of the Hardtack test series. This flash "lit up the entire sky for a moment, a dirty orange light flashing through the clouds," visible even 200 miles east of Bikini (61).

During their escorted journey to Kwajalein (from which Reynolds was flown to Hawaii), Reynolds talked with his two coast guard keepers. As the two guardsmen warmed to the *Phoenix* crew, they told Reynolds of their routine assignments "replacing damaged buoys and marine installations affected by the bomb tests." When Reynolds expressed concern about their high levels of routine radiation exposure, they dismissed it, telling him that their superiors had told them that "a man can take one hundred roentgens per hour without harm" for five or six hours at a time. Although Reynolds produced his copy of Shubert and Lapp's *Radiation: What It Is and How It Affects You* and showed them data disproving what they had been told, they still rejected his analysis of their risk. Instead, one of the men recounted how

> some of the men, in order to get leave, cheat by putting the radiation badges
> issued them—which are usually worn on the shirt—into their shoes. Since the
> deck is radioactive, they get a much higher exposure record that way, in a
> short while. What [the guardsmen] didn't seem to realize is that the feet are
> attached to the body, and if the deck is the most radioactive place on the boat,
> the badges should be placed in the shoes. (Reynolds 1961:63)

But the sailors discounted Reynolds's scientific knowledge of the effects of radiation as a form of foolish superstition.

This interaction illuminates how cultural protocols of order and propriety could so easily override objective scientific findings. These two servicemen were not about to believe the data produced by Reynolds—a specialist in these studies. They were content to superstitiously rely on information coming from their chain of command's representation of the world. Reynolds's rule breaking—even as an act designed to reduce health risks—signified untrustworthiness. This reaction illustrates one possible negative outcome of engaging in such protests. Raising awareness of potential dangers caused Reynolds to be designated a dissident outlaw, and this label made it easier for many to dismiss the scientific and humanistic complaints made by Reynolds and others. As an early member of the scientific community to adopt such drastic tactics, Reynolds was easily labeled as a deviant. But such stigma did not diminish the scientific findings on which he based his dramatic and drastic protests.

Reynolds's trial in Hawaii proceeded quickly. The federal court in Honolulu found him guilty of "violat[ing] the Atomic Energy Commission's order forbidding nationals from entering [a nuclear] test area" (FBI n.d.). The FBI maintained an ongoing interest in Reynolds's trial (FBI 1958). At the sentencing hearing, Reynolds told the court that the drastic acts of his government required drastic counteractions. He stated that the AEC was "playing false with the American public. For the first time in the history of American science, a scientist had to read the title of a report, then read who wrote it, and then try to determine where it came from, before he could properly evaluate the content of a so-called scientific paper" (Reynolds 1961:141). The judge in the case was not moved by Reynolds's stance and told him, "[Y]ou may be a good scientist, but you are a pretty poor citizen" and then sentenced him to two years confinement, with six months to be served under incarceration and a year and a half probation (147–48).

When Reynolds's lawyer won an appeal (over issues of denial of council) in the Ninth Circuit Court of Appeals, the federal prosecutors tried Reynolds again. During the second trial, Reynolds had much better legal representation and an impressive list of expert witnesses to argue his case, including Linus Pauling. But the judge would not allow testimony from the experts. He ruled it would detract from the salient legal issues before the court.

Though the prosecution had lost key documents from the first trial, the judge allowed the case to proceed. Reynolds's new lawyer, John Silard, argued that to find Reynolds guilty, the jury had to believe he had entered the testing zone willfully for a bad purpose. In his closing statement, Silard pressed the argument, telling the jury that when considering Reynolds's decision to break the law and cross into the testing zone,

> You must find that that was a willful, bad purpose.... You cannot find it.... If you find it, then in our opinion you will be violating the instructions that the Court will give you as to the meaning of willfulness. And without that willfulness Earle Reynolds, as His Honor will tell you, must be found not guilty. That is what he will tell you.... That is the single issue I pose to you, and I hope in your deliberations you will honestly come to your best conclusion on that subject. And that is all that Dr. Reynolds asks you to do in this case. (Reynolds 1961:226)

Even though the prosecuting attorney inadvertently argued during his summation that Reynolds had believed at the time of his offense that his actions were lawful, the judge's final instructions to the jury fell short of the narrow charge recommended by John Silard, and the jury once again found Reynolds guilty.

In Reynolds's statement to the court at his sentencing hearing, he showed deference to the judge and the proceedings. He explained that he chose to protest by attempting to disrupt the nuclear weapons test because "it would have been impossible for me to have been a good scientist, and at the same time a good citizen, as I understand the term, without taking the action which I took" (Reynolds 1961:232). The second sentence was even more severe than the first: a two-year sentence including a six-month prison term and five years of probation instead of eighteen months. When Silard appealed the second verdict, he requested that the judge rescind his order that Reynolds not travel outside of Hawaii. Supreme Court justice William O. Douglas ruled on November 2, 1959, that Reynolds could leave the state.[3]

The two guilty verdicts against Reynolds added to his fame. Funds for his legal defense and appeals came in from peace activists and progressive citizens from across the country. Famous journalists such as Norman Cousins wrote passionate articles about his cause (Cousins 1958). Reynolds's newfound celebrity took him by surprise. As a result of the second trial, newspapers across the United States wrote editorials praising Reynolds's moral resolve. Even in the conservative US heartland, editorialists appreciated that his acts of conscience were neither ill-informed nor foolish. An editorial in Ohio's *Fayette Review* stated: "If Dr. Reynolds is a 'crackpot' then so are all the rest of the scientists and intellects who have worked for the betterment of the human condition. He is not worried about politics but about people.... We stand behind him in his fight and urge you to also" (Reynolds 1961:258). Perhaps the highest praise Reynolds earned came in 1959 from Martin Luther King Jr., who wrote to Reynolds: "[Y]ou are pioneering for peace and rank in my book with Thoreau and Gandhi" (250).

Though increasingly identified as a political activist, Reynolds still viewed himself as an active scholar. In December 1959, while waiting on his appeal, Reynolds presented a paper titled "Irradiation and Human Evolution" at the annual meeting of the American Anthropological Association in Mexico City.[4] Though his recent guilty verdict was publicly known, he found that his old friends and colleagues (including Fred Eggan, W. W. Howells, and Clyde Kluckhohn) were all cordial to him. But he noticed there was,

> however, no discussion of my "outside" affairs, and to an anthropologist every-
> thing beyond his narrow specialty is outside; and I sensed, at times, a rather
> polite avoidance of touching on any topic which might be "embarrassing." In
> some cases this was due simply to the fact that the person just didn't have
> close contact with the outside world, a condition I can understand so well,
> having lived that way myself for a long, long time. (Reynolds 1961:252)

There were some exceptions to this general avoidance of discussing Reynolds's political problems and the implications of his radiation research, but Reynolds experienced a tinge of melancholy upon realizing that his colleagues were coming to regard him as a dangerous outsider.

In February 1960, Earle Reynolds visited the Atom Bomb Museum in Hiroshima. Among the exhibits, he found one prepared by his old employer, ABCC, on its research program. Reynolds was disturbed to see that a new goal had been added to the commission's original charges of studying the effects of radiation and exploring the scientific and medical uses of radiation. This new goal was the propagandistic objective of reducing "unnecessary fear by substituting known for the unknown" (Reynolds 1961:263).

The following day, Reynolds met with the new ABCC director, Dr. George B. Darling. During their conversation, Darling indicated that he didn't know much about Reynolds's work but had heard that a graduate student at the University of Michigan was writing his dissertation using Reynolds's data. At a lunch with some ABCC staff, mention was made of one of Reynolds's ABCC reports. Dr. Beebe, a commission statistician, "said quite casually, 'Oh, yes, that's the report that was suppressed, isn't it?'" (Reynolds 1961:265). Further inquiry determined that ABCC had suppressed his 1954 "Report on a Three-Year Study (1951–1953), of the Growth and Development of Hiroshima Children Exposed to the Atomic Bomb" after he left the agency. Beebe told Reynolds he had heard there was something wrong with the statistical analysis in the report. Reynolds later had it independently confirmed that there was nothing wrong with his statistical analysis when he consulted University of Michigan doctoral student John V. Nehemias, who had analyzed Reynolds's data and reached the same conclusions (Nehemias 1960). Indeed, it was the well-supported *conclusions*—on the extent of damage done to generations of Hiroshima survivors due to the bomb's radiation—not any problems with methods or statistical analysis that had led to the suppression of the report. When Reynolds sought advice from prominent scientists about what he should do about the suppression of his report, they generally told him to forget about it, as any fuss he raised would reflect poorly on him. Reynolds took these suggestions very bitterly, and this further distanced him from the political bureaucracy of academia that so marred the independence of scientific inquiry (Reynolds 1961:272–75, 1963a).

That scientific findings indicating grave dangers were suppressed raises questions about what course of action a scientist like Reynolds *should* or can take under such conditions of secret research. Issues of secrecy and national security would have prevented Reynolds from going public with his suppressed findings, and had Reynolds remained working within the comfortable bureaucratic setting of ABCC and continued to produce findings so at odds with the desired outcomes of the commission, he would have missed promotions or been disciplined. Political forces created a gravitational pull that narrowed the range of acceptable interpretations of data. Such limits are within the range of what Thomas Kuhn called "normal science," but such limits during wartime had serious consequences for those exposed to radioactive fallout.

On December 29, 1960, the Ninth Federal Court of Appeals unanimously overturned the lower court ruling against Reynolds, finding that the law Reynolds "was convicted of violating was not authorized by the statute under which it was purportedly issued and was therefore invalid." Reynolds had been correct in his initial interpretation of the law of the sea: the AEC had no legal authority to prevent Reynolds from entering the testing ground. An editorial in *The Nation* hoped that Reynolds had

> the wherewithal to carry his next conviction up to the United States Supreme Court...for it would be stimulating to see how the Supreme Court—well aware as the Court is that this nation of ours in years past has fought valiantly to defend the freedom of the seas—would view this lonesome trespass on a vast section of the world's largest ocean marked only by pinpoints on a map. All other trespasses may be forgiven, but this one, never. (*The Nation* 1961)

Though Reynolds's trials and appeals were expensive and stressful, in the end the experience only made him more comfortable in engaging in civil disobedience to oppose US military policies (Reynolds 1963b, 1968). In 1961 Reynolds returned to Japan to teach at the Hiroshima Women's College, where he continued to research the medical consequences for children exposed to radioactive fallout from nuclear weapons tests. While Reynolds's protests were popular among the Japanese public, the Japanese government did not approve of such disruptive acts. Even as Japanese culture was growing united in its opposition to nuclear weapons, the Japanese government had neither the desire nor the ability to clash with Washington over nuclear weapons issues.

Hiroshima and Russian Pilgrimages

In the fall of 1961, as Reynolds prepared to sail from Hiroshima to Vladivostok to protest a new series of Russian nuclear weapons tests, a US State Department official contacted him

> to make certain he fully understood the risks of sailing into the territory of a foreign government without appropriate visa or other permission. Reynolds expressed appreciation for the interest shown; said he was aware of the risks; and intended to issue a statement that the venture was entirely a private one and that he had no desire to create an international incident or embarrassment to the American Government. He relieved the American Government of any duty or responsibility with regard to protection or assistance. (FBI 1967b:3)

As the *Phoenix* approached the Soviet coast, Soviet patrol boats stopped the boat just 3 miles off shore. Soviet officials spoke with Reynolds for two hours before politely refusing him permission to enter the port and also refusing to accept Reynolds's petitions protesting Soviet tests of atomic weapons. Newspapers around the world reported these events with great interest. In the press, Reynolds highlighted the fact that "he was arrested by American authorities at En-I-we-tok, but merely turned back by the Soviets" (FBI 1967b:4). The FBI was not amused, and for good reason: the press clippings in Reynolds's FBI file establish that his protests brought press summaries of his research on Hiroshima survivors to a global audience.

Much of the US government's surveillance and handling of Reynolds and his projects occurred without his awareness. For example, a classified confidential document dated January 23, 1962, from the US Consulate General in Osaka to the Department of State in Washington, DC, reported on plans, which the consulate had learned about in a Japanese newspaper, to "send two A-bomb survivors on a tour of the US and Europe as a 'Hiroshima Peace Pilgrimage,' appealing for a ban of nuclear weapons." The document continued:

> In view of the leftist and anti-American orientation of the most powerful anti-nuclear-weapon groups in Japan, especially of the Gensuikyo (Japan Council for Prohibition of Atomic and Hydrogen Bombs), it appears possible that the persons chosen to make the trip may prove ineligible for visas as Communists or members of front organizations. Although Dr. Reynolds is not himself a Communist or sympathizer and recently publicly opposed the policy statements of the pro-Soviet wing of Gensuikyo, we have no reason to believe that he is politically sophisticated or knowledgeable enough to be able to detect and exclude pro-Communist candidates. (FBI 1962a:1)

The report concluded that if the Department of State refused to grant the pilgrims visas, it could "expect considerable pressure" from an international coalition of anti-nuclear activists. The report closed with a caution that "since we wish to avoid giving Dr. Reynolds any indication of approval or disapproval of his project, we do not intend publicly to show any interest in it until we receive the visa applications" (FBI 1962a:2). Not wanting to reveal that such a protest was significant enough to impact the State Department, the department officially ignored the peace pilgrimage as a few activists toured the United States and spoke to groups meeting at college campuses, community centers, and churches.

A few months later, in September 1962, Reynolds teamed with a group of international peaceniks on *Everyman III*, a poorly maintained ship of questionable seaworthiness. The crew planned to make port in Leningrad and then travel by train to Moscow, where crew members would present peace pamphlets to Soviet citizens and leaders. The FBI was very interested in this trip and gathered information from an informer, who recorded one public talk in which Reynolds recounted how his anthropological work with Hiroshima survivors had led him to resign his position with ABCC:

> Now, the 1945 children of Hiroshima are adults, and [I] have been doing a follow-up job on them for the US Government. Now, however, my relationship to the US Government has undergone a mutation, shall we say; and I am now working under the sponsorship of some private individuals, who had underwritten my research.
>
> I am also interested in instituting in Hiroshima work on the science of peace. This was [a] delicate matter because of the Japanese Government, but when the President of Hiroshima University agreed to sponsor the work, we could develop a sound program and set about raising money for it. Then, a call came to go around the world, to be Skipper of "Everyman III" in an attempt to get to Leningrad with our peace message. I did not want to go as my work at Hiroshima seemed to be of paramount importance, but I could not refuse; I felt I must accept the mandate, even though it might be a wild-goose chase. (FBI 1962b)

Everyman III's crew, carrying fifty thousand Russian-language pamphlets advocating the cessation of nuclear tests, sailed from England to Stockholm, then on to Leningrad Harbor, where Soviet harbor patrol boats stopped and detained them for not having visas. An FBI report based on one of Reynolds's public talks contained an amusing narrative of *Everyman III*'s arrival in Leningrad:

> Representatives from the Leningrad Peace Committee arrived, and we were told we could have a conference on a nearby ship—so we walked up the dock about 50 yards, under strong guard, and boarded a Soviet Ship. This was the only time we set foot on Soviet soil.

From 9:00 p.m. to 4:00 a.m., we had a meeting with various groups, and defined areas in which we could agree and areas in which we could not agree. Then we were escorted back to our boat and the Soviet Peace Committee thought we might get our visas—but later on we were told we would not get them.

It was the immigration officers who said we would not be allowed to enter the Soviet Union, and that we must leave at once; nor could we speak to the people or distribute literature. We tried to get word through to the Soviet Peace Committee, but were not able to deliver our manifesto, as the soldiers on our boat never left us alone for one moment. They were very civil and pleasant, but always there and firm.

Then, a Soviet boat came and towed us away from the dock. But we had promised our supporters to go to Leningrad, and we determined to leave no stone unturned to accomplish our purpose. A couple of our young men jumped in and tried to swim ashore, but were brought back.

Then our Russian-speaking crew member shouted through a loudspeaker, "We came to talk to you, and you will not listen; we came as friends, and you have treated us as enemies." Then, we put up our large banners in three languages.

Then, when they said we had to go, we knocked out some of the sea cocks so that water came into the hull; and, after the pilot came aboard, he found the ship was sinking, and they threatened to tie us up and put us down in the hold. They did tie us up for 28 hours, and then left us in charge of four guards while they tried to stop the water coming in. We had made one leak so that it took them a long while to find it. For 8 days they anchored us at five different anchorages, and all the while we were pleasant but non-cooperative.

All this while our personal relations were friendly—they sang songs with us and played chess, but never let us out of their sight. After 8 days, they escorted us into international waters, and we returned to Stockholm. (FBI 1962b:5–6)

Though the crew had not completed their initial goals, the resulting publicity in the international press further spread their message of alarm and resistance. Reynolds returned to Japan to teach anthropology and continue his human radiation and fallout studies.

"Like Slaves": Okinawa and the Culture of Occupation

In the winter of 1963, Reynolds sailed from Hiroshima to Okinawa to renew his tourist visa; some suggest that he made the renewal in Okinawa to avoid the scrutiny he would have received in Tokyo because of his increased activism. The Okinawa Council for the Prohibition of Atomic and Hydrogen Bombs sponsored a lecture by Reynolds entitled "Various Problems with Democracy on Okinawa." An army intelligence agent recorded this lecture and later produced a transcription for inclusion in Reynolds's FBI surveillance file.

Reynolds began his talk with a discussion of a 1954 incident in which the Japanese fishing boat *Lucky Dragon* was blasted with radiation during a US nuclear weapons test of a 17-megaton bomb at Bikini Atoll. The incident caused radiation sickness and death among the crew and raised Japanese awareness that US military forces were indifferent to the health impacts of atomic testing on the Japanese people and their fishing grounds. The *Lucky Dragon* incident brought a widespread outcry from the Japanese public and inspired Takeo Murata and Ishiro Honda to create *Godzilla*, the campy Japanese golem of America's reckless nuclear policies. Reynolds's discussion of *Lucky Dragon* seemed designed to spark emotional reactions in his audience. Reynolds reminded his audience that the United States never apologized to Japan for the *Lucky Dragon* incident and then launched into a critique of nuclear tests.

Reynolds remarked on the nature of Okinawa's state of unfreedom, describing what he had seen of the US occupation of Okinawa, with barbed-wire enclosures, seizure of land, and the establishment of enclosed occupation compounds. Reynolds said that "Okinawa is a military-occupied country, and there is no democracy in a military-occupied country. Americans are here to protect America. When it comes to government, governments are very selfish and do not concern themselves with the welfare of other governments and peoples" (see Price 2004a).

If one removes the moralistic elements of Reynolds's description and analysis of the US occupation of Okinawa, one can find a shared analysis in the CIA's own secret internal descriptions of the problems of the occupation. A June 1960 confidential CIA report on the Ryukyu Islands found that

> Ryukyuans resent US occupation of 10.8% of the total arable land in the islands, and this issue provides the most visible irritant to relations between USCAR and the local population. Although agitation results from any US attempt to acquire additional land, the issue has been temporarily quieted by changing US payment from a lump sum for indefinite leases to rental fees negotiated every five years. Connected to this issue is pacifist objection to introduction to missiles, which also necessitates acquisition of additional land. (CIA 1960)

But while Reynolds's and the CIA's analysis aligned in their views of the dynamics of occupation, the CIA and US military sought a smoother occupation, while Reynolds sought local self-determination.

Sailing to North Vietnam and China

On February 12, 1967, one of Reynolds's crew members (whose identity was redacted by FBI censors) wrote Alexis Johnson, the US ambassador to Japan, of plans to violate US laws by sailing to North Vietnam to deliver $20,000 worth of banned medical supplies. Reynolds's crew member told Johnson:

> We plan to sail from here to Hiroshima as soon as we can get masted and rigged, arriving there about February 22, staying about two days to take on

medical aid cargo for the North Vietnam Red Cross—the gift of thousands of people, mostly American Quakers. Some of the leading physicians of Hiroshima, assisted by religious leaders and atom bomb survivors, are preparing the civilian relief kits for us. We also carry messages of friendship and hope for peace from many Americans and Japanese, particularly school children, for the children and people of North Vietnam.... We believe we are fulfilling a patriotic duty in the best sense, as well as a high religious leading. In a way, this is an experiment in the quest for non-violent ways to solve world problems in place of war. And we are prepared to pay the ultimate price if necessary, just as is the traditional patriot soldier fighting for his country. (FBI 1967a)

The State Department warned Reynolds and the crew of the *Phoenix* that they risked $10,000 fines and decade-long prison sentences if they violated US prohibitions governing travel to North Vietnam. The State Department informed Reynolds that

> travel without properly validated passports is grounds for revocation or cancellation; that it is unlawful for United States Nationals to engage in unlicensed transactions with [North] Vietnam; that it is a violation of United States law to sail any United States documented ship to North Vietnam or to take cargo so destined aboard; and that their proposed voyage is hazardous for sailing vessels because of weather and entry into an area of military combat operations. (FBI 1967b:7)

After some delays in setting sail, on March 30, 1967, the *Phoenix* arrived in Hai-phong and delivered extensive medical supplies. Upon return to Japan, the passports of five US crew members were revoked, and Reynolds was ordered to return to the United States. The trip generated international publicity as newspapers and magazines, including *Look*, published a favorable pictorial piece on the trip (Massar and Hedgepeth 1967). The FBI intensified its monitoring campaign on Reynolds and the *Phoenix* crew's movements and communications (see, e.g., FBI 1967c). But Reynolds's message of humanitarian opposition to US military policies was reaching the public. Still no charges were filed against Reynolds, and he was allowed to remain in Japan.

Reynolds and his second wife, Akie, attempted to sail to China in August 1968, but Japanese authorities stopped the *Phoenix* and forced it to return to Japan, where Akie was charged with immigration violations and Earle was charged as an accomplice. These charges were later dropped. The next year, Reynolds and five US crew members sailed the *Phoenix* on an uninvited People to People Goodwill Visit to China (FBI 1969a). The FBI reported that Reynolds met up with a Chinese patrol ship before reaching China (FBI 1969b). The *Phoenix* crew said they wished to visit China to bring messages of peace from the West; the Chinese crew ordered them back to Japan (FBI 1969c). A classified confidential report on this trip in Reynolds's State Department file records that the *Phoenix* told of their need for supplies to make the return journey. They were refused and told to depart immediately. Undaunted by adversity and hoping to emulate its legendary namesake, the *Phoenix* loitered just outside the claimed Chinese territorial waters. Hours later it was approached by another, smaller patrol boat which asked about the *Phoenix*'s supply needs. The Americans seized on the appearance of new faces to reiterate the argument for allowing them entry into China, but were cut short by an officer who told them not to talk politics (…a hidden capitalist "roader") and demanded to know whether or not they wanted supplies. (FBI 1969b:4)

The Chinese sailors were interested in the *Phoenix* crew, but there was minimal contact between the two ships. The Chinese gunboat eventually gave *Phoenix* some needed fuel oil and sent the crew home, advising them to "go back and join in the American struggle" (FBI 1969c).

Once Reynolds returned to Japan, he found himself in continual trouble. His Hiroshima research eventually came to an end in 1970, when he was expelled from Japan as an "undesirable alien." The FBI has not released all documents relating to these events, but it seems likely the FBI and State Department played a covert role in the deportation. As Reynolds told the *San Francisco Chronicle*, he "was not the first, and not the last foreigner to be deported for pacifism" (FBI 1970a).

In 1970 Earle and Akie Reynolds sailed the *Phoenix* back the United States. The FBI legal attaché in Tokyo sent reports on Earle Reynolds to J. Edgar Hoover, and the FBI continued to monitor Reynolds's political activities back in the United States (FBI 1970b). Reynolds continued to use his research on the devastating biological effects of the Hiroshima and Nagasaki bombings to speak out against the nuclear arms race (Reynolds 1977, 1981). He became a dignified leader and spokesperson for the movement to end the wars in Southeast Asia. In later life, he and Akie moved outside Santa Cruz, California, where they worked as caretakers at a Quaker retreat center and he occasionally taught college courses. After the death of his wife in 1994, he moved near his daughter in southern California, where he lived until his death in 1998 (see UCSC 1999; Wittman 1987).

Reynolds and the Wages of Scientific Activism

Touching living bodies that have been severely damaged by the actions of one's country tends to change people—though the nature of this change is far from universal. Some individuals reacted to their contact with nuclear horror by clinically compartmentalizing their reactions. Others, such as Reynolds, take personal action to confront the madness of weapons of mass destruction in a direct if not successful (given the escalation of arms production) manner.[5] Reynolds understood that inaction was itself an action contributing to the problems of nuclear proliferation. Reynolds's work had an impact on the global community through the coverage of his protests in the press and on the scientific community through his papers and talks on the biological consequences of nuclear tests and nuclear war. Reynolds's message of the physical dangers of fallout to humans helped establish the international nuclear weapons protest movement. Reynolds's first protests and the resulting court battles were key events in the establishment of the international scientific community's opposition to nuclear weapons testing. These acts helped paved the way for Physicians for Social Responsibility to formally oppose the atmospheric testing of nuclear weapons in 1961 and for the Nobel Committee to award the 1962 Peace Prize to Linus Pauling for his nuclear disarmament efforts.

Earle Reynolds's struggles help us reconsider the limits of normal roles for "applied" or "action" anthropology. Reynolds's activist-applied anthropology radically unhitched mission from employment. His story illustrates how applied research can unleash knowledge that bears a weight of uncomfortable responsibility—a responsibility that if acted upon can lead anthropologists to undertake duty-bound actions contributing to the endangerment of their careers. That it seems unusual to consider the outlaw Reynolds an applied anthropologist tells us more about the ethical banality we encounter in our work in mainstream applied anthropology than it does about Reynolds. Reynolds provided valuable contributions to peace efforts as the US government paid others to prepare for nuclear annihilation. It is important to recognize that efforts were possible only outside the traditional employment venues of academia. Had Reynolds taken harsh public stances or actions while employed as a professor of anthropology at a public or private institution, it seems certain he would have jeopardized his job.[6]

While many elements of Reynolds's life were extraordinary, the basic problems he faced in trying to reconcile the interests of his employer and those of the population he studied are similar to many of the essential dilemmas faced by all of us working as applied anthropologists. All anthropologists face choices concerning whether efforts to effect change are best focused on working inside or outside extant power structures. For Reynolds, the choice became clear with time, and he paid for his opposition with a chunk of his career. That few contemporary anthropologists know of him is part of the lesson of Earle Reynolds: his acts of heroism sent him to the margins. His message of danger was itself hazardous and demanded that he be kept at a distance from the halls of academia or outside the borders of respectable mainstream employment. For Reynolds, inaction was a form of action contributing to the problems he studied.[7]

Reynolds was no less an anthropologist than one working as a management consultant in the corporate workplace. But Reynolds's work limited his employability and distanced him from many of his anthropological colleagues. Reynolds's work for the ABCC was just as political as his antinuclear protests, but it was the latter work that limited his employability. There were plenty of anthropologists who did not worry about the military's use of their research as they did linguistic research or ergonomic designs for flight suits and seats of aircraft that might be used to deliver more bombs like those dropped on the people Reynolds had studied in Hiroshima (Nader 1997a, 1997b; Price 1998a, 1998b, 2002). Not only were scholars engaged in these enterprises not subjected to the marginalization that Reynolds was, but they advanced upon career paths that bestowed them with financial security and social prestige.

That Reynolds refused to censor himself and instead engaged in activism does not mean he stopped engaging in science—it simply means he refused to succumb to the weighty gravitational forces that beckon scholars to not speak out on controversial issues, even when their research demands brutal critiques. Professional settings institutionally desensitize us to the consequences of our work and the rewards for remaining silent, or for working within respectable and ineffective bureaucratic structures. As Laura Nader observes, anthropologists

> need to think deeply about…desensitization. Desensitization is what occurred in Nazi Germany and allowed genocide. It trained into those fueling the various genocides in the contemporary scene. Genocide is not solely part of national fabrics and internal happenings in nations, it is also embedded in war. The total unconcern with the consequences of one-sided military action—whether by the US or its allies in Iraq, or the US in Libya or Sudan, or the Israelis in Lebanon, or the "allied" forces in Afghanistan—is fed by silences that at bottom may be about deeply embedded racism against Arabs and Islamic countries more generally, a cultural racism in the guise of Orientalism about which most anthropologists have had little to say, contrary to positions they have taken elsewhere. (Nader 2001:167)

The secrecy of this work contributed to scientists' desensitization. The environment of secrecy surrounding the work of ABCC damaged the scientific process to such a degree that evaluations of the dangers presented by nuclear weapons were not subject to the sort of open scrutiny required by the scientific process. As Robert Merton observed, "[T]he institutional conception of science as part of the public domain is linked with the imperative for communication of findings. Secrecy is the antithesis of this norm: full and open communication its enactment" (Merton 1968:611). Secret science easily becomes damaged science, and when national security policies are allowed to hold sway over the acceptance of official reports, there are few options for dissenting scientists working within the system.

There is general widespread confusion about the nature of science's "neutrality" and the possibility or appropriateness of activist science. This confusion adds to an academic climate promoting timidity and acquiescence to science policies that support status-quo findings upheld by governmental agencies regardless of the harm such policies portend for people. It is vital to recognize that despite Reynolds's unusual actions and his political advocacy, he never ceased being an applied scientist.

After I presented a paper on Earle Reynolds's activism at the 2004 annual meeting of the American Association for the Advancement of Science, a disgruntled reporter from *Newsday* objected to my description of Reynolds the activist as a scientist in good standing. The reporter insisted that scientists who become involved in political advocacy forfeit their standing as scientists because they have abandoned their commitment to impartiality—a hallmark of scientific observations. In replying to the reporter, panel member Laura Nader and I argued that notions of impartial scientists had been dispensed with decades ago and that his point was undermined by the fact that no one questions the scientific "neutrality" of scientists committed to *supporting* the nuclear arms industry. While these points have merit, a superior rebuttal was supplied from the conference floor by a senior mathematician from Yale, who stood and told the reporter that the hallmarks of science were not found in political neutrality. Instead, they were measured by whether or not the observations, measurements, and theories provided by a scholar had high *reliability* (meaning that other scholars could repeat the measures and get similar results) and *validity* (meaning the scholar had measured what he or she thought he or she was measuring) and whether or not the scholar had engaged in adequate theory testing. By the mathematician's measure, Reynolds had not failed any of the criteria for being a good scientist. She added that being a scientist did not remove anyone from the responsibilities of citizenship.

The reporter did not seem to appreciate these distinctions, but they are key ones for understanding the continuity between Reynolds's research, politics, and life—and for bridging prevalent disconnects between science and public policy. As Earle Reynolds argued at the sentencing hearing for his second trial, "It would have been impossible for me to have been a good scientist, and at the same time a good citizen, as I understand the term, without taking the action which I took." Reynolds understood that there are public duties embedded in scientific knowledge and that science without consideration of the public good is folly.

Notes

This paper benefited from conversations with and critiques from David Aberle, Margot Backus, Alexander Cockburn, Barbara Rose Johnston, Laura Nader, Bill Peace, Midge Price, Jessica Renshaw, Ted Reynolds, Tim Reynolds, Eric Ross, Jeff St. Clair, and Roger Snider.

1. As part of a larger research project, I have accessed more than forty thousand pages of FBI documents relating to anthropology in the Cold War. Most of these documents record surveillance and harassment campaigns directed at activist anthropologists who, like Reynolds, were fighting for progressive social changes (see Price 1997, 2002, 2004b).

2. For an example of Reynolds's early physical anthropological research, see Reynolds 1950.

3. The legal point clarified by Justice Douglas was that since the judge and prosecutor in the trial had agreed that Reynolds posed no flight risk, not allowing him to travel was a punitive measure that goes against the spirit and function of the bail system (see Reynolds 1961:242–43).

4. In September 1959, after his second trial in Hawaii, Reynolds received correspondence from his friend Kent Vickery at Columbia University, advising him that because of his guilty verdict, "the departments in some state universities may be a bit reluctant to risk legislative antagonism, but...in most of the private colleges and universities, the reaction might on balance be favorable rather than otherwise" (Reynolds 1961:237).

5. The sickness and death of many Hiroshima victims impacted Earle Reynolds and his family, but the death of twelve-year-old Sadako Sasaki (commemorated at Hiroshima's Peace Park) seems to have deeply touched Reynolds.

6. This finding is in accordance with "Ross's Second Law of Academic Freedom," which states, "An aca-

demic institution's blatant disregard for academic freedom varies in direct proportion to the size of a university's endowment" (personal correspondence with author, May 20, 2005).

7. The negative consequences to academic careers from such activism remain with us in the present (see Frank 2005).

References

ABCC. *See* Atomic Bomb Casualty Commission

Atomic Bomb Casualty Commission
1952   Research meeting. March 24, 1952. RG 32, box 3092, folder MH 15-21.

BAAA. *See* Bulletin of the American Anthropological Association

Bulletin of the American Anthropological Association
1954   News of People and Research. Bulletin of the American Anthropological Association 2(3):6–7.

Central Intelligence Agency
1960   Ryukyu Islands (Okinawa), Classified Confidential Report. CIA report. NLE MR case number 2000-69.

CIA. *See* Central Intelligence Agency

Cousins, Norman
1958   Earle Reynolds and His Phoenix. Saturday Review 41:26–27.

Department of Energy (files released to David Price under the Freedom of Information Act)
1951   Letter from Grant Taylor to Bugher, August 17, 1951. Document number 9806190003.
1952   Box 2922, folder MRA 7, Hardtack V. 3.
1958   DOE 61A1524, box 36.

DOE. *See* Department of Energy

FBI. *See* Federal Bureau of Investigation

Federal Bureau of Investigation (files released to David Price under the Freedom of Information Act)
n.d.   HQ 117-2236-3.
1958   HQ 117-2236-8, September 3.
1962a   HQ 117-2236-10, January 23.
1962b   HQ 100-437334-13, December 11.
1967a   HQ 100-437334-41.
1967b   HQ 100-437334-47, April 28.
1967c   HQ 100-437334-48.
1969a   HQ 100-437334-81.
1969b   HQ 100-437334-92:4.

1969c   HQ 100-437334-93.

1970a   HQ 100-437334-81.

1970b   HQ 100-437334-95.

Frank, Joshua

2005   Without Cause: Yale Fires an Acclaimed Anarchist Scholar. Electronic document, http://www.counterpunch.org/frank05132005.html, accessed May 13, 2005.

Massar, Ivan, and William Hedgepeth

1967   A Troubling Voyage to North Vietnam. Look 31(13):17–21.

Merton, Robert

1968   Social Theory and Social Structure. New York: Free Press.

Nader, Laura

1997a   The Phantom Factor: Impact of the Cold War on Anthropology. *In* The Cold War and the University. Noam Chomsky, Ira Katznelson, R. C. Lewontin, David Montgomery, Laura Nader, Richard Ohmann, Ray Siever, Immanuel Wallerstein, and Howard Zinn, eds. Pp. 107–46. New York: New Press.

1997b   Postscript on the Phantom Factor—More Ethnography of Anthropology. General Anthropology 4(1):1–8.

2001   Breaking the Silence—Politics and Professional Autonomy. Anthropological Quarterly 75(1):161–69.

The Nation

1961   The Trespasser. The Nation 192:22–23.

Nehemias, John V.

1960   The Effect of Atomic Bomb Radiations upon the Growth of Children Present at Hiroshima on August 6, 1945. PhD dissertation, University of Michigan, Ann Arbor.

NRC. *See* Nuclear Regulatory Commission

Nuclear Regulatory Commission (records released to David Price under the Freedom of Information Act)

1958   Document number 61A1524, box 36, page 11, June 30, 1958.

Price, David H.

1997   Anthropological Research and the Freedom of Information Act. Cultural Anthropology Methods 9(1):12–15.

1998a   Cold War Anthropology: Collaborators and Victims of the National Security State. Identities 4(3–4):389–430.

1998b   Earle L. Reynolds. Anthropology Newsletter 39(6):29.

2002   Interlopers and Invited Guests: On Anthropology's Witting and Unwitting Links to Intelligence Agencies. Anthropology Today 18(6):16–21.

2004a   "Like Slaves": Anthropological Notes on Occupation. Electronic document, http://www.counterpunch.org/price01062004.html, accessed October 16, 2006.

2004b   Threatening Anthropology—McCarthyism and the FBI's Surveillance of Activist
        Anthropologists. Durham, NC: Duke University Press.

Reynolds, Earle

1950   Distribution of Subcutaneous Fat in Childhood and Adolescence. Society for
        Research in Child Developments 15:509.
1951   Growth and Development Program of the Atomic Bomb Casualty Commission.
        Washington, DC: Atomic Bomb Casualty Commission.
1952   Growth and Development Program of the Atomic Bomb Casualty Commission.
        Washington, DC: Atomic Bomb Casualty Commission.
1954a   Report on a Three-Year Study (1951–1953) of the Growth and Development of
        Hiroshima Children Exposed to the Atomic Bomb. Washington, DC: National
        Research Councils, Atomic Bomb Casualty Commission.
1954b   Growth and Development Program of the Atomic Bomb Casualty Commission.
        Nippon Shonika Gakkai Gasshi 58:699–709.
1960   Irradiation and Human Evolution. *In* The Process of Human Evolution. Gabriel
        Lasker, ed. Pp. 89–108. Detroit: Wayne State University.
1961   The Forbidden Voyage. New York: David McKay Company, Inc.
1963a   The Hiroshima Hibakusha. Paper presented at Sixty-second Annual Meeting of the
        American Anthropological Association, San Francisco, November.
1963b   Letter from Japan. Peace News, March 1. FBI file HQ 100-437334-81.
1968   The Phoenix. Quaker Life, August. FBI file HQ 100-437334-81.
1977   Earle-ly Warnings about Nuclear Threat. Resource Center for Nonviolence
        Newsletter, July–August. FBI file HQ 100-437334-81.
1981   The First Seriatin Study of Human Growth and Middle Aging. American Journal of
        Physical Anthropology 54:23–24.

Reynolds, Earle, and Barbara Reynolds

1962   All in the Same Boat. New York: D. McKay.

UCSC. *See* **University of California, Santa Cruz**

University of California, Santa Cruz

1999   Pursuit of Peace: An Online Exhibit from the Earle and Akie Reynolds Archive.
        Electronic document, http://library.ucsc.edu/oac/exhibits/web120/, accessed October
        16, 2006.

Wittman, S. A.

1987   Voyage of a Peace Activist. The Progressive, February: 16.

f o u r

There Are No Peripheries to Humanity

Northern Alaska Nuclear Dumping and the Iñupiat's Search for Redress

Edith Turner

Summary: Arctic nations are beginning to band together to prevent their sparsely inhabited lands from being used as a rubbish dump for pollutants (see Schneider 1996) and for what metropolitan countries are most scared of and most want to dump elsewhere—nuclear waste. But in the moral climate of the earth, no human community is expendable. One may not touch even arctic lands. A young university student does not have to die because a government chooses to kill her, as happened when the Atomic Energy Commission dumped experimental nuclear material near her village. She was innocent. "Center" and "periphery" are no more: not only has economic globalization reached us, but the value system of the globe also.

Preliminary Observations about Fieldwork Itself

Victor Turner has a great respect for fieldwork. He believed rightly that anthropologists should supply a primary source of valid material for other readers, as literal as possible—a source that would be available whatever the interpretation and discussion that followed (personal communication). In the era of globalization, the need for fieldwork still holds and is even greater for the very reasons that societies are no longer stale. When evaluating what an individual actually says, it is no longer assumed that his or her words represent what the society says. Now, the *drift* of a social situation, recognized by the people themselves and the ethnographer to be revolving in a general way around society's "Archimedean point," is as near as we can get. In this article, the material of which is based on the reactions of the northern Alaskan Iñupiat branch of the Inuit people to the extremely deleterious effects of localized radioactive pollution, I am trying to sense, in that key situation, the effect of the drift. Though the events in which I was caught up appear to be political, my work could not be termed political anthropology. Because of the intimacy of relationships in the small village and my developing research on healing there, I found myself working at the level of the anthropology of experience, in this case, suffering in sympathy with the sick, becoming angry on their behalf, and even finding an odd sympathy with one of them who had died.

Narrative as Method in the Era of Globalization

In order to press home the reality of the conflicting circumstances that confront peripheral people—and their anthropologists—in the era of globalization, it is more than ever necessary when depicting the exigencies of the people that humanistic principles are deployed—that is, to frame the action, to frame the particulars. From what kind of fieldwork is this anthropology derived? Fieldwork "happens" best—often apparently by chance—when anthropologists find themselves in a situation where everything they have learned and felt under their skin about a society—through being immersed in it for some time and having begun to truly appreciate what it values—becomes curiously irradiated, which is much the same effect that societies achieve when organizing themselves in carnival, ritual, or in some big protest. *Then*, when anthropologists of quality, deeply informed, convey in narrative in words just as they experienced it, that narrative becomes a classic in the discipline's canon. There are also many such passages in the older literature, showing that our forebears did truly experience along with their field people, as in the classic "Balinese Cockfight" of Clifford Geertz. The hard work of establishing findings, then documenting them and correlating them with other features of society and other societies, using all kinds of sources, is crowned by such a passage.

Now, before the gaze of fieldworkers, the realities of globalization are cutting their girders and machine lines across the delicate kinship veins and arteries of human interconnectedness—which are not "structures" or "systems" but, in the case of kinship, blood-fed reproductive cells with their huge emotional load—in other words, the ineradicable umbilical cord that joins all of us to this world. The sacred land itself, often scarred by tribal war: it is cut across by oil fields, nuclear dumping, first-world property encroachments. This is especially true in the far north. The account that follows, based on arctic fieldwork, shows human activity in the context of nuclear dumping.

Fieldwork in the Era of Globalization

In 1987 I went to Point Hope, northern Alaska, to study Native healing. I knew that the Iñupiat, Yup'ik, and Siberian Yup'ik of Saint Lawrence Island had sent troupes of dancers to Washington from time to time. The dancing of the "Eskimos" was admired down in the south, and they were chosen for the president's inauguration. This much was global. I knew too that in order to complete the long journey to Point Hope, where I heard many healers lived, I would be taking planes, not dogsleds. There was modern transportation. In the Arctic there was a clinic connected by satellite phone to the far-off hospital. One of the healers in Point Hope worked regularly on a contract basis in the outpatients' clinic in the big village of Kotzebue. The mail came in by air every day. We were well on in the twentieth century.

Mid-century histories of northern Alaska record as a minor point that the region was of importance in the Cold War after World War II. Therefore there were military installations all along the northern Arctic Slope. I vaguely recall how in 1958 the US Atomic Energy Commission planned to do what in the climate of the day seemed rather exciting. They were going to create a huge crater next to the ocean, using nuclear explosions, so as to make a harbor for seagoing vessels. This was "Project Chariot" (see Foote 1961). But for some reason the project was abandoned.

Be that as it may, in 1987 when I arrived, Point Hope was a small isolated village of 680 people living in one hundred prefabricated houses beside a mostly frozen ocean. Subsistence hunting was their main occupation. I sat with the people, visiting neighbors' homes when a healing was in progress and going to church when testimony was being given, which was often. I learned a little bit about what it was like to heal. There could be detected in the process a certain level of spirit power that fascinated me.

After several months I began to see this village as the center of the world; time was doing different things to me. The rest of the world's sense of time and its activities began to look unreal. In the village, late at night in January 1988, I wrote,

> I feel a sense of something like a strong magnet dragging me into a set of powers or valences that have now become obvious to me, yet even so they're different from what I originally expected. They don't seem different now, just ordinary. But when I watch carefully in Point Hope I seem to see the rest of the world moving back behind our village. Our world here is obvious to us and the other world is falling behind. What happens here in Point Hope is everyday experience to us. Yet it's we who are moving. The whole village seems to be moving considerably in advance of the world down below. There's the knowledge of Dorcus the healer, and the cases she's describing; her showing me how to heal [not that I wanted a career in it, but for me to understand her healing, it was necessary for her to show me how in a minor way]; my feeling Mina's backache so clearly through her padded parka—and she even said my working on it made her feel better: it all follows a distinct and recognizable pattern, but I've not been aware of the pattern before. I'm fascinated by

being able to sense that definite hysterical "Burr" that sick flesh in a human body gives out, a signal to the human hands that contact the place and can "hear" the message. A pleading signal for those hands to take out the trouble. This healing is immediate, given, and practical; no mental "visualization" is required because the hands see.

This effect of being lost in the fieldwork also happened to me in Africa (Turner 1987:108). One goes into the field, becomes lost in it, and then one may wake up with a start to find oneself in the modern scene after all.

As it happened, matters in Point Hope were breaking open on a wider arena—because history itself on a worldwide scale had broken into the peace of Point Hope. Just as in the thirties, forties, and fifties the village had been ravaged by deadly measles and tuberculosis from the south (the marks were still on the village), so now my sense of the village quietly riding through time was disturbed—as the people themselves were disturbed—by a threat that had been growing since the sixties, cancer. My landlady Joanna found that her painful shoulder was not healing. The doctors told her it was cancer of the bone. Amos, the prime whaling captain, had something of the sort wrong with his previously injured leg. I said to myself, "So much has changed with these people. They seem to be at the mercy of modern life. What can be the cause of this trouble?" I went to the Point Hope clinic and leaned over the counter. The health aide and I chatted about poor Joanna and Amos.

"What's the cause of the cancer, do you think? Why is there so much of it here?"

"The figures are nothing out of the ordinary," she said. "They've always been like that."

People were becoming sad about Joanna. On Easter Sunday, 1988, the church was packed. An old woman carried the cross up to the altar, stepping very slowly—which started the motion on its way. Ten children were baptized, including three children of Ernie Frankson, practitioner of the old religion. Ernie himself was present. The first hymn was all about flowers and trees with their leaves, suitable for Easter in Western Christian countries. As for us in Point Hope, we were a hundred miles north of the tree line. There were no leaves or flowers around us, only snow. But there was light—sunlight blazing through the windows.

I was sitting next to Joanna, as I always did. We went up to take communion, Joanna walking behind me. I turned after receiving it and walked back to my pew. A moment later Joanna returned from her communion, tears running down her face. I tenderly touched her good hand to comfort her.

"What is it, Joanna?"

"I saw Paula up there, Paula!" she whispered. She pointed at the sanctuary.

"Oh Joanna!" I said, holding my chin in amazement, gazing at the empty space. Paula Tukumavik was her sister, dead from cancer for many years. "Why, that's good, Joanna." So Paula was not gone forever.

Kaglik, a fundamentalist and a believer in Oral Roberts, told me a little later that

God had come in a vision to Amos and Joanna, and that they were cured. Nevertheless, they both later died and were bitterly mourned.

Still, the cause of sickness in Point Hope remained a mystery. Everyone knew that Project Chariot had been abandoned. No one had exploded any bombs. In fact, as I discovered, the resistance that the village had mounted in the sixties had prevented the fulfillment of the project; and that same spirit of resistance had the effect of engendering Native protection movements up and down the state.

Very slowly I began to take notice. My main study of healing (Turner 1989, 1996) traced a local method that was turning out to be a good one and even helped people in minor cases of small cancer nodules. But the major cases of cancer defeated the traditional healers. Only fundamentalist Christians hoped for healing in such cases. Kaglik may not have seen that Joanna's and Amos's visions were probably connection to their nearness to death. The darkness of this story shows how the village had been tilted down, half-submerged under the "forces of history," as Marx called them. And in that darkness souls were connecting in their traditional way to the underworld of the dead. I myself came back on a short visit in 1990 and sensed Joanna herself in the pew at the church—a year after she had died. I felt she was sitting beside me, and said seriously, under my breath, "Glad you're here."

It was not until 1991 that Rex Tuzroyluk, a Western-trained Iñupiaq biologist, and I tried to total up the cancer score.[1] Rex said there had been ten cancer deaths in the previous two years. He was puzzled. He pulled out an old clipping about Project Chariot that clearly demonstrated the mentality of the Atomic Energy Commission and the US Army. The project has been invented by Edward Teller, supposedly as a way to "beat swords into plowshares," under his notorious "Plowshares" scheme. When I read the clipping I realized that the site was at Ogotoruk Creek, Cape Thompson, only 31 miles south, on the best caribou grazing land—and caribou meat was the second staple of the Iñupiat. I thought, "The area for the project was so near the village. Who'd dare to go up and see what they left behind?" Rex said there had also been a US Army base just to the west of the new village site of Point Hope, on land that drained into what had been the drinking pond for the previous village site. Had toxic wastes such as PCB spilt there, Rex wondered, causing illness over a long term among the inhabitants? There were reports among villagers of having seen personnel burying canisters. At Rex's suggestion I wrote anxiously to many agencies on the matter, and from the Environmental Protection Agency and the state Department of Environmental Conservation I received the explanation that the illness was caused by people's bad lifestyle. They meant by this that the people were smoking too much, using drugs, and consuming alcohol and junk food. There were similar responses from the Native Health Service at the North Slope Borough. The Army Corps of Engineers stated outright—what we found afterward to be a lie—that there was no toxic waste left in the area.

I was puzzled. It was the lifestyle? Why was the lifestyle supposed to be so much worse in Point Hope than among, for example, many of the wild students I knew down below, or in any village in the lower forty-eight states where the shopping carts are full of junk food and cigarettes? Presumably, if it were a matter of lifestyle the people in the small towns of the lower forty-eight ought to be dying of cancer at the same rate as in Point Hope. I began to think that sooner or later I would have to find out what US cancer rates were.

But others in Point Hope were not waiting. During my visit in the summer of 1991, Caroline Nashookpuk, the Point Hope representative to the North Slope Borough on matters of health, told the villagers at the Elders' Conference that she knew something was wrong and was looking into the matter. It should be noted that during that year the Elders' Conference was moderately attended and featured the usual discussions of concerns about drugs and drunkenness, education issues, and the like, with the usual unexceptional resolutions at the end.

That summer Rex and his wife Piquk took me outside their house and showed me a seal stretched in the gravel that looked strange. Its hair was not gray but an orange color, wrong-looking. This orange color was not caused by oil contamination: the EPA office in Anchorage informed us that oil contamination results in black discoloration. I took pictures. Connie Oomituck reported to me later that people had been finding tumors in seals and caribou.

By my next visit in June 1992, matters had changed again. What really upset me was seeing how old Barbara Lane, who had been over-quiet last year at the elders' lunch, now sat hardly moving in the corner next to her healthy old husband. She had further fallen in upon herself. She looked yellow and ate little. We learned later it was a brain tumor.

This year the Elders' Conference seemed to have teeth. Irma Oktollik was chairperson. Through this conference, which constituted a town meeting, the people talked repeatedly about the need for immediate action, and there was a determination to unite and hold the line for their village. Caroline was busy trying to coerce the Native Health Service to investigate the pollution that was the cause of the cancer, but responses of the white-run service were extremely slow.

This was June 1992. During those summer months a researcher named Dan O'Neill of the University of Alaska at Fairbanks was busy in the archives of the university library, conducting an investigation of the old Project Chariot activities of 1958–1963, which everyone knew by now was a project designed to threaten Soviet Russia during the Cold War. While turning over the material he discovered documents describing the illegal experimental dumping of 15,000 pounds of radioactive soil at the Chariot site in 1962, *after* the project had been officially abandoned. The material was brought in from the Nevada test sites, specifically for the purpose of experimentation, and secretly positioned in a loose dump without the legally required containers. This was executed under the cover of the withdrawal from the Chariot site.

In the middle of August 1992, the nine villages of the North Slope received the information that Dan O'Neill had revealed. Rex Tuzroyluk told me about it on the phone.

"Edie, when the news came out I went around to my mom's and she just sat and wouldn't talk to me." Her daughter, Rex's youngest sister Tuzzy—a brilliant university student—had recently died of cancer. When Piquk, who was not well herself, came on the phone, she also sounded in shock. I said to her, "They have to move that dump. But where will they put it, shoot it out into space?"

"Dump it on Washington, DC," she said.

Thus began the story, a true account, of events that joined my field community with perhaps the most serious issue of our day, radioactive pollution, and brought some of the villagers to the center of the world, Washington, DC

Politics were changing rapidly. In the middle of this whirlwind of news, Jack Schaefer, the village's self-made lawyer, said on the phone, "We've done it, we've designated ourselves, 'The Native Village of Point Hope.'"

"Great." ("Native Village" was another title for the Indian Reorganization Act [IRA] body, which had the full rights of a Native Reserve and sovereignty under the federal government, not under the politically conservative state of Alaska.) So Point Hope in effect had become an elective village holding all the IRA powers. This body proceeded to buy back 90 percent of the land from its previous owner, the village corporation, a body that had been in danger of bankruptcy and forced sale, so now the land would remain permanently under the control of the Native Village or "tribal government"—a brilliant "castling" move, as in chess. This was what Thomas Berger had passionately recommended in his book *Village Journey* (1985), written as a warning against the possible fate of Native lands under the Alaska Native Claims Settlement Act of 1971, or ANCSA. Accordingly, in Point Hope, Ernie Frankson, a key leader, and after him Jack Schaefer, became presidents of the Native Village.

So already fear of the dump was leading the village toward a more secure self-determination. It was a process that had been developing since 1963 in resistance to white encroachment.

The news came through that on learning of the dump revelations, Jack and other leaders from Point Hope had come to Anchorage and had been interviewed by the *Anchorage Daily News*, September 6, 1992.

Rex Tuzroyluk was immediately appointed as monitor for the Tikigaq Native Corporation because, as he said in his report of September 14, 1992:

> The general public at Point Hope is concerned about the quality of information reaching them. They have been given little information about what radioactivity is, where it comes from, what it does, and how it is detected. They need information about the half-life of the radioactive isotopes that are reported to be in the dump. The initial objective is to determine how far there is immediate danger to people, animals, and the environment from radioactive material on the site and to determine if any surface or subsurface conditions might remain hazardous in the future.

> On September 9 a group of investigating officials from the outside walked up

the Ogotoruk Creek and investigated all by themselves. They reported that they tested the site on the surface with a scintillator [a sensitive Geiger counter] and found no radiation.

On September 11, Rex Tuzroyluk and a group of Iñupiat, plus a white Army Engineer expert on radiation, Willard Ferrell, and two white environmental experts, Scott Holmes and Ron Short, went to the site to investigate the dump mound. We walked to the site carrying three electric rod drivers for making holes. When we arrived at the mound, I measured its dimensions by my stride, which is accurate. It was 42 ft. by 40 ft. and 6 ft. high. The outside men, who judged by eye, said it was 30 ft. by 32. ft.

We drove a hole into the mound with an augur. Ron Short read the Geiger counter reading at the base of the hole. It read 3 at first. We went down 2? feet. When the Geiger counter was shoved in the hole it read 6.2. We tried again. It flickered once. I saw it, Rex saw it, Rock saw it, and Luke saw it [all Iñupiat]. I did not get the number. Willard Ferrell said he got 1.3. But he said, "Let's get out of here." This is what really got us. He said, "This is it. Cover the Hole. Let's get out of here." He had no doubt in his mind we did hit something here. That's what he told us.

Willard, after the flicker, would not go out and try the other side of the mound. He would not say this in the public meeting.

It should be noted that there is a pond right next to the mound. In my experience it thaws down to 8 ft. around and at the bottom of a pond. This was the water source closest to the mound and no samples were taken there.

I respect Willard Ferrell but he is not telling us everything.

Their final report to Mayor Ray Koonuk was that they have determined they have to investigate further with the proper equipment.

The point is that the Army Corps of Engineers has this information. Yet very little of it comes to Point Hope. If they have been so concerned about persons and the environment why did they not give information about how radiation works and how to detect it? (Tuzroyluk 1992)

Describing the feeling in Point Hope itself, Jack Schaefer reported, "On October 9, 100 angry and fearful residents of Point Hope met at their community center. George Kingik made a speech in which he declared: 'The Jews in the Holocaust were treated better than we were. The Jews knew it was coming.'"

The Iñupiat North Slope Borough Assembly, mainly elected by Iñupiat, also put in its protest against the dumping. Committees were formed at the village and borough level, and after a time Iñupiat policy began to develop. News came through from Washington that the Department of Energy promised to clean up the dump at a cost of one million dollars. One could see polarization in the activities involving the small village of Point Hope: the village on the one side, and the nation's capital on the other. Events continually spanned the gap. For the malaise that was afflicting the village was also to be seen in the nation during the years when the dump existed; the two malaises derived from the same source—that is, the results of Western industrial and military policies, policies that affected us all.

In January 1993 I received a phone call in the middle of teaching freshmen undergraduates the course "Ritual and Symbol," which included my lugging a heavy drum into the classroom for a performance of a girl's initiation. The call was from the Iñupiat village. Jack Schaefer of Point Hope, Jesse Kaleak of Barrow, who was mayor of the North Slope Borough at the time, his assistant Johnny Aiken, and other Iñupiat and some friendly lawyers were meeting in New York City with a number of North American Native leaders to put their various cases to the United Nations. Boutros Boutros-Ghali, then secretary-general, had agreed to give an audience to leaders of indigenous minority communities. Jack telephoned and asked me to come. Getting Steve Sharp, a northernist anthropologist, to take my class, I made the long journey into the city and found Jack at a high-rise hotel.

Jack had arrived from Point Hope fresh from cutting up seal meat. His hands were stained with the indelible dark red blood of seals, and his fingernails were clogged. He had split his leather jacket right down the back. I sewed up his jacket in the hotel room, using the small skin-sewing stitches that Molly Oktollik had taught me the first year I was there. We went off to find the others and had a meeting. Jack, self-taught lawyer that he was, had already armed the others with stacks of very frightening information. For instance, Peggy, the Native Village secretary had seen *four* other dumps just like the one that O'Neill had reported; experimental medical tablets containing radioactive substances had been given to Anaktuvak Pass Iñupiat without any explanation; and army-supply nuclear generators enclosed in a mere 1-inch shell had been abandoned up and down the North Slope when the DEW line (Distant Early Warning) army posts were closed down. The latter were dangerous objects, at risk of opening in the melting and freezing conditions on the Slope. These were all true horrors. I went among my Iñupiat friends hunched and ashamed, willing to follow them up the elevator in the huge rectangular building of the United Nations and sit as inconspicuously as I could in front of Boutros Boutros-Ghali while he listened to Iroquois, Plains Indians, Natives from Nevada, Hawaiians, and ourselves, the Iñupiat, telling wrongs. We had no pull, no majority vote; we were quite helpless. Even I told Boutros-Ghali of these wrongs. Now I find myself saying "we," for writing which I have been reprimanded in the past. Disobedient as ever, I still say "we." How could I stand over with the whites and say about my friends, "they"?

Here then is what fieldwork can do in the age of globalization—what it simply did to me: it put me on the Iñupiat's side in their venture into the political heart of the world. And the Iñupiat were as formal and eloquent as they ever were in their elders' conferences, and in ages before that, in their *qalgi* (meeting centers), those underground domed sod houses. Afterward, Boutros-Ghali, looking like an old and selfish turtle, informed the meeting that he was setting up an office of the United Nations at Geneva to be devoted to the interests of indigenous minorities, those without a United Nations vote. This was good! The man belied his looks. (Now, in 1996, it became apparent that Boutros-Ghali designated this whole decade, the 1990s, as "the Decade of the Indigenous Peoples.")

Finally, we all grouped around the secretary-general and had our photographs taken, the anthropologist too.

When this was over, Jack came down with me to my home in Charlottesville, Virginia, to await an appointment with two Alaskan senators in Washington and with officials at the Department of Energy. He had to wait for five weeks. Here, Jack's presence constituted a case of a personage from the field arriving at the anthropologist's end of the enterprise—creating a reversal. Jack became interested in Charlottesville, and keenly interested in what the University of Virginia had to offer that might help his people in their struggle to make an obdurate government undertake a thorough investigation of all the dumps. He borrowed many books on nuclear pollution and nuclear law on my library card. We made inquiries around the science faculty for those who understood long-term radioactivity problems. Jack gave a talk in my class on these problems, and on the Iñupiat's need for self-determination, and he met many of the anthropology faculty.

A friendly nuclear physicist also invited us to visit the University of Virginia's nuclear reactor on the university grounds, originally established as a teaching tool for students. We drove up past the students' dining hall and Slaughter Gymnasium and turned right through a half mile of trees. We saw a sign saying NUCLEAR REACTOR, and by the road a small 50-foot pond, then a building. At the entrance at the back of the building our friend met us. It was an oldish building—it must have been built in around 1960. The offices were clean but needed a coat of paint. Our friend took us to the Geiger counter in the passage and told us to put our hands in the sensor to check our existing levels of radiation. They were low. He then opened a double door and led us into a brightly lit hall. First we saw a walkway and a railing on the left; up against the wall on the right were dumped two or three long rods. Our friend drew our attention to what was over the railing on the left. It was a pool, looking like a swimming pool. But unusually deep. He pointed to the far right end, deep down. Connections led to the depths and to rods visible deep below; and out from the rods in the water swam a brilliant blue color, filling a third of the lower waters. The blue color. I had heard about that, from descriptions of Madame Curie's life. Jack and I drew back.

"It's quite safe," said the scientist by my side. I did not reply because I was trembling inside. I had heard such words before.[2] We left the hall and rechecked with the Geiger counter. Mercifully the readings showed no increase. Later, I read how this reactor had been subsequently inspected and come under criticism.

Meanwhile, as I discovered later, in Alaska on February 23, 1993, the state epidemiologist, Dr. John Middaugh, made a statement referring to the Point Hope dump: "There has been no evidence of radiation impact on the health problems of the local residents."[3] And later in the letter: "The plan to excavate the Cape Thompson site should be abandoned"—that is, the plan to remove the dump. What then had caused all the cancer I had seen among the villagers of Point Hope?

May 17, 1993. At last, after six weeks' delay, the Department of Energy (DOE) made arrangements for the Iñupiat group to do their business at their office. Appointments also came through with the Alaska senators at the Senate building. It was at DOE that I first started suffering from an auto-immune syndrome, with many aches and pains.[4] So my story, even at a personal level, was a dark one.

Again in Washington, the Iñupiat met with their lawyers to set up the DOE inquiry and decide strategy. We were to meet there with one Tom Gerusky, who headed the nuclear problem affairs office. The Atomic Energy Commission had long since ceased to exist, and the Nuclear Regulatory Commission did not take responsibility for the past; it was the Army Corps of Engineers that was responsible in this matter to DOE—so it was to DOE that we would have to go. This department was no longer located in Washington but was out in Maryland, an expensive taxi ride away. I went with Jack—we were late—and I slammed down the forty-five dollars and wrote it off as tax-deductible. Was this research? It was an interesting question.

The small episode of the taxi fare opens up the question of what it is that anthropologists do in the field. If we are not asking questions all the time—and contemporary fieldworkers are learning not to do so—we will have to go about our research by making real, actual friends, and committing ourselves to acts of friendship.[5] Now is this research? I would say yes. It is personal, but of course all fieldwork is personal, and such is the case with fieldwork anywhere on the globe. When Clifford Geertz was chased from the cockfight by the Balinese police, he was simply in the same situation as the Balinese, for a time. When one is acting in the field, one is acting as a real person.

In this matter of radioactivity, I had the same intentions as Jack and the delegation when we visited Washington. Thus it can be seen that a major element of fieldwork is that the people *need* you; you will become their representative. There is a very interesting cross-positioning of roles here that happens constantly in our present age of globalization, the age of the growth of reflexivity everywhere. It is likely to become a truism in the twenty-first century, so that anthropologists of any nation will be questioned by other nations, often more questioned than questioning, and more in demand as "reflectors" of each culture's true meanings.

To continue the story: DOE is housed in a recently built and manicured large office complex in a field outside of Germantown, Maryland. Jack and I found a classic flight of steps around the side, entered, and walked down a long corridor. The place was throttling, tense. Jack and I looked at each other, reading the signs on the walls. Down a long side corridor we found a person who could tell us the way. At last we came to a door, which when we opened revealed a semi-dark conference room full of people—Tom Gerusky and his numerous assistants, and there were our friends, Jesse Kaleak, Ray Koonuk, Johnny Aiken, and the others. This "Tom," as he chose to be called, was in the process of scolding the Iñupiat for submitting a requirement that

DOE, in addition to the removal of the dump, should mount a much wider investigation into other radioactive dumping. (Gerusky was quite adamant. At this point, I wonder why that was.)

"No," he was saying. "The one million dollars is all you'll get. That's for clearing the dump. Don't expect any more investigations." And his assistant lugged out a huge memorandum, a thousand pages long, he told us, and started reading about how those who were going to take away the dump would wear such and such protective clothing, and so on, interminably.

I broke in, intensely irritated (unlike the outwardly cool Iñupiat). "What's all this about protecting the white men doing the clearing away? What about the *cancer* now existing in the village? You don't seem to be interested in that at all. Of course there has to be an investigation." This caused a certain hiatus in the reading. Slides illustrating the same material as the memo were put on instead. Jack beside me was shifting his feet. "Let's get out of here," he said. "We'll walk out."

"Okay."

The two of us achieved quite a good "walk-out" effect, stony-faced, with heads erect.

In the corridor, Jack told me how Gerusky had been persistently slithery in his dealings with him. I shuddered. Who was this Gerusky? I now had a terrible headache and my limbs hurt. When I got back to my lodgings I threw up.

Nevertheless we still had two senators to see. Our Iñupiat friends had also left DOE soon after we did, and were equally seething.[6]

Our Alaska senators were hard to locate. At last we found ourselves outside Ted Stevens's office at the secretary's desk. To Jack's easygoing inquiries, he found out that the office had known about the dump from way back. Jack withdrew quietly, much shaken. "Why did he never say anything?" Stevens had sworn he knew nothing about any pollution.[7]

So now the Iñupiat had arrived at the heart of the government and were finding lies and subterfuge firsthand. I followed where my friends led. I was finding these things firsthand too.

Stevens's legislative assistant, David Lundquist, was in his office, and I had a word with him about another case of dumping. The government was offering the Mescalero Apache of Arizona millions of dollars for education and other needs if they would accept nuclear waste on their land. I said to Lundquist, "That is immoral."

I remember his riposte. "You're a bleeding heart."

I turned away, both sick and proud. My heart did bleed.[8]

Eventually we followed our guide through a long tunnel to the Senate itself. Three business-suited gentlemen were walking in front of us. "That's Edward Teller," said the guide, pointing to one of them. This Edward Teller, the "Father of the Atom Bomb," was just another fleshy man. Why was he so at home here at the Senate?[9]

We did meet Stevens, and we also met Senator Murkowski. It was hard to choose between them. Each of their private Senate chambers was large, full of luxury and fine portraits, antique chairs, beautiful things. Every now and then the senator concerned would be called to the floor to vote, hurrying into the huge chamber we had glimpsed while walking around the corridor on its periphery. At Senator Stevens's chambers, Jack in his mended jacket and four-days'-worn T-shirt gave his appeal with his educated dignity. He told the senator about the dumps and the sickness, and described what he was also worried about, the 2-foot-wide metal pipes the hunters had discovered that reached deep into the ground on the Chariot site, visible to this day, stuffed with a bit of dirt. "They definitely need investigation," Jack told the senator.

"They would never drill so wide," said Stevens, flustered. "It's impossible! Why would they want to do something like that?" Here was another denial. The constituency of this senator, back in Alaska, was four-fifths white, the rest Native. These four-fifths would not want to hear what Jack said. In our own minds, to this day the question repeats itself, "What size [were?] the nuclear bombs the Chariot team had intended to place underground at Ogotoruk Creek, then detonate? Have we any information about the plans and how far they went?" This matter went beyond the fears of a small village, whose troubles were less, after all, than those of the Marshall Islands.[10]

Shortly after the conclusion of these meetings, I was due to fly to Anchorage and give a paper on the dump and people's reactions to it at the Alaska Anthropological Association annual meetings (April 1993). First I visited Point Hope. The mood there was black. All the authorities were denying that the dump had anything to do with people's ill health. In any discussion of the dump, the people doubted that the government would actually do what was necessary and move the material. Barbara Lane was dead, and her husband Jacob, who had been an important man as long as his wife was alive, could no longer run a whaleboat and had given up his captaincy to his daughter. He was now unshaven. Many men had let their beards grow. There was more trash lying about in the village. None of the villagers seemed to be able to lift up their heads. There had been insult; the government had been found to play them false. These people embodied the oldest village in America—did no one honor even that? No one from outside cared about that, and dumped nuclear waste on them that would kill them. That gray-black mood was something I did not like to see. I myself was unhappy, embroiled in the dreadful results of globalization.

It was obvious that I had to do some real compiling of figures. My friend Connie knew about many of the cases, Piquk also. Everyone was talking about the latest people in trouble: someone new was suffering the familiar pain—another was in for surgery. I quickly came up with thirty-seven cases. Dr. Bowerman of the Native Health Hospital in Barrow was able to trace an excess of seventy deaths from cancer in Point Hope between 1969 and 1993 (the village was smaller in earlier years). This translated as an average of fifty-seven per thousand per year.[11] The death rate from cancer in 1950, before the dump, was four per thousand—so that the recent rate represented a more than fourteen-fold increase. Why the difference between those periods? Nearly every agency to which we appealed argued that it was caused by the people's lifestyle.

Nevertheless, a year after the dump had first been discovered, the Department of

Energy did remove it, commenting that it was done so that the people of Point Hope would feel better. It would be of psychological benefit.

It was not until 1995 that the government medical authorities came to a new conclusion: the high rate of cancer in Point Hope was indisputably caused by the local radioactive pollution. In October 1995, Rex came on the phone to tell me that he and Caroline, Mayor Ray, and the mayor of the North Slope, George Ahmaogak, had been asked to Washington to the White House because President Clinton wished to apologize to Point Hope village representatives for the previous administrations' illegal acts.

"Wonderful!" I said, and thought, "About time."

I drove up to Washington when the group finished at the White House to see them and have dinner. I was to meet them at their hotel and we would drive to Union Station, where the lawyers were waiting for us at a restaurant.

In the hotel, there was Caroline, beaming and full of energy as usual. We hugged comprehensively. Rex and all of them were happy. Then for the restaurant. When we got to the door, it was pouring with rain. We bundled into my car and set forth. But I took some kind of wrong turn. Twice we found ourselves approaching Dupont Circle, each time in a different direction. Why? I peered through the steaming, wiper-wracked windshield. Okay, now we were on Constitution Avenue.

"It must be east," I muttered. "The station is east of the Capitol"—or so I thought. The folks in the car seemed pretty happy, whatever. I was soon far to the east on Constitution Avenue and decided to turn back—taking the wrong way on a one-way street. Now the Eskimos took over. "Eh-eh-eh-eh-eh! You can't do that."

"Edie, you have to go west," said Ray. "Take this road." How did he know? Caroline and the others were laughing now; I do not think they wanted this journey to end. Ray and Caroline took over the directions and we soon found ourselves in the parking lot on the roof of the station, and descended to meet our friends, who had only just arrived. At dinner, plans were at last made for the hoped-for investigations. Even compensation was mentioned.

And so now we find ourselves in 1996, an era of the reflexivity of our friends in the field. When I go into the field now, it is really like going home, where everyone knows you, and they take it for granted you will turn up some time or other. "Hi Edie. Welcome home"—this is in the store at Point Hope, with snow outside. Snow. That is the natural stuff to find lying outside. The squeak of my sneakers in the snow is what I have been missing—the kids wanting me to play, their little faces turned up like cups, a bit unsteady and about to spill in fun, the smell of doughnuts Molly had just cooked, and she throws one toward me in the time-honored habitual gesture of Iñupiat ritual giving. Her eyebrows are raised and winsome and thoughtful; she is glad to see me. Then suddenly sighs. It's her son, who committed suicide last year. John, her husband, says "No don't, Molly. Come on, don't." She tries to fight it down, but the sad look is still there. (But Molly did not know, the day I was there, that a few days into the future, after I left, she would catch a whale. That is how they put it:

Molly caught a whale. "The woman catches the whale," so the mystery goes. Molly does not call me on the phone or I would have heard all about it, not just the bare news from Piquk. Now Molly can get over her sorrow better; now she will be very busy.) Back in Molly's house I give two-year-old Joanna a "snowmobile ride" on my knee, and get quite excited myself.[12]

They have just announced on the Oktolliks' TV the loss of Ron Brown (this was March 31, 1996), and John tells me about it; he has to jog my memory as to who Ron Brown is. Now I see it is a disaster.

John Oktollik knows more about Bosnia than I do.

They keep looking out the window where they can see the south shore. Is there a water cloud hanging above the open sea? The weather is warm for the area, and muggy, 26 degrees Fahrenheit, and the wind is from the south, blowing the ice against the shore. There will be no whales, for there is no water for the whale to come through. But wait, next day, what happens?—and it will not happen without the whole village *doing it*. The wind is the trouble, the wind is still wrong, from the south.

What happened was this. After church on Sunday a call came through on the CB, heard at Molly's, that there was going to be a rogation (prayer service, dull in my experience) in the church at 3:00. I thought I had better go. The voice went on, "Any volunteers to bring a boat into the church?" Aha! I remembered how they brought a boat into the church the first year I was there, and how they blessed it in the hope of catching whales. I remembered the whaling captains all standing in the sanctuary. I left Molly's and wandered outside in the snow to watch. Over a stretch of snow beside Seymour's house, I saw men collecting around a skin boat, which still rested on its high rack. But not for long; they were manhandling it down and onto a sled. I had to run to keep the boat in view as it glided through the streets, pulled by snowmobile, then to the side of the church. I came up behind panting, and saw again the captains with five of their young sons heaving and blundering the boat off the sled. Then they took the sled and smartly passed it into the church and parked it up the aisle in the sanctuary, and afterward took the boat itself through the church entrance, sideways, with banging and side-slipping, until they could get it through the door and the right way up again, then up the aisle; and sled and boat were set as on ice and on sea, in church—where the altar boy was in the act of changing the colored altar cloth for a white one. Whales like white. The preacher wore white. The paddles were all scoured white and set upright, as when a whale is caught, in the position of the "catch" signal to other boats.

The church was filling quickly. All twenty-two whaling captains, including the prime one, Henry Nashookpuk (known for his unspoken gifts), stood in two ranks on each side of the boat. The preacher stood at the prow and began. We sang of the good things from the sea, "The whales and all that move in the waters," "The sea is his and he made it," and "When I in awesome wonder consider all the worlds," songs that brought tears to the eyes of many of us, Molly, Emma, myself—and others, so Emma said. Then the captains came forward to the boat and put their hands on the gunwale, all around, and their wives behind them. (It was just a 16-foot boat.) The congregation went up and put their hands on the wives, and so on. Then we all began praying for whales. The sound arose till my eyes were starting out of my head. I prayed like mad—there were weird cryings from the crowd, with arms whirling on high. The strength rose and rose and rose. Edie, I told myself, you've never been in a religious event like this! I look over to where Henry's face appeared. It was calm—and faintly happy. I quieted, and soon the hullabaloo was over, and we finished with one more hymn, most of us in a state of cold chill. The congregation started to leave, the men took the boat down and out the door, and I went gingerly over the snowy step myself, to find Molly waiting to walk back with me. As we passed the end of the church and came into the open, there it was. The wind had changed to the north. It blew icy and fresh from far up the village and fell freely on our cheeks and upon the south shore. It would blow the ice away and there would be water. No one said a word.

The next day there was water, and the men went down on the ice to break trail across the ice toward the open water. By Tuesday there were several crews down at the water, watching. Several whales were seen. And as I said, Piquk phoned me a week after I got home and said Molly had her whale. Henry and John Tingook also caught whales.

So the people's efforts were rewarded by a favorable north wind. Obviously the Iñupiat had regained their powers. The whale was once more the center of their life, their Archimedean point. The point had swung back into position. The event of "changing the wind" was caused by the prayers, while the possibility of the event was also caused by the prayers. One should refer back in time for the roots of this process. The desire and need for the whaling way of life and the relationship with these animals were what motivated the fight for health and self-recognition (the antipollution struggle); the presidential apology and subsequent improved economy won by the villagers gave birth to the strength to make the Christian-shamanic prayer, which gave birth to the whales' arrival. For the villagers, therefore, the possibility of catching a whale engendered the whale—through ordeal. It reinforced the villagers' knowledge of the whale as a spiritual animal.

My own interpretation, long since self-weaned from exclusive faith in either positivism or the "one-faith-only" idea, was that this was the old and excellent shamanism. This Christian shamanism had altered the weather. Such an interpretation shows the integration of past and present, and also shows the way such nonmaterial power works, even across times and spaces that seem too vast for connection.

* * *

Before I left Point Hope, I went to see Caroline: we gave each other another great hug. "Do you remember that ride in the rain?" was the first thing she said, and collapsed with mirth. We have a minor shared memory here that neither of us will ever forget. I was also conscious that her own memory of Washington was the more vivid of the two, due to all the efforts she and the others had made in the past and because of the presidential apology.

Globalization has greatly affected not only peripheral peoples but anthropology itself. Shared memories and shared experiences are a serious side of it. The actual, not virtual, participation in cross-traveling possibilities for both sides—not only one way, but both ways—is another. This actual participation has to be recorded as a kind of Evans-Pritchardian history. These are not "observers'" social facts, but participant-based, political, life-and-death social facts, and they concern action. We are not writing societies; this time they seem to be bent on writing us, so as to correct the balance and achieve justice for themselves on global terms.

It is the turn of events that dictates what we should write. A society grows and ramifies somewhere, the stranger approaches (and the more informed the stranger is, the more drastic are the events that seem to befall him or her)—then, in all manner of speaking, all hell breaks loose. It is as if in the modern, extremely fluid state of all societies, the entry of that conscious particle, the anthropologist, is enough to start one or two small chain reactions, to tip the balance here and there just enough for reflexivity to seethe and burgeon. To "correct" this is not the point—it is not a matter for concern, for it seems to be the true role of anthropologists, perhaps insignificant but necessary role in the global situation, just as certain kinds of communication cells are necessary in a living body.

In conclusion, one will have to see my stories as piecemeal affairs, none directly illustrating how globalization affects fieldwork. One cannot tie down Boutros-Ghali's turtle look, the extraordinary coziness of the Union Station restaurant after the rain-bombarded journey, or Rex standing in light snow at Cape Thompson after seeing the Geiger counter flicker, to a theory of globalization. Maybe Wallerstein (1974) understood globalization. But he was no fieldworker. Fieldworkers know the global feel firsthand, in those absurd particularities. Humanistic anthropologists for better or worse are following this path, often following people in the field about in these people's efforts to preserve their autonomy. There is some kind of antiradioactivity effect here. The little unseen particle of humanism might be able to protect the twenty-first century from the total annihilation of our umbilical connection with each other. The girders and power lines have only one kind of power.

The Iñupiat live far up in the north. Nevertheless it was they who kept the interlacing connection going with the center of power in Washington. Circumstances impelled them to connect. Globalization for them did not take the form of the relatively harmless effects of world capitalism, but derived from the boiling kind of hysterical power (driven by hidden capitalism on both sides) that brought about the Cold War between two mighty states. Here globalization hit an innocent village, and drew its desperate representatives to the capital. These representatives have mandated that the peripheries of the planet will not do for the dumping of harmful garbage, because people live there.

Notes

This paper would have been impossible without the major help and research of Jack Schaefer and Rex Tuzroyluk (the latter is now president of the North Slope Borough Assembly). The friendship of these two means much to me. Warm thanks also go to Piquk Tuzroyluk for her friendship and hospitality. I thank the friend who allowed us to see the University of Virginia nuclear reactors. Many others have aided the production of the essay, especially Steve Sharp. Thanks to all.

For the sake of privacy I have changed the names of some of the sick in Point Hope.

1. Iñupiaq is the singular of the word Iñupiat.

2. In 1958 in Manchester, England, where I was living, there occurred what is now termed the Windscale disaster, in which an experimental atomic pile about 11 miles from the city leaked radioactivity. At the time, the British government announced that the danger was very slight. In 1959 I gave birth to a Down syndrome baby, Lucy, who died after five months. The news was released sixteen years later that there had been many abnormal births in Manchester during the same period.

3. Letter to Kevin Cabble, Department of Energy, Nevada, from Alaska governor Hickel's office.

4. After three years, this trouble, polymyalgia rheumatica, was eventually cured.

5. There are many ethnographies that recount how researchers either had to apologize to their patient field discussants for beleaguering them with incessant questions, or discovered early in their fieldwork the offense that the practice of questioning gives. There are signs that in anthropology this penchant for the questionnaire is giving way. In sociology it is on the increase.

6. Now, certain of the recalcitrant DOE officials have been sacked, and Tom Gerusky no longer has his position.

7. Yet anthropologist Harry Stephen Sharp—my friend Steve of the "Ritual and Symbol" class—later revealed that when he was stationed at army bases at Fairbanks and Fort Wainwright in 1971–72, talk of the existence of the dump was commonplace among the men. It is ironic that at that date Vic Turner and I were in Ireland studying pilgrimage, unaware of these future events, while Steve Sharp—a future anthropologist who was to help me with "Ritual and Symbol"—was stationed in the middle of damning evidence, unable to help, uneasy like his comrades.

8. Years later the Apache did accept their offer. There were many complications, not all of which are clear. Many of the Apache are still protesting the decision. As I write (November 16, 1996) the dumping is due to take place in three weeks (Marta Weigle, personal communication).

9. Teller had been to see Stevens and his legislative assistant, David Lundquist.

10. Jack Schaefer and his group shared a lawyer who had worked effectively on the problems and rights of the Marshall Islanders, the people who had been most afflicted by nuclear testing in the South Pacific.

11. The death rate from cancer in the whole of the United States in 1980 was 1.8 per 1,000.

12. The name Joanna was not given in the way we might do, to keep a family name going. The people have a strong sense of reincarnation. For them, this was the dead Joanna returned for a better try at life.

References

Anchorage Daily News
1992   Nuclear Waste Dump Discovered. Anchorage Daily News, September 6: 1.

Berger, Thomas R.
1985   Village Journey: The Report of the Alaska Native Land Review Commission. New York: Hill and Wang.

Foote, Donald Charles

1961   A Human Geographical Study in North-West Alaska: Final Report of the Human Geographical Studies Program of the United States Atomic Energy Commission, Project Chariot. Cambridge, MA: Atomic Energy Commission.

Middaugh, John

1993   Letter to Kevin Cabble, Department of Energy, Nevada, from Alaska governor Hickel's office, February 23.

Schneider, Howard

1996   Arctic Nations Discuss Cleanup: Group Moves to Protect Native Peoples, Wildlife from World's Pollution. Washington Post, September 21: A15.

Turner, Edith

1987   The Spirit and the Drum. Tucson: University of Arizona Press.

1989   From Shamans to Healers: The Survival of an Iñupiat Eskimo Skill. Anthropologica 31(1):3–24.

1996   The Hands Feel It: Healing and Spirit Process among a Northern Alaska People. DeKalb: Northern Illinois University Press.

Tuzroyluk, Rex

1992   The Nuclear Waste Dump at Chariot. Point Hope, AK: Tikigaq Native Corporation.

Wallerstein, Immanuel M.

1974   The Modern World System. New York: Academic Press.

f i v e
Uranium Mining and Milling
Navajo Experiences in the American Southwest

Barbara Rose Johnston, Susan E. Dawson,
and Gary E. Madsen

Uranium is found in trace quantities everywhere on earth. Rock containing uranium is mined, crushed, and processed in a mill, where it is then leached, generally using an acidic or alkaline leach, dried, and barreled. The resulting uranium oxide powder is typically yellow in color, and when this "yellowcake" is further processed and enriched, it is used to fuel nuclear power plants. With additional processing, the highly enriched fuel can serve as the fissile core of a nuclear bomb. This chapter explores some of the legacy issues associated with uranium mining and milling, with a focus on the human costs of producing yellowcake on Navajo lands in the American Southwest.

The element uranium was discovered in 1789 by a chemist analyzing the components of pitchblende ore from a German mine. A French scientist first isolated pure uranium in 1841. In the United States, uranium was first mined as a component of pitchblende ore in 1871, when 200 pounds of ore from a Denver, Colorado, mine were sent to London for research on possible industrial applications. In 1898 French scientists Pierre and Marie Curie isolated radium from pitchblende, describing it as a daughter of uranium decay. That same year, low-grade uranium, vanadium, and radium were found in carnotite, a mineral containing red and yellow ores used as body paint by early Navajo and Ute Indians on the Colorado Plateau. These discoveries triggered a prospecting boom in southeastern Utah, whose radium mines became a major source of ore for the Curies (Hahne 1989).

Outside of research, medical treatments, and luminous paint, demand for radium proved over time to be limited, and when high-grade ores were located and developed in the Belgian Congo in the 1920s, the market price for radium plummeted, prompting abandonment of many US mines. Canadian production at Great Bear Lake began in the mid-1930s, and when production outstripped market demand in 1937, the Belgian Congo mines were closed. One year later, US researchers discovered a military weapons application for vanadium: it adds tensile strength and elasticity to molten steel. This discovery prompted re-mining of tailings piles near abandoned radium mines, the reopening of a vanadium mine in southeastern Utah in 1938, and, beginning in 1939, renewed exploration of the Navajo Reservation (Ringholz 1989).

When German physicists Otto Hahn and Fritz Strassmann successfully demonstrated a technique to split the uranium atom and generate energy in 1938, the scientific and military establishment took note. By 1939–40, uranium weapons research was being conducted in Germany, the Soviet Union, France, Canada, Great Britain, Japan, and the United States, through its radiological warfare program in the Chemical Warfare Department and its Manhattan Project (Miller 1986).

In the United States, whose available supply was limited to materials in tailings piles and the small amount mined on the Colorado Plateau, 90 percent of the uranium eventually used in the Manhattan Project was imported from Canada and the Belgian Congo, with smaller amounts obtained from mines in South Africa. Recognizing the urgent need to develop a national supply of uranium, the government established a covert program to mine uranium from vanadium dumps and to survey the Colorado Plateau in search of new lodes. In late 1940, shortly after Germany began its occupation of Belgium, the twenty-year stockpile was transferred from the Congo to the United States and stored in a warehouse on Staten Island. In 1942 this stockpile of 1,200 tons of uranium was turned over to the US Army and processed at the Canadian Chalk River facility (Edwards 1997). In late 1942, the US Geological Survey completed its classified survey of the Colorado Plateau, and from 1943 to 1945 approximately 76,000 pounds of uranium oxide for the Manhattan Project were secretly recovered from tailings piles on the Navajo Reservation (Chenoweth 1997; DOE 2005). In 1944–45, following a uranium mining agreement negotiated by the British with the South African government, some 40,000 tons of uranium oxide were imported to the United States from South Africa (Fischer 1990; Horton 1999).

Germany also made great efforts to locate and protect uranium stocks, advancing into Czechoslovakian Sudentenland and in 1938 taking control of the Joachimstal uranium mines, the world's first known source of uranium. The Germans used slave labor to work these mines, and the German firm Auerwerke used slave labor from the Sachsenhausen concentration camp to process uranium at the Oranienburg works near Berlin (Preston 2006:162–63).[1]

After World War II, the US Congress approved the 1946 Energy Act, establishing the Atomic Energy Commission (AEC). In 1947 the AEC opened offices in Colorado, New Mexico, and Utah, publishing advice on uranium prospecting and offering a $10,000 discovery bonus for high-grade deposits. In the decade that followed, "uranium fever" swept the United States. In 1953 alone, Americans bought thirty-five thousand Geiger counters. Finding uranium, according to Gordon Dean, chairman of the AEC from 1950 to 1953, became a patriotic duty: "The security of the free world may depend upon such a simple thing as people keeping their eyes open. Every American oil man looking for 'black gold' in a foreign jungle is derelict in his duty to his country if he hasn't at least mastered the basic information on the geology of uranium. And the same applies to every mountain climber, every big game hunter, and for that matter, every butterfly catcher" (Caufield 1989:75). By 1958 there were seventy-five hundred reports of uranium finds in the United States, with 850 underground and 200 open-pit mines producing uranium (Brugge and Goble 2002; World Information Service on Energy 2004).

With their intimate knowledge of the land, Native Americans played a significant role in locating uranium sources in the American Southwest. Shown samples of numerous types of uranium-bearing ore, many Native Americans were able to lead miners to areas where years before they had seen similar rocks. Significant deposits were found in the Colorado Plateau, a 120,000-square-mile region known as the Four Corners (where Colorado, Utah, Arizona, and New Mexico come together) and home to the largest concentration of Native Americans remaining in North America: the Navajo, Southern Ute, Ute Mountain, Hopi, Zuni, Laguna, Acoma, and several other Pueblo nations (Brugge and Goble 2002; Caufield 1989). This chapter focuses on the Navajo people who live on 26,110 square miles of land and number approximately 270,000 residents (Utah Division of Indian Affairs 2006).

In late 1949 and early 1950, Henry Doyle, a US Public Health Service (USPHS) sanitary engineer, conducted the earliest study of uranium miners on the Navajo Nation. This exploratory study examined working conditions and radiation exposures in several mines leased by the Vanadium Corporation of America (VCA). According to Doyle:

> In general, standard mining practices were being used at these properties and all drilling was being done wet. There was no source of water in the immediate vicinity of these mines. Water for the drills was being hauled by a truck from a spring approximately three miles away. No change house, toilets, showers, or drinking water was available to the workers at these mines. It is my understanding that the US Bureau of Mines made a safety inspection in June 1949 and recommended that change houses and basic sanitation facilities be made available at these sites. No action on this recommendation has been taken by the Vanadium Corporation of America and it is my understanding that they have doubts that the facilities would be used by the Indians if they were provided. (Doyle 1950:2)

Furthermore, Doyle found that the Navajo workers were not given pre-employment examinations, and there was no medical program for the miners. Doyle also assessed working conditions in radium mines. He noted that none of the mines had mechanical ventilation or even crosscuts in the mineshafts providing limited natural ventilation. In addition, radon samples from these mines identified concentrations 4 to 750 times the accepted maximum allowable concentration of 10^{-8} curies per cubic meter (Doyle 1950).

While the ore was on Native American lands, the rights to exploit and profit from this scarce and rare mineral were granted by the US federal government to private commercial operators (Allen 1989). For example, in 1952 the Department of Interior's Bureau of Indian Affairs awarded a uranium-mining contract to Kerr-McGee Corporation. The contract was negotiated by federal agents and then presented as a job-creating initiative to the Navajo Tribal Council. The council, without receiving information on the nature of uranium mining or its known dangers, endorsed the contract, and Kerr-McGee hired one hundred Navajo miners to work at two-thirds the off-reservation pay scale. An additional three hundred to five hundred miners were employed in "independent mining" operations supported by the Small Business Administration. These workers mined shallow (50 feet or less) deposits of rich uranium ore, which was sold in small lots to the AEC buying station located behind the Kerr-McGee milling facility (Tso and Shields 1980:13).

Under the 1946 Atomic Energy Act, the AEC controlled the uranium industry. No one else was permitted to own uranium; all that was mined had to be sold to the AEC, and the AEC declared itself not responsible for protecting the health of miners. Despite government awareness that uranium mining was a dangerous business that posed a high degree of health risk for workers and area residents, this information was not communicated to workers or residents. Thus, in the AEC's 1951 *Prospecting for Uranium*, there is no reference to radiation except to say that "the radioactivity contained in rocks is not dangerous to humans unless such rocks are held in close contact with the skin for very long periods of time" (AEC 1951).

At the end of the 1950s, the government ended the uranium-prospecting boom, announcing that it would buy uranium only from existing deposits. By that time, Kerr-McGee had rights to about one-quarter of the known US reserves. The AEC continued to purchase uranium up until the late 1960s, when it decided it had enough to meet weapons development needs. The US federal government continued to purchase uranium for nuclear fuel needs until 1971, when the commercial nuclear industry was able to directly acquire its fuel source (Brugge and Goble 2002).

Dirty Business

The nuclear fuel cycle involves four different industrial processes: mining, milling (producing uranium oxides commonly called yellowcake), enrichment, and fuel fabrication. These industrial processes all generate hazardous by-products, in the form of

radon gas and radioactive dust. The human health risks associated with these hazardous by-products have been known for a long time.

As early as 1546, miners of uranium-bearing pitchblende in the Erzgebirge
Mountains of central Europe were reported to have an unusually high incidence of fatal
lung disease. Cases of lung cancer in uranium miners were first clinically and anatom-
ically diagnosed in Germany in 1879. In 1824 Christian Gmelin published findings
from his research on the acute and chronic health effects of uranyl nitrate, chloride, and
sulphate in dogs and rabbits. By the early 1900s, uranium had been shown to increase
glucose secretion and was being administered as a therapeutic agent for diabetes
(Hodge et al. 1973). In 1913 a study reported that of the 665 uranium miners who
worked at the Schneeberg mines in the Erzgebirge Mountains in southern Germany
and died between 1876 and 1912, 40 percent had died of lung cancer. Because there
was little silicosis in these cases, investigators concluded that the most probable cause
of the lung cancer was radiation from radon and its daughters (Axelson 1995). Studies
of Czechoslovakian uranium miners found, in addition to fatal lung disease, significant increases in the rate of miscarriage, cleft palate, and other birth defects. These
studies suggested a simple and cheap way to reduce the danger by installing adequate
mine ventilation, which by the 1930s was required by the Czechoslovakian government. By 1942, with additional studies documenting the relationship between radiation exposure and lung cancer among pitchblende miners, the French had begun
installing ventilation systems in their uranium mines (Cunningham and Saigo
1990:362).

The health risks associated with uranium mining and the causal relationship
between mining and lung cancer were known and cited in Manhattan Project studies
on the biomedical effects of radiation. In 1942 Wilhelm C. Hueper published a review
of the literature on the European miners, suggesting that radon gas was implicated in
causing lung cancer. When the US Advisory Committee on Human Radiation
Experiments (ACHRE) reviewed the case of radiation experimentation involving uranium miners in its 1994 report, it noted:

> At the time its own program began, the AEC had many reasons for concern
> that the experience of the Czech and German miners portended excess lung
> cancer deaths for uranium miners in the United States. The factors included
> the following: (1) No respected scientist challenged the finding that the Czech
> and German miners had an elevated rate of lung cancer; (2) these findings were
> well known to the American decision makers; (3) as Hueper points out,
> genetic and nonoccupational factors could be rejected; and (4) radon standards
> existed for other industries, and there was no reason to think that conditions in
> mines ruled out the need for such standards. (ACHRE 1996:356)

Not only was the AEC aware that uranium mining posed significant health risks, with
the assistance of the USPHS, it was actively monitoring radon levels in the mines,
finding higher levels than those reported in the European mines (Holaday 1950). In

Figure 5.1. As illustrated in this 1947 "health physics" poster produced by Oak Ridge National Laboratory, efforts were made to educate and protect the scientists, engineers, and technicians who refined uranium and developed the fuel for reactors and bombs. Credit: Photo courtesy of Oak Ridge Associated Universities

1952 a federal mine inspector at the Shiprock, New Mexico, facility discovered that the ventilation fans in the mine's primary shaft were not working. Returning in 1955, the same inspector noted that the fans ran out of fuel during his visit. By 1959 USPHS monitors documented radiation levels in the Shiprock facility at an estimated ninety to one hundred times the permissible limits for worker safety (DOE 2005).

Navajo miners in the 1950s and 1960s worked in dusty mine shafts, eating their lunch there, drinking water from sources inside the mine, and returning home to their families wearing dust-covered radioactive clothing. According to testimony by George Kelly, a Navajo miner who spoke in 1979 to a US Senate committee, "Inside the interior of the mine was a nasty area, smoky, especially after the dynamite explodes. We run out of the mine and spend five minutes here and there and were chased back in to remove the dirt by hand in little train carts.... The water inside the mine was used as drinking water, no air ventilators, however. The air ventilators were used only when the mine inspectors came and after the mine inspectors leave, the air ventilators were shut off." Another Navajo miner, Phillip Harrison, states: "[W]hen I went to work [in 1969], I was never told anything inside the mine would be hazardous to my health later. It really surprised us to find out after so many years that it would turn out like this, that it would kill a lot of people. They said nothing about radiations or safety, things like that. We had no idea at all" (Caufield 1989:78–79).

Beginning in 1949, the USPHS monitored the health of uranium miners, conducting epidemiologic studies to determine the health effects of radiation. In exchange for the mining company's list of miners' names, the USPHS agreed that its doctors would not divulge the potential health hazards to the workers, nor would they inform those who became ill that their illnesses were radiation related (*Begay et al. v. United States*, 591 F. Supp. 991 [D. AZ (1985)], court document 84-2462). In reviewing the available evidence in 1994, ACHRE concluded "that an insufficient effort was made by the federal government to mitigate the hazard to uranium miners through early ventilation of the mines, and that as a result miners died" (ACHRE 1996:254).

Since 1940 more than fifteen thousand people have worked in the mines or processing mills in the Southwest (Saleem 2003). They include an estimated three thousand Navajo who worked, at one point or another, in the approximately twelve hundred mines scattered across the Four Corners region. Many more thousands of Navajo and Pueblo Indian families lived near uranium mine and mill operations and tailings and have been exposed to contaminated water, dust, and radon gas. Many developed radiation-related diseases.

Epidemiologic studies of uranium miners over the years have demonstrated a number of harsh facts. Of the 150 or so Navajo miners who worked at the Shiprock facility, 18 had died of radiation-induced cancer by 1975, an additional 20 were dead by 1980 of the same disease, and another 95 had contracted serious respiratory ailments and cancers (Samet et al. 1984). Studies have also identified miscarriages, cleft palates, and other birth defects as health effects related to uranium mining and exposure to contaminated environs. For example, a review of medical records for 13,329 Navajo born in the Shiprock, New Mexico, area (1964–81) determined statistically significant associations between uranium exposure and unfavorable birth outcomes when (a) the mother lived near tailings or mine dumps, (b) the father had a lengthy work tenure, and (c) either parent worked in the Shiprock electronics assembly plant (Shields et al. 1992). In addition to the association between uranium exposure and birth defects, this study raises important questions concerning the role of cumulative exposure to radiogenic substances and the possibility of synergistic effects.

Because underground uranium miners were considered to have greater risks associated with their employment than other workers, including surface miners, millers, and ore transporters, those employed in the aboveground occupations did not receive similar attention. Consequently, there were no long-term studies of the surface miners and ore transporters. Only a few epidemiologic studies have been conducted on uranium millers (see Archer et al. 1973; Pinkerton et al. 2004; Thun et al. 1985; Wagoner et al. 1964; Waxweiler et al. 1983). Taken together, these health studies identified several health problems associated with the milling process. These included statistically significant elevations of certain nonmalignant respiratory diseases, lymphatic and hematopoietic cancers other than leukemia, and nonsignificant elevations (meaning increased incidence at slightly less than the threshold for statistical significance) of lung cancer and chronic renal disease. These diseases were identified with exposures to uranium, silica, and vanadium dusts and chemicals used in the processing of the ore (see Archer et al. 1956; Pinkerton et al. 2004).

None of the epidemiologic studies of uranium millers have focused on American Indian populations. This has been a significant omission, since several tribes have uranium mills on or near their lands, and many American Indians were employed in milling operations. More than forty uranium mills operated in the western United States from the late 1940s through the 1980s, generally employing 100 to 150 workers at any one time. On the Navajo Nation, there were four privately owned mill companies, which operated during the 1950s and 1960s and employed primarily Navajo workers. While precise figures are unknown, the total number of Navajo and other American Indian uranium millworkers, both on and off the reservations, probably numbered in the thousands.

In addition to hazards and exposures within the milling process, each mill produced a significant amount of tailings—the by-product of refining the ore. Such tailings have provided an additional source of radioactive exposure to workers, community members, and the larger environment through contamination of the air, groundwater, streams, and soil.

Many southwestern uranium deposits were played out by 1970. Other mining operations were abandoned because the market for uranium oxide was at an all-time low and extraction costs exceeded the market return. When Kerr-McGee closed its Shiprock mill operation and pulled out of the community, it left behind some 70 acres of raw uranium tailings containing approximately 80 percent of the original radioactivity found in uranium ore. These tailings were piled in huge mounds less than 60 feet from the San Juan River—the only significant surface water for some fifteen thousand people in the Shiprock area. The tailings pile was also within 1 mile of a day-care center, public schools, the Shiprock business district, and cultivated farmlands (Brugge and Goble 2002; Tso and Shields 1980:13).

Furthermore, in July 1979, the United Nuclear Corporation's mill tailings dam near Church Rock, New Mexico, broke under pressure and released more than 93 million gallons of radioactive water and 1,000 tons of contaminated sediment into the Río Puerco (EPA 2005; World Information Service on Energy 2004). Outside of the nuclear weapons testing program, the Church Rock disaster is the largest release of radioactive materials in the continental United States (Saleem 2003).

According to a US congressional investigation, United Nuclear had known of cracks in the dam structure at least two months before the break but had made no effort to make repairs (US Congress, House Interior and Insular Affairs Committee 1979). About seventeen hundred Navajo were immediately affected, and their single water source was severely contaminated. Sheep and other livestock were found to be heavily contaminated with higher-than-normal levels of lead-210, polonium-210, thorium-230, and radium-236. Indian Health Service area director William Mohler advised Native Americans to continue to eat their livestock but to avoid consuming organ tissues, where radioactive toxins were expected to lodge most heavily. Three years later, Church Rock sheepherders were still having difficulty locating commercial markets for their mutton: the animals were deemed safe by the government for Native American consumption but unsafe for non-Indians in New York and London. United Nuclear refused to supply emergency food and water to the community and argued for more than a year before agreeing to pay a minimal out-of-court settlement (US Congress, House Interior and Insular Affairs Committee 1979). The mill was closed in 1982, and due to seepage from the tailings and off-site migration of radiological and chemical contaminants in groundwater, the site was placed on the Superfund National Priorities List in 1983. Groundwater remediation efforts began in 1989, and while mine tailings have been stabilized, cleanup has not proceeded to the point where the site can be removed from the list (EPA 2005). In 2003 the Navajo Nation Environmental Protection Agency conducted assessments of soil, water, and air contamination at the Church Rock site and in the homes and surrounding region. It found radiological contaminants in water, soil, and some homes built with rocks from the tailings piles (Craig 2003).

Some of the consequences of federal failures to protect the health of uranium workers, their families, and residents were explored in anthropological fieldwork conducted by Susan Dawson on the Navajo Reservation in 1989 (Dawson 1992). Some fifty-five Navajo households and thirty-three key informants were interviewed over a four-month period to determine the psychological and financial needs of Navajo families with uncompensated occupational illnesses. Dawson identified whether or not the families had applied for workers' compensation or filed lawsuits; documented whether or not the families had applied to entitlement programs; determined the extent to which the families' needs were being met through compensation; and tried to understand the day-to-day lifestyle of Navajo families that had experienced occupational illness.

The respondents in this study provided consistent descriptions of working conditions from the 1940s through the 1970s. Several problems were identified, including the lack of engineering controls (for example, mine ventilation), personal protective equipment, and worker-safety education and training. Several miners explained that they were forced to enter the mines directly after blasting, when the mines were filled with smoke and dust. White workers were not forced to do so, according to the respondents. All workers reported that at no time during their employment were they informed of the dangers of radiation, nor were they informed of their rights under state workers' compensation laws when they became ill. The respondents also indicated that workers were not even aware that radiation existed. The workers spoke little or no English and believed that the uranium companies had their best interests in mind. One Navajo supervisor, who spoke at a reservation chapter meeting, said he had been trained for his role as foreman with one of the mining companies. He was informed explicitly about the dangers of radiation but was told specifically not to inform the workers under his supervision that they were in danger.

Miners' families often traveled with the miners and lived in housing established for them directly on the sites. The majority of the respondents worked only as miners; however, a small number worked as millworkers, processing raw uranium ore. Both those who mined and those who milled reported that they used water from the area for drinking, bathing, washing, and household uses. Children played on the tailings and mine wastes from the work sites, even using the mines as their play areas. Livestock grazed in these areas, drinking the water and huddling in abandoned mines for warmth during winter months.

A common characteristic evident in all the interviews was the lack of basic social service benefits or knowledge of how to gain access to social and legal services. Only twelve of the respondents (out of fifty-five experiencing radiation-related health effects) had filed lawsuits, and only eleven had filed workers' compensation claims. Prior to their illnesses, forty-one families reported that at no time had they received government assistance or social services. After their health problems were diagnosed, twenty-seven families reported receiving some form of governmental or social assistance.

Most families interviewed lived in rural, remote areas and often lacked transportation or the financial means to buy gasoline; they relied on relatives to assist them. Many respondents found social service and legal systems too complicated with bureaucratic entanglements, so they did not access them at all or gave up early on in the process. One respondent could not keep up with ongoing appointments to qualify for disability because she did not have transportation; she consequently discontinued her visits. Of the twenty-two individuals eligible for Social Security benefits, only five reported receiving this entitlement. One widow, when asked why she did not file for benefits, explained that she felt intimidated by the process because she was told she had to write letters. She had no stationary or stamps and could not write in English, so she decided against it. Thirty-nine respondents had not entered claims for workers' compensation, saying they did not think they were eligible.

Factors inhibiting the ability of Navajo uranium miners and their families to claim or gain compensation primarily involved, for one reason or another, lack of information about the dangers of uranium mining, the dangers of living in uranium-contaminated settings, the nature of illnesses resulting from radiation exposure, the existence of or eligibility for workers' compensation and social services, and the nature of grievance procedures—time limitations and requirements for victims to prove work-related injury created restrictive barriers.

Gaining entry into the bureaucratic maze of grievance procedures required (among other things) knowledge of their existence, knowledge of eligibility rules, and knowl-

Figure 5.2. Reclaimed mill site at Rare Metals, Tuba City, Arizona, Diné Nation. Credit: Photo by Gary Madsen

edge of the English language, as well as literacy skills and access to transportation. It is significant to note that informants indicated concern over the possibility that there may have been traditional families (workers or family members) on the reservation who were never apprised in comprehensible terms that their illnesses may have been caused by working in a radiation-related industry. This lack of information would have kept them from entering the grievance and compensation process.

Millworkers Study

In 1990 Dawson presented the findings of the above study to a Senate committee meeting in Shiprock on the Navajo Nation. She gave testimony on the mental health impacts experienced by Navajo underground uranium miners and their families (US Congress, Senate Committee on Energy and Natural Resources 1990). This hearing was held to gather testimony concerning proposed federal radiation compensation legislation. After Dawson testified, several Navajo uranium millers approached her. They requested that they also be studied, since at the time of the hearing, millworker exposures and health issues were not reflected in the proposed compensation legislation. This request became the impetus for a millworkers study conducted by Dawson, Gary Madsen, and Bryan Spykerman during the fall of 1992 on the Navajo Nation and in the following year among non-Indians who worked in Utah and Colorado.

Data were gathered from eighty-three American Indians (almost all Navajo) and eighty-seven non-Indians through in-person interviews of millers or their survivors.

Table 5.1. Proximity to Uranium Mines and Materials

	Navajo	Non-Indian
Lived within one-half mile of uranium mine	34%	18%
Lived within one-half mile of uranium mill	76%	20%
Children played near a mine or mill	38%	12%
Brought uranium materials home	58%	47%

Adapted from table 4, Madsen et al. 1996

Questions concerned millworking conditions, including perceived radiation exposures; self-reported health histories; psychosocial impacts; and environmental exposures to respondents and their families (see Dawson and Madsen 1995; Dawson, Madsen, and Spykerman 1997; Madsen et al. 1996).

The studies indicated that a vast majority of workers were never warned about the radiation hazards associated with millwork, experienced significant exposures to ore and yellowcake dust during their employment (the Nuclear Regulatory Commission in 1986 noted that uranium dust presented the most significant hazard for the workers) (Nuclear Regulatory Commission 1986), accumulated ore dust on their clothing, and took their clothing off the work site, allowing for possible exposures to both their families and the larger community. Regarding the entire sample, the most frequently reported health problems were shortness of breath, persistent cough, lung cancer, emphysema, silicosis, pulmonary fibrosis, and pneumoconiosis. These symptoms and diagnosed diseases were consistent with the ore and yellowcake dust conditions experienced by the workers.

Differences between the Navajo respondents and the non-Indians were also found. The Navajo millers (82 percent) were more than twice as likely as the non-Indians (33 percent) to attribute their health problems to their millwork environment. Also, 60 percent of the Indians noted experiencing anxiety or depression that they related to their physical health problems, as compared to about 40 percent of the non-Indian respondents (see Dawson, Madsen, and Spykerman 1997; Madsen et al. 1996).

The studies also identified larger environmental issues. Here, too, there were differences between Navajo and Anglo respondents.

Overall, these larger environmental exposures suggest that the Navajo millers and their families experienced greater risks than did the non-Indians. More research needs to be initiated to study the impacts of uranium mining and milling on worker families and other community members who have lived in proximity to sites.

Navajo Activism

Due to the lengthy latency period between exposures and the development of health problems, it was not until people began to manifest illnesses and to die that the workers and their families began to question the health effects of their uranium employment. The Navajo, in particular, had unique obstacles related to the recognition of radiation-related problems, which were likely shared by other American Indian tribes. For example, the Navajo language lacked the terms to define and describe radiation and radiogenic effects. So unlike the Anglo population, the Navajo needed to develop a nuclear lexicon. It was especially difficult for workers early on to attribute their health problems to their uranium work. Many believed that their lung problems, for instance, were related to breaking a taboo in the natural world—for example, standing next to where lightning had struck. By not making the connection between their health problems and their work, the workers and their survivors could not apply for workers' compensation or other disability and survivors' benefits. In addition, for traditional Navajo people, it is taboo to talk about deceased people (Charley et al. 2004; Dawson 1992; Dawson, Charley, and Harrison 1997).

Beginning in the early 1970s, with the appearance of deaths and health problems, a network of Navajo activists emerged. They included former workers, family members of workers, and health professionals. The latter were associated with the US Indian Health Service. They were at the forefront of educating Navajo workers and their families about radiation-related work exposures, health problems, and redress (Charley et al. 2004; Dawson, Charley, and Harrison 1997).

We suggest that the way they approached these problems can provide others with a useful model for addressing the needs for environmental justice. The Navajo employed a variety of approaches including the following:

- Navajo health representatives identified uranium workers' illnesses initially through the Navajo Nation's Community Health Representatives program, a federally funded tribal health advocacy program.

- Four support groups—two for miners and two for millers—provided a support base and dissemination of information. A fifth group was recently created to assist uranium workers' families in seeking redress for their perceived radiation-related health problems.

- One of the support groups evolved into the Navajo Office of Uranium Workers, which became an important registry for workers and their families for research and compensation.

- The Uranium Education Program at the Navajo Nation's Diné College was established, with funding provided by the National Institute of Environmental Health Sciences. An important component of the work involved translating nuclear technological terms into the Navajo language and dialects (see Charley et al. 2004).

- Legislative lobbying for redress and compensation aided greatly in the passage of the Radiation Exposure Compensation Act of 1990 and the amendments of 2000 (Dawson, Charley, and Harrison 1997).

These programs were effective because many Navajo activists were involved in more than one of the above activities over a long period of time. The Navajo were highly successful in organizing and bringing about change for the Navajo workers and their families. They became a model for other workers off the reservation, providing them with tactics and techniques for organizing around nuclear issues.

Conclusion

Today, the Navajo Nation is experiencing a health crisis of epidemic proportions, which many believe to be the result of hosting uranium mining and milling operations and the failure of the federal government to protect its citizens. The US government failed to meet its legal and moral obligations to miners and millworkers in three ways. First, the government was negligent by not informing the workers of the inherent health risks of uranium miners; second, the government failed to provide compensation to the workers and their families for the deaths and illnesses resulting from uranium exposure; and third, the ecological damage created by uranium mining and milling processes was not addressed for an extended period of time, creating further health hazards. Had full disclosure been given to the Navajo workers, their families, and residents, the respondents could have made rational decisions regarding their health and employment.

To a limited degree, as illustrated in other chapters in this book, these grievances are addressed inasmuch as the provisions of the 1990 Radiation Exposure Compensation Act and its 2000 amendments allow. The act provides compassionate payment for Navajo underground uranium miners or their widows, as well as residents exposed to downwind radiation from nuclear weapons testing. However, as discussed elsewhere in this volume, efforts to compensate for pain and suffering of radiation-related disease provide, at best, an imperfect remedy for the select few recognized as meeting the standards of exposure.

The legacy of Cold War–era uranium production on the Navajo Nation involves much more than a struggle over the health problems of individual workers, their families, or area residents exposed to hazardous conditions in days gone by. The wastes from mining and milling include long-lived radiogenic hazards that contaminate, and will continue to contaminate, the soil, water, and air for years to come. Perhaps the most profound remedial actions have been those taken by members of the Navajo Nation and its government, whose struggle to document the effects of uranium mining and secure accountability and appropriate remedy has included community-based advocacy as well as the formation and evolving strength of the Navajo Environmental Protection Agency. Federal and state efforts to identify hazards, come up with remedial plans, and implement those plans are conducted in partnership with the Navajo Nation. And when these efforts fail to provide meaningful and effective remedy, the Navajo Nation has taken additional steps on its own. The most powerful example of remedy is the resolution passed by the Navajo Tribal Council on April 29, 2005. With this act (Diné Natural Resources Protection Act 2005), the Navajo Nation has created the legal means to prohibit the resumption of uranium mining on Navajo lands, citing the severe health impacts Navajo workers have already incurred and concern that existing technologies do not provide sufficient safeguards to ensure the health and well-being of the people and their environs.

This discussion of uranium mining, and its impact on Navajo lives and futures, resonates with the experiences of communities around the world that have played or play host to uranium mining. The distinct difference in this case is that the US government has acknowledged limited culpability for the human health problems resulting from uranium exposure and attempted some form of remediation. The situation is very different for most other uranium miners and resident peoples in places where uranium mining is often unregulated, the environmental hazards of production are ignored, and mining is conducted by multinational corporations whose labor and environmental practices would be illegal at "home."

Notes

Portions of this chapter first appeared in "Resource Use and Abuse on Native American Land: Uranium Mining in the American Southwest," by Barbara Rose Johnston and Susan Dawson, chapter 14 in *Who Pays the Price? The Sociocultural Context of Environmental Crisis*, edited by Barbara Rose Johnston (Washington, DC: Island Press, 1994). This chapter is a greatly expanded and revised version and was written with the financial support of the John T. and Catherine D. MacArthur Foundation through a research and writing grant, "Considering the Consequential Damages of Nuclear War Legacies," to the Center for Political Ecology (2004–05). Special thanks are given to Barbara Rylko-Bauer for providing last-minute research support.

1. It is unclear from Preston's book what sources were used to support her account of slave labor in the uranium mines and processing plant. However, the German firm Auerwerke is mentioned as exploiting slave labor from the Sachsenhausen concentration camp (Simpson 1995:308) and from Ravensbrück, a concentration camp for women located about 50 miles north of Berlin (Morrison 2000:208). In interviewing her mother, a survivor of three Nazi concentration camps, anthropologist Barbara Rylko-Bauer reports:

> "While my mother was interred at Ravensbrück, she underwent a selection conducted by an SS officer who had come from Oranienburg. She recalls him examining her teeth and gums, her hands, and then making a mark on her forehead with some sort of crayon. She was selected as part of a transport of women who were being sent to Oranienburg to work in some military-related plant. She later found out that this was considered almost like a death sentence, because many prisoners got sick and even died and there was a high risk of some kind of poisoning, she thinks maybe lead poisoning. My mother was saved from this fate by a former medical school classmate of hers, named Dr. Adamska, who was working as a prisoner-assistant to the Nazi physician in Ravensbrück. When Adamska saw her in the long line of naked women waiting to be examined prior to their transfer, she convinced the Nazi doctor to declare my mother unfit for labor. So she was sent back to her barracks and did not join this other group that was sent off to Oranienburg." (Barbara Rylko-Bauer, personal communication with author, August 25, 2006)

As for the mines in Czechoslovakia, after the war, German POWs were forced to work there, under the terms of the Czechoslovak-Soviet Agreement of 1945, until late 1949, when the Czech government was forced by the terms of the agreement to return them to Germany. Thereafter, labor for the mines was provided by political prisoners and others interned by representatives of the communist government. Prison labor was used in these and other uranium mines in the region until they closed in 1961 (Dvořák 2006). This use of forced labor was not unique. In Sillamäe, an Estonian town on the Gulf of Finland, the Soviet Union established a uranium processing facility and mined uranium shale deposits using forced labor. By the late 1940s, some "16,000 prisoners and convicts, and a 10,000 man forced-labor unit consisting mainly of Baltic conscripts who had served in the German army" worked there. Of this number, an estimated 79 percent were prisoners of war and criminal convicts, 19 percent were soldiers serving various kinds of punishment, and 2 percent were free labor (Maremäe et al. 2003:17).

References

ACHRE. *See* Advisory Committee on Human Radiation Experiments

Advisory Committee on Human Radiation Experiments
1996   Final Report of the Advisory Committee on Human Radiation Experiments. New York: Oxford University Press.

AEC. *See* Atomic Energy Commission

Allen, Mark
1989   North American Control of Tribal Resource Development in the Context of Federal Trust and Self-Determination. Boston College Environmental Affairs Law Review 16:857–95.

Archer, Victor E., S. E. Miller, Duncan A. Holaday, and Henry N. Doyle
1956   Health Protection of Uranium Miners and Millers. AMA Archives of Industrial Health 14:48–55.

Archer, Victor E., Joseph K. Wagoner, and Frank E. Lundin
1973   Cancer Mortality among Uranium Mill Workers. Journal of Occupational Medicine 15(1):11–14.

Atomic Energy Commission
1951   Prospecting for Uranium. Washington, DC: US Government Printing Office.

Axelson, Olaf
1995   Cancer Risks from Exposure to Radon in Houses. Environmental Health Perspectives 103, Supplement 2:37–43.

Brugge, Doug, and Rob Goble
2002   The History of Uranium Mining and the Navajo People. American Journal of Public Health 92:1410–19.

Caufield, Catherine
1989   Multiple Exposures: Chronicles of the Radiation Age. Toronto: Stoddart.

Charley, Perry H., Susan E. Dawson, Gary E. Madsen, and Bryan R. Spykerman
2004   Navajo Uranium Education Programs: The Search for Environmental Justice. Journal of Applied Environmental Education Communication 3(2):101–08.

Chenoweth, W. L.
1997   Raw Materials Activities of the Manhattan Project on the Colorado Plateau: Nonrenewable Resources 6(1):33–41.

Craig, Vivian
2003   Church Rock Uranium Monitoring Project. Electronic document, http://www. crcpd.org/radon/Nashville/100703-1400_craig.ppt, accessed October 25, 2006.

Cunningham, William P., and Barbara Woodworth Saigo
1990   Environmental Science: A Global Concern. Dubuque, IA: Wm. C. Brown.

Dawson, Susan E.
1992   Navajo Uranium Mining Workers and the Effects of Occupational Illnesses: A Case Study. Human Organization 51(4):389–97.

Dawson, Susan E., Perry E. Charley, and Philip Harrison
1997   Advocacy and Social Action among Navajo Uranium Workers and Their Families. *In* Social Work in Health Settings: Practice in Context. Toba Schwaber Kerson, ed. Pp. 391–407. New York: Haworth.

Dawson, Susan E., and Gary E. Madsen
1995   American Indian Uranium Millworkers: The Perceived Effects of Chronic Occupational Exposure. Journal of Health and Social Policy 7(2):19–31.

Dawson, Susan E., Gary E. Madsen, and Bryan R. Spykerman
1997   Public Health Issues Concerning American Indian and Non-Indian Uranium Millworkers. Journal of Health and Social Policy 8(3):41–56.

Department of Energy
2005   Shiprock Mill Site. Electronic document, http://www.eia.doe.gov/cneaf/nuclear/ page/umtra/shiprock_title1.html, accessed February 25, 2006.

Diné Natural Resources Protection Act of 2005
2005   An Act Relating to Resources, and Diné Fundamental Law; Enacting the Diné Natural Resource Protection Act of 2005; Amending Title 18 of the Navajo Nation Code. Resolution of the Navajo Nation Council, 20th Navajo Nation Council— Third Year, 2005. Electronic document, http://www.sric.org/uranium/DNRPA.pdf, accessed October 25, 2006.

DOE. *See* **Department of Energy**

Doyle, Henry H.
1950   Survey of Uranium Mines on Navajo Reservation. Unpublished report.

Dvořák, Tomás

2006   Uranium Mining versus the "Purging" of the Borderlands: German Labour in the
        Jáchymov Mines in the Late 1940s and Early 1950s. Soudobé de`jiny
        12(3–4):627–71.

Edwards, Gordon

1997   How Uranium from Great Bear Lake Ended up in A-Bombs. Electronic document,
        http://www.ccnr.org/uranium_events, accessed October 25, 2006.

Environmental Protection Agency

2005   United Nuclear Corporation, McKinley County, New Mexico. Electronic document,
        http://www.epa.gov/earth1r6/6sf/pdffiles/0600819.pdf, accessed October 25, 2006.

EPA. *See* Environmental Protection Agency

Fischer, David

1990   South Africa: As a Nuclear Supplier. *In* International Nuclear Trade and
        Nonproliferation: The Challenges of the Emerging Suppliers. W. C. Potter, ed.
        P. 273. Toronto: Lexington Books.

Hahne, F. J.

1989   Early Uranium Mining in the United States. Electronic document,
        http://www.world-nuclear.org/usumin.htm, accessed October 25, 2006.

Hodge, H. C., J. N. Stannard, and J. B. Hursh

1973   Handbook of Experimental Pharmacology. Berlin: Springer-Verlag.

Holaday, Duncan

1950   Letter, Duncan Holaday to Chief, Industrial Hygiene, 20 November 1950 (Radon
        and External Radiation Studies in Uranium Mines). ACHRE document IND-
        091394-B.

Horton, Roy E.

1999   Out of (South) Africa: Pretoria's Nuclear Weapons Experience. Electronic document,
        http://www.usafa.af.mil/df/inss/OCP/ocp27.pdf, accessed October 25, 2006.

Hueper, William C.

1942   Occupational Tumors and Allied Diseases. Springfield, IL: C. C. Thomas.

Johnston, Barbara Rose, and Susan Dawson

1994   Resource Use and Abuse on Native American Land: Uranium Mining in the
        American Southwest. *In* Who Pays the Price? The Sociocultural Context of
        Environmental Crisis. Barbara Rose Johnston, ed. Pp. 142–53. Washington, DC:
        Island Press.

Madsen, Gary E., Susan E. Dawson, and Bryan R. Spykerman

1996   Perceived Occupational and Environmental Exposures: A Case Study of Former
        Uranium Millworkers. Environment and Behavior 28(5):571–90.

Maremäe, Ello, Hain Tankler, Henno Putnik, and Ilge Maalmann, eds.
2003   Historical Survey of Nuclear Non-proliferation in Estonia, 1946–1995. Report prepared for the International Atomic Energy Agency. Tallinn, Estonia: Estonia Radiation Protection Centre and the Swedish Nuclear Power Inspectorate.

McElroy, N., and A. Brodsky
1986   Training Manual for Uranium Mill Workers on Health Protection from Uranium. Washington, DC: Nuclear Regulatory Commission.

Miller, Richard L.
1986   Under the Cloud: The Decades of Nuclear Testing. New York: Free Press.

Morrison, Jack G.
2000   Ravensbrück: Everyday Life in a Women's Concentration Camp, 1939–1945. Princeton, NJ: Markus Wiener Publishers.

Pinkerton, Lynne E., Thomas F. Bloom, M. J. Hein, and Elizabeth M. Ward
2004   Mortality among a Cohort of Uranium Mill Workers: An Update. Occupational and Environmental Medicine 61:57–64.

Preston, Diana
2006   Before the Fallout: From Marie Curie to Hiroshima. New York: Berkeley Books.

Ringholz, Raye C.
1989   Uranium Frenzy: Boom and Bust on the Colorado Plateau. Electronic document, http://www.onlineutah.com/uraniumhistory.shtml, accessed February 10, 2005.

Saleem, H. Ali
2003   Mining, the Environment, and Indigenous Development Conflicts. Tucson: University of Arizona Press.

Samet, J. M., D. M. Kutvirt, R. J. Waxweiler, and C. R. Key
1984   Uranium Mining and Lung Cancer among Navajo Men. New England Journal of Medicine 310:1481–84.

Shields, L. M., W. H. Wiese, B. J. Skipper, B. Charley, and L. Banally
1992   Navajo Birth Outcomes in the Shiprock Uranium Mining Area. Health Physics 63(5):542–51.

Simpson, Christopher
1995   The Splendid Blond Beast: Money, Law, and Genocide in the Twentieth Century. Monroe, ME: Common Courage Press.

Thun, Michael J., Dean B. Baker, Kyle Steenland, Alexander B. Smith, William Halperin, and Thomas Berl
1985   Renal Toxicity in Uranium Mill Workers. Scandinavian Journal of Work and Environmental Health 11:83–90.

Tso, Harold, and Lora Magnum Shields
1980   Navajo Mining Operations: Early Hazards and Recent Interventions. New Mexico Journal of Science 12(1):13.

US Congress. House of Representatives. Committee on Interior and Insular Affairs. Subcommittee on Energy and the Environment

1979   Mill Tailings Dam Break at Church Rock, New Mexico (Church Rock hearings). 96th Cong., October 22.

US Congress. Senate. Committee on Energy and Natural Resources. Mineral Resources Development and Production Subcommittee

1990   Testimony of Earl Mettler on impacts of past uranium mining practices, 101st Cong. 2d Sess.

Utah Division of Indian Affairs

2006   Diné (Navajo Nation). Electronic document, http://indian.utah.gov/ utah_tribes_today/dine.html, accessed October 26, 2006.

Wagoner, Joseph K., Victor E. Archer, Benjamin E. Carroll, Duncan A. Holaday, and Pope A. Lawrence

1964   Mortality Patterns among US Uranium Miners and Millers, 1950 through 1962. Journal of the National Cancer Institute 32(4):787–801.

Waxweiler, Richard J., Victor E. Archer, Robert J. Roscoe, Arthur Watanabe, Michael J. Thun

1983   Mortality Patterns among a Retrospective Cohort of Uranium Mill Workers. Proceedings of the Sixteenth Midyear Topical Meeting of the Health Physics Society. Albuquerque, NM: Health Physics Society.

World Information Service on Energy

2004   Chronology of Uranium Tailings Dam Failures. Electronic document, http://www.wise-uranium.org/mdafu.html, accessed October 25, 2006.

s i x
Uranium Mine Workers, Atomic Downwinders, and the Radiation Exposure Compensation Act (RECA)
The Nuclear Legacy

Susan E. Dawson and Gary E. Madsen

Since September 11, 2001, government officials have attempted to tighten national security in the United States. In addition to creating a new administrative agency, Homeland Security, and passing the Patriot Act, the federal government has renewed its emphasis on nuclear weapons development. At the same time, recent threats of terrorism and breaches in information security at the nuclear research facility in Los Alamos, New Mexico, have heightened concern about maintaining the security of the entire nuclear research and development program (Associated Press 2004; Emery 2004; Holmes 2004). Security violations also led the Nuclear Regulatory Commission (NRC) to announce in 2004 that security problems at nuclear plants would no longer be made public, so that such information would not be available to terrorists (Rulon 2004). The failure of the United States to persuade North Korea and Iran to abandon their emerging nuclear weapons programs presents another threat (Dickey et al. 2006; Bernstein 2005; Sanger 2004). Indeed, North Korea announced in February 2005 that it actually possesses nuclear weapons (T. Johnson 2005), not just the capacity to make them, and substantiated this claim with a nuclear test in October 2006.

Citing national security concerns, the Bush administration in 2003 requested and received from Congress $42.8 million for research and development for a new generation of nuclear weapons. Funding requests in 2004 included $36.5 million to develop more low-yield nuclear weapons, such as the Robust Nuclear Earth Penetrator (RNEP) bomb, or bunker-buster bomb; $29.8 million for a new nuclear bomb factory; and $30 million to upgrade the Nevada Test Site (HEAL Utah 2004). Because of strong opposition among downwinders (people exposed to atomic fallout from previous nuclear testing) and congressional leaders such as Representative Jim Matheson (D-UT), Congress did not fund these requests (Gehrke 2004; Lofholm 2005). The 2006 federal budget initially included research funding for the bunker-buster bomb; however, this bomb was eliminated in favor of conventional weapons (Burr 2005).

The uranium mining industry in the United States is experiencing a resurgence, thanks to efforts to revive the development of nuclear power plants and nuclear weapons and to meet global production demands worldwide. The industry has largely been on hold since the 1990s, when the price of uranium plummeted. Uranium was selling for approximately $43 a pound in May 2006 (Fahys 2005; Kosich 2006; Oberbeck 2006a, 2006b), up from about $7 a pound in 2001. By December 2006, the price had risen to $60 a pound. The Cotter Company of Colorado reopened one of its uranium mines in 2004 and plans to open additional mines in the future. If the price of uranium continues to escalate, more mines may resume operations (Lofholm 2005). Unfortunately, this combination of the possible resumption of nuclear testing, renewed uranium mining, and increased security may create a climate similar to that of the Cold War period (the 1940s through the 1980s), in which the United States and the Soviet Union produced and tested nuclear weapons in an atmosphere of utmost secrecy.

The US uranium mining and atomic testing that began in the post–World War II era, the subsequent scientific studies of radiation-induced health effects, and the struggle to win compensation for the victims offer some lessons that contemporary policy makers would do well to heed. During this period of nuclear weapons production and testing, a lack of safety precautions and risk notification by the government and industry resulted in large-scale health problems and deaths of citizens and workers, culminating in a large-scale technological, human-made, disaster that we can ill afford to repeat. The implications of this disaster may best be understood by examining the historical context of US uranium mining and nuclear testing.

Uranium Mining in the United States

Extensive uranium mining began in the western United States in the late 1940s. Thousands of mines had operated by the early 1980s, chiefly on the Colorado Plateau. Ninety-two percent of western mines were clustered there, including 325 in Arizona, 1,276 in Colorado, 215 in New Mexico, 1,197 in Utah, and 280 in Wyoming, for a total of 3,293. In the 1950s and 1960s, Colorado and Utah produced most of the nation's uranium ore, but in the 1970s and 1980s production shifted to New Mexico and Wyoming (Yih et al. 1995).

Between 1950 and 1989, US mines—both surface and underground—produced more than 225 million tons of uranium ore (DOE 1991). This activity heavily affected a number of American Indian nations. For example, the Navajo Nation, which encompasses portions of Arizona, New Mexico, and Utah, had more than a thousand mines (Dawson et al. 1997), whereas Laguna Pueblo, 40 miles west of Albuquerque, New Mexico, hosted the Jackpile Mine, the largest open-pit uranium mine in the United States.

The Atomic Energy Commission (AEC), established in 1946, was the only purchaser of uranium for nuclear weapons from 1948 until 1970 (DOE 1991). To put it another way, private US uranium mining companies had only one buyer: the federal government. This situation changed in 1964, when Congress enacted the Private Ownership of Special Nuclear Materials Act to provide for the production of nuclear power plants and arrangements between the AEC and private energy companies (DOE 1991).

We do not know how many workers in all have worked in uranium mining. Archer and colleagues estimate that in 1945 there were approximately 350 uranium miners in the United States, increasing to 550 in 1950. By 1955 more than twenty-one hundred miners held jobs in uranium mines, and by 1960 that figure had climbed to fifty-seven hundred (Archer et al. 1962). After 1960, thousands still worked in the mines, until their numbers fell significantly when the industry essentially ceased operations at the end of the 1980s (DOE 1991).

To understand the US uranium mining experience, it is important to present a history of uranium mining and health issues in Europe.

The Impact of Uranium Mining on Miners' Health

Uranium mining was not new when it began in the United States in the 1940s; Europeans had mined uranium in the late nineteenth century, and the adverse consequences for miners' health rapidly became evident. During the latter part of the 1800s, an active uranium mining industry existed in the Erzgebirge Mountains, a region between eastern Germany and the present Czech Republic. The Schneeberg mines in Germany (Saxony) began in the fifteen century. The Joachimsthal mines in Jáchymov in what is now the Czech Republic (Czechoslovakia and Bohemia) opened in the sixteenth century. At that time, these mines produced arsenic, bismuth, cobalt, copper, iron, nickel, and silver. By the late nineteenth century, they had turned to pitchblende for uranium dyes, especially in the Jáchymov region. By the twentieth century, the prize was radium. (For a history of the European experience, see ACHRE 1996; Holaday and Doyle 1952; Hueper 1942; Lorenz 1944; Ringholz 2002.)

A substantial number of the Erzgebirge region miners died of a lung disease known as *Bergkrankheit*, or "mountain disease." Härting and Hesse (1879) first diagnosed it as lung cancer. They found that 75 percent of all deaths among mine employees had resulted from lung cancer but that the incidence was lower for mine carpenters and masons than for miners. The study showed that miners developed lung cancer over a lengthy latency period of approximately twenty years. Research during the 1920s and 1930s generally supported the link between uranium mine work and lung cancer (see Hueper 1942; Lorenz 1944). To reduce risks associated with radiation exposures, mining companies built mechanical ventilation systems beginning in the 1930s (Bhounek 1970).

In the early 1940s, two prominent US medical researchers, Wilhelm Hueper and Egon Lorenz, summarized the Erzgebirge uranium miner studies. Hueper, an Austrian émigré, became the first director of the environmental cancer section of the National Cancer Institute (NCI). After reviewing the literature, he concluded that radiation caused the European miners' lung cancer, ruling out genetic, work, and nonwork factors (ACHRE 1996; Hueper 1942). Medical researchers in the United States did not unanimously accept Hueper's conclusions. Lorenz, a senior biophysicist at the NCI, published his own review of the literature on European miners, noting, "Whereas in former years pneumoconiosis in combination with arsenic and cobalt was assumed to be the cause of this cancer, today the radioactivity of the ore and the radon content of the air in the mines are generally considered to be the primary cause" (Lorenz 1944:5).

Lorenz emphasized other factors that might have caused the miners' lung cancer, including a possible hereditary predisposition. In addition, he observed that the measured doses of radon gas from the European mines did not seem to be high enough to cause health problems.

It was not until 1951 that two researchers, William Bale and John Harley, explained this discrepancy. They identified the importance of the decay products of radon (radon daughters, or progeny), which can attach themselves to mine dust. Miners inhaled and concentrated these products in lung tissue, with the result that delivered doses were up to one hundred times higher than the amount of radon gas alone indicated (Archer et al. 2004). Mechanical ventilation in the mines could significantly reduce the radon daughter risks to the miners by dispersing them (Holaday 1969).

By the late 1940s, there was growing evidence, based upon a pilot study by AEC medical researchers Merril Eisenbud and Bernie Wolf, that the "European experience" was likely to play out among US uranium miners (Eisenbud and Wolf 1948; Ringholz 2002). In response to these concerns, the US Public Health Service (USPHS) began what eventually became a massive study of US underground uranium miners during the summer seasons of 1950 and 1951. Duncan Holaday, a senior sanitary engineer with the USPHS, served as the principal investigator. The study had two interrelated goals: (1) to identify uranium mine environmental exposures, and (2) to conduct a medical evaluation of the miners (Holaday, David, and Doyle 1952; Holaday and Doyle 1952).

According to Holaday, the role of the USPHS was to gather and disseminate data concerning the uranium experience. The agency had no authority to shut down mines if they were not complying with health and safety regulations. Nor could USPHS investigators enter privately owned mines without permission of the owners. To get data, the USPHS agreed not to warn miners of radiation hazards or inform them directly of the health study findings. Even as late as 1960, a USPHS medical consent form failed to apprise miners about the risk of lung cancer and other health problems related to working with radiation in mines. Holaday later stated that the USPHS procedure was routine and had been followed in previous industrial studies (ACHRE 1996). The muzzling of the researchers and the latency of the lung damage caused by uranium mining made it impossible early on for miners to recognize a connection between work exposures and health problems. According to the Advisory Committee on Human Radiation Experiments, "Had they been better informed, they could have sought help in publicizing the fact that working conditions in the mines were extremely hazardous, which might have resulted in some mines being ventilated earlier than they were" (ACHRE 1996:365).

USPHS researchers presented the initial findings of the study in two different reports, the *Progress Report* of January 1952 and the *Interim Report* of May 1952, both focusing on uranium mine and mill exposure levels on the Colorado Plateau (Holaday and Doyle 1952; Holaday et al. 1952). Summarizing the exposure data from forty-eight mines, Holaday and Doyle reported exceptionally high concentrations of radon. Moreover, they compared these radiation levels with those in the European studies and found that the median level of radiation exposures in US mines was higher than exposure levels found to be related to lung cancer among the European miners (Holaday and Doyle 1952).

Greatly concerned by the excessive radon daughter levels in the mines, the researchers organized two conferences in August 1951 at the USPHS Salt Lake City Field Station. Representatives from the AEC, the US Geological Survey, and the US Bureau of Mines; technical experts from eight mining companies; and representatives of five state health departments attended. During these meetings, USPHS researchers presented information regarding mine study findings, radon measuring techniques, and ways to reduce mine radon levels using mechanical ventilation (Holaday and Doyle 1952).

The medical side of the study consisted of giving miners physical examinations, including chest X-rays and urine and blood analyses. The researchers found "no clear-cut etiologic or pathologic patterns" and noted that a majority of the workers had been employed for just a short time. Since an extensive latency period characterized the diseases that European miners had suffered, the absence of strong evidence of mine-induced disease in the Americans was not surprising (Holaday et al. 1952:6).

Almost thirty years after the *Interim Report* appeared, Holaday testified in a deposition given to Stewart Udall, attorney and secretary of the interior under the Kennedy and Johnson administrations. Holaday spoke about a document he had written in 1964, in which he stated:

> It is now 14 years since the uranium study was started. At times, this project
> has been quite active; for other periods it has been quiescent. The study was
> undertaken with the belief that all that was required was the evaluation of
> environmental conditions in the industry and comparison of the results of the

studies with the data on human experience which was available in the literature. Measures to control the exposures of the workers to toxic materials could
then be recommended. This belief was a delusion. (Holaday 1981:26)

Udall was then a private attorney. He brought two lawsuits on behalf of uranium
miners.

After the reports were issued in the early 1950s, there was some progress made in
reducing radiation risks in uranium mines. Some mine owners improved ventilation,
and the states of Colorado, New Mexico, and Utah established minimum standards for
radon concentrations; however, enforcement was generally inadequate, and AEC commissioners did not move to establish national standards regarding radon exposure limits. When Udall asked Holaday in 1981 whether AEC officials took recommendations
made in the early 1950s seriously, Holaday said, "There was no reaction from them"
(Holaday 1981:28). The AEC position, later stated by Jesse Johnson, director of the
AEC's Raw Materials Division, was that the AEC had no authority to regulate uranium
mines (J. Johnson 1959), despite the fact that the AEC did regulate beryllium (ACHRE
1996; Ringholz 2002). Not until 1971 did the Environmental Protection Agency
(EPA) adopt a more stringent federal standard on mine exposures (Cross et al. 1974).
This action was prompted by a growing awareness by the miners and the public of the
health problems associated with the uranium mining industry (Eichstaedt 1994).

Despite the lack of an official response from the AEC to its recommendations, the
USPHS continued to study the Colorado Plateau uranium miners, adding new miners
to the study in 1951, 1953, 1954, 1957, and 1960 (Archer et al. 1962). Researchers
gathered baseline health data for each miner so that investigators could develop a mortality assessment. In this way, the causes of miners' deaths as reported on death certificates could be compared with a control group of males of similar age and ethnicity in
the states where the miners worked. The study eventually included approximately four
thousand American Indian and non-Indian underground uranium miners. The major
problem with this type of study was that the miner had to die for comparisons to be
made.

In the 1970s, the study was transferred to the National Institute for Occupational
Safety and Health (NIOSH). The first publication showing a statistically significant
excess of lung cancer deaths among uranium miners appeared in the *Journal of
Occupational Medicine* in 1962 (Archer et al. 1962). Further investigations produced
several other published reports including Archer 1981; Archer, Gillam, and Wagoner
1976; Archer, Wagoner, and Lundin 1973; Holaday, Archer, and Lundin 1968;
Hornung and Meinhardt 1987; Lundin et al. 1969; Lundin et al. 1971; Roscoe 1997;
Roscoe et al. 1995; and Wagoner et al. 1964. Reports that included the USPHS findings, along with pertinent data from other studies, also appeared in print (see Archer
et al. 2004; Gofman 1981; Lubin et al. 1994; National Academy of Sciences 1988).

Cumulatively, the uranium miner studies produced several important findings.
They demonstrated a linear relationship between cumulative exposure levels and lung
cancer, with the cancer risk per unit of exposure in the lower cumulative radiation

categories greater than in the higher ones. In other words, cancer-causing radon progeny are more efficient at causing cancer at lower levels than higher ones (see Archer 1981; Gofman 1981; Hornung and Meinhardt 1987; Lubin et al. 1994; Lundin et al. 1971). The studies also documented an extensive latency period of about twenty years between exposure and health outcomes. In addition, whether or not a person smoked did not explain the positive relationship between exposure and lung cancer; however, smokers who were also miners had a shorter latency period than did exposed nonsmokers (see Archer et al. 2004; Lundin et al. 1969; Roscoe et al. 1989).

But the higher incidence of lung cancer among uranium miners was only part of the story. Beginning with the 1952 USPHS *Interim Report*, evidence showed that uranium miners were also developing nonmalignant respiratory disease (Holaday et al. 1952). The longitudinal progression of the study data confirmed this finding. For example, Roscoe's 1997 update found statistically significant excesses of lung cancer, pneumoconiosis, tuberculosis, chronic obstructive respiratory disease, emphysema, benign and unspecified tumors, and diseases of the blood and blood-forming organs among miners (Roscoe 1997).

While we focused on the USPHS-NIOSH study, other significant contributions to the literature concerning uranium mining and health effects included studies conducted largely in New Mexico and on the Navajo Nation (Gottlieb and Husen 1982; Mapel et al. 1997; Samet, Kutvirt et al. 1984; Samet, Young et al. 1984; Samet et al. 1991; Samet et al. 1994). In general, these studies both supplemented and complemented the aforementioned research.

Miners were not the only people affected by the US nuclear weapons and power industries. In the next section we will review the history and pertinent studies of the atomic downwinders, focusing on radioactive fallout produced by the Nevada Test Site.

US Atomic Downwinders

Shortly after World War II ended with the detonation of atomic bombs at Hiroshima and Nagasaki, the US military needed to know much more about the environmental and human impacts of the new technology. The military undertook a nuclear testing program in the Marshall Islands, Micronesia, that lasted from July 1946 to August 1958. In the end, the United States conducted sixty-seven nuclear tests at Bikini and Enewetak (Republic of the Marshall Islands 2005). Even though government officials considered the Pacific testing successful, having the test site outside the continental United States posed a range of problems, including difficulties in transporting service personnel and materials and maintaining a high level of security. Therefore, the US military began a search in 1947 for a test site within the continental United States, resulting eventually in the selection of the Nevada Proving Ground, later known as the Nevada Test Site (Titus 1986).

From 1951 through 1992, the United States conducted one hundred atmospheric and more than eight hundred underground nuclear tests at the Nevada Test Site (Boutté 2002; Makhijani et al. 1995). Despite plentiful evidence from previous scientific research indicating the dangers of such tests for people within reach of the fallout, the AEC did not make health and safety a top priority during the nuclear testing program. Agency officials ignored studies demonstrating the adverse health effects of radium, including research on Madame Curie's work and the radium dial painters (see Clark 1997; Reid 1974). As Fradkin wrote:

> As the tests got underway at the Nevada Site in 1951, it was known within
> the scientific community that radiation caused superficial injuries, leukemia,
> malignant tumors, genetic defects, and such miscellaneous ailments as
> cataracts, obesity, impaired fertility, and shortened lifespans. Also, an associa-
> tion had been found between the fallout from the Hiroshima and Nagasaki
> bombs and leukemia. (1989:183)

The exposure of a broad public to radiation raises different questions than exposure of workers in nuclear-power-related industries, and protection from radiation becomes far more difficult. For example, whereas children are not allowed to work in the uranium industry, they still can be exposed to fallout or other forms of environmental radiation. In addition, exposure of the general public can involve significantly larger numbers of people than exposure of worker populations (*Irene Allen et al. v. United States*, Civil No. C 79-0515-J, 1984).

Unfortunately, just as the government agencies involved failed to notify the uranium miners of the risks they faced, they also failed to warn the public about nuclear testing, even those directly in harm's way. The AEC used several tactics to promote nuclear testing, invoking the need for protection against the communist threat and the potential for peaceful uses of atomic energy. Despite the existence of evidence to the contrary, the agency told people that fallout was safe and any exposures would not result in long-term health problems (Titus 1986). The AEC's public information program received close scrutiny during the *Irene Allen et al. v. United States* case, in which atomic downwinders sued the United States for redress. Judge Bruce S. Jenkins summarized the evidence as follows:

> This court is convinced that that part of the program of public safety, the pub-
> lic information program was badly flawed, and that during the operation of
> that program, the information given to the off-site public as to the long-term
> biological consequences of exposure to ionizing radiation was woefully defi-
> cient—indeed, essentially non-existent…[and] failed to adequately, contempo-
> raneously, and thoroughly measure and monitor such fallout so as to be able to
> inform persons at risk of the extent of the hazard faced by each. (315–16)

In addition to ignoring the research that existed, the AEC did not have sufficient knowledge to evaluate the dangers posed by nuclear testing. At the beginning of the testing program, the agency believed that radioactive fallout would spread throughout the global atmosphere. In reality, air currents and other atmospheric conditions, such as rainstorms, created radioactive hot spots, so that specific places suffered higher concentrations of radiation. Furthermore, the AEC emphasized that people would be exposed to radiation externally for the most part—on the skin—rather than by ingesting it through such sources as milk and food (Metzger 1972). Citing Representative Chet Holifield as quoted in the *New York Times*, Metzger wrote: "Representative Holifield branded the AEC 'grossly tardy and negligent' in telling the nation the truth about fallout from atomic tests. He accused the AEC of intentionally playing down the effects and dangers of radiation" (86).

Several epidemiologic studies occurred between the early 1960s and the 1990s, including studies by Weiss in 1961, Knapp in 1963, and the Centers for Disease Control in 1965 (see Ball 1986; Beck and Krey 1983; C. Johnson 1984; Kerber et al. 1993; Lyon 1979; Rallison et al. 1974; Stevens et al. 1990). The geographic focus of these studies was the states of Arizona, Nevada, and Utah, which were immediately downwind of the Nevada Test Site. The publications *Justice Downwind* (Ball 1986), *Under the Cloud* (Miller 1986), *Fallout* (Fradkin 1989), and "The United States" in *Nuclear Wastelands* (Makhijani et al. 1995) describe the studies and their findings within this historical period. Researchers cumulatively found a relationship between fallout exposures and increasing leukemia, thyroid cancer, and certain other cancers. In this chapter, we did not discuss nuclear testing with onsite participants because they were not a focus of our research.

Unfortunately, the AEC held up public access to the early studies by Weiss and Knapp. The 1961 Weiss study report suggested that, for those living in southwestern Utah, fallout contributed to an increase in leukemia deaths. AEC personnel received the report for review in 1961 but did not release it publicly until 1978, for fear, in part, that its release might threaten the nuclear testing program (see Ball 1986). Moreover, Knapp's 1963 study of fallout contaminants in fresh milk was also sequestered until 1978, when journalists succeeded in forcing the AEC to release it in response to Freedom of Information Act requests (see Ball 1986). These early studies provided evidence that US continental testing program fallout contributed to significant health problems, yet the AEC continued to assure the public that fallout was essentially harmless.

Controversy concerning the extent of fallout and its health effects continues to this day. Scientists and concerned citizens became increasingly worried in the 1980s that the atmospheric tests in Nevada had produced excessive levels of fallout that had not been studied adequately. Miller (1986) demonstrated that fallout trajectories blanketed major portions of the United States. (See map 6.1.)

In the late 1980s, Congress mandated, under Public Law 97-414, a national study to indicate exposures of the US public to iodine-131 fallout from Nevada nuclear atmospheric bomb tests conducted during the 1950s and 1960s. The NCI conducted this study and in 1997 released a report showing that the major pathways of exposure to iodine-131 were drinking cow's milk (considered the single most important route);

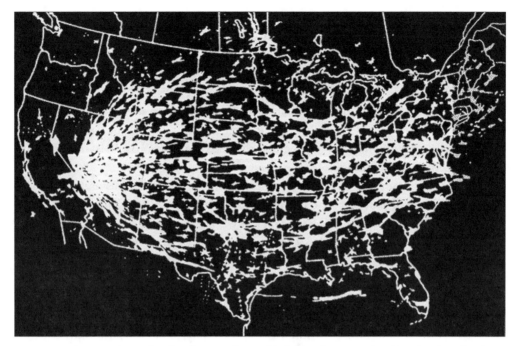

Map 6.1. This map by Richard Miller was first published in his 1986 book Under the Cloud. Miller used publicly accessible records to trace the significant movement across the United States of fallout from nuclear weapons detonated at the Nevada Proving Ground. Miller's map does not include fallout from subsurface tests or from nuclear detonations outside the continental United States.

breathing contaminated air; and eating contaminated foods such as cottage cheese, eggs, goat's milk, and leafy vegetables. The NCI also identified counties in the states of Colorado, Idaho, Montana, South Dakota, and Utah that had the highest concentrations of fallout (NCI 1997). These geographic areas indicate a much larger area of heavy fallout than what Congress considered when it wrote compensation legislation for fallout victims.

Scientific Studies and Reparations

Scientific studies, including those we have documented in this chapter, played a major role in providing evidence of the connection between exposures and health outcomes that could be used in court to claim redress for people who suffered from radiation produced in nuclear weapons programs. Yet the limitations of science and the fact-finding process meant it took a very long time for miners and downwinders to substantiate their claims of radiation-induced illness. Government agency secrecy, latency, sample size and levels of significance in epidemiologic studies, and differences among scientific publication venues all present major challenges to those investigating the relationship between uranium exposure and health outcomes.

Government Agency Secrecy

Some of the early studies that sounded the alarm about radiation-related health problems among miners and downwinders did not reach the public for many years because government entities refused to make them public. The early USPHS reports circulated among government and uranium industry personnel, but miners never saw them. Indeed, the USPHS gained access to private mines only after agreeing not to disclose the hazards of radiation exposures to workers. Only in the 1960s and afterward did miners begin to be notified of the risks they faced at work.

Miners and mines now fall under jurisdiction of the Mine Safety and Health Administration (MSHA), created in 1969. MSHA is similar to the Occupational Safety and Health Administration, created in 1970 to provide and enforce health and safety regulations. The AEC suppressed the 1961 Weiss study of leukemia in Utah and the 1963 Knapp study of radioactive iodine in the food chain. Neither became available to the public until 1978 (see Ball 1986). Secrecy not only meant the continuation of nuclear mining and testing and the poisoning of growing numbers of people but also retarded the development of scientific knowledge, since the majority of scientists had no access to pioneering studies for many years.

Latency

Two types of epidemiologic study are critical to establishing the link between radiation exposures and health outcomes: cohort studies, which compare the health outcomes of those who are exposed with the outcomes of those who are less or not exposed; and case-control studies, which compare people with health problems with those who are well (see Sumner et al. 1995). These two research designs are invaluable in making connections between exposure and health outcomes when studying communicable diseases that have a short period between exposure and outcome. But these methodologies do not work as well when a lengthy latency period is involved. According to Gofman:

> Radiation-induced cancer was the first disease to add a new dimension to this
> problem of cause and effect. This new dimension has been fiercely resisted in
> many quarters, even ridiculed, in the face of a mountain of evidence that the
> time period between insult and disease can be measured in decades, not days,
> weeks, or months. (1981:107)

This situation points out the need to develop stringent exposure standards as a precautionary measure when dealing with toxic substances rather than waiting for, in this case, radiation-induced illness and death. Merril Eisenbud, a former industrial hygienist who worked for the AEC, commented that it is important to develop a conservative exposure standard when dealing with workers who are exposed to toxic materials and then to lower it by five to ten times as a performance standard (see Udall 1994). Early on, Eisenbud and colleagues at the AEC's New York operations office recommended that the AEC include health protection requirements for miners in their contracts with mine operators, but the recommendation was never adopted (see ACHRE 1996).

Archer and colleagues reported the latest evidence on latency among US underground uranium miners: the average latency period was about twenty-five years for former miners who were nonsmokers and nineteen for smokers, based on a review of 821 lung-cancer cases among the miners since 1947. The authors concluded that by the government "disregarding the European radon mine exposures and waiting for strong evidence of lung cancer among US uranium miners (ignoring the exposures occurring while waiting during the latency period), the epidemic became inevitable" (Archer et al. 2004:480).

Sample Size and Statistical Significance

Generally, it is impractical for researchers to study an entire population exposed to environmental toxins such as uranium. Typical studies involve taking a sample of a population exposed to radiation and comparing death or illness rates of this sample with one not exposed, the control group. If a control group is unavailable, the exposed group is compared with comparable vital statistics of a region. Since samples do not include everyone in a population, if one were to take multiple, randomly drawn samples one at a time from the same population, there would be random variation from sample to sample. Yet the objective is to determine whether a difference between exposed and unexposed people indicates a true difference or is due to random variation.

To be confident that a difference between exposed and unexposed people reflects actual differences, the researcher applies a statistical formula called a test of statistical significance. Generally, researchers require statistical significance at least meeting the .05 level. The .05 standard means that the probability of a true difference between exposed and unexposed people is ninety-five chances out of one hundred, or nineteen chances out of twenty. In other words, the chance of being wrong is only five out of one hundred or one chance in twenty. This level of statistical significance is more likely to occur with a larger sample size than with a smaller one for a given difference between exposed and unexposed people because the chance variation is less for a larger sample than a smaller one. For example, if a sample of one thousand uranium miners experienced ten deaths from lung cancer, compared with two deaths among a control group of nonminers, this eight-person difference would more likely yield statistical significance with this size sample than with one of only a few hundred. The USPHS study of underground uranium miners, which began in 1950, involved a sample of several thousand workers. Even with this large sample, it took until 1959 for white miners with three or more years of work experience (a subsample of 907) to document a statistically significant elevation of lung cancer. Had this sample been considerably smaller, the elevated levels of lung cancer would not have been statistically significant until more miners had died of the disease.

Brown and Mikkelsen suggest that the standards of proof of statistical significance generally used by medical researchers are too stringent. They argue: "To achieve scientific statements of probability requires more evidence than is necessary to state that something should be done to minimize a health threat" (1990:134). We agree with Brown and Mikkelson when life-and-death issues are at stake. Action should be taken to reduce exposures to toxins to the lowest levels possible even when there are elevated health problems among the exposed sample that do not reach the .05 level. Unfortunately, the commonly accepted standard makes it difficult for small populations to establish statistical significance relating toxic exposures to health outcomes. According to Gofman:

> Some seemingly brainwashed scientists have become such slaves to statistics that they really think that 1 chance in 19 (the 5.26% level of significance) is *meaningfully* or perhaps *magically* different from 1 chance in 20. So we find otherwise serious scientists writing such rubbish as "this result was not found to be significant," when if probed, they will tell you that the findings were at the 5.26% level of significance. (1981:811)

Differences in Scientific Publication Venues

Another critical obstacle for anyone researching the literature on radiation exposures and attendant health problems is the difficulty in obtaining certain scientific publications. In our research on uranium miners and downwinders, we gathered information from the in-house publications of government agencies, which are often not readily available to the public; proceedings from professional meetings, which are not readily available to nonmembers; books and professional journal articles, available chiefly in university libraries; and legal transcripts from court proceedings, available through local, state, and federal court systems. Of all these materials, books and scholarly journal articles were the most accessible. Some government sources were unavailable until then secretary of energy Hazel O'Leary released them to the public in the early 1990s.

The difficulty in getting copies of some publications meant that we expended considerable effort in constructing a coherent understanding of what happened to the miners and downwinders because of gaps in the evidence from documents we could not obtain. These missing or hard-to-access reports were significant obstacles for activists and lawyers seeking compensation for damages from mining and fallout.

To give an example of the difficulties of finding information, we interviewed a medical researcher, one of several authors of an important health agency report, who never saw the final report even after it was published in the 1980s. When we discovered the report in the 1990s, we showed it to the surprised researcher. Furthermore, a major study that we received from another researcher and presented as part of congressional testimony was published only in the proceedings of a professional meeting.

Therefore, it was not as widely disseminated as it would have been if it were published as a journal article. The congressional committee was unaware of the report, even though it had been published years before (US Congress, House Judiciary Committee 1998). Given the difficulty of finding and compiling these data, even when the government is not trying to keep them secret, the average citizen often finds the discovery process overwhelming.

The Struggle for Radiation Victims' Redress

In addition to the collection of scientific evidence of the connection between radiation exposures and health outcomes, attorneys, congressional leaders, journalists, and worker and community activists have worked tirelessly over many years to provide redress for radiation victims. These individuals have made a concerted effort to bring the issue to the public's attention. We will discuss briefly some of these major developments related to miners and downwinders.

In the mid-1970s and 1980s, people whose health had been damaged by nuclear development began to sue the government, and scientific radiation studies began to be used as evidence to determine compensation (see Ball 1986, 1993). The possibility of lawsuits and reparations developed out of grassroots support groups for those who felt they were radiation victims. The downwinders' Committee of Survivors, established at the end of 1978; the Navajo uranium miners' Red Valley Uranium Radiation Victims Committee, founded in 1984; and the Mexican Water Uranium Committee, established in 1985, were among the earliest support groups. Utah citizens also organized grassroots groups, such as Citizens Call, founded by Janet Gordon in 1978, and the Downwinders, which Preston Jay Truman created in 1980. In the same year, Bennie Levy, an ironworker at the Nevada Test Site, organized the Nevada Test Site Workers Victims' Association. These groups testified at lawsuits and congressional committee hearings, educated citizens and workers about radiation issues, developed registries of radiation victims, and provided general support to victims and their families (see Ball 1986; Charley et al. 2004; Dawson et al. 1997).

Journalists played a major role in apprising the radiation victims, the general public, and policy makers about radiation-industry health hazards. The *Denver Post* published some of the earliest journalistic accounts between 1957 and 1967. The first articles reported on the possible connection between mine radioactivity and lung cancer, and by 1967 reporters had documented a more definitive connection between the two (see Pearson 1975). Furthermore, J. V. Reistrup, a science, space, and energy reporter at the *Washington Post*, became aware of underground uranium miners dying of lung cancer. In 1967, after visiting Nucla, Colorado, where he interviewed a dying miner, Reistrup wrote an article for the *Post* in which he documented the workers' plight. He also interviewed Duncan Holaday and Victor Archer, researchers in the USPHS study, who told Reistrup about the mounting illnesses and deaths of uranium miners (see Eichstaedt 1994). In 1977 the *Deseret News* of Salt Lake City ran a series of articles about fallout experienced by residents of Saint George, Utah, a city in the state's southwestern corner. The articles identified the connection between nuclear fallout and the development of such diseases as cancer, leukemia, and thyroid problems (see Miller 1986).

Beginning in the 1960s, some of the uranium miners who became ill sought redress through workers' compensation claims, which proved largely unsuccessful. While Colorado and New Mexico recognized that radiation exposure was a hazard of uranium mining and therefore an occupational illness, Utah did not recognize this category of illness, so uranium miners and their families could not file claims appealing for benefits (Eichstaedt 1994). In congressional testimony, Earl Mettler, a New Mexico attorney, recognized that workers' compensation claims presented several problems, including a very low rate of claimant success, limited benefits, and short statutes of limitation. Mettler stated, "Thus, whether viewed in terms of the number of cases that are successful or the level of compensation received, workers' compensation does not provide an adequate remedy" (US Congress, Senate Energy and Natural Resources Committee 1990:177).

In 1979 attorneys Stewart Udall and Bill Mahoney visited some of the Navajo widows and documented their plight. They filed a lawsuit on behalf of the Navajo uranium miners, *John H. Begay et al. v. United States*, on December 15, 1979 (see Ringholz 2002). Udall and associates also filed a lawsuit on behalf of non-Indian uranium miners, *Sylvia Barnson et al. v. Foote Mineral Col, Vandium Corporation, and the United States*. These miners had worked in the Four Corners area of Arizona, Colorado, New Mexico, and Utah.

Addressing the harms done to people who had not worked in the mines, Dan Bushnell filed a lawsuit, *Bulloch v. United States*, on behalf of southern Utah ranchers whose sheep had died in large numbers due to fallout (see Fuller 1984). Joining forces with attorneys David M. Bell, Dale Haralson, Ralph E. Hunsaker, and J. MacArthur Wright, Udall filed the major case concerning human fallout victims, *Irene Allen et al. v. United States*, in 1982. One of the major stumbling blocks to all these cases was the discretionary function exception of the Federal Torts Claim Act (FTCA). This exception gave the government broad immunity from tort suits (Ball 1986).

In a landmark decision of 1984 in the Allen case, Judge Bruce Jenkins ruled favorably for ten of the twenty-four plaintiffs (Ball 1986). However, the Tenth Circuit Court reversed Jenkins's judgment in 1986, upholding the discretionary function exception of the FTCA. The US Supreme Court denied hearing an appeal from the appellate court, thus ending the plaintiffs' legal challenges. The other radiation-related lawsuits also failed based on the same legal point (Fradkin 1989). Despite the fact that the legal efforts were unsuccessful overall, they added an additional source of scientific evidence and testimony from victims and their families that supported causal linkages between radiation exposures and health problems. (For a discussion of the uranium lawsuits, see Ball 1986, 1993; Eichstaedt 1994; Fradkin 1989; Ringholz 2002; and Udall 1994.)

Congressional Efforts: The Radiation Exposure Compensation Act

The struggle for compensation also took place in Congress. Senator Edward Kennedy (D-MA) introduced the first piece of compensation legislation, the Radiation Compensation Act of 1979, or Senate 1965. According to Ball:

> [I]t was an effort to amend the Federal Tort Claims Act to make the United States liable for damages to individuals who were recklessly endangered by governmental actions and omissions. Covered in the proposal were the civilian downwinders and the miners who worked in a Four Corners uranium mine between 1947 and 1961. (1993:83)

The Senate failed to enact Kennedy's bill. In 1981 Senator Orrin Hatch (R-UT) introduced a new compensation bill, Senate 1483, which the executive branch strongly opposed by summoning what Ball called "a mass of persons to testify against the proposed legislation. Bureaucrats in the Reagan administration, especially from the Departments of Energy and Defense and the Veterans Association, argued against Senate 1483" (1993:85). The Hatch bill met the same fate as the earlier Kennedy bill, but Hatch was persistent and reintroduced a modified bill called the Radiogenic Cancer Compensation Act of 1983, or Senate 921. This bill, unlike the two previous ones, had no formal hearings and never made it out of the Senate Labor and Human Relations Committee (see Ball 1993).

Finally, in 1989 Hatch and Representative Wayne Owens (D-UT) introduced legislation that culminated in the passage of the Radiation Exposure Compensation Act (RECA), signed into law by President George H. W. Bush on October 15, 1990, and amended in 2000. The 1990 RECA legislation provided benefits to underground uranium miners, atomic downwinders, and nuclear test site participants. Administered by the Department of Justice (DOJ), RECA provided compassionate payment to those meeting eligibility requirements, including documented radiation-related illnesses and exposures. The legislation was unique in that Congress, in addition to providing compensation, also apologized on behalf of the nation to victims and their families.

The passage of the 1990 RECA bill was largely due to extensive lobbying efforts by activists, attorneys, legislators, scientists, and radiation victims. Senator Hatch and Representative Owens, working jointly, had written a more moderate bill than the previous three efforts. Ball states:

> The legislation came about because, in large part, the public was being made aware, on a fairly regular basis, of the dangers to the health of many hundreds of thousands of civilians in the continental United States as a consequence of implementing the risky national security technology policies that had been in existence for over forty years. The 1990 RECA criteria turned out to be more stringent for claimants than the available scientific evidence indicated they

should be.... For example, the act set the required levels of radiation exposure so high that many sufferers could not qualify for compensation. (1993:87)

According to Brugge and Goble,

> [U]sing the consensus risk estimates of the time from BEIR IV, RECA criteria meant that former workers with lung cancer had to have a risk of six times normal for lung cancer if they were non-smokers, and fifteen times normal if they were smokers. These were extremely stringent conditions for qualification for compensation. (2003:389)

In addition, the downwind geographic areas designated for coverage under RECA were limited. Furthermore, surface miners, millworkers, and ore transporters were not eligible for consideration.

The DOJ also established other stringent eligibility requirements for claimants applying for RECA. For example, initially the officials administering the act did not recognize the validity of traditional Navajo marriages, which did not have formal documentation. The DOJ required marriage licenses as proof of marriage for widows of deceased miners. Also, the act required that all medical records, such as birth and death records, be certified and original copies. Many traditional Navajo elders did not have birth certificates, let alone original records. Often, they had only copies of certain documents such as death certificates. These issues were not fully rectified until the 2000 amendments were passed, and then only through the efforts of attorneys and activists. (For a full discussion of problems associated with 1990 RECA, see Brugge and Goble 2003; Dawson and Madsen 2000; Eichstaedt 1994.)

In the ten years after the passage of RECA, grassroots efforts resurfaced to amend it. These efforts included the Western States RECA Reform Coalition, an umbrella organization for a large number of local grassroots organizations. The lobbying efforts culminated in the introduction of four pieces of legislation in 1999 and passage of the Radiation Exposure Compensation Act amendments of 2000 on July 10, 2000 (Brugge and Goble 2003). The amendments extended the geographic areas for compensation for downwinders and added surface miners, millworkers, and ore transporters to those eligible for compensation. Miners who had smoking histories were no longer required to have significantly higher levels of exposure than nonsmokers to be eligible for compensation. In fact, the changes to RECA made miners eligible if they had either forty working level months (a measurement of radiation exposure) or had established mine employment for one year. The list of compensable diseases was extended to include a wider range of ailments, and certain medical criteria were made less stringent for potential claimants (Department of Justice 2006). For a summary of claims as of January 18, 2006, see table 6.1.

Downwinders are eligible to receive $50,000 in compensation; onsite participants $75,000; and uranium miners, millers, and ore transporters $100,000. Shortly after Congress passed the RECA amendments of 2000, it passed the Energy Employees

Table 6.1. Count of Claims

Claim Type	# Approved	$ Approved
Downwinder	9,805	$490,220,000
Onsite Participant	960	68,460,816
Uranium Miner	3,800	379,298,560
Uranium Miller	738	73,800,000
Ore Transporter	143	14,300,000
Total	15,446	$1,026,079,376

Department of Justice 2006

Occupational Illness Compensation Program Act (EEOICPA) in October 2000. Under the act, administered by the Department of Labor, miners, millers, and ore transporters who have already won a RECA claim are entitled to an additional $50,000. In the future, such beneficiaries will receive a total of $150,000 (Department of Labor 2003). The combination of RECA and EEOICPA has resulted in compensation awards totaling over $1 billion.

Present Issues Concerning RECA and Compensation

Despite the passage of the RECA amendments of 2000, concern about exposures and compensation persists among purported victims and their advocates. RECA now allows downwinders only in certain counties in Arizona, Nevada, and Utah to be eligible for compensation, even though the 1997 NCI study identified certain counties in Colorado, Idaho, Montana, South Dakota, and Utah as having the highest per-capita thyroid doses from the Nevada Test Site nuclear tests (NCI 1997). Blaine, Custer, Gem, and Lemhi counties in Idaho received heavier doses of iodine-131 than some Utah counties that qualify for RECA (Smith 2004). Idaho downwinders have organized to demand a change in RECA to make fallout victims in that state eligible for compensation. Furthermore, Idaho health officials have instituted a preliminary study to examine whether there is a relationship between multiple sclerosis and nuclear fallout in Idaho (Associated Press 2005).

The National Academy of Sciences has recently held meetings to discuss possibly expanding the geographic areas defined as being downwind in RECA. But once again information circulates among only a small group of officials and academics, and remedies are slow in coming. According to Preston Truman of Lava Hot Springs, Idaho, president of Downwinders, "it's not just Idaho. You've got western Montana, sections of western Colorado, northwest New Mexico, Iowa and upstate New York all with high fallout doses, but not only are they not covered, they haven't been told about this study" (Smith 2004).

More community studies need to be conducted to investigate possible health problems experienced by people who live or have lived in proximity to sources of radioactive exposures. In 1996 the Navajo Nation established a large-scale educational program to apprise its residents of environmental contamination left by the extensive mining and milling of the 1950s and 1960s. According to Charley:

> Uranium mining and milling has left large areas of the Navajo reservation contaminated with abandoned mines, mine waste, and mill tailings and associated radioactive contaminants. There are well documented problems with lung cancer and silicosis in former uranium miners, and there is great concern between uranium millers and other Navajos who reside near contaminated areas about late effects of radiation exposures from these sources. (2000:1)

RECA also excludes post-1971 uranium workers. Only those who were employed in uranium mining, milling, and truck hauling prior to 1972 are eligible for compensation. This cut-off date was based upon government liability related to the federal government procurement program, which ended in 1970 (Madsen and Dawson 2005). Recent scientific evidence suggests that the exposure-limit regulation the EPA adopted in 1971 was not stringent enough to adequately protect underground mine workers over their cumulative working careers (see Archer et al. 1980; Lubin et al. 1994; Madsen and Dawson 2005; National Academy of Sciences 1988). Advocates had lobbied for the inclusion of post-1971 workers in the 2000 amendments to RECA, but Congress declined to include them. The lobbying efforts for changes in the 2000 RECA amendments placed the greatest emphasis on earlier uranium workers.

Summary: Lessons Learned

The Cold War period of uranium production and testing has been a wide-scale human-caused disaster, resulting in widespread illness and death primarily from chronic low levels of radiation. Many scientists in the early nuclear era believed there was a threshold dose of radiation that, if not exceeded, would not cause health problems. As Gofman has explained, these advocates of a threshold dose did not accept a linear relationship between radiation exposures and the development of health problems. Unfortunately, the assumption that the body has mechanisms to repair damage from low doses did not withstand scientific research. Drawing on studies of radiation victims since the 1940s, Gofman concluded, "Therefore, scientifically it is thoroughly reasonable to say that cancer and leukemia induction by radiation is proportional to dose right down to the lowest conceivable doses" (1981:411).

The people presently opposing the possible resumptions of nuclear testing and uranium mining have reason to be concerned. Activist groups, including the Eastern Navajo Allottee Association and the Eastern Navajo Diné Against Uranium Mining are working diligently to stop uranium mining on the Navajo Nation, while the Healthy Environment Alliance of Utah has lobbied against the resumption of nuclear bomb building and testing. Hopefully, history will not repeat itself, and the lessons learned from the Cold War and its aftermath will be translated into sound public policy concerning uranium mining and nuclear weapons testing.

References

ACHRE. *See* Advisory Committee on Human Radiation Experiments

Advisory Committee on Human Radiation Experiments
1996   Final Report of the Advisory Committee on Human Radiation Experiments. New York: Oxford University Press.

Archer, Victor E.
1981   Health Concerns in Uranium Mining and Milling. Journal of Occupational Medicine 23(7):502–05.

Archer, Victor E., Teresa Coons, Geno Saccomanno, and Dae-Yong Hong
2004   Latency and the Lung Cancer Epidemic among United States Uranium Miners. Health Physics 87(5):480–89.

Archer, Victor E., J. Dean Gillam, and Joseph K. Wagoner
1976   Respiratory Disease Mortality among Uranium Miners. Annals of the New York Academy of Sciences 271:280–93.

Archer, Victor E., Harold J. Magnuson, Duncan A. Holaday, and Pope A. Lawrence
1962   Hazards to Health in Uranium Mining and Milling. Journal of Occupational Medicine 4(2):55–60.

Archer, Victor E., Neal Nelson, Frank E. Lundin Jr., Joseph K. Wagoner, Arthur S. Watanabe, David M. Scott, Roy M. Fleming, Robert W. Wheeler, Max B. Slade, and Cherie Hutchison
1980   The Risk of Lung Cancer among Underground Miners of Uranium-bearing Ores. NIOSH study group report. Rockville, MD: National Institute for Occupational Safety and Health.

Archer, Victor E., Joseph K. Wagoner, and Frank E. Lundin
1973   Lung Cancer among Uranium Miners in the United States. Health Physics 25:351–71.

Associated Press
2004   Workers Put on Leave as Los Alamos Probes Missing Data, Injury. Salt Lake Tribune, July 23: A5.
2005   MS–Nuke Test Links to Be Probed. Salt Lake Tribune, February 11: A7.

Ball, Howard
1986   Justice Downwind: America's Atomic Testing Program in the 1950s. New York: Oxford University Press.

1993   *Cancer Factories: America's Tragic Quest for Uranium Self-Sufficiency.* Westport, CT: Greenwood Press.

Beck, Harold L., and Philip W. Krey
1983   Radiation Exposures in Utah from the Nevada Nuclear Tests. *Science* 220:18–24.

Bernstein, Richard.
2005   Iran Is Reported to Continue Nuclear Activity. *New York Times,* November 18:A6.

Bhounek, F.
1970   History of the Exposure of Miners to Radon. *Health Physics* 19:56–57.

Boutté, Marie I.
2002   Compensating for Health: The Acts and Outcomes of Atomic Testing. *Human Organization* 61(1):41–50.

Brown, Phil, and Edwin J. Mikkelsen
1990   *No Safe Place: Toxic Waste, Leukemia, and Community Action.* Berkeley: University of California Press.

Brugge, Doug, and Rob Goble
2003   The Radiation Exposure Compensation Act: What Is Fair? *New Solutions* 13(4):385–97.

Burr, Thomas
2005   Funds to Develop Bunker Buster N-bomb Scrapped. *Salt Lake Tribune,* October 25: C5.

Charley, Perry H.
2000   *Navajo Environmental Health Program: Partnership for Health Community.* A Report to the Navajo Nation Health and Social Services Committee. Shiprock, NM: Diné College, Uranium Education Program.

Charley, Perry H., Susan E. Dawson, Gary E. Madsen, and Bryan R. Spykerman
2004   Navajo Uranium Education Programs: The Search for Environmental Justice. *Journal of Applied Environmental Education Communication* 3(2):101–08.

Clark, Claudia
1997   *Radium Girls: Women and Industrial Health Reform, 1910–1935.* Chapel Hill: University of North Carolina Press.

Cross, F. T., C. H. Bloomster, P. L. Hendrickson, B. L. Hooper, J. A. Merrill, I. C. Nelson, and B. O. Stuart
1974   Evaluation of Methods for Setting Occupational Health Standards for Uranium Miners. A Research Report for the National Institute for Occupational Safety and Health. Richland, WA: Battelle, Pacific Northwest Laboratories.

Dawson, Susan E., Perry E. Charley, and Philip Harrison
1997   Advocacy and Social Action among Navajo Uranium Workers and Their Families. *In Social Work in Health Settings: Practice in Context.* Toba Schwaber Kerson, ed. Pp. 391–407. New York: Haworth.

Dawson, Susan E., and Gary E. Madsen
2000   Worker Activism and Environmental Justice: The Black Lung and Radiation Compensation Programs. Tulane Studies in Social Welfare 21–22:209–28.

Department of Energy
1991   Uranium Industry Annual 1990. Washington, DC: Department of Energy.

Department of Justice
2006   Radiation Exposure Compensation System. Claims to Date Summary of Claims Received by 01/19/2006. All Claims. Electronic document, http://www.usdoj.gov/civil/omp/omi/Tre_SysClaimsToDateSum.pdf, accessed January 20, 2006.

Department of Labor
2003   Energy Employees Occupational Illness Compensation Program Act. US Code 42.

Dickey, Christopher, Maziar Bahari, and Babak Dehghanpisheh
2006   Iran's Rogue Rage. Electronic document, http://www.msnbc.msn.com/id/10858242/site/newsweek, accessed November 9, 2006.

Eichstaedt, Peter H.
1994   If You Poison Us: Uranium and Native Americans. Santa Fe, NM: Red Crane Books.

Eisenbud, Merril, and Bernie Wolf
1948   Medical Survey of Colorado Raw Materials Area. Washington, DC: Atomic Energy Commission.

Emery, Erin
2004   Colorado Senator Proposes Firing Los Alamos Manager. Salt Lake Tribune, July 25: A9.

Fahys, Judy
2005   Japan Sending Trainloads of Toxins to Utah. Salt Lake Tribune, October 5: A1.

Fradkin, Philip L.
1989   Fallout: An American Nuclear Tragedy. Tucson: University of Arizona Press.

Fuller, John G.
1984   The Day We Bombed Utah. New York: Signet.

Gehrke, Robert
2004   Bill Hailed as Win for Downwind Utahns. Salt Lake Tribune, November 21: B1.

Gofman, John W.
1981   Radiation and Human Health: A Comprehensive Investigation of the Evidence Relating Low-Level Radiation to Cancer and Other Diseases. San Francisco: Sierra Club Books.

Gottlieb, Leon S., and Laverne A. Husen
1982   Lung Cancer among Navajo Uranium Miners. Chest 81:449–52.

Härting, F. H., and W. Hesse

1879   Der Lungenkrebs, Die Bergkrankheit In Den Schneeberger Gruben. Vierteljahrsschrift Für Gerichtliche Medizin Und Öffentliches Sanitätswesen 30:296–308; 31:102–29, 313–37.

HEAL Utah

2004   Will History Repeat Itself? The Smokeout Summer 6. Electronic document, http://www.healutah.org, accessed February 10, 2005.

Holaday, Duncan

1969   History of the Exposure of Miners to Radon. Health Physics 16:547–52.

1981   Deposition of Duncan A. Holaday to Stewart Udall. November 1981. Phoenix: John A. Brabec and Associates.

Holaday, Duncan A., Victor E. Archer, and Frank E. Lundin

1968   A Summary of United States Exposure Experiences in the Uranium Mining Industry, from Symposium on Diagnosis and Treatment of Deposited Radionuclides. Monographs on Nuclear Medicine and Biology 2:451–56.

Holaday, Duncan A., Wilfred D. David, and Henry N. Doyle

1952   Interim Report of a Health Study of the Uranium Mines and Mills. Washington DC: Federal Security Agency, US Public Health Service, Division of Occupational Health and the Colorado State Department of Public Health.

Holaday, Duncan A., and Henry N. Doyle

1952   Progress Report (July 1950–December 1951) on the Health Study in the Uranium Mines and Mills. Salt Lake City: US Public Health Service.

Holmes, Sue Major

2004   Energy Department Restricts Use of Computer Disks. Salt Lake Tribune, July 24: A5.

Hornung, Richard W., and Theodore J. Meinhardt

1987   Quantitative Risk Assessment of Lung Cancer in US Uranium Miners. Health Physics 52:417–30.

Hueper, William C.

1942   Occupational Tumors and Allied Diseases. Springfield, IL: C. C. Thomas.

Johnson, Carl J.

1984   Cancer Incidence in an Area of Radioactive Fallout Downwind of the Nevada Test Site. Journal of the American Medical Association 251(2):230–36.

Johnson, Jesse C.

1959   Radiation Hazards in Uranium Mines and Mills. Paper delivered to the American Mining Congress, Denver, September 16.

Johnson, Tim

2005   North Korea Claims Nukes. Salt Lake Tribune, February 11: A1.

Kerber, R. A., J. E. Till, S. L. Simon, J. L. Lyon, D. C. Thomas, S. Preston-Martin,
M. L. Rallison, R. D. Lloyd, and W. Stevens
1993   A Cohort Study of Thyroid Disease in Relation to Fallout from Nuclear Weapons
        Testing. Journal of the American Medical Association 270:2076–82.

Kosich, D.
2006   Uranium Radiates Investment Heat. Electronic document,
        http://www.mineweb.net/sections/energy/76397.htm, accessed January 9, 2006.

Lofholm, Nancy
2005   Uranium Revival: Demand Returns and Companies Reopen Mines in the Southwest.
        Albuquerque Sunday Journal, January 9: I1.

Lorenz, Egon
1944   Radioactivity and Lung Cancer: A Critical Review of Lung Cancer in the Miners of
        Schneeberg and Joachimsthal. Journal of the National Cancer Institute 5:1–15.

Lubin, Jay H., John D. Boice Jr., Christer Edling, Richard W. Hornung,
Geoffrey Howe, Emil Kunz, Robert A. Kusiak et al.
1994   Radon and Lung Cancer Risk: A Joint Analysis of 11 Underground Miners Studies.
        Washington, DC: Department of Health, Education and Welfare.

Lundin, Frank E., Jr., J. William Lloyd, Elizabeth M. Smith, Victor E. Archer, and
Duncan A. Holaday
1969   Mortality of Uranium Miners in Relation to Radiation Exposure, Hard-rock Mining
        and Cigarette Smoking—1950 through September 1967. Health Physics
        16:571–78.

Lundin, Frank E., Joseph K. Wagoner, and Victor E. Archer
1971   Radon Daughter Exposure and Respiratory Cancer Quantitative and Temporal
        Aspects: Report from the Epidemiological Study of United States Uranium Miners.
        Washington, DC: Department of Health, Education, and Welfare, Public Health
        Service.

Lyon, Joseph L., Melville Lauber, John W. Gardner, and King Udall
1979   Childhood Leukemias Associated with Fallout from Nuclear Testing. New England
        Journal of Medicine 300:397–99.

Madsen, Gary E., and Susan E. Dawson
2005   Unfinished Business: Radiation Exposure Compensation Act (RECA) for Post-1971
        US Uranium Underground Miners. Journal of Health and Social Policy 19(4).

Makhijani, Arjun, A. James Ruttenber, Ellen Kennedy, and Richard Clapp
1995   The United States. In Nuclear Wastelands: A Global Guide to Nuclear Weapons
        Production and Its Health and Environmental Effects. Arjun Makhijani, Howard
        Hu, and Katherine Yih, eds. Pp. 169–284. Cambridge, MA: MIT Press.

Mapel, Douglas W., David B. Coultas, David S. James, William C. Hunt,
Christine A. Stidley, and Frank D. Gilliland
1997   Ethnic Differences in the Prevalence of Nonmalignant Respiratory Disease among

Uranium Miners. American Journal of Public Health 87(5):833–38.

Metzger, H. Peter
1972   The Atomic Establishment. New York: Simon and Schuster.

Miller, Richard L.
1986   Under the Cloud: The Decades of Nuclear Testing. New York: Free Press.

National Academy of Sciences
1988   Report of the Committee on the Biological Effects of Ionizing Radiation. Health
        Effects of Exposures to Low Levels of Ionizing Radiation. Washington, DC: National
        Academy Press.

National Cancer Institute
1997   Estimated Exposures and Thyroid Doses Received by the American People from
        Iodine-131 in Fallout Following Nevada Atmospheric Nuclear Bomb Tests.
        Washington, DC: US Government Printing Office.

NCI. *See* **National Cancer Institute**

Oberbeck, Steven
2006a   Canadians Stake Claim to Utah's Uranium. Salt Lake Tribune, January 10: E1.
2006b   Uranium Mining May Restart. Salt Lake Tribune, June 16: C10.

Pearson, Jessica S.
1975   A Sociological Analysis of the Reduction of Hazardous Radiation in Uranium Mines.
        Salt Lake City: Department of Health, Education and Welfare/National Institute for
        Occupational Safety and Health.

**Rallison, Marvin, Blown M. Dobbyns, F. Raymond Keating, Joseph E. Rall, and
Frank H. Tyler**
1974   Thyroid Disease in Children. American Journal of Medicine 56:457.

Reid, Robert
1974   Marie Curie. New York: Signet.

Republic of the Marshall Islands
2005   Nuclear Testing in the Marshall Islands: A Chronology of Events. Electronic docu-
        ment, http://www.rmiembassyus.org/nuclear/chronology.html, accessed January 28.

Ringholz, Raye C.
2002   Uranium Frenzy: Saga of the Nuclear West. Logan: Utah State University Press.

Roscoe, Robert J.
1997   An Update of Mortality from All Causes among White Uranium Miners from the
        Colorado Plateau Study Group. American Journal of Industrial Medicine 31:211–22.

Roscoe, Robert J., James A. Deddens, Alberto Salvan, and Teresa M. Schnorr
1995   Mortality among Navajo Uranium Miners. American Journal of Public Health
        85(4):535–40.

Roscoe, Robert J., Kyle Steenland, William E. Halperin, James J. Beaumont, and Richard J. Waxweiler

1989   Lung Cancer Mortality among Nonsmoking Uranium Miners Exposed to Radon Daughters. Journal of the American Medical Association 262:629–33.

Rulon, Malia

2004   Feds Will Keep Public in Dark about Plants. Salt Lake Tribune, August 5: A11.

Samet, J. M., D. M. Kutvirt, R. J. Waxweiler, and C. R. Key

1984   Uranium Mining and Lung Cancer among Navajo Men. New England Journal of Medicine 310:1481–84.

Samet, Jonathan M., D. R. Pathak, Marion V. Morgan, David B. Coultas, David S. James, and William C. Hunt

1994   Silicosis and Lung Cancer Risk in Underground Uranium Miners. Health Physics 66(4):450–53.

Samet, Jonathan M., D. R. Pathak, Marion V. Morgan, Charles R. Key, A. A. Valdivia, and Jay H. Lubin

1991   Lung Cancer Mortality and Exposure to Radon Progeny in a Cohort of New Mexico Underground Uranium Miners. Health Physics 61(6):745–52.

Samet, Jonathan M., Rebecca A. Young, Marion V. Morgan, Charles G. Humble, Gary R. Epler, and Theresa C. McLoud

1984   Prevalence Survey of Respiratory Abnormalities in New Mexico Uranium Miners. Health Physics 46(2):361–70.

Sanger, David E.

2004   Iran, N. Korea Progressing with Nuke Programs. Salt Lake Tribune, August 8: A4.

Smith, Christopher

2004   Idaho Downwinders Want Fallout Hearing. Salt Lake Tribune, September 11: A3.

Stevens, W., D. C. Thomas, and J. L. Lyons

1990   Leukemia in Utah and Radioactive Fallout from the Nevada Test Site. Journal of the American Medical Association 264(5):585–91.

Sumner, David, Howard Hu, and Alistair Woodward

1995   Health Hazards of Nuclear Weapons Production. *In* Nuclear Wastelands: A Global Guide to Nuclear Weapons Production and Its Health and Environmental Effects. Arjun Makhijani, Howard Hu, and Katherine Yih, eds. Pp. 65–104. Cambridge, MA: MIT Press.

Titus, A. Costandina

1986   Bombs in the Backyard: Atomic Testing and American Politics. Reno: University of Nevada Press.

Udall, Stewart L.

1994   The Myths of August: A Personal Exploration of Our Tragic Cold War Affair with the Atom. New York: Pantheon Books.

US Congress. House of Representatives. Committee on the Judiciary. Subcommittee
on Immigration and Claims
1998   Testimony of Susan E. Dawson, PhD, and Gary E. Madsen, PhD. 105th Cong. 2d
        sess. June 25.

US Congress. Senate. Committee on Energy and Natural Resources. Mineral
Resources Development and Production Subcommittee
1990   Testimony of Earl Mettler on impacts of past uranium mining practices, 101st
        Cong. 2d Sess.

Wagoner, Joseph K., Victor E. Archer, Benjamin E. Carroll, Duncan A. Holaday,
and Pope A. Lawrence
1964   Mortality Patterns among US Uranium Miners and Millers, 1950 through 1962.
        Journal of the National Cancer Institute 32(4):787–801.

Yih, Katherine, Albert Donnay, Annalee Yassi, A. James Ruttenber, and Scott Saleska
1995   Uranium Mining and Milling for Military Purposes. In Nuclear Wastelands: A
        Global Guide to Nuclear Weapons Production and Its Health and Environmental
        Effects. Arjun Makhijani, Howard Hu, and Katherine Yih, eds. Pp. 105–68.
        Cambridge, MA: MIT Press.

seven

Hanford, Tribal Risks, and Public Health in an Era of Forced Federalism

Edward Liebow

For American Indians and Alaska Natives, the Cold War's legacy has been one of environmental contamination, financial duress, and formidable barriers to much-needed health and social services. Most of the US Cold War arsenal was produced and tested at facilities deliberately located away from major population centers—in the heart of Native America. Cold War–era weapons production has left dangerous by-products that must be stabilized and disposed of. In a few dramatic cases, Native peoples may have been exposed intentionally to ionizing radiation, asked to bear a significant local burden in the service of national interests.

As the other chapters in this volume eloquently testify, the Hanford (Washington) Nuclear Reservation was not alone in contaminating the environment. The arms race imposed an enormous local burden not just at weapons labs and production facilities in the United States but also in western and southern Australia, Micronesia, French Polynesia, Siberia, western China, India, Pakistan, and across the Arctic. In other words, wherever a nuclear military power glows on the world map, one can expect to find a marginalized region within its national boundaries or colonial territories with its very own bands of nuclear Natives.

What has been done and what can be done to redress these problems? This chapter summarizes the work of social and environmental-health scientists over the last fifteen years among Pacific Northwest tribal groups that share air and watersheds

145

contaminated by Cold War–era Hanford nuclear-weapons-production activities. It places this work in the context of the institutional locus and research design of initiatives designed to investigate the nature and extent of Hanford-related health and environmental harm and the "forced federalism" of the 1980s and 1990s. In concluding, it reflects critically on the adversarial "blame-affixing" style of investigation typical of such programs. This style springs from the belief that before there can be a remedy, there must first be a responsible party identified and called to account. If observed effects defy adequate causal attribution, even the best-intentioned of government officials can do little, even as the harmful effects and the need for a remedy persist. Dispensing with the need to nail the perpetrator shifts our focus away from finding the "bad guy" (for example, the government, the military-industrial complex) and acknowledges that complicity, and therefore responsibility, is widely shared.

Legacy of the Cold War for Native Americans

The US strategy of spending the Soviet bloc into submission diverted public funds away from Native Americans, for whom the US government serves as a fiduciary trustee. Neglecting Native peoples to pay for other programs is hardly new. During Ulysses Grant's post–Civil War presidency, the nearly bankrupt Reconstruction Congress sought help in bearing the cost of administering Indian affairs by enlisting missionary societies, the original faith-based organization–government partnership. World War II nearly emptied the federal treasury again, and the Cold War era saw congressional attempts to cut expenses by terminating the nation's trust relationship with tribal governments. "Terminated" tribes such as the Menominee of Wisconsin and the Klamath of Oregon plummeted overnight from modest prosperity into abject poverty.

Health care services, which in the 1950s had finally begun realizing the benefits of an overdue reorganization of federal Indian administration, were passed off to the Indian Health Service, a poor stepcousin public health agency. All involved openly acknowledged that its funding covered only one-half to two-thirds of the health care that Native peoples needed. Education and housing services later suffered the same shameful fate.

Much of whatever meager capital Native peoples have managed to accumulate since the late nineteenth century the Interior Department has lost in an accounting haze that is probably less the result of malice or indifference than the inevitable outcome of a chronically understaffed and ill-equipped agency. Over the decades, the Interior Department saw its resources ebb and collect in pools across Washington's Potomac River in the glass-and-steel office towers of Crystal City and Fairfax County, where the Defense Department sowed the Soviets' demise.

Facing Hanford's Legacy

The US federal government's neglect, underfunding, and effort to end its trust obligations to Native tribes have had particularly harmful results when combined with the development and production of nuclear weapons. The Hanford site occupies about 560 square miles in southeastern Washington State. The US government facilities were established there as part of the Manhattan Project, code name for the World War II program that built the atomic weapons that destroyed Hiroshima and Nagasaki. Two parallel efforts—one to build a uranium bomb, the other to build a plutonium bomb—began in 1942. Given security concerns and little certainty about the feasibility of large-scale production of weapons-grade fuel, the Manhattan Project hedged its bets by using two different places. Scientists at a facility in Oak Ridge, Tennessee, used a mechanical separation method known as gaseous diffusion to extract uranium fuel. At Hanford scientists used a chemical separation method that involved dipping plutonium rods into a witches' brew of powerful solvents. Oak Ridge fueled the Hiroshima weapon. Hanford fueled the Nagasaki weapon.

The federal government shrouded Hanford in secrecy, keeping it off-limits to the public. Its releases, however, could not be contained within its 560-square-mile area. Over the period 1944–72, Hanford released about 25 million curies of radioactive contamination into the environment.[1] Releases came in two distinct forms:

1. *airborne releases*, for the most part a normal by-product of chemical reactions used to separate weapons-grade plutonium from enriched uranium reactor rods;[2] and

2. *river-borne releases*, the result of both accidental releases and normal operations that used Columbia River water to cool weapons-production reactor cores.

The largest volume of airborne releases came during Hanford's first two years of operation, when the push to produce the Nagasaki weapon was greatest. The end of World War II allowed Hanford to slow its production pace somewhat and to install safeguards that reduced off-site releases. Even so, substantial airborne releases continued well into the 1950s, while river-borne releases reached their peak in the early 1960s, when all nine production reactors were on the job.

The airborne releases consisted of a number of very short-lived radioisotopes, along with iodine-131 (I-131), an unstable isotope of iodine-129 that has a half-life of about eight days. In other words, if a kilogram of I-131 is released into the atmosphere and scattered by the wind, eight days later 500 grams remain (the rest having been transformed into the stable iodine-129). Another eight days later, 250 grams remain, and by about two months after the initial release, less than 1 percent of the originally released radioactive I-131 remains. This fact is important because just about all the iodine to which the human body is exposed is taken up by the thyroid gland. The thyroid gland makes hormones to regulate the rate at which the body carries out its normal functions. While thyroid diseases are quite widespread among Americans (about 7 percent of the US population has thyroid disease, and about 40 percent of adults have growths on their thyroid glands that can be felt by hand or detected with a sonogram [Wu 2000:38]), exposure to radioactive I-131 can contribute to thyroid disease and in rare instances thyroid cancer.

Figure 7.1. Postwar residents in nearby cities identified closely with the Hanford nuclear works as the lifeblood of the local economy. Credit Edward Liebow

The river-borne releases included almost two dozen different radioactive chemicals, most of which have half-lives measured in small fractions of seconds. However, some have much longer half-lives and therefore remain available in the environment to result in human exposures. Among the radioactive chemicals released from Hanford into the river, isotopes of arsenic, phosphorus, neptunium, zinc, sodium, and strontium are known to be important contributors to human health risks, largely because of how closely they resemble stable chemicals that the body uses (Grogan et al. 2002). Once absorbed by the body, the radioactive decay process bombards healthy tissue and can disrupt the normal ways cells function. With a long enough exposure to enough of these radioactive materials, immune systems can be compromised, birth defects can result, and the risk of certain cancers, especially thyroid and bone cancers, can increase.

A turning point for Hanford's tribal neighbors came in 1978, when the Carter administration enacted the Nuclear Nonproliferation Act. This law promised that in the United States, nuclear materials from commercial power plants would not be recycled for the production of nuclear weapons and would have to be disposed of in some other way. Looking for that other way, a National Academy of Sciences study led to the 1982 Nuclear Waste Policy Act, which said that since this highly dangerous material cannot be recycled for weapons, it should be stored behind a suitable geological barrier to prevent it from reentering the biosphere. After all, lawmakers reasoned, rock is much more likely than human institutions to remain intact over the tens of thousands of years this material will take to decay to a harmless state. As it happens, Hanford sits atop a basalt rock formation. The site returned to public awareness and

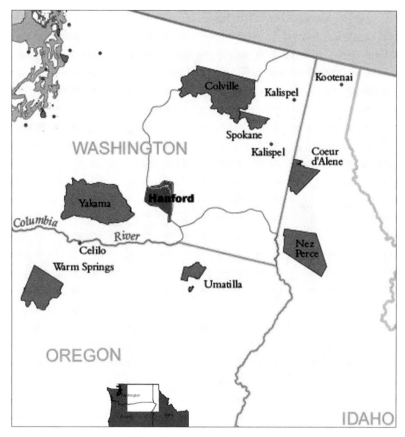

Map 7.1. The lands of the nine member tribes of the Intertribal Council on Hanford Health Projects in relation to the Hanford Nuclear Reservation. Credit: Edward Liebow

in the 1980s became the center of debates over whether it would be suitable as a permanent nuclear waste storage site.

Hanford's tribal neighbors, in particular, had a strong interest in what had been going on at Hanford since the 1940s (see map 7.1). Long before Indian reservations were created in the mid-1800s, the tribes used resources from throughout the Columbia River Plateau region later contaminated by Hanford. The Columbia River and its tributaries were at the heart of long-established grounds for hunting, fishing, food gathering, and medicine gathering, as well as social interaction networks. The Hanford Reach of the Columbia River, the confluence of the Columbia, Yakima, and Snake rivers, and the falls above and below today's Hanford site were all important places for fishing and social gathering.

Under pressure from US westward expansion, the tribal groups of the Columbia Basin ceded millions of acres in present-day Washington, Oregon, and Idaho. The US government forced the region's Native peoples to relocate their settlements to reservations. Nevertheless, the tribes negotiated legal agreements that protected their rights to pursue their traditional lifestyles on the ceded lands.[3]

As the government withdrew the Hanford site from public use in the 1940s, officials offered vague assurances to tribal leaders that their rights to use this land would be restored after the war ended. Instead, the onset of the Cold War brought an expansion of the plutonium production program. National security prevented all access to the site, including the tribes' rights to hunt and fish there.

In the 1980s, national imperatives—now to create storage facilities for nuclear waste—continued to block the tribes' access to these lands. As Hanford received increasingly serious consideration as a permanent nuclear waste storage site, three tribes (the Nez Percé, Umatilla, and Yakama) were designated as "affected tribes" for the purposes of the Nuclear Waste Policy Act. The "affected" designation enabled the three tribes to become much more closely involved in Department of Energy (DOE) activities at Hanford. As a result, the tribes developed an institutional capacity for dealing with the inordinately complex process of cleaning up what many observers have termed one of the most polluted places on the planet.

The Nuclear Waste Policy Act was amended in 1987, eliminating Hanford as the commercial spent-fuel repository site. But even this policy change could not reverse the transformation set in motion by the repository program. By then, negotiations were underway between the DOE, the Environmental Protection Agency, and the State of Washington to create a cleanup agreement eventually consummated in 1989. Although the federal agencies and state government did not invite any tribes to be official parties to this agreement, tribal representatives were included on the Hanford Advisory Board, which was granted oversight authority in a number of planning and budgetary matters.[4] The federal panel convened to make sense of the thousands of documents released in 1986 (which revealed publicly for the first time the magnitude of Hanford contamination) also included tribal representatives.

The panel raised the question of the potential health effects from this contamination and recommended launching two studies: the Hanford Environmental Dose Reconstruction Project (HEDR), to estimate radiation doses individuals received from off-site Hanford releases; and the Hanford Thyroid Disease Study (HTDS), to determine whether airborne radioactive iodine had any discernible health effects, since it was by far the largest persistent source of Hanford radiation that accumulated off-site. Both of these public health projects required tribal involvement, although the nature and extent of this involvement was not specified at first.

The Battelle Pacific Northwest National Laboratory received a $12 million contract from the DOE to conduct the HEDR project in 1989. A Technical Steering Panel, with members appointed by the governors of Washington, Oregon, and Idaho, supervised the study. It was only after several of these appointees pointed out the importance of tribal representation that the Native groups gained a seat at the table. At the Technical Steering Panel's direction, Battelle established subcontracts with eight tribes (later another tribe was added for a total of nine) in 1990.[5] These subcontracts reflected the tribes' perspective that the information needed for estimating radiation doses from the pursuit of distinctive traditional lifestyles (for example, locations for gathering medicinal plants, family-controlled hunting and fishing spots) was extremely sensitive and that history strongly undermined the tribes' confidence that nonmembers would afford this information the protections it required. Thus the tribes wanted to protect their sovereignty in the context of public health research while also developing the capacity to ensure the scientific integrity of this research.

Unfortunately, the language of the subcontracts did not ensure the smooth functioning of the project. Soon after Battelle and the tribes agreed to the subcontracts, Battelle subcontracting officials and their tribal counterparts disagreed about a number of administrative matters. One Technical Steering Panel member worked extensively to resolve these conflicts and assembled the Native American Working Group in 1990 when it became apparent that substantive technical matters played an equally significant role in the conflicts with Battelle.[6] Working group members consisted of representatives from the tribes' health or natural-resource-management organizations. Generally, the tribal representatives did not believe that the models that shaped the investigation were sensitive enough to distinctive tribal traditions that may have led to elevated radiation exposures for the region's Indian people. For example, the models placed a heavy emphasis on exposures from eating contaminated foods (ingestion), while underemphasizing inhalation and skin absorption as important exposure pathways. The importance of ingestion pathways increases in direct proportion to the amount of time one spends indoors in a well-insulated building. Tribal critics charged that Eurocentric assumptions about how much time people spent out of doors led modelers to overlook these other exposure routes. Similarly, participation in sweats and the ritual use of smoke are distinctive to tribal traditions, creating lifestyle-related risks that tribal critics charged were overlooked in models designed to estimate exposures. Between 1991 and 1995, the Native American Working Group met quarterly in conjunction with the Technical Steering Panel's quarterly meetings.

The Public Health Practice Training Program

The Native American Working Group's early meetings made it clear that no outsider organization could expect to come to the tribes and produce reliable and valid dosimetry-related data, but the tribes would require some assistance to build the capacity to do the research themselves. The Centers for Disease Control (CDC) entered into a memorandum of agreement with its US Public Health Service cousin, the Indian Health Service, to create a training program for the specific purpose of enhancing the capacities of the Native American Working Group's member tribes in public health research and related activities. Five groups of trainees completed the yearlong Public Health Practice Training program between 1991 and 1997.

This training program was a qualified success (Liebow 1997). A cadre of thirty-seven trainees from the nine tribes completed the course. Six tribal members who completed the course went on to complete advanced degree programs. For those who went back to their tribal health department positions, the impact on their respective tribes extended beyond environmental health and radiation exposures to a number of practical areas of public health. For example, the course resulted in a grant application that funded a tribal position to work on baby-bottle tooth-decay prevention, and the development of automated databases to replace outmoded record-keeping technologies.

Students who successfully completed the program also reported that their training placed them in a better position to evaluate research proposals submitted by outsiders (some tribes are approached frequently with such requests), manage the work of outside contractors retained to extend the technical expertise of tribal staff, assess job candidates for public health positions, establish and supervise a tribal institutional review board, and enhance their skills in data collection and analysis.

American Indian Tribes and the Hanford Thyroid Disease Study

With the revelations about Hanford's vast releases of radioactive iodine, in 1990 the CDC awarded the Seattle-based Fred Hutchinson Cancer Research Center a $10 million contract to conduct the HTDS. The authorizing language that provided funding for this study specifically required that thyroid disease among Native Americans be studied.

However, no study focusing on thyroid disease among Native Americans was ever completed. The Native American Working Group, the CDC, and the HTDS project team decided early on that the study of Native Americans, if it were to take place, would need to have the same specific aim and statistical power as if it had been established for the study of thyroid disease in the general population. That is, it needed to determine whether the risk of thyroid disease increased due to Hanford's I-131 releases.

As with the study of the general population, the researchers had to determine whether it would be feasible to detect an increase in thyroid disease among Native Americans that could conclusively be attributed to Hanford I-131 exposures. To determine the feasibility of the study, researchers had to establish a suitable study design, establish guidelines for assessing the feasibility of completing the study as designed, and estimate doses of radiation that representative individuals might have received and the size of the population from which a sample might be drawn.

The study design chosen for the general population was a "retrospective cohort" design.[7] The HTDS project team's epidemiological experts determined this would be the most statistically robust approach to establishing a link between Hanford radiation and thyroid disease. In their judgment, with the support of the tribes, it would not be appropriate to use a less statistically robust design for the Native American component, which would relegate the Native component to some "second-class" status. But after extensive analysis using data summaries supplied by eight of the nine tribes, the HTDS project team recommended to the CDC that a "retrospective cohort" study could not be done among Native Americans living near Hanford because too few members of the nine tribes were in the right age groups to yield an adequate level of statistical power in examining the relationship between dose and risk of thyroid disease. In other words, to see an increased level of thyroid disease among Indian people who had a higher dose from Hanford, and a lower level of thyroid disease among Indian people who had received lower Hanford doses, you would need a much larger number of people. This is a classic problem among the small-scale communities with which anthropologists often work—there are simply too few people to apply conventional epidemiological approaches and come up with statistically convincing results.

In the epidemiologists' view, there was no point in doing a study of this sort if it did not yield statistically meaningful results, because it would probably produce a negative conclusion (for example, "Hanford had no effect on thyroid disease among the region's Indian people") when the study was actually inconclusive. The tribes reluctantly agreed in 1999 that it would not be to their benefit to have a great deal of time and money spent only to arrive at an inconclusive result that appeared to be negative.

To get some good out of the thyroid study, the tribes briefly considered the possibility of undertaking epidemiology studies using other designs, including descriptive studies to characterize the historical incidence of thyroid diseases among tribal members, case-control studies to look for differences between the circumstances surrounding tribal members with thyroid disease and other tribal members, and methodological work to improve the epidemiologists' tools for working with small populations. But all these options had significant weaknesses or were ineligible for funding under the existing agreements with and between government agencies.

A descriptive study would have established for each tribe a baseline trend for tribal health planning purposes, but such a study would not necessarily associate thyroid disease among tribal members with Hanford radiation exposures. The DOE-DHHS (Department of Health and Human Services) memorandum of understanding that covered the study specifically required health studies to be tied to Hanford.

A case-control study would have determined whether an association existed between Hanford radiation exposures and cases of thyroid disease among tribal members. The limitations of this approach are many, however. Some tribes did not have any individuals who fit a specific case definition and so could not have participated in the study or benefited from its findings. The number of cases in other tribes would have been so small that scientists would have received the results of case-control comparisons skeptically. More important, a study that simply established an association between thyroid disease and Hanford radiation exposures would do little, by itself, to benefit individuals sick with thyroid disease.

As an alternative to epidemiology studies, the tribes decided to press for intervention services. They reasoned that instead of spending a great deal of money for studies, why not invest in screening tribal members for thyroid disease and treating those for whom screening results indicated a need? But the tribes could not get funding for medical screening. Strenuous efforts were made for several years to get Congress to appropriate funds for a medical screening program—all to no avail.[8]

No epidemiology studies occurred because the populations were too small for adequate statistical power. No medical services were provided because no agency of the US Public Health Service (USPHS) would "take ownership" of the problem. They would not take ownership because even if the public health problem existed (and we don't know whether it existed because the basic descriptive epidemiology has never been done due to funding shortages), it could not be attributed confidently to the DOE's activities at Hanford.

The Hanford Health Information Network's Tribal Services Program

The conflict-riddled HEDR and HTDS projects were not the only efforts to determine the impact of Hanford's off-site releases on its neighbors. In 1991 the DOE's Office of Environment, Health and Safety issued a grant to the Washington State Department of Health Services to fund the Hanford Health Information Network (HHIN). It was already apparent to state officials that information from the federally funded public health activities described above would not be forthcoming for several years, so HHIN represented a state government response on behalf of the Hanford region's residents. The states of Washington, Oregon, and Idaho could make valuable contributions to educating the public about the health effects of ionizing radiation and heightening the awareness of regional health care providers. The funding proposal for HHIN included a Tribal Services Program. The Northwest Area Portland (Oregon) Indian Health Board received a contract for this program, and it promptly set up its own tribal advisory board. Many of this board's initial members were also members of the Native American Working Group established for the HEDR project.

The HHIN worked closely with the Washington State Department of Health to build an Individual Dose Assessment program. This task involved taking the computerized I-131 dose model produced by the HEDR project and adding a survey that individuals could complete. The survey asked questions about where people lived and what they ate during the period when airborne I-131 releases were at their peak. The computer model was then run with these individualized data, and individuals received a printout reporting a likely dose range. Although the project was conceived as a "dial-a-dose" program that would be easy to use and produce results instantly, after it was finally implemented in 1998, it took about a year between the time an individual supplied his or her personal information and when he or she received a dose estimate and accompanying explanation back from the state health department. Despite requests from the Tribal Services Program and the Intertribal Council on Hanford Health Projects, the survey, as designed by the state health departments, did not ask for information about individuals' ethnic backgrounds or tribal affiliations. We have no way of knowing how many tribal members sought or received individualized dose assessments (Cedar River Associates 2000).

Indian Tribes and the Consortium for Risk Evaluation with Stakeholder Participation

In 1994 the DOE's Office of Environmental Management issued a $35 million grant to the Consortium for Risk Evaluation with Stakeholder Participation (CRESP). Medical, environmental, and occupational health scientists at the University of Washington and at several New Jersey–based institutes of higher learning participated in the consortium. The New Jersey–based members focused primarily on the DOE's Savannah River site in South Carolina, while the University of Washington–based members focused mainly on the Hanford site. Tribal members participated in consortium activities beginning in 1995 as part of the consortium's outreach programs rather than as collaborators in the "scientific" investigations. CRESP hosted two invitation-only meetings focusing on tribal concerns—one in Seattle in 1995 and the other at the Umatilla Indian Reservation in 1998. Due in part to the DOE's sponsorship, and partly because of the administrative effort to work simultaneously with nine tribes, these meetings, and other tribal participation in subsequent outreach activities, involved only the three tribes originally designated as "affected" for the restricted purposes of the Nuclear Waste Policy Act. Despite the broad range of health- and safety-related issues that CRESP considered within its domain, the other six tribes acknowledged to have a stake in Hanford-related environmental-health activities had very little interaction with the consortium.

As the consortium itself observed, "[O]ne of the best ways to understand the work of CRESP is to look at the publications of CRESP researchers." Out of more than six hundred published journal articles and book chapters produced by CRESP authors as of November 2004, not a single one focused on Hanford's tribal neighbors.[9]

Indian Tribes and the Agency for Toxic Substances and Disease Registry

The most recent opportunity for tribal involvement in Hanford-related environmental-health activities came through the USPHS's Agency for Toxic Substances and Disease Registry (ATSDR). Congress originally established this agency through Superfund legislation to examine health risks associated with sites on the Superfund National Priorities List for cleanup. Hanford has several National Priorities List sites, as do other parts of the DOE's nuclear-weapons-production complex. Given the number of public health assessments and other public health activities that could potentially arise at these sites, ATSDR and the CDC agreed to combine forces in 1995 to create an advisory commission for involving the public—and state and local governments—in overseeing site-specific public health activities. At Hanford, public involvement took the shape of the Hanford Health Effects Subcommittee. The nine tribal members of the Intertribal Council on Hanford Health Projects were invited to serve as ex officio members of the subcommittee.[10] In addition, two positions reserved for Native

Americans—but not officially representing any tribal government—were filled in 1998.

In 1997 ATSDR funded a cooperative agreement program designed to support tribes in their environmental-health capacity-building efforts over a five-year period. But the funds for the first year of the program were disappointingly modest (each tribe received less than $17,000), and the agency restricted the tribes to assessing the need to improve their capacity to address environmental-health issues. ATSDR officials and tribal representatives anticipated that in the program's next four years, tribes would have the opportunity to create the institutional capacities identified as necessary during the needs-assessment phase. But, as had happened so often before, the promised funding fell short or fell through. Funding for the program's second year was delayed by two years, and the government provided only a tiny amount for the following years—just enough to support travel to meetings to discuss the lack of funding to do any substantive work.

One of ATSDR's main tools for carrying out its mission is called a public health assessment, which follows a regulation-driven set of guidelines for determining its geographic scope, the nature of the data to be collected, pathways to be examined, and so forth. The public health assessment process is generally restricted to secondary data, and in Hanford's case it was arbitrarily limited by ATSDR epidemiologists to a geographic domain that excluded tribal residential centers, despite information from the HEDR project that demonstrated the need for less restrictive borders. Just as important, but more subtle in its effect, the secondary-data limitation penalized the region's tribal members because most data-collection efforts concerning Hanford historically have failed to collect information about race and ethnicity among affected populations, failed to over-sample in areas with known concentrations of tribal residents to assure adequate statistical power in epidemiological analyses, failed to examine pathways of distinctive interest to tribal groups, and failed to acknowledge diversity among the region's tribal residents with respect to lifestyles and health status.

As a result of these multiple failures, the Hanford Public Health Assessment results issued to date say, in effect, that no data are available to suggest adverse impacts to the region's Indian people. As with the thyroid disease study, the inadequacies of the research design and the lack of funding for better approaches have hobbled the investigation. From a tribal perspective, no data are available only because the issue didn't matter much to those who controlled the science at the time, and no funds are available to produce new data.

ATSDR had planned to make a substantial investment in medical monitoring for some of the region's residents. The medical monitoring program aimed to provide surveillance of thyroid abnormalities for people living where airborne iodine-131 doses were the greatest. However, ATSDR designed an eligibility area that included only the Spokane Tribe among all of Hanford's tribal neighbors. Members of other neighboring tribes would have had to establish their eligibility individually, through the Individual Dose Assessment program. That program, as its manager acknowledged, was not designed to account for distinctive traditional lifestyles, and what its design limitations meant for tribal participation in the medical monitoring program was not clear. ATSDR officials said they wanted to find suitable public health activities to meet the needs of tribes who were not eligible to participate in the medical monitoring program. However, the agency was dependent on the DOE for its Hanford-related funding, and funding restrictions imposed by the DOE ultimately prevented the implementation of any medical monitoring program.

Considering these repeated failures, ATSDR has a significant credibility problem. From a tribal perspective, the agency has demonstrated a fundamental inability to deliver on its promises (for example, restricted first-year funding, a two-year delay in delivery of second-year funding, effective exclusion for most tribes from the planned medical monitoring program, inability of public health assessment design to attend to tribal information needs). This track record has left little basis for confidence that the program's original goals are likely to be realized.

Unfinished Business

The Technical Steering Panel completed its work in 1995, but it recognized that several unfinished tasks required further efforts. Several of these involved social scientists. Social scientists were singled out because, aside from the Indian people themselves, the only technical specialists actively advocating on behalf of tribal interests have been the social scientists involved—not the epidemiologists, the toxicologists, the health physicists, the atmospheric scientists, or the fish scientists.

Shortly after the HEDR project began, the CDC asked University of Washington professor Eugene Hunn to provide detailed information based on his research on Native foods, plants, settlement patterns, and fishing practices on the Columbia (see, e.g., Hunn 1991). The University of Colorado's Deward Walker had been involved with the Technical Steering Panel from the very beginning. A tireless advocate for protecting tribal members' health and building tribal organizational capacities for public health, education, and environmental protection, Walker also lent his considerable archive of unpublished field notes to help document fisheries production and consumption levels and fishing sites along the Columbia River system (Walker and Pritchard 1999).

Hunn's and Walker's information proved enormously helpful in subsequent work to improve the dose model for river-borne contamination (Grogan et al. 2002). Researchers had based their initial estimates of Hanford's releases on an elaborate model for airborne releases but a rather simplistic model for river-borne releases. Five of the tribes (Colville, Spokane, Kalispel, Kootenai, and Coeur D'Alene) are primarily "downwind" tribes. That is, doses of Hanford radiation these tribes' members received had a greater contribution from airborne I-131 and less of a contribution from a host of river-borne chemicals. By contrast, members of the Nez Percé, Umatilla, Warm Springs, and Yakama tribes are known to have consumed large quantities of fish that had to swim through Hanford effluent to get to tribal fishing sites. These tribes' members likely received higher doses from the river pathway. The most recent work with the tribes has sought to make the river model more useful in public health activities. Additional research is under way to expand the list of radioactive chemicals traced through the environment, refine the way in which statistical uncertainties are incorporated by the model, and make possible the calculation of organ-specific rather than whole-body doses.

In 1995 the CDC hired LTG Associates, a research and consulting firm whose principals are social scientists, to complete a survey of dairy owners in Hanford's vicinity to fill gaps in milk-production records and make more accurate estimates about where milk consumed by area residents was produced. Consumption of milk and dairy products is important in reconstructing airborne I-131 doses because milk is consumed fresh. Grazing dairy cattle consume any airborne I-131 deposited on pasture grass and pass it on to people through their milk before it has a chance to decay. The report ultimately concluded that not enough information was available to produce more accurate milk-consumption estimates (LTG Associates 1998). Too much time had passed, and reliable records simply did not exist.

The CDC hired William Willard, a professor of American Studies at Washington State University, to collect historical evidence about Hispanic field hands and migrant laborers who might have received prolonged exposures to Hanford releases because of their extended periods of work outdoors. Willard's work has not been published, but reports to the Technical Steering Panel's Task Completion Group indicate that documentation is very sparse concerning Hispanics in the area at the time of the peak releases. Of note are some anecdotal accounts of Japanese Americans working in the orchards of the Columbia, Snake, and lower Yakima river valleys during this time, but no one has undertaken to study this population. Such a study may prove useful because orchard work at the time would have had much in common with Native subsistence practices, especially in terms of time spent out-of-doors and away from the protective shielding of well-insulated buildings.

Medical anthropologist Marie Boutté of the University of Nevada–Reno (whose contribution to this volume is in chapter 9) has long been involved in community-based research around the Nevada Test Site and proposed Yucca Mountain repository site (see, e.g., Boutté 2002). Because of her expertise, the CDC and ATSDR invited her to join the Hanford Health Effects Subcommittee, where she has provided expert social science review of Hanford study plans and preliminary findings.

Lowell Sever, a biological anthropologist and epidemiologist first with Battelle and then with the University of Texas School of Public Health, performed a series of epidemiological studies examining the relationship between radiation exposures and birth defects among children born in Hanford's vicinity (Sever 1995; Sever et al. 1988). This research found that the higher the radiation dose received by parents before their children were born, the more likely the children were to be born with neural tube defects. Defects of the neural tube—which develops into the spinal cord and brain—occur when the tube fails to close completely during the early stages of pregnancy.

Sever and his colleagues investigated whether rates of birth defects among infants in the Hanford area were higher than expected, potentially because of exposure to radioactivity from Hanford operations. They determined the rates of certain birth defects for counties near Hanford and found that although the overall rate of birth defects was not greater than expected, the rate of certain neural tube defects was increased. The researchers compared the study group to other radiation-exposed groups. They considered the Hanford doses too low to account for radiation exposure causing the elevated rates of neural tube defects. The researchers did not have an explanation for the elevated rates but proposed that exposure to agricultural chemicals be considered.

Conclusion

This sprawling historical landscape has several key features. As the Cold War came to a dramatic end in the 1990s, the lid of secrecy about Hanford's contaminated legacy of weapons production blew off, and the magnitude of local burdens borne by Native peoples in the name of national interests became evident. The federal and affected state governments made an enormous investment in environmental and health studies aimed at more precisely characterizing these burdens to determine whether public health interventions might be justified. For the first time, non-Native officials took halting steps to involve affected Native peoples in the investigative work.

Although the involvement of the tribes in these projects is a step forward, from the vantage point of a longtime observer, I find a significant degree of coercion in the way the tribes became involved and participated in the government studies. I believe this coercive quality derives from the adversarial model of blame-affixing risk research that our policy-making institutions favor.

The coercive quality of Native peoples' involvement in the Hanford health studies threatens to subvert the principle of self-determination that has informed federal Indian policy since the 1970s. In delegating their authority to state governments, the DOE and the DHHS effectively abdicated the federal government's trust responsibility to Native tribes. State governments treated the tribes not as sovereign nations but as stakeholder groups no different from other non-Native communities affected by the Hanford releases. If the tribes wanted a role in design and implementation of the research projects on which any hope of remedial action depended, they had to accept the primary role of state governments and, ultimately, accept the states' recommendations for action.

The coercion, then, is an unintended consequence of devolution of federal powers to the states during the Reagan–Bush era, amplified during the Clinton and second Bush administrations. I say "unintended" because the Reagan, first Bush, and Clinton administrations each affirmed a government-to-government policy for interacting with tribal governments rather than funneling all dealings with tribes through the

Bureau of Indian Affairs. At the same time, however, as Corntassel points out, "an era of 'Forced Federalism'…compels Indian nations to negotiate their jurisdictional status regarding taxation, gaming, hunting and fishing rights, and other areas of resource management with state governments which have historically shown disregard for the sovereignty of Indian nations" (2001:2).

In other words, as the Cold War was ending and federal officials made plans for delivering the so-called peace dividend, the US federal government reallocated much of its responsibility for environmental protection and fundamental health and human services investments to the states, without regard for the implications this shift would have for tribal sovereignty. At the same time it was professing to honor "government-to-government" interactions with tribal sovereigns, the federal government was ridding itself of the means to do so.

Tribal involvement in public health activities at Hanford has been narrow in scope, piecemeal, and poorly funded. The federal government has provided little or no support for health interventions designed to attend to specific local circumstances, leaving Pacific Northwest tribes at the mercy of the glacially paced State of Washington for dose-related information that they need to determine an appropriate course of action.

If this sounds like a critique of the federal and state governments, it is—but perhaps not for the usual reasons. The problem rests not with an indifferent and encumbered bureaucracy. No, the problem rests in subscribing to what I have termed elsewhere the "blame-affixing adversarial model" of risk research (Liebow 2002). This model reflects a legalistic principle of fairness: "When something goes wrong, we must identify the guilty party and make her or him pay to set things right." This same principle is a cornerstone of US environmental law: the polluter pays.

The problem with this model is that if the guilt of the alleged guilty party cannot be established with any confidence, or if the party no longer exists, then *nobody* pays, and nothing gets fixed.

To address the health and environmental costs of nuclear weapons production, we simply have to get beyond blame and reframe the problem. Some of the observed harms that Native peoples of the Pacific Northwest (and indeed nuclear Natives everywhere) suffer defy adequate causal attribution. But our inability to identify a single villain does not do away with the harmful effects, nor does it eliminate the need for remedy.

If we try to get beyond blame, we have a much better chance of setting things right. The ultimate goal in making decisions about how best to reduce risk and harm is to do so *fairly*, but not in a legal sense. Local values of fairness will prevail, and decision makers should anticipate (rather than be surprised by or dismissive of) the possibility that different local constituents will clash over what a "fair outcome" is. The problem is not one of affixing blame (who is at fault?) among the parties who disagree. Instead, the problem is one of transforming an unproductive conflict into a productive one. To do so, specialists must relinquish sole authority to determine the legitimacy of problems raised, and they must recognize that their introspection is not an adequate substitute for direct observation of how potentially affected persons judge the burdens and benefits associated with the deployment of dangerous technologies in the name of national defense.

If the Cold War has taught us anything, it has taught us that we must dispense with the need to name the guilty party that caused such substantial harms among us. Complicity is widely shared. A public investment in public health remedies for disenfranchised peoples is required—not because our government institutions are racist but because they are institutions of a racist society that must work its way back from the brink of darkness.

Notes

1. For comparison's sake, the Three Mile Island nuclear power plant accident in 1979 released between 16 and 24 million curies of iodine-131. The 1986 accident at the Chernobyl plant released between 35 and 49 million curies of iodine-131. The nuclear bomb fallout from aboveground tests at the Nevada Test Site (1951–63) released approximately 150 million curies of iodine-131 (Heeb 1994; Heeb and Bates 1994).

2. I say "for the most part" because at least one intentional release of radioactive iodine is well documented. It took place over three days in 1949 to calibrate observational equipment and is known in Hanford lore as the Green Run.

3. For example, treaties reserved Indians' rights to fish at "all the usual and accustomed places." The treaties also protected the privilege to hunt, gather foods and medicines, and graze livestock on "open and unclaimed lands" within areas ceded to the US government.

4. Eventually, the Nez Percé, Umatilla, and Yakama each received substantial funding from the DOE for technical review of environmental and cultural resource–management activities associated with the Hanford site and a comprehensive review of the federal government's uses and abuses of the Columbia River.

5. The Kootenai Tribe of Idaho was not included originally. In 1994 the Kootenai were added to the Native American Working Group, with acknowledgment that their reservation and resident membership were squarely within the HEDR modeling domain.

6. The Native American Working Group was transformed into the Intertribal Council on Hanford Health Projects (ICHHP) in 1994 with the adoption of bylaws and an operations plan endorsed by resolution of the governing bodies of each of the nine tribal members: the Coeur D'Alene Tribe, the Colville Confederated Tribes, the Confederated Tribes of the Umatilla Indian Reservation, the Confederated Tribes and Bands of the Warm Springs Indian Reservation, the Kalispel Tribe, the Kootenai Tribe of Idaho, the Nez Percé Tribe, the Spokane Tribe, and the Yakama Indian Nation. Map 7.1 shows the locations of ICHHP member tribes in relation to the Hanford site and the Columbia River.

7. Epidemiologists use a "retrospective cohort" study design when they want to measure the relative risk of developing a disease as a result of being exposed to an identifiable hazard. Subjects are selected on the basis of whether they have been exposed—in this case, individuals born in the fifteen counties nearest to Hanford during 1944, 1945, and 1946. Their subsequent disease status is compared: Do they have thyroid disease now? If they are no longer living, did they die as a result of thyroid disease? (Kopecky et al. 2004).

8. See *Seattle Post-Intelligencer* 1998.

9. The CRESP website has a searchable database of all its publications (http://www.cresp.org/products.html). The database includes one unpublished 1997 "outreach" workshop proceedings document. The only two peer-reviewed publications having to do with Native Americans are

from investigations associated with the DOE facility at the Idaho National Engineering Laboratory in south-eastern Idaho.

10. Because the subcommittee is chartered with the authority of the Federal Advisory Committee Act, its members are considered "temporary federal employees" while discharging their subcommittee responsibilities, and they are subject to specific legal prohibitions against representing any other governmental jurisdiction while doing so. Thus, for the tribal representatives—as well as representatives of the respective state governments—their presence at subcommittee meetings was in an ex officio, nonvoting capacity.

References

Agency for Toxic Substances and Disease Registry
1998   Estimation of Health Risk Based on Revised Estimates of HEDR Doses for Maximum Representative Individuals Consuming Fish and Waterfowl from the Columbia River: An Evaluation of HEDR Reports on the Columbia River Pathway. Atlanta: Department of Health and Human Services.

Boutté, Marie I.
2002   Compensating for Health: The Acts and Outcomes of Atomic Testing. Human Organization 61(1):41–50.

Cedar River Associates Consulting, Inc.
2000   Hanford Individual Dose Assessment Project, Final Report, December 2000. Electronic document, http://www.doh.wa.gov/EHP/rp/hanford-ida-final.doc, accessed October 23, 2006.

Corntassel, Jeff J.
2001   "Deadliest Enemies" or Partners in the "Utmost Good Faith": Conflict Resolution Strategies for Indian Nation/State Disputes in an Era of Forced Federalism. Paper presented at the Annual Meeting of the American Political Science Association, San Francisco, August 29.

Grogan, Helen, Arthur Rood, Jill Weber Aaneson, and Edward Liebow
2002   A Risk-based Screening Analysis for Radionuclides Released to the Columbia River from Past Activities at the US Department of Energy Nuclear Weapons Site in Hanford, Washington. Atlanta: Centers for Disease Control and Prevention, Radiation Studies Branch.

Heeb, C. M.
1994   Radionuclide Releases to the Atmosphere from Hanford Operations, 1944–1972. PNWD-2222 HEDR, January 1994. Richland, WA: Battelle Pacific Northwest Laboratories.

Heeb, C. M., and D. J. Bates
1994   Radionuclide Releases to the Columbia River from Hanford Operations, 1944–1971. PNWD-2223 HEDR, January 1994. Richland, WA: Battelle Pacific Northwest Laboratories.

Hunn, Eugene S.

1991   NCH'I WANA, the Big River: Mid-Columbia People and Their Land. Seattle: University of Washington Press.

Kopecky, Kenneth J., Scott Davis, Thomas E. Hamilton, Mark Saporito, and Lynn Onstad

2004   Estimation of Thyroid Radiation Doses for the Hanford Thyroid Disease Study: Results and Implications for Statistical Power of the Epidemiological Analyses. Health Physics 87(1):15–32.

Liebow, Edward B.

1997   An Evaluation of CDC's Community-Based Public Health Practice Training Program. Prepared for the Centers for Disease Control and Prevention, Region X, Seattle. Contract No. 200-97-0921. Seattle, WA: Centers for Disease Control.

2002   Environmental Anthropology. *In* The Handbook of Environmental Psychology: Environmental Psychology to Make a Difference. R. Bechtel and A. Churchman, eds. Pp. 147–59. New York: Wiley and Sons.

LTG Associates

1998   Milk Producers Survey Final Report. Prepared for the Centers for Disease Control and Prevention, Radiation Studies Branch, Atlanta. Contract No. 200-95-0906. Atlanta: Centers for Disease Control.

Seattle Post-Intelligencer

1998   Congress Denies Money to Check Health of Hanford Downwinders. October 5: B3.

Sever, L. E.

1995   Looking for Causes of Neural Tube Defects: Where Does the Environment Fit In? Environmental Health Perspectives 103, suppl. 6:165–71.

Sever, L. E., N. A. Hessol, E. S. Gilbert, and J. M. McIntyre

1988   The Prevalence at Birth of Congenital Malformations in Communities Near the Hanford Site. American Journal of Epidemiology 127(2):243–54.

Walker, Deward E., Jr., and Lawrence W. Pritchard

1999   Estimated Radiation Doses to Yakama Tribal Fishermen: A Test Application of the Columbia River Dosimetry Model Developed for the Hanford Environmental Dose Reconstruction Project. Boulder, CO: Walker Research Group, Ltd.

Wu, Patricia

2000   Thyroid Disease and Diabetes. Clinical Diabetes 18(1):38–42.

e i g h t
From Cold War Complex
to Nature Preserve

Diagnosing the Breakdown
of a Multi-Stakeholder Decision Process
and Its Consequences for Rocky Flats

Theresa Satterfield and Joshua Levin

Rocky Flats Environmental Technology Site sits on a mesa 16 miles north and west of Denver, Colorado, in the western United States. Due to its proximity to Denver, in 1995 the US Department of Energy (DOE) named Rocky Flats the most dangerous facility in the nation's Cold War complex of nuclear weapons production sites. Operating from 1952 through 1989, the plant manufactured the detonating devices at the core of hydrogen bombs. In January 1992, following a series of protests against the plant, an FBI raid, and subsequent charges of safety violations, the DOE announced that production at Rocky Flats would permanently cease. As recently as 1993, the plant housed more than 14 tons of plutonium (some in metal, the rest in compounds and mixtures) and more than 7 tons of highly enriched uranium. In 1994 the DOE, in conjunction with EG&G (the aerospace and engineering corporation that had previously held the Department of Defense production contracts at Rocky Flats) estimated that cleanup would cost $36 billion and projected an astonishing fifty years for cleanup after closure. In 1997 Energy Secretary Federico Péna (a former Denver mayor), announced that instead of EG&G, Kaiser-Hill would be responsible for a $7.3 billion cleanup and closure, scheduled for 2006.

In early 2005, an article in the *Bulletin of the Atomic Scientists* observed that regulatory law allows for considerable latitude in compliance regarding the cleanup of Rocky Flats (Moore 2005). In the most recent period, the DOE decided that the site

Figure 8.1. Barrels of nuclear waste were frequently stored outside, where they corroded and leaked radionuclides into the soil and water. Photo courtesy of the US Department of Energy, Rocky Flats/DOE, 1962

would become a wildlife refuge, thereby "rebranding" Rocky Flats as a benign nature preserve while simultaneously avoiding the more stringent cleanup standards necessary when residential or agricultural use is expected. The contracted cleanup itself was constrained early on by a limited budget that could be realized only at the expense of a "legal" yet suboptimal soil cleanup level. That is, a "within-budget" cleanup was achieved by altering the depths at which cleanup would occur. Surface soil up to a depth of 3 feet would be cleaned to 50 picocuries of plutonium per gram of soil; whereas soil between 3 and 6 feet deep could contain as much as 1,000 picocuries of plutonium per gram of soil. No limit was set for levels below 6 feet. To place these guidelines in perspective, the plutonium standard for the Nevada Test Site is 200 picocuries per gram of soil, whereas 10 picocuries is slated for cleanup at the Lawrence Livermore Laboratory in California's Bay Area. In the words of the above-cited article, "Plutonium-239 has a half-life of 24,400 years. To allow high levels of it to remain in the site's soil, which will likely be stirred up by humans and animals in the long term, demonstrates a wanton disregard for the well-being of unsuspecting future generations" (54).

An abiding puzzle for this chapter is understanding how this outcome occurred. To a certain extent, such an outcome depends on the silencing or watering down of public scrutiny of cleanup. Yet Rocky Flats was well known as a site of protest in the 1980s and a model of public participation in cleanup decisions in the decades that followed (Whicker 2004). We contend that the quiescence of public scrutiny did not happen by overtly coercive actions; nor was public scrutiny suppressed per se. Rather, in time, public-participation efforts aimed at guiding a thorough cleanup broke down in that the capacity to resist undesirable outcomes and maintain the integrity of a collective community voice was diminished. What follows herein is an effort to diagnose that breakdown. Using our ethnographic record, we propose a breakdown "trajectory" applicable to Rocky Flats and possibly useful to those studying public participation or in need of diagnostic tools that help explain at what stage and why public participation sometimes fails. To this end, this chapter also echoes the findings of chapters herein by Liebow; Johnston, Dawson, and Madsen; and Dawson and Madsen, all of whom detail the legacy and plethora of scientific studies of impacts that obfuscate rather than reveal or articulate pressing community concerns and injuries.

Our particular thesis is that public participation at Rocky Flats came to be replaced early on with a program of old-style risk communication, understood here as "all we have to do is teach them the science" literacy training, and agreement will follow. This approach was "successful" to the extent that much of the involved public achieved an impressive level of technical sophistication. However, this demonstrated scientific literacy did not lead to diminished conflict or agreement about how to manage the risks posed by residual contaminants at the site. Instead, improved stakeholder understanding of the risk estimates, as well as most facets of risk assessment, appeared coterminous with increased conflict and a crisis in confidence in the participation process itself. We find that the periods of concentrated conflict, stress, and intermittent paralysis of public participation in decision making at Rocky Flats were produced by a lack of transparency as concerns budgetary limitations and by the difficulty regulatory agents, the contractor, and the involved public all had in addressing the tradeoffs intrinsic to the cleanup. A tradeoff can be thought of as a decision about how much of what to do when and where (Gregory 2000). Discussion became paralyzed by this tradeoff avoidance because the very values or ethical positions central to the tradeoff dilemma had to masquerade as scientific points about different cleanup options. This situation in turn produced two central outcomes: First, these masquerading or "fugitive" values fostered a competitive (and sometimes detrimental) exploitation by all parties of technical expertise; second, the opportunity for democratic public involvement was eroded by the near-constant reconstitution of public groups into lay specialists and experts only as part of an elusive effort to realize technical agreement about cleanup decisions. We suspect that this pattern is not unique to Rocky Flats and thus conclude with an explanatory schema or trajectory of breakdown that might help prevent similar problems at other DOE sites, many of which have yet to be remediated.

Methods and Context

The arguments provided herein are based on field observations at stakeholder meetings and interviews with key stakeholders. Field observations involved attendance at ongoing group meetings for an eighteen-month period. Thirty-five interviews were conducted by occasionally one and usually both of the chapter's authors; the specific interviewees and their group affiliations are listed in table 8.1. Interviewees included virtually all parties active in public involvement during the study period—namely staff, individual citizens, and activists affiliated with the Citizen's Advisory Board (CAB); appointed representatives of surrounding municipal governments (organized as the Rocky Flats Council of Local Governments); and representatives of Kaiser-Hill (the cleanup contractor), the DOE, the Environmental Protection Agency (EPA), and the Colorado Department of Public Health and Education. Further interviews included key representatives from the Rocky Flats Cleanup Agreement Focus Group (RFCA Focus Group) and the Radionuclide Soil Action Level Working Group, as well as the Decontamination and Decommissioning Working Group, the Stewardship Working Group, and the Rocky Flats History Project.

Our initial mandate in beginning the study was to observe and describe the process of public involvement at the site. Early on, it was evident that virtually all involved stakeholders were discontent with the public participation program. Interviews thus focused on the reported (retrospective) histories of participation, the technical and democratic problems of cleanup, specific events or qualities that characterized the local experience of public involvement, and stakeholder expectations as to how decisions should be (or had been) made.

Regulatory Law, Public Science, and Scientific Literacy at Rocky Flats

Regulatory law, as set out by the EPA, currently requires that the radiation risks to which the public is exposed fall within a 10^{-4} to 10^{-6} risk range—that is, a 1 in 10,000 to 1 in 1,000,000 cancer-mortality risk. Estimating low-dose impacts has historically been based on the "linear hypothesis," wherein extrapolations from high-dose exposure (such as that suffered by victims of the 1945 bombings of Hiroshima and Nagasaki) are used to project low-dose exposure.[1] The estimations seek designations of comparatively safe doses, yet extrapolations from "high" to "low" also suggest that all levels of exposure are, to varying degrees, detrimental to human health. By 1980 several prominent regulatory scientists argued that the linear model was "not appropriate...[because] adverse health effects increased very gradually at low doses and followed a linear model only at much higher levels" (Walker 2000:101). As of the mid-1990s, dramatically different opinions existed on the question of low-dose effects. Some "held that even the energy in very low doses of radiation could damage DNA strands in cells [and that] mutations that occurred in this way could lead to cancer"

Table 8.1. Number and Group Affiliation of Interviewees

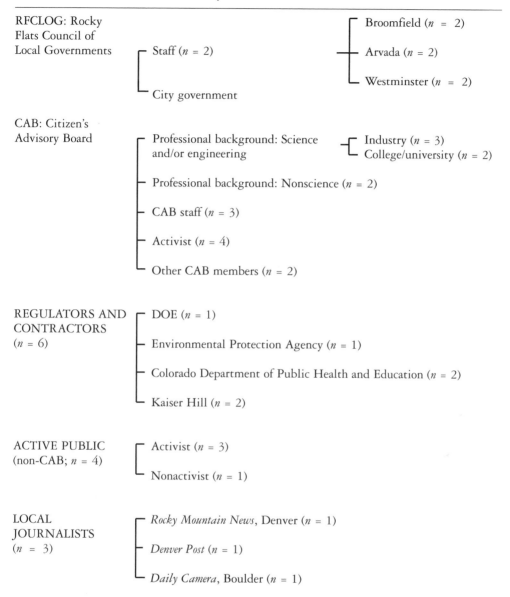

RFCLOG: Rocky Flats Council of Local Governments

- Staff (n = 2)
- City government
  - Broomfield (n = 2)
  - Arvada (n = 2)
  - Westminster (n = 2)

CAB: Citizen's Advisory Board

- Professional background: Science and/or engineering
  - Industry (n = 3)
  - College/university (n = 2)
- Professional background: Nonscience (n = 2)
- CAB staff (n = 3)
- Activist (n = 4)
- Other CAB members (n = 2)

REGULATORS AND CONTRACTORS (n = 6)

- DOE (n = 1)
- Environmental Protection Agency (n = 1)
- Colorado Department of Public Health and Education (n = 2)
- Kaiser Hill (n = 2)

ACTIVE PUBLIC (non-CAB; n = 4)

- Activist (n = 3)
- Nonactivist (n = 1)

LOCAL JOURNALISTS (n = 3)

- *Rocky Mountain News*, Denver (n = 1)
- *Denver Post* (n = 1)
- *Daily Camera*, Boulder (n = 1)

RELATED DISCUSSION AND SPIN-OFF GROUPS

- Decommissioning and Decontamination Working Group (mainly staff scientists and key literate public stakeholders)
- RSAL Working Group (mainly scientifically literate CAB members)
- RFCA Focus Group (mainly CAB and RFCLOG members and Kaiser-Hill representatives)
- Stewardship Working Group
- RF History Project

N = 35

(143). Others held that "cells had amazingly sophisticated repair mechanisms" and that "small doses of radiation [might even be] beneficial" (144).

Paralleling this expert argument, many scholars have noted that contestations about the legitimacy of science are now ubiquitous in public life and that we have indeed entered the age of debates about risk (Beck 1992, 1999; Krimsky and Golding 1992; Wynne 1996; Yearley 2000). This fact is most evident when the matter at hand involves nuclear or chemical exposures, or more recently genetically modified technologies (Wynne 2001). For instance, much of the public disagrees with the expert community about the safety of radioactive isotopes if the source or location of those materials is also associated with weapons development, nuclear power, and nuclear waste. Moreover, it is well established that much of the general public distrusts government agencies assigned with the management of these technologies (see, e.g., Slovic 1999). Scientists and regulators have often viewed this distrust and difference of opinion as (1) a problem of scientific and technical illiteracy on the public's part (a failure to understand the science and hence a fearful or resistant attitude) and/or (2) a problem of poor education and communication on the part of experts. This view persists despite the growing expertise in risk communication (Morgan et al. 2002; National Research Council 1996) and the many calling for public involvement at the earliest possible stages and openly rejecting the "public deficit" model of citizen knowledge (Irwin and Wynn 1996; Jasanoff and Wynne 1998).[2]

At Rocky Flats, the long-standing dialogue between the DOE, EPA, and multiple citizens produced an "involved public" with an impressive level of technical expertise as concerns both cleanup operations and probabilistic risk estimates. Questions about the effects of varied decommissioning strategies, the implications of wind patterns on contamination dispersal in future open space, and the long-term health effects of low-dose exposure from different levels of plutonium concentration in the soil were oft and articulately debated. Across all interviews with nonspecialist members of the involved public, only one offered "inaccurate" information about the behavioral attributes of radiation or the meaning of the linear hypothesis, background radiation, exposure pathways, comparative risk ratings, and the probabilistic ranges of risks that mattered for regulatory purposes. Most understood the difference between alpha particles and gamma rays and the kinds of mitigating protection each required. Importantly, most participants were dose sensitive in that they understood fully the relationship between dose and hazard (Kraus et al. 1992). Some could recite the comparative risks of different naturally and non-naturally occurring forms of radiation exposure as an expression of either millirem dose annually or cumulative lifetime dose. Discussions of dose tended, in fact, toward the more arcane and context-specific influences of exposure, such as the duration and intensity of exposure (chronic versus acute), pathways of inhalation or ingestion, physical attributes of the contaminant (gamma ray or alpha particle), and the age or vulnerability of the dose recipient.

It is difficult to determine precisely when and how this high epistemological standard and accompanying technical discourse among public participants were established at Rocky Flats. Indeed, some degree of specialization is to be expected across all groups engaged in what has been termed citizen or public science (Irwin 1995). But at Rocky Flats, two additional points are relevant. First, a more technically amenable and focused Citizen's Advisory Board (CAB) appears to have replaced the activist climate that succeeded in shutting down the plant and pressing the DOE for a thorough cleanup between the early and late 1990s. Several longtime CAB members identified a gradual decrease in community and antinuclear activism among CAB participants and attendees at open meetings. One explained:

> There were a lot of people who had been historically involved from an activist perspective. That wasn't all that was on the CAB, but that certainly influenced the sort of flavor of it. We have a lot more now who have no historical connection to the work at the site, or the issue in any way. And some who I would characterize as being probably more conservative.

Second, as the site began to approach a 2006 or thereafter cessation of cleanup, the pressure to resolve some of the more trenchant debates—debates about how safe was safe enough, how best to proceed with the decommissioning of buildings and the decontamination of soil, and the viability of institutional controls for monitoring residual risks—escalated.

In this tense decision-necessary climate, the "rationalizing" forces of science were expected to resolve these debates. Advocating the "best available science" as a guiding principle for cleanup decisions is a laudable goal, and cleanup—most would agree—should be guided by a high standard of technical rigor. But such efforts do not necessarily forge a more effective public process. Indeed, high technical competency across nonspecialist stakeholders may well be an indicator of increased conflict.

Ultimately, we found that it was not a failure of scientific literacy at Rocky Flats—that is, a failure for the involved public to "understand what is meant by the numbers"—that exacerbated conflicts about cleanup (Fischhoff 1995). Rather, it was a problem of tradeoff paralysis. That is, across all interviews and all meetings of the period, one single variable appeared to drive most of the conflict, stress, and at times breakdowns of public meetings at Rocky Flats. This variable was the pronounced difficulty that representatives of the DOE and the EPA, the contractor (Kaiser-Hill), and the involved public had in both addressing and reconciling the tradeoffs intrinsic to cleanup. A sometimes-agonizing struggle (locally referred to as "brain damage" or the hard work of public discussion) evolved from efforts to resist, avoid, or circumvent any real and ostensible limitations on cleanup of the site and hence efforts to resist making difficult tradeoffs involving particular gains or sacrifices.

The tradeoff impasse at Rocky Flats was as follows: Vocal critics of proposed cleanup activities rejected fiscal and temporal limitations and maintained that the agencies and contractor must spend whatever it took to clean up the site. In contrast, agency representatives and the contractor consistently worked from the assumption that they would pursue the best possible cleanup within the limitations of available time (a cleanup deadline of 2006) and, importantly, funding. Clear statements regarding these divergent views follow. For example, one member of the CAB stated that negotiations implying tradeoffs were patently moot:

> You know, this whole issue about what the cleanup level's gonna be. I don't
> get that. I'm like, are you gonna clean it up or are you not gonna clean it up.
> Why are we negotiating what the cleanup level's gonna be? I don't get that. If
> I can go out there with a Geiger counter when you're gone, am I gonna get a
> click? What, what are we, what are we negotiating?

Whereas a key agency representative from the DOE stated the following during an interview:

> It's all about this tradeoff. But certain groups reject the timeline and reject the
> budget. The fact is that the fiscal constraints to this contract are so blatantly
> real that we just have to emphasize: Seven billion[3] dollars is what [Rocky Flats
> is] getting, it's irresponsible to ask for more. And that message has been con-
> veyed by the congressional office, [and] on a one-on-one basis to some key peo-
> ple. But, you know, the way I look at it is: the government has basically said
> that they're willing to give Rocky Flats seven billion dollars to clean this place
> up. And that's a whole lot of money. And we can get a great cleanup for that.
> And there's a lot of possible outcomes on what the end-state looks like.

Over the multiyear period of public involvement at Rocky Flats, the necessity of making time and cost limitations clear was chronically impaired. To some extent, the contractor and the two agencies found themselves in a quandary by virtue of the expectation that they could minimize public conflict and simultaneously cope with a wide range of technical and financial uncertainties. In regard to the first expectation—minimizing public conflict—we were explicitly informed by agency personnel that the DOE and Congress had produced an agreement that guaranteed yearly appropriation of funds for the Rocky Flats cleanup as long as three conditions were met: (1) that the cleanup be completed by 2006; (2) that the cost and scope of the cleanup be contained to the allocated 1997 amount; and (3) that conflict in the community be curtailed (particularly given the history of public protest at Rocky Flats). This agreement, made in trust, was validated de facto through ongoing annual appropriations to Rocky Flats, but as those funds were "conditional," the contractor and agencies had to "minimize conflict" while meeting bottom-line budget limitations regardless of any certainty that cleanup could actually be achieved with the available resources and within the agreed-upon timeline.

Those who study the difficulty people have making tradeoffs recognize that decisions become vastly more complicated when the degree of uncertainty about whether actions taken will deliver the desired consequences is high (Gregory 2002). The complexity of tradeoff considerations and their intersection with a heightened scientific discourse was nowhere more evident than in the multiyear discussion among stakeholders about radionuclide soil action level, or RSAL. This level refers to the maximum volume of radioactive materials found in the soil above which cleanup or removal of that soil is required. The implications for where the RSAL is set at Rocky Flats are enormous, as soil cleanup represents the single largest and likely most expensive remediation action at the site. Yet determining a RSAL level is a complex and uncertain science. Anticipated exposure doses from soil depend on a wide set of variables and assumptions including but not limited to:

- Wind patterns, hydrology, soil morphology, slope, and so on, each of which contribute to a particular pattern of soil migration and contaminant concentration within and beyond the site

- Expectations about the typical future users of the site (suburban residents, subsistence ranchers, recreational users of open space, or dirt-eating children)[4]

- User activities and hence their rate of inhalation or ingestion-derived exposure

- Setting a safe maximum annual dose (a difficult task given the uncertainties of hypothetical dose reconstructions and the heterogeneity of contaminant concentration).

The DOE had initially proposed a maximum allowable plutonium RSAL of 651 picocuries per gram ($pCig^{-1}$) of soil. Those rallying for a conservative RSAL (and hence a more thorough cleanup of soil) hoped that the "subsistence farmer" ("resident rancher") affiliated with the 35 $pCig^{-1}$ would become the prototypical future user. (A resident rancher was defined as a person who lived full-time on the land and would grow and consume products from that land.) Others promoted less conservative scenarios, including RSALs for a wildlife worker and a recreationalist. (A wildlife worker would manage the open space refuge that Rocky Flats would become, spending approximately forty hours a week on the land. A recreationalist might only occasionally hike, jog, or mountain bike on the same land.) Specialist and nonspecialist parties worked closely on these questions for three years, yet impasse persisted because in part the contractor and especially the DOE were ambivalent about making the cost/time/RSAL tradeoff explicit. During interviews, agency parties and the contractor represented the concrete reality of fiscal constraints as self-evident and thus not worthy of public discussion. Yet their silence on this point during public meetings helped create a suspicion vacuum wherein several members of the public regarded the agents as having actively concealed the "true" nature of the fundamentally limiting "time and cost" variables. A ubiquitous manifestation of this situation was widespread suspicion about the possibility of "behind-closed-door" negotiations. The assumption was that, at the moment of contracting an initial budget, federal parties had acted unethically and against the well-being of the local community and that under these "clandestinely established" budgetary constraints, public participation was nothing more than a vacuous gesture.

Interestingly, and despite the DOE and contractor's position that the fiscal limitations, hence the necessary tradeoffs, ought to have been self-evident, explicit discussion of tradeoffs did not occur until late in the second year of RSAL discussions. The meeting was significant enough for the DOE project manager to describe the exchange as a "momentous discussion" and to characterize it as "throwing a dead rat on the table"—the dead rat being the fundamental limitations posed by a cost ceiling and hence the need for tradeoffs. The exchange recorded below occurred midway through the meeting; it begins with a longtime citizen-participant in discussions about the future user of the site:

> *Citizen:* This is presumably a dead horse but I hope it is not.... The RAC study [the study that produced an estimated RSAL of 35 pCig^{-1}] used a resident rancher because it is most conservative.[5] Is that [possibility] really dead? We can't possibly say what will happen in five hundred years.

> *EPA staff:* We base our assessment on reasonable maximum risk, but I don't think a [resident] rancher is that—I won't tell my boss that. Plus, a wildlife-refuge worker is still conservative and reasonable.

> *Citizen:* Would Christopher Columbus have been able to tell us how we are going to use the US in five hundred years?... That is totally unreasonable for you to say that it is reasonable.

> *DOE staff:* The agencies are constrained by laws, regulations, and policy. Furthermore, we have to strike a balance here between what can be done in this place, at this time, and with this money.... To put it bluntly, the RAC study was "unconstrained." We don't have that freedom. In the interest of intellectual honesty, we have to work within these limitations.

The DOE representative's emphasis on "intellectually honesty" brought the fiscal constraints around cleanup out from the shadows of "technical" and "scientific" discussions of RSAL and future-use determinations. Through this candor, he attempted to include the attending public in the burden of these constraints so that more detailed decisions concerning tradeoffs within the established limitations could begin to be addressed. His candor was greeted with suspicion, however, as heretofore discussion of cost tradeoffs in the form of budgetary limitations had been absent. All RSAL discussions had been couched in the language of technical defensibility of the RSAL modeling studies.

At the next public meeting, the above moment of candor was no longer evident; avoidance of discussions of tradeoffs and the underpinning budgetary limitations were again the prevailing norm. On the new occasion (below), the lack of transparency about tradeoffs leads participants to doubt the legitimacy of their participation in the first place. Note in particular that the speaker's comments reflect his now-derailed expectation that as an active public participant, his comments will be influential and his stated awareness that the limits of the cleanup were predetermined by political and economic decisions beyond any citizen sphere of influence. This view is forcefully expressed below in veiled accusations of foul play and open statements of dissatisfaction that lead, eventually, to the request that citizens be permitted an opportunity to address the "real" principals—decision makers (that is, members of Congress responsible for the initial budget allocation):

> The decision-making process is a lot more complicated, and there is a lot of subtlety, and there are a lot of pressures that are hidden to the people that come to these meetings. One of the reasons that I am interested in having a meeting with the principals [those in Congress responsible for allocating the cleanup budget] is because I think that they're entitled to hear from people that are unhappy with some of the decisions we've already been told have been made. They're entitled to hear from us, not just from the coordinators [onsite agency personnel]. The coordinators are clearly not the only decision makers about the soil action levels—despite the kind of neat logic of your presentations. Take one item—which is the decision I've heard criticized a great deal, and that's the decision about the [future-user] scenario that will be employed for calculating the soil action levels. We've been told that decision has been made. There's a good bit of unhappiness in this room about that decision and in the people that come to these meetings. And I suspect that there will be, beyond this, when the news is available to people about the decision that has supposedly been made. But how—I'm really, I'm really, really interested, how that decision was made. Who made it? If we can understand who is weighing in, then we know that we need to approach those people…'cause those people are participating in the decision. I really, I really want to know. I think we're entitled to know.

The EPA representative responds to the accusation that RSAL levels were predetermined. In so doing, he articulates the regulatory rationale for the decision and argues that although the decision may not be consistent with the priorities of critics, the public voice has nevertheless been central to the decision-making process. It is instructive to note that in this subsequent exchange, all earlier efforts to discuss tradeoffs have been dropped; discussion has returned to or been converted to a debate about the technical defensibility of different future-user scenarios. A discourse of policy and scientific standards is used to neutralize the underlying tradeoff conflict:

> *DOE staff:* I think the retort is a bit disingenuous. There's been a lot of process to decide what assumptions we should use to develop the numbers. We agreed that we needed to make assumptions about land use to develop the numbers. We ultimately, as a result of this process, are developing like five or six sets of numbers. And that's great. But the principal recommendations on things like land use, or the risk or dose basis for the number, are not coming from the principals. We're not all sitting around in our showers and just deciding what sounds good. There's been a lot of process here. There's been the working group. There's meetings—technical meetings every day. And so ultimately it comes to convergence at some point. When this came up [previously], I didn't

want to mislead you; say, "No, it's wide open. We got the whole table and anything goes." Could a [RSAL] number anywhere on that table come out? Yes. Do we think that the number is going to probably coincide with the row that says "wildlife refuge worker"? That's probably going to be our recommendation unless some new information comes to bear that just throws that out the window. So, semantically, has a decision been made? No. Does it look like the Rocky Flats Cleanup Agreement principals are going to recommend that scenario as the basis for the RSAL. Yes.

Citizen: You're going 'round in circles. Someone wrote down in the write-up, whatever you call it—that was a decision. Now we are trying to find out who made that decision?

DOE staff: No, you're hearing what you want to hear. There's been a lot of process to develop information to determine what the most likely future land use would be. It doesn't mean that the outcome was always the one you wanted, but you absolutely influenced how these decisions were made.

To summarize these points, a central part of the above-sited trust compact made with Rocky Flats federal (congressional) parties was that budgetary and time limitations would be met at the same time that public dissatisfaction would be contained. Given this mandate, the cost limitations eventually had to be broached by agency personnel local to Rocky Flats. Yet some public participants reacted so strongly and suspiciously to the meeting wherein the suggestion of a cost tradeoff was made explicit that thereafter mention of tradeoff limitations were again avoided. Discussions of tradeoffs were also quickly and easily converted to accusations of deal brokering between Congress and the agencies. To both avoid public controversy and cope with numerous technical unknowns, the central issue of economic and temporal limitations was not, and perhaps could not be, addressed directly. Instead, it was couched within the language of the RSAL and future-user decisions. This sublimation of the basic conflict provided the only means though which discussion could proceed and anticipated public resistance could be postponed and contained.

Why do tradeoffs so matter? Practically speaking, tradeoffs are difficult because they are linked to ethical positions. We care, often deeply, about achieving outcome A over outcome B because the former is seen as fulfilling a desired value or ethical position more fully than the latter (Gregory 2002). Achieving one objective or valued goal comes at the cost of giving up something else of importance. This situation is most evident in the RSAL debate where the enduring conflict involved the identity of the "future user." At stake here is a fundamental ethical, not technical, concern: Should the RSAL level be based on protecting the health of the most vulnerable future user (a child or rancher) or the health of the average citizen (a visitor or temporary wildlife worker)? Yet rather than discussing the tradeoffs so as to render explicit the values or ethical position of different participants, public discussion fell into the default position of trying to utilize scientific debate to defuse tradeoff conflict. The RSAL discussions became paralyzed by the sublimated value issues because the ethical positions central to the tradeoff dilemma had to masquerade as points about the scientific defensibility of RSAL modeling parameters. Critical members of the involved public also responded negatively and with suspicion to the DOE's introduction of cost tradeoffs precisely because they were being asked to engage in a "taboo" or nonnegotiable tradeoff, borrowing Fiske and Tetlock's (1997) term (see also Baron and Leshner 2000; Baron and Spranca 1997).

Taboo tradeoffs arise when people are asked to pit an important ethic intrinsic to a tradeoff against a qualitatively different category of value. Such tradeoffs lead respondents to believe they must sacrifice a deeply held principle in order to participate in any negotiation, tradeoff, or decision process. This is particularly the case when strongly held normative positions from one sphere of life (for example, beliefs about justice, fairness, and democracy) come up against utilitarian values such as cost or time concerns. Such tradeoffs are often regarded as undermining the integrity of the first set of values (justice, fairness, etc.). For example, to compare or evaluate the importance of one's children in juxtaposition to the cost of raising them is morally offensive to most people. Acts of this kind reflect back to those making the tradeoff something "ugly" about themselves or their personal integrity precisely because they are asked to behave as though they are willing to transgress important norms, including the idea that "parenthood-childhood is priceless." In the Rocky Flats case, public participants acted on the premise that they were being asked to "sacrifice" human health for "dollars." Moreover, when faced with tradeoffs that are actually or ostensibly taboo, people often react with a common set of "hallmark" reactions. Several of the hallmarks, identified by Baron and Spranca (1997) and Fiske and Tetlock (1997), were evident at Rocky Flats:

Absolutism or Quantitative Insensitivity

This is the "all-or-nothing" quality of responses to taboo tradeoffs. It can be understood as the tendency to believe that a small-scale expression of an act is just as bad as a large-scale one. The woman quoted above who negated negotiations with a concise "Are you going to clean it up or not?" is a case in point. Under these circumstances, it becomes very difficult to discuss the "wisdom" of variations in scale. In the RSAL case, the DOE began with a comparatively high RSAL number (651 pCig^{-1}). What followed, save for a brief and then erased discussion, was several years of public effort to criticize the technical viability of that number and in so doing to "use science" to drive the number as low as possible. This is a perfectly understandable strategic reaction. But is it wise for those involved? If the DOE had discussed, early and clearly, the cost limitations within which they were working, a different conversation might have occurred. Driving the RSAL as low as strategically possible through the development of studies of user models (for example, the resident rancher at 35 pCig^{-1}) might have been replaced by a better quality conversation on cost and scale. For instance, if a soil cleanup based on a 35 pCig^{-1} RSAL were to cost X dollars while a 40 pCig^{-1} RSAL would cost 30 percent less yet represent only an infinitesimal change in health risk, it might be wise to spend the 30 percent saved elsewhere. (There are often diminishing returns for dollars spent—that is, the first half of dollars spent realizes huge gains whereas the second half of gain-per-dollar outcome is much poorer.) That 30 percent expenditure might have gone to realize a better health-protecting gain (the value behind the tradeoff) elsewhere.

Resistance

People often refuse to believe they must face a tradeoff in the first place and thus suspend the tradeoff/decision-making process until a more palatable option can be found. There were many expressions of this pattern at Rocky Flats. Most obviously, the wish to talk to federal parties responsible for the initial budget was driven in part by tradeoff resistance and by participants' understandable reluctance to accept as given a limited cleanup in the absence of legitimate discussion of the historical basis of those limits. In the words of one CAB member protesting against cost and regulatory limitations: "This can be influenced by the community, and you could make these kinds of recommendations to your bosses [reject the limitations on our behalf]. That is not how this decision has to be made."

The Slippery Slope Dilemma

This is the belief (and sometimes very real possibility) that any move in a particular direction will lead to or is symbolic of devastating future outcomes. The slippery slope problem is akin to legal decisions established on the basis of a minor infraction but ultimately contentious because they hint at the undermining of such inalienable rights as equality across all persons or free speech. This dilemma was well represented at Rocky Flats by the widespread fear that a poor RSAL would set a dangerous precedent for all other as yet unremediated sites in the DOE complex.

Given the thorny nature of some tradeoffs, those whose regulatory mandate is to ensure that the tradeoffs are made must develop tactics to cope with the "perilous social predicament of attempting a taboo tradeoff."[6] Equally, they must address the sense of betrayal and "indignation of observers who learn that sacrosanct normative boundaries have been transgressed" (Fiske and Tetlock 1997:285). This quandary often means that agency representatives (the tradeoff brokers) must adapt several tactics to deflect blame and ensure peace. These tactics include compartmentalizing categories of discussion by explicitly invoking distinctions between spheres of consideration and negating the possibility of discussing two linked points simultaneously (saying, for example, "That's a justice concern; we're only talking here about technical issues"). Other tactics involve obfuscating the tradeoff and procrastination (257). This last point is taken up further in the section below.

Fugitive Values and the Paralysis of Public Discussion

Thus far we have sketched out some evidence for a particular sequence of behavior in the Rocky Flats case. First, a state of proficient or increased scientific literacy among public participants was widely evident. While positive in some respects, this state can also be attributed to the heightened attention granted to technical discussion of cleanup options due to the belief that a more rational, hence scientific discussion of posed options would serve to diffuse the escalating emotional climate engendered by difficult decision processes and the related problem of tradeoff avoidance. The most important aspect of this problem is the perennial "bogged-down" state it produces. Wishing that public discussion venues be cleansed of all but technical discussions does not make it so. Many risk scholars have clearly and repeatedly demonstrated that all risk debates are at their core value or ethical debates and thus it is virtually impossible to suspend or eliminate (nontechnical) aspects of the debate. But when attempted, what invariably surfaces instead is a bogged-down state, manifest at Rocky Flats as a three-year debate and restudy of the technical defensibility of the soil action level (a point also elaborated below). This bogged-down state is in fact a state of "fugitive values." The deeply embedded value positions that make the decision and tradeoff processes difficult in the first place go underground but do not go away. Instead, they entangle and even paralyze public discussion precisely because they infuse every point of discussion about ostensibly technical problems. These values in operation are fugitive in the sense that they move from place to place and appear in a fleeting form without ever being brought into the open where they can often be put to constructive (and ultimately more democratic) use.

Consider, for example, a public meeting at Rocky Flats that we attended early in the study period. At this meeting, the facilitator announced unambiguously that all discussions in the meeting were to remain focused on technical points. "Value-driven discussions" were isolated and excluded as "explicitly off-limits." Similarly, most public participants recognized that over time a silencing of value positions had taken place. However, agreement among public parties on whether this outcome was pejorative or successful was mixed. Some CAB members regretted, although tacitly accepted, the fact that value or ethical debates had been eliminated as viable points of discussion:

> Well, in the past there's been a lot of ethical, moral, philosophical discussion.
> If you look back at statements by the advisory board, [we made] sure that we
> put that up front. [But] I think DOE actually did try pretty hard to move the
> public away from that. A lot of what you get [now] is: "Well we've had all of
> that, we've had the moral and philosophical, but now it's a science decision."
> And that's really dominated the past two years.

In another case, the necessity of eliminating justice or related ethical concerns from discussion was described, quite literally, as a painful state:

> I think it's especially painful for the activists who are concerned not only about
> technical stuff, but also about peace and justice stuff. They've got to speak in
> one dialect [a scientific one] but not the other dialect in which they are fluent
> [an ethically based one].

Others openly complained that the silencing of value positions was insufficiently complete to the extent that they viewed stakeholder meetings as having descended into a chaos of competitive agenda setting:

> There's a place for that [ethical considerations], but when it starts to hinder
> the CAB process, then I think it's not right, I think it's counterproductive.

Regardless of whether participants believe that the silencing of ethical positions is a "good" or "bad" outcome, it remains the case that rendering value positions fugitive exhausts both human and fiscal resources. It can also produce unexpected consequences. First, it is exhausting for those who willingly volunteer their time as public participants to find that the group is "getting nowhere" or "spinning its wheels." Public discussion is often reduced to tedious and nonproductive talk, a point not missed by those involved. In the words of a CAB member:

> They think it's a good process because there's lots and lots of words and lots
> and lots and lots of time, and that's called public participation, and it is public
> participation and it's just, it's just like a sponge, it's absorbing huge amounts
> of human energy.

Second, under these fugitive-value/tradeoff-avoidant conditions, wherein distinctions (to the extent possible) between "technical debates" and "ethical conflicts" are not made and the objectives of participants are redirected into debates about the technical merits of alternative cleanup actions, public participants must and do resort to the only available option: they become entangled in a troublesome good-science/bad-science debate. And they likely attack the scientific studies that are the basis for different cleanup options and seek to hire independently conducted studies of their own. This is not to suggest that conducting independent studies or reviews is wrong. Historically, there has been an undeniable, indeed heinous legacy of deception on the part of the DOE regarding the impact of its operations on public health. But if such studies are based solely on distrust they may end up redoing already adequate studies for reassurance when greater attention to the ethical concerns of different groups might reveal the necessity of other equally important studies.

At Rocky Flats, at those points where irreconcilability of scientific interpretations threatened to paralyze cleanup, new studies were conducted and new data were collected based on the premise that new and better science would resolve lingering concerns because science is naively regarded as immune from political manipulation. In actuality, advocates for ever-safer and more thorough cleanup standards are pitted against those who defend a lesser standard as scientifically robust and legally defensible—to wit, both sides claim to possess the scientific upper hand. Many recognize and even enjoy the fallacy of this argument. During an interview, one CAB member noted that everyone appeared to believe that

> the problem [of growing conflict] has a technical solution. The goal [they believe] is to use the best technical and scientific procedures and evidence possible to generate the best possible technical solution. So it's sort of like a good-science/bad-science dilemma. I think there have been real powerful moments where DOE has found itself funding, to its credit, things whose outcomes it could not have predicted.... So one of the things I've tried to learn is the different ways the DOE is conflicted about its own imperatives and responsibilities.... Science is something that has previously been used in ways that [to me] are criminal [for example, weapons production]. Literally [now] I've seen it get used jujitsu, aikido-like, against them.

Again, the RSAL debate provides the best case in point. Recall that initially the DOE posed and defended a RSAL for plutonium of 651 picocuries per gram. The question any level tries to address is, given particular land-use scenarios, what risk exposure is safe enough? The volume of plutonium remaining in the soil is converted, depending on said use conditions, to a probabilistic risk range that meets the EPA's health-safety standards. (Again, the minimum standard is a 10^{-4}, whereas the upper level of the range sits at 10^{-6}.) The CAB could not agree on a unified position to present to the DOE. Members were deeply divided and had no means for reconciling their own profound ideological and ethical differences. There were those who thought the original RSAL numbers were, quoting a CAB staff member, "based on enough scientific process that...they must be safe," and those who thought "they were the worst numbers ever."

Those who argued for the higher numbers believed that regulatory agencies could, by and large, be trusted and that the posed standard was safe enough. Setting an unnecessarily stringent standard at Rocky Flats, they argued, wasted public funds. Critical members of the public stated that a 651 level would not ensure the safety of more vulnerable populations—namely, young people, whose biological systems are still developing; people with compromised immune systems; and future generations whose potential behavior on the land cannot be predicted—and thus the only defensible plan was a conservative one. But as the concerns on both parts were essentially value based or ethical in nature—they pertained to ideas about one's social responsibility to the public and future generations, or about the "rightness" of protecting some people less well than others—they were off-limits. Instead, attention focused on the technical viability of the DOE's initial results and the need to recalculate RSAL and risk estimates.

After considerable expense ($400,000) and time, new studies recalculated RSAL numbers reflecting the complete range of end users. At the low end of the possible range, the (new) numbers were well under 40 $pCig^{-1}$, depending on the specifics of calculation inputs and the identity of the end user. The lowest number in the range (10 pCig^{-1}) was produced for the identity or end user known as "child of a resident rancher." Such a child might play in and eat soil and would also be fed food grown in the soil during his or her key developmental years. But even the probable wildlife worker corresponded to a much lower number. Ultimately, at Rocky Flats the critical public appeared to recognize that the realization of their competing ethical positions (however well disguised) depended largely on their technical strategy, their capacity to criticize the RSAL models, and their ability to present compelling or competing scientific evidence to support their positions.

Although the DOE consented to financing the second study, it was, in the words of one CAB member, deeply "fearful [because of the cost implications] that the number would go down too far" and "horrified" when it did.

In the end, the consequences of tradeoff avoidance, the heightened technical discourse it inspired, and the disruptive play of fugitive values were all detrimental to the very democratic goal of public participation. That is, as tradeoff avoidance and decision paralysis persisted, the roles and even presence of different public discussion groups were compromised, and a successive chain of "spin-off" groups emerged. Firstly and gradually, the CAB's role was diminished. Such a shift is not necessarily a product of agency sleight of hand; public participants appeared fully aware that a pattern of open public involvement representing the diversity of opinion (and skill) embodied in the CAB was replaced by involvement by a smaller, more technically literate group:

> The Citizen's Advisory Board is not nearly as knowledgeable. People like myself [one of a more knowledgeable subset or core group of CAB members] are paying a whole [lot] less attention to the process of the advisory board than to the process of the focus group, because I think that's where the real discussion is happening.... We became very very involved with the soil action level because we were knowledgeable about this particular highly technical stuff.

Other CAB members, while aware of their diminished access to direct participation, were deeply critical of this shift and identified in particular: (a) the relocation of substantive discussion to other groups and (b) the social pressures within the CAB as concerned scientific or technical literacy. Several members of the CAB clearly articulated both points, as illustrated by the successive quotes below:

> They have all these committees that break out and then the committees give their reports. I think part of what I'd do to help with involvement and, and an understanding of the science, I would start holding committee meetings housed within our meetings on the important stuff, um, like the RSAL stuff. I would have that group [RFCA Focus Group] integrated into the monthly [CAB] meeting. I would stop all of this nonsense reporting [back to the group] crap that wastes our time.

> The whole organizational structure of the CAB, I think, is ineffective. You
> don't involve the citizens within the structure that they have now. There's no
> process for making a board member feel welcome. There's no process of help-
> ing a board member through the intimidation of the science. I have no idea
> what these committees do because I can't read the reports. The reports are all
> like this heavy-duty science stuff. And I'm not going to read twenty pages of
> science that I don't understand and get to the end of it and go "I have no idea
> what I just read."

Ultimately, it became unclear as to just where those citizens who did not or could not articulate their concerns in a fully scientific and technical idiom fit. Many simply remained silent observers until they felt confident enough to speak. One noted that a "freeze settled over the group" when the implications of certain technical discussions were neither "fully understood" nor "fully explored." It would then take "someone with considerable guts" to say: "What exactly do you mean by that? At which point the other person acts offended or kind of patronizing or something."

Others observed that tension during meetings, if and when ideas were voiced by those less technically literate, was common:

> You should see some of the body language that goes on around [here] when a
> citizen is talking about something that we know is not right. Instead of saying
> to this guy, "Your points have [merit]," no one responds. They [meeting
> chairs] just say "Oh, thank you very much." That's not citizen participation,
> that's BS. You just bullshitted this guy. You gave him his time in the sun, you
> gave him the microphone, he expressed a concern. You, all your body language
> just made fun of this guy. That is the CAB's definition of citizen participation,
> but it's not my definition.

Each of the above quotes indicates that as the CAB's role diminished, an ever-more-versed segment of the public was proceeding with more substantive technical discussions in venues extrinsic to and thereafter operating as de facto substitutes for the CAB. Each of these new groups tended to be smaller and more focused so as to have a greater chance at reaching agreement and confining discussion to increasingly esoteric technical content. Specifically, as the CAB's central role diminished, three successive groups emerged to fill the vacuum. First emerged the Rocky Flats Council of Local Governments (RFCLOG); comprised of local (mayoral) elected officials and their staff, the council was said to be more representative than the CAB of the surrounding civic population and also more sensitive to the restrictions on the RSAL and other decisions imposed by state, city, and county regulations. Second to emerge was the RFCA Focus Group; it was comprised of technically literate (and educationally credentialed) members of the above two civic groups (the CAB and RFCLOG), as well as Kaiser-Hill staff and DOE and EPA representatives and scientists. RFCA was justified as necessary because too many CAB members had neither the time nor the skill to "properly" understand the nuances of the science and the policy limitations set out in the cleanup agreement. Speaking specifically about the new RFCA Focus Group, an involved CAB member and trained PhD scientist identified the group as a much-anticipated opportunity to "really discuss the technical issues." The specific aim was to resolve differences about RSAL levels through extensive technical debate. But the RFCA Focus Group was not the panacea that many hoped for—a forum for rational scientifically astute discussion. Many complained, in the words of one scientifically trained CAB member, that it, too, was "bogged down" and "totally dysfunctional" due to "people's political agendas." Finally, as the RFCA Focus Group approached decision paralysis around the good-science/bad-science debate concerning the very high versus very low soil action level, the Radionuclide Soil Action Level Working Group emerged. That is, as stakeholders could not manage the diversity of opinion on RSALs within their ranks, the DOE called for a "technical" review of the second and third (low RSAL) studies. The convening of this new working group served to limit the complicating role of the fugitive ethical-cum-technical division and (DOE hoped) challenge the plummeting and hence cleanup-costly RSAL numbers with not tradeoff discussions but further calculations and technical review.

With the establishment of increasingly technical groups, it was assumed that upon resolution of the technical debate, an "announce and defend" or "teach the public the numbers" format for public discussion would follow. To wit, "literate" group members would communicate their findings to the "less-educated" members of the public:

> We've got a special work session planned to talk to others [less "literate" mem-
> bers of the CAB] about the calculations. We've done the work, and we're
> going to bring the results of the working group back to the CAB. But what
> we're going to do with the CAB, is try to educate the members as to how the
> numbers were calculated. And then see if we can put together a recommenda-
> tion [on RSALs for DOE], and hopefully we can get a recommendation fast.

Regardless of motive, what occurred at Rocky Flats was a long and drawn-out pattern of group mutations, where an ever-more-versed segment of the involved public, along with the agencies' science and policy staff, came to stand in for public discussion and involvement. In the process, an important democratic principle—the need for a diverse CAB to deliberate and debate the means for achieving the best outcome for the public—was pitted against the ideal and elusive pursuit of scientific literary and hence (it was argued) reasoned debate. Invariably, at Rocky Flats much of the legitimacy and integrity of the former democratic principle was sacrificed.

Discussion—The Dynamics of the Breakdown of Public Participation at Rocky Flats

Previous studies of risk have shed light on how risks are conceived and how risks become amplified in public life. A very small set of studies evaluating (critically and not) different public-participation experiments is available (Arvai et al. 2001; Beierle 2002; Pelltier et al. 1999; Renn et al. 1995; Sunstein 2000; Webler 1997). Ample anecdotal evidence and some published evidence also show that stakeholder groups addressing radiation risks often fail to reach consensus or super-majority support (Easterling and Kunreuther 1995). Finally, a number of early studies highlight the differing ethical positions held by disputing parties in risk debates (Jasanoff 1999; Nelkin 1992). Nelkin, in particular, has found that while disputes about science as it is applied to regulatory policy are often motivated by political or moral values, the debates themselves remain preoccupied with technical questions. The value complexity of debates is matched by their strategic complexity as "moral arguments are combined with extensive use of technical expertise…and technical expertise becomes a resource exploited by all parties to justify competing moral and political claims" (Nelkin 1995:452–53).

But as yet there exists little systematic effort to document ethnographically the specific processes (including the complex interplay of ethical positions and knowledge-driven arguments) that lead to discussion paralysis across stakeholders and the resultant influence of those processes on public involvement—its shape, its characteristics, and its perceived legitimacy. In the substantive portions of this paper, we have drawn on field interviews and observations at Rocky Flats to provide a descriptive portrait of the dynamics of risk and science controversies in public-participation contexts. What follows here is a summary of this description in the form of processual schema. The aim is to develop a trajectory-based framework that can accommodate the complex details of cases such as Rocky Flats for the purposes of cross-case comparisons and, ultimately, necessary restructuring of public participation.

Figure 8.2 posits that in the Rocky Flats case, two types of pressure (boxes 1 and 2, horizontally displayed on the left-hand side of the diagram) were exerted. They in turn produced four primary consequences or outcomes (boxes 3 through 6, vertically displayed on the right side of the diagram).

Box 1—Decision Parameters

The first two boxes denote the "pressures" that emerge when decision parameters are imposed on public participants and the actions under discussion involve a high degree of uncertainty. First, there exist numerous epistemological and engineering uncertainties about the health effects and technical possibility of cleanup. At Rocky Flats, Kaiser-Hill was among the first to take on the task of cleaning up one of the many nuclear arsenal sites within the DOE complex. It invested considerable time and resources in preparing and negotiating a contract with the federal government and likely budgeted for numerous contingency or worst-case scenarios. It is telling that the first cost estimate for cleanup, put forth by EG&G in 1990, was $36 billion; the estimated cleanup deadline was seventy years, or a 2060 closure date. This earlier estimate is nearly five times Kaiser-Hill's $7 billion-plus budget and schedule. The gross

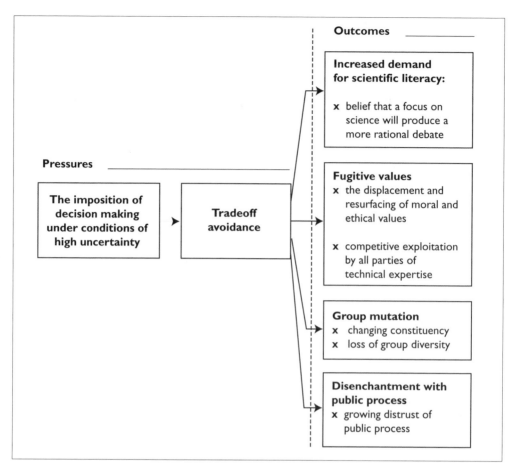

Figure 8.2. Diagnosing the breakdown of deliberative processes.

discrepancy in estimates likely indicates that it is difficult at best to know with even a modicum of precision what cleanup will involve, what technologies will be used or developed to conduct the necessary decontamination and decommissioning of the site, how long it will take, and how much it will cost. During the period of study, stakeholders widely acknowledged that Kaiser-Hill was over budget and behind schedule. The uncertainties placed the contractor and the client (DOE) in a position of heightened and chronic vigilance with regard to costs and schedule. This vigilance came into direct conflict with efforts to set RSALs because the final RSAL could dramatically compromise the overall budget (and because there was concern that a low RSAL at Rocky Flats would set a dangerous cost precedent at future sites in the complex).

Box 2—Tradeoff Pressures and Avoidance

Cost limitations and temporal deadlines are a given in any project of this kind. Moreover, those most responsible for site decisions know only too well that tradeoffs must be made to achieve the end goal of cleanup. But it is invariably difficult for regulators to voice candidly and consistently the necessity of tradeoffs and to address them head-on with full recognition of what making such tradeoffs involves. This difficulty is due in part to agency fears that it will come across as assigning a monetary value to human life. More broadly, there are many socially and psychologically compelling reasons why such tradeoffs are regarded as morally and emotionally complex. These problems are augmented by the fact that regulators fail to recognize that it is virtually impossible to make tradeoffs without clearly addressing the ethical positions or values that underpin why one option is selected over and above other competing options (Gregory 2002).

These two phenomena—boxes 1 and 2 (decision parameters under uncertainty and tradeoff avoidance)—converge to exert extraordinary pressure on the capacity for a diverse body such as the CAB and the many linked participatory groups to operate. Several outcomes thus emerge.

Box 3—Increased Demand for Scientific Literacy

The increased pressure and tension exerted by a climate of tradeoff avoidance and decision making under financial uncertainty were met by elevating expectations for scientific literacy under the guise that the more problematic value considerations could be cleansed from the discussion and a more rational debate across stakeholders would thereafter prevail.

Box 4—Fugitive Values

When ethical considerations are increasingly sublimated, value differences across stakeholders do not go away; rather they become "fugitive" forces in the discussion. Points about value are forced to masquerade as technical points, encouraging more than is necessary the competitive exploitation of technical expertise by all parties. At Rocky Flats this situation was most clearly demonstrated during the protracted debate about RSALs and the excessive restudy and recalculation of RSAL levels.

Boxes 5 and 6—Group Mutation and Disenchantment with Public Process

As the interplay of tradeoff avoidance, fugitive values, and a "science-only" discussion persists, the role of public discussion groups is compromised. New groups emerge, each more highly specialized and more highly focused on technical points of discussion. The assumption is that these new modified specialist groups will resolve their differences and, having done so, will "educate" or convince the larger involved group accordingly. In the process, the very principle of a diverse citizen board and democratic public involvement is undermined, and widespread disenchantment ensues.

Conclusion

Understanding the nature, practice, and expectations of public-participation programs is a difficult task. In particular, little is known about the sequential or processual trajectory of how and why efforts to involve an interested public in specific discussions about risk management and remediation programs stumble or fail. For instance, when and under what conditions do they suffer periods of protracted paralysis? Why are they sometimes forced to deviate from their initial democratic, multi-stakeholder (and intrinsically democratic) good intentions?

Risk scholars have argued vehemently that risk debates are value debates, and that as such, involving the public in risk-management decision processes is essential though variable across political cultures (Jasanoff 2005; National Research Council 1996). Less academically, there are now any number of practitioners who consider themselves experts at facilitating public involvement. While the general trend toward public involvement should be applauded for its fundamentally democratic spirit, it is not the case that *any* public involvement is good involvement. Increasingly, federal agencies are embracing participatory groups with little or no knowledge of how to structure that involvement or little or poor use of the often very good recommendations emerging from applied social scientists. Instead, among those who follow public-involvement efforts, there is increasing talk of a backlash against public involvement because so many efforts exhaust all social and fiscal resources yet fail to produce a decision outcome supported by the vast majority, or ideally all involved stakeholders.

Without better diagnostic evidence of the kind ethnography can produce, there is little basis for improving the operation of the myriad deliberation exercises underway or for instructing federal agencies on the importance of good-quality, well-structured public involvement. More importantly, the Rocky Flats case demonstrates clearly that any public-participation effort that fails to (a) properly and systematically address the fundamental importance of making tradeoffs and decision parameters clear *and* (b) openly debate and analyze the ethical positions with which those tradeoffs are associated will likely lead to a breakdown in public involvement. Further, an insistence on greater technical literacy has some benefits, but if that "literacy" is the product of naive efforts to minimize conflict, it will only serve to obfuscate the more fundamental ethical conflict at play and eventually erode the possibility of meaningful involvement across a demographically and educationally diverse public.

Notes

1. See especially David Price's chapter herein on the Hiroshima–Nagasaki tragedies and the influence of those events on the scientific and activist career of Earle Reynolds, who, Price argues, found that science served only to render invisible the mortality and suffering of a human community.

2. Irwin has argued that despite public groups' considerable discontent with science as practiced in the context of controversial hazards (radiation, bovine spongiform encephalopathy—popularly known as mad cow disease—and so forth), the prevailing approach to policy decisions remains modernist. Science, he argues, "does indeed construct the definition of risk issues and all other concerns, including alternative forms of understanding and different value structures, become peripheral (1995:62). Here he draws on Habermas's account of the "technocratic consciousness," which "reflects not the sundering of an ethical situation but the repression of ethics as such as a category of life" (62).

3. The overall budget for cleanup was earlier stated as $7.3 billion; the amount cited here includes only estimation of cost and does not include Kaiser-Hill's profit margin for the project. That profit will go up or down depending on unanticipated costs, as well as costs to the company for fines levied due to time overruns and related unmet contractual obligations.

4. It is, of course, difficult to manage for the future when dealing with material (for example, plutonium-239) with a half-life of 24,065 years.

5. RAC stands for the Risk Assessment Corporation, the consulting group responsible for the CAB-initiated study of RSALs.

6. We do not mean to suggest that these are consciously manipulative responses but rather a normal human response to an uneasy situation.

References

Arvai, Joseph L., Robin Gregory, and Timothy L. McDaniels
2001   Testing a Structured Decision Approach: Value Focused Thinking for Deliberative Risk Communication. Risk Analysis 21:1065–76.

Baron, Jonathan, and Sarah Leshner
2000   How Serious Are Expressions of Protected Values? Journal of Experimental Psychology 6:183–94.

Baron, Jonathan, and Mark Spranca
1997   Protected Values. Organizational Behavior and Human Decision Processes 70:1–16.

Beck, Ulrich
1992   Risk Society: Towards a New Modernity. London: Sage Publications.
1999   World Risk Society. Cambridge: Polity Press.

Beierle, Thomas C.
2002   The Quality of Stakeholder-based Decisions. Risk Analysis 22:739–49.

Easterling, Doug, and Howard Kunreuther
1995   The Dilemma of Siting a High-Level Nuclear Waste Repository. Boston: Kluwer Academic.

Fischhoff, Baruch
1995   Risk Perception and Communication Unplugged: Twenty Years of Process. Risk Analysis 15:137–45.

Fiske, Alan P., and Philip E. Tetlock

1997   Taboo Trade-offs: Reactions to Transactions That Transgress Spheres of Justice. Political Psychology 18:255–97.

Gregory, Robin

2000   Using Stakeholder Values to Make Smarter Decisions. Environment 42:34–44.

2002   Incorporating Value Trade-offs into Community-Based Environmental Risk Decisions. Environmental Values 11:461–88.

Irwin, Alan

1995   Citizen Science: A Study of People, Expertise, and Sustainable Development. London: Routledge.

Irwin, Alan, and Brian Wynne, eds.

1996   Misunderstanding Science? The Public Reconstruction of Science and Technology. Cambridge: Cambridge University Press.

Jasanoff, Sheila

1999   The Songlines of Risk. Environmental Risk 8:127–34.

2005   Designs on Nature: Science and Democracy in Europe and the United States. Princeton, NJ: Princeton University Press.

Jasanoff, Sheila, and Brian Wynne

1998   Science and Decision Making. *In* Human Choice and Climate Change. S. Raynor and E. Malone, eds. Pp. 1–87. Washington, DC: Batelle Press.

Kraus, Nancy, Torbjörn Malmfors, and Paul Slovic

1992   Intuitive Toxicology: Expert and Lay Judgments of Chemical Risks. Risk Analysis 12:215–32.

Krimsky, Sheldon, and Dominic Golding

1992   Social Theories of Risk. Westport, CT: Praeger-Greenwood.

Moore, LeRoy

2005   Rocky Flats: The Bait-and-Switch Cleanup. Bulletin of the Atomic Scientists 61:50–57.

Morgan, Granger, Baruch Fischhoff, Anne Bostrom, and Cynthia J. Atman

2002   Risk Communication: A Mental Models Approach. New York: Cambridge University Press.

National Research Council

1996   Understanding Risk: Informing Decisions in a Democratic Society. Washington, DC: National Academy Press.

Nelkin, Dorothy

1992   Controversy: Politics of Technical Decisions. Newbury Park, CA: Sage Publications.

1995   Science Controversies: The Dynamics of Public Disputes in the United States. *In* The Handbook of Science and Technology Studies. S. Jasanoff, G. Murkle, I. Petersen, and T. Pinch, eds. Pp. 444–56. Thousand Oaks, CA: Sage Publications.

Pelltier, David, Vivica Kraak, Christine McCullum, Ulla Uusitallo, and Robert Rich
1999   The Shaping of Collective Values through Deliberative Democracy: An Empirical Study of New York's North Country. Policy Sciences 32:103–31.

Renn, Ortwin, Thomas Webler, and Peter Wiedemann
1995   Fairness and Competence in Citizen Participation: Evaluating Models for Environmental Discourse. Dordrecht, Netherlands: Kluwer Academic.

Slovic, Paul
1999   Trust, Emotion, Sex, Politics, and Science: Surveying the Risk-Assessment Battlefield. Risk Analysis 19:689–701.

Sunstein, Cass R.
2000   Deliberative Trouble? Why Groups Go to Extremes. Yale Law Journal 110:71–119.

Walker, Samuel
2000   Permissible Dose. Berkeley: University of California Press.

Webler, Thomas
1997   Organizing Public Participation: A Critical Review of Three Handbooks. Human Ecology Review 3:245–54.

Whicker, F. Ward
2004   Avoiding Destructive Remediation at DOE Sites. Science 303:1615–16.

Wynne, Brian
1996   Misunderstood Misunderstandings. *In* Misunderstanding Science? The Public Reconstruction of Science and Technology. A. Irwin and B. Wynne, eds. Pp. 19–46. Cambridge: Cambridge University Press.
2001   Creating Public Alienation: Expert Cultures on Risk and Ethics on GMOs. Science as Culture 10:445–81.

Yearley, Steven
2000   Making Systematic Sense of Public Discontents with Expert Knowledge: Two Analytical Approaches and a Case Study. Public Understanding of Science 9:105–22.

n i n e
Health Assessment Downwind
Past Abuses Shadow Future Indicators

Marie I. Boutté

The Nevada Test Site (NTS), where more nuclear weapons have been detonated than any other place on earth, lies in the desert of Nye County, Nevada, some 70 miles northwest of Las Vegas. It covers 1,350 square miles, or approximately 850,000 acres. The Atomic Energy Commission (AEC) selected the site for nuclear testing in 1950, in part because the land was already under complete federal control, few people lived in the surrounding area, it had low rainfall and predictable winds, and it would be easy to protect from enemies if necessary. On January 27, 1951, an air force plane dropped a 21-kiloton bomb named Able, which exploded 1,060 feet above the desert in an area known as Frenchman Flat, thus conducting the first atmospheric test at the NTS. One woman, ten years old at the time and living about 100 miles away, remembered the day this way: "The first blast came without any warning. We were awakened out of a sound sleep. No one was even informed it was going to happen. We lived in an old two-story home. It broke out several of our windows and cracked our house on two sides the full length of the house" (Miller 1986:89; US Congress, Senate Labor and Human Resources Committee 1982:22).

In this chapter, I want to put a personal face on the experiences of downwinders to illustrate how proposed activities, such as transportation and storage of high-level nuclear waste at Yucca Mountain, located on the northwestern edge of the NTS, may further affect their health and relationship with the federal government. First, I give a brief history of the people and rural communities exposed to nuclear radiation from weapons testing at the NTS and their dealings with the federal government in regard to this exposure.[1] Second, I describe the steps taken by Nevada's Nuclear Waste Projects Office (NWPO) to implement a Community Health Assessment Project as part of its oversight activities at Yucca Mountain and the role I played as an anthropologist in this endeavor. Third, I discuss how the past legacy of radiation exposure continues to place a shadow over the lives of downwinders and complicates collection of health data for future assessment of health impacts. Finally, I make recommendations for multiple assessment tools that would provide a more comprehensive picture of health effects from Nevada's past legacy of nuclear exposure and its potential future legacy from Yucca Mountain.

Unfortunately, the problem of radiation does not exist only in the past for Nevada residents. Currently, the Department of Energy (DOE) is studying Yucca Mountain as a possible repository for spent fuel and other high-level radioactive wastes (HLW) from commercial nuclear power plants and DOE defense facilities. Should all expected inventories be disposed of at Yucca Mountain, the site could eventually hold 70,000 tons of wastes, and all of it has to be transported there via rail or trucks. These activities have significant implications for once again exposing residents of Nevada and others to ionizing radiation, and they present new challenges for identifying and monitoring the health effects of such exposures. As was the case in the early 1950s, Nevada's health agencies have no capabilities for identifying exposures or monitoring Yucca Mountain health impacts, nor have they taken any interest in developing such capabilities. With this writing, I aim to contribute to efforts to alter this situation.

Atomic Assault Brings a Litany of Trouble Downwind

In the early 1950s, more than one hundred thousand men, women, and children were scattered in the rural communities east of the NTS, in the downwind areas of Arizona, Nevada, and Utah (Ball 1986:59). Their way of life was situated predominately in the heartland of the Mormon Church, and the church was the bedrock of their social, economic, political, and religious existence. During the years of atmospheric testing, from 1951 to 1962, most Mormons lived a life of self-sufficiency as ranchers, and much of the legacy of nuclear testing is embedded in this self-sufficient lifestyle. This is how one woman described how her family met their daily needs during those years: "We had three cows at the time that we milked, we drank all the milk, which is one of the worst things, and then, of course, I made butter and sometimes cheese. I always raised a big garden and we ate our own meat, so we had it all." She went on to say that "there was no way of getting away from it. They never came and told us not to do this, so we lived right under it. I have pictures here that prove it.... You could see where the cloud was coming in with the radiation of a blast" (Gallagher 1993:117). Another resident described family life at that time this way: "Our family was economically low.

We didn't have indoor plumbing. We didn't have a telephone. We did all our entertainment living in the hills of St. George [Utah]. We had our little huts on the hillside, played in irrigation ditches. It was a great way to grow up. After a bomb, there would be the fallout, fine like flour, kind of grayish white. We would play like that was our snow" (157).

At the time, most Mormons in these communities did not use tobacco, alcohol, tea, or coffee, as directed by church doctrine. They thought the US Constitution and the United States were divine in origin, thus they considered themselves patriotic, good citizens (Gallagher 1993:xxix). In general, they were a noncomplaining people, not in the habit of questioning those in authority such as church leaders and the federal government. They supported the government's program of nuclear testing, even feeling a sense of pride in having such an important defense program right in their backyard (Ball 1986:56). In fact, many went out on a regular basis to watch the bomb blasts and mushroom clouds as they passed overhead. One man who lived downwind said it was "[q]uite a unique experience for us hillbillies here in a one-horse town to go out and see something like that" (Gallagher 1993:134). Another said, "We'd get up to watch it and hear it and watch the pink cloud go over. We thought it was something to see, something great" (138). Even schoolchildren were sent outside to watch the effects of bombs blasting as part of their science classes. If anyone in these rural communities dared to complain or protest the atomic assault from the NTS, their neighbors often called them eccentric, unpatriotic, or even communist.

The AEC gave its Nevada neighbors plenty to observe in the 1950s and 1960s. Able was one of the smallest of the one hundred atmospheric tests detonated at the NTS between 1951 and 1962; the largest was the 74-kiloton Hood test, fired on from a balloon at 1,500 feet on July 5, 1957, at Yucca Flat. Shots Simon and Harry were among the worst "dirty bombs," those that deposited the most radioactive fallout downwind (Ball 1986:66). Simon, detonated from a tower in April 1953, had a yield (total effective energy released) of 43 kilotons, way over the AEC's projected yield of 35 kilotons. This particular bomb sent a band of nuclear debris over 80 miles wide across communities downwind from the NTS (Miller 1986:170). Harry, a 32-kiloton bomb detonated from a tower in May 1953—famously known as Dirty Harry— deposited an extraordinary amount of contamination off-site (Fradkin 1989:21). The heavy fallout readings from Simon and Dirty Harry led the AEC to set up roadblocks, halt traffic, and check vehicles downwind of the blasts for radiation. Radio announcements warned people to stay indoors while the fallout from Dirty Harry passed over. But such warnings were rare. In May 1953, right after the AEC detonated Harry, the agency experimented with "airburst" bombs, where the fireball does not touch the ground prior to reaching its maximum luminosity. One such device was Grable, a 15-kiloton bomb fired from a 280 mm cannon (DOE 1994, 1995). Thus those living in proximity to the NTS during the years of atmospheric testing occupied a virtual war zone, where bombs were dropped from airplanes, fired from cannons, and detonated from steel and wooden towers. All around them, soldiers on atomic maneuvers

Figure 9.1. Small Boy event, July 14, 1962, Frenchmen Flats, Area 5, Nevada Test Site; view looking north from official observer point. Small Boy was part of Operation Dominic II, a test series involving detonation of four bombs to obtain information on the electromagnetic pulse effects of nuclear weapons. An estimated twenty-nine hundred military and civilian personnel were present for these tests. The relatively low-yield test of July 14 resulted in the formation of a radioactive cloud that moved east from surface ground zero and crossed Highway 93 south of Alamo, Nevada. During the night of July 14 and the morning of July 15, the cloud moved further east into Utah. Isotopes identified in the release included radioactive iodine, some 1,100 picocuries of I-131 per cubic meter of air, and 3,500 picocuries of I-131 per liter recorded in milk at Caliente, Nevada. The maximum total radioactivity recorded was 140,000 picocuries of gross beta activity per cubic meter of air in Elko, Nevada. Photo courtesy of National Nuclear Security Administration/Nevada Site Office

marched toward ground zero, and military and weather planes buzzed overhead, monitoring wind and fallout patterns.

In 1963 the Limited Test Ban Treaty prohibited atmospheric testing, so atomic testing at the NTS moved underground. The AEC detonated just over eight hundred additional bombs in shafts, tunnels, and craters. Underground tests sometimes "vented," releasing radioactive particles into the air, and crater explosions sometimes threw out tons of radioactive dirt and debris that Nevada's winds carried off-site. A crater shot named Sedan, a 104-kiloton thermonuclear device detonated in July 1962, lifted 12 million tons of radioactive dirt, stone, and dust into the air (DOE 1994; Goin 1991). The downwind community of Ely, Nevada, had to turn its streetlights on at four o'clock in the afternoon when the bomb's large radioactive cloud passed over (Fradkin 1989:136). The biggest bomb ever detonated at the NTS in terms of yield was Boxcar, a 1.3-megaton underground test conducted in April 1968 in an area known as Pahute Mesa (DOE 1991).

The wind carried radioactive fallout from atomic testing at the NTS all across the United States, but communities and ranches in southeastern Nevada, southwestern Utah, and northwestern Arizona were especially hard hit (Kerber et al. 1993). (See map 6.1) Soon after weapons testing began at the NTS, downwind communities raised concerns about the immediate and long-term health effects of fallout exposure. Despite their patriotic commitment to the government's nuclear testing program, those living downwind from the NTS soon began to suffer a long list of health problems. Not long after testing started, subtle clues appeared that the atomic fallout might be causing something unusual to happen, first to the environment and then to residents and their children. People began noticing that wildlife, from deer to birds, thinned from expansive rangelands regularly dusted with fallout from the NTS (Wasserman and Solomon 1982:64). At the same time they found ulcerated burns on their cattle and horses, and their pet dogs and rabbits died or had offspring with deformities. Foliage and vegetable gardens began rotting. "That year when we raised the garden," one woman remembered, "we noticed the squash and tomatoes would get this light stuff on them, the leaves would get white and crusty and the squash would be all yucky and the tomatoes did the same thing. It kind of spread around the garden. We ate them, the ones that were good" (Gallagher 1993:138). People also suspected something was amiss in the early years of testing when their Geiger counters, bought in the hopes of getting rich from uranium prospecting, began giving off unusually high readings in their homes and backyards. When thousands of sheep abruptly became sick and died, and others were born with deformities, suspicions of trouble turned to certainty for most downwinders. The sheeps' death produced a real sense of collective consciousness of the danger of fallout.

Two years after atmospheric testing began, during the spring and summer of 1953, some 11,710 sheep were grazing in an area approximately 40 miles north to 160 miles east of the NTS. Between March 17 and June 4 of that year, Operation Upshot-Knothole exposed these sheep to massive amounts of radiation. Eleven tests emitted a total of 252 kilotons of nuclear fission products as radioactive fallout. Out of these 11,710 exposed sheep, 1,420 lambing ewes (12.1 percent) and 2,970 new lambs (25.4 percent) died (US Congress, House Interstate and Foreign Commerce Committee 1980:3). These figures do not account for the number of lambs born with deformities. One rancher described such lambs this way: "Have you ever seen a five-legged lamb? I did. Have you ever seen a one-eyed lamb? I did.... Have you ever seen a young animal that was born completely rotten? I did. They'd be bare. I had little lambs born that absolutely didn't have one speck of wool on their bodies. They were transparent and you could see their little hearts a-beatin' until they died. I never seen anything like that in my whole life until then and I've been in the sheep business from the time I was a little boy on the farm" (Gallagher 1993:275–76). This rancher went on to say, "I bet there wasn't one sheep that was out there in '53 that didn't die within two years because I was buying sheep all the time to replace them. They kept on going down and down and down. It breaks you. It broke me. I had to mortgage my house to buy more sheep to start out again. It took me 15 years to pay it off. It completely broke my brother-in-law.... He was never able to crawl out of it after that, and finally he died of cancer in his fifties" (276).

In 1955 sheep ranchers filed suit against the government in federal court in Salt Lake City. This lawsuit was the first attempt to seek compensation for losses from radiation released from the government's nuclear arms industry. However, the court denied the ranchers' claim, based on the government's argument that fallout levels were too low to have resulted in the sheep deaths. Some twenty-five years later, in 1980, the House Committee on Interstate and Foreign Commerce investigated the sheep deaths and concluded that the AEC had knowingly disregarded and covered up evidence correlating the deaths of the sheep to radiation exposure. Federal and state veterinarians had measured lethal doses of radiation in the organs of dead and dying animals, but the AEC had suppressed the reports (Gallagher 1993:xvii). The committee also concluded that the government had wrongly denied compensation to the sheep ranchers for their losses (US Congress, House Interstate and Foreign Commerce Committee 1980:13). With the committee's findings to back them up, in 1982 the ranchers went back to court, asking that the earlier judgment be set aside and that a new trial be scheduled. The judge who had presided over the 1955 case was still on the bench, and he vacated the 1956 judgment, ordered the government to pay court costs of about $120,000, and scheduled a new trial (Titus 1986:123). The judge also found that the AEC had perpetrated a fraud upon the court and said that a remedy must be granted to the ranchers, even at that late date. Unfortunately for the ranchers, in May of 1985 the US Court of Appeals rejected these findings and canceled the new trial. Once again, the court sided against the ranchers and in favor of the government. Stewart Udall, former secretary of the interior and an attorney, who represented many downwinders in their lawsuits against the government, had this to say about how the court of appeals handled the ranchers' claim: "Chief Judge Oliver Seth sought to close the door on this shabby chapter of American jurisprudence. Yet, many scholars who have studied the rationale this jurist used consider the outcome of this appeal a gross miscarriage of justice" (Udall 1994:216).

While the downwinders' environment and livelihood were being atomically assaulted, so was their health, although at first they had no inkling of the damage because the federal government repeatedly told them in its massive publicity campaigns that the fallout was harmless. Also, the physicians in the area knew nothing of radiation effects when downwinders went for consultation. Often, the first signs of trouble for people exposed to fallout were the same as for their animals—burns on their skin: "[M]y wife, her skin, her hands, arms, neck, face, anything that was exposed just turned a beet red. I thought probably she had a sunburn, but Oleta wasn't the type to develop a sunburn.... She got a severe headache, and nausea, diarrhea, really miserable. We drove out to the hospital and the doctor said, 'Well it looks like sunburn, but then it doesn't.'" This husband went on to explain what happened to his wife four weeks later: "All at once she let out the most ungodly scream, and I run in there and there's about half her hair layin' in the washbasin!...the hair had just slipped right off! She was in a state of panic, and I did the best I could to comfort her, but that hair never did grow back. She'd work her hair back and over and cover up the best she could, but anytime she'd ever go out in public she'd always wear a hat" (Gallagher 1993:134).

After the assaults that resulted in acute radiation sickness came the assault on women's ability to bear children. Many suffered sterility, multiple miscarriages, and children with birth defects. This situation was especially devastating to Mormon families and communities, which prized large numbers of children: "All of a sudden everybody we knew or somebody they knew or were related to was having miscarriages at five or six months along, or their babies were dying on them and I said something has got to be going crazy here. It's just not normal. I thought they put something in the water! It was all through the valley here, a strange widespread thing." One woman had an abnormal pregnancy and had to have a D and C procedure at six months: "My husband was there and [the doctor] showed him what he had taken out of my uterus. There were little grapelike cysts. My husband said it looked like a bunch of peeled grapes. [The doctor] couldn't give an explanation of what caused it. There was a girl from BYU studying to be a nurse who called me and she said she had had a couple of them in a row. She was doing a thesis on it" (Gallagher 1993:143). Some children survived but were born with terrible, life-threatening deformities: "It was a little boy, and from the hips down the legs were all shriveled up and black. It lived for a couple of hours. It would have been completely paralyzed in the legs. Or they would have had to take them off had it lived. That was a seven-and-a half-month baby. It was 1953" (118). One father said, "I remember when my boy was born with a birth defect, right after when all this happened.... His face was a massive hole and they had to put all these pieces of his face back together. I could see down his throat, everything was just turned inside out, his face curled out and it was horrible. I wanted to die. I wanted him to die. I didn't want him to live because I thought there was no way that he could ever make it. I remember going outside the hospital, laying on the grass and just crying and sobbing over it" (165). In addition to these atrocities on human life, schoolrooms in downwind communities began filling up with children who were physically and mentally handicapped: "We had seven retarded children born through that time, more than we had ever known in this area in the whole history of Parowan" (180). "We had a lot of mental retardation. This had become very apparent early in 1956.... Now we say they are Down's syndrome, and in those days they were Mongolian idiots... there's a difference.... We had all these children that needed special education, who were not only slightly retarded. They were severely retarded. It really struck us. We said they were all born during that time, how come?" (162). A woman told Gallagher in 1988: "Here in Enterprise [Utah] three or four years ago there were three Down's syndrome babies born in one year, children of adults who were children during the testing" (139). Thus it appeared that the nuclear legacy from the NTS was being passed down in the following generations, or so downwinders believed.

From the mid-1950s to early 1960s, as radioactive fallout undermined men and women's ability to conceive and bear healthy children, clusters of cancers sprang up, especially among children and young people, in predominantly rural Mormon communities where cancer had been practically unknown prior to 1951. Mothers and morticians were among the first to notice the unusual number of leukemia cases. One mortician interviewed by Gallagher (1993:149) reported his shock at a sudden surge in deaths from leukemia in Saint George, Utah, in the mid-1950s. He had to teach his employees new embalming techniques to prepare the small bodies of the wasted children brought to him.

One leukemia cluster that occurred in Fredonia, Arizona, had important consequences later on for the whole downwind population (Boutté 2004). Fredonia, a town about 200 miles from the NTS, had a population of 643 in 1960. Four cases of leukemia occurred there between 1960 and 1965; no cases of leukemia had been reported in Fredonia during the entire previous decade (Wasserman and Solomon 1982:63). In 1966 the Leukemia Unit of the US Public Health Service (USPHS) conducted an epidemiological study in Fredonia and confirmed the increased incidence of leukemia. The results of the study were not made public, however. In a memorandum marked "For Administrative Use Only, Not for Publication," dated August 4, 1966, the director of the Leukemia Unit, Dr. Clark Heath, noted that "this number of cases is approximately 20 times greater than expected" (Heath 1966:2). The findings were eventually made public in 1979, when congressional hearings were held on health effects of low-level radiation and government documents were declassified, especially those of the AEC (US Congress, House Interstate and Foreign Commerce Committee 1979). The federal health bureaucracy, closely allied with the weapons testing bureaucracy, did not make available the results of a number of studies of leukemia and thyroid disease carried out in the downwind zone until the late 1970s (Fradkin 1989:40).

It was the cluster of leukemia in Fredonia in the early 1960s that caused one mother and three widows to launch a movement in the mid-1970s seeking redress from the federal government for health effects of radioactive fallout. The efforts by these women and other early advocates for the exposed led to both groundbreaking lawsuits and federal compensation legislation (Boutté 2004). Fradkin, in his book *Fallout: An American Nuclear Tragedy*, notes that while Mormon women are supposed to be docile and passive, "it was the women of Fredonia and the other small towns and hamlets who, once they suspected a link between the tests and cancer, organized the challenge to the government and were the loudest and most vocal in their protests" (1989:31–32). Fradkin suggests that perhaps the women "felt the keenest loss, the greatest abandonment by death," and it was perhaps the women "who intuitively sensed the threat to future generations from the legacy of the tests." In contrast, he notes that the men of the region were mute, suggesting that they "felt their livelihoods most threatened by the disclosure that the area had once been poisoned" (32). However, it came to pass that the whole world learned that the area had been poisoned.

Some evidence of the terrible consequences of nuclear testing emerged during the same years in which downwinders lost their faith in the government and began to sue. In 1963 hearings before the Joint Committee on Atomic Energy raised the possibility of adverse health effects from fallout. As a result, the federal government carried out a series of epidemiological studies—first by the USPHS Bureau of Radiologic Health and later by the National Cancer Institute and Department of Health and Human Services (Wachholz 1990). These studies focused primarily on the incidence of thyroid disease and leukemia and were essentially completed in the early 1990s, although results continue to be published periodically in scientific journals. Health researchers have thoroughly criticized these studies because of the lack of good baseline health data on which to base them. However, the general findings tended to support an association between exposure to fallout and an excess of thyroid neoplasms in residents downwind from the NTS and a relationship between fallout and some types of leukemia (Boutté 1997a, 1997b). In 1990 Congress acknowledged the causal relationship between atomic fallout and a number of adverse health effects, enacting the Radiation Exposure Compensation Act (RECA). Nevertheless, lack of pretesting baseline health information continues to make it difficult to determine just how widespread and serious fallout and health effects are within exposed populations. This absence of usable data has made it very difficult for downwinders to obtain radiation compensation.

RECA recognized thirteen "compensable" diseases for downwinders: leukemia; myeloma; lymphomas (other than Hodgkin's disease); and primary cancer of the thyroid, breast (for females), esophagus, stomach, pharynx, small intestines, pancreas, bile ducts, gall bladder, and liver. The amended RECA of 2000 added cancer of the lung, brain, colon, ovary, urinary bladder, and salivary gland. It also made cancer of the breast for males compensable (Boutté 2002). However, there was no compensation for miscarriages, birth defects, mental retardation, mental anguish, and all the other health effects that downwinders see as their legacy of fallout exposure.

When the federal government offered the downwinders compensation in the form of money and an apology for the hardships endured from atmospheric testing, many thought the government had finally acknowledged and taken responsibility for what had happened to them. Little did they know how insincere the apology would be and how difficult it would be to get the money. In 2002 I published an article in *Human Organization* (Boutté 2002) outlining three major problems that downwinders have had in getting compensation under RECA. The first is the strict and rigid criteria for eligibility, where the problem lies generally with the specificity or type of compensable disease and less so with geographical area or time frame as dictated in the law. The fact that RECA 2000 added six more compensable categories of cancers to the original thirteen was seen as a positive effort on behalf of the government, but the law still left out a wide variety of other health problems that downwinders feel ought to be covered. The second problem that RECA presents for downwinders is the complexity of the application process; compiling the necessary detailed medical records and proof of residence from so many years ago frequently requires the help of an attorney experienced in compensation issues. The third problem is the amount of compensation: $50,000. Downwinders are not only adamant about the fact that $50,000 is a small amount for one's health and life, but they also see this payment as an injustice when other exposed groups, such as uranium miners and test site workers, get substantially more money for their exposures. These three problems do not even start to address the central issue of having the radiation compensation program administered by the Department of Justice, the very federal entity that fought the downwinders from the very beginning in their quest for justice and compensation.

Community Health Assessment Project

In 1994 the NWPO began a health impacts initiative as part of its Yucca Mountain oversight program, and the office hired me as a cultural-medical anthropologist to set the plan in motion. In all, I was involved in three phases of this initiative. In the first phase, I carried out an extensive literature review to get the "lay of the land" in terms of the health effects of radiation; survey the earlier health studies of people living near the NTS, as well as studies of analogous situations; and assess the strengths and weaknesses of the various methodologies used in such studies. I also read congressional hearings on health effects of radiation, oral histories, and illness narratives of people exposed to radiation (Boutté 1994). Reading this material enabled me to construct the picture of downwinders that I presented in the previous section, and it made me give serious thought to how this past history of radiation exposure could and did shed light on potential problems for future health studies.

The second phase in the health studies initiative began in July 1995. I consulted on research design with national experts from the Centers for Disease Control and Prevention and leading universities. In a meeting held in Chicago, this panel of experts recommended that I include four components in a health-effects impact program: health assessment, health monitoring, environmental assessment, and environmental monitoring. Following this meeting, in December 1995 I began a series of consultations and meetings with various Nevada state agencies that could give input on and possibly implement these components. In general, these meetings and consultations were not fruitful in that the agencies showed a general lack of interest in the overall health-effects project. This situation was due in part to a lack of funds and personnel. In addition, nuclear issues in Nevada are seen as political issues, and thus environmental and health agencies avoid them whenever possible. After initiating and carrying out the first two phases, I focused exclusively on the health assessment component, which became the third step in Nevada's Yucca Mountain health-effects initiative.

I began the health assessment component by generally surveying nine Nevada communities close to Yucca Mountain (Indian Springs, Pahrump, Amargosa Valley, Beatty, Caliente, Panaca, Pioche, Alamo, and Mesquite) for the purpose of selecting a community first for a general medical ethnography and later for a pilot household health survey. The medical ethnography was intended to provide an overall view of the sociocultural context of the community and how general health issues and resources fit within this context. The household health survey was a way to begin to identify specific health problems of individuals and families within the community. To choose a site, I asked the following questions: How likely was the community to be impacted by transportation and storage of nuclear waste at Yucca Mountain and in what fashion? What had been the community's past history of exposure to hazardous waste, radiation, and other forms of environmental pollution? Were health personnel located in the community and did they express an interest in participating in a health impact assessment project? Would community leaders such as town council members and county commissioners support such a project? Did the community have organized groups that perhaps could serve as a conduit for recruiting and advertising the project? Was the community homogeneous or heterogeneous in terms of demographics? And was housing available for research staff?

I chose the township of Caliente in Lincoln County as the site for the medical ethnography and pilot household study because it satisfied most of the questions that framed the assessment. Of major importance was the fact that the federal government had designated Lincoln County an "affected unit of government" in regard to Yucca Mountain impacts. Because the town is bisected by the Union Pacific Railroad and US Highway 93, a lot of high-level nuclear waste will pass through it if the Yucca Mountain storage facility is approved. Caliente also stands downwind from the NTS, so residents there participated in the earlier epidemiological studies and are eligible for compensation under RECA. In addition, I came across a poem early on in my fieldwork that helped turn my attention to this particular community. The poem was written in 1993 by a woman named Margaret Sibley, whose grandfather had died of cancer in Caliente. With her permission, I print the first stanza of her poem, titled "The Government's Biggest Sin":

> The cool breeze and fresh air, a small town atmosphere.
> Caliente is a beautiful place.

Its name came from the warmth of the water,
Not from the heat of the sun's face.
Yet, since the nuclear years of the "Arms Race"
Caliente is not such a nice place.
The radiation level is, of course, too high.
It has caused many family members and friends to die.
Cancer is the leading disease, which plagues the people here.
It is what everyone has come to fear.

In 1995 I began collecting data in Caliente for a general medical ethnography of the community. I spent one full month in the community in 1995 and made several shorter trips there during 1996 and 1997. As in the community site-selection process, I formulated a number of questions as I launched the medical ethnography. I grouped the questions under such topics as health data information systems (What health data are currently being collected and where are the data located? How are data collected and by whom? Can the data be used to formulate a general health profile?); health care resources and utilization of resources; perceptions of health problems; historical background on toxic and hazardous exposures; and general demography and lifestyles in the community as they relate to health. Data were collected primarily through participant observation, key informant interviews, and archival research. In general, during this phase of research there was much community support of the fieldwork. But during my stay in 1995, there was tension in the community over a resolution by county commissioners that supported the temporary storage of high-level nuclear waste in Lincoln County. The State of Nevada threatened a lawsuit to stop the resolution. A recall initiative against a county commissioner who supported the resolution circulated through the community. Whether or not this tension and political climate influenced the qualitative data I collected was hard to assess, but a great deal of my time was spent clarifying my goals and objectives and establishing rapport with community leaders on both sides of the debate. These efforts were generally successful, but I was consistently asked by residents if "the governor had sent me out there to spy on Lincoln County."

In January and May 2000, I returned to Caliente with a research assistant to carry out a household health survey designed as only a pilot study in terms of developing fieldwork strategies and testing the instrument for its usefulness in establishing some community baseline health data. First we selected the best method for random sampling. The Caliente Utilities Customers' List (dated November 9, 1999) was the best tool, as it was the most inclusive list of Caliente resident addresses available. After obtaining the list through approval by Caliente city hall staff, we numbered each of the 792 listed addresses sequentially and drew a total of 105 addresses (50 in January and 55 in May) by using a random number table (Kirk 1990:650–51). The goal was to have a total research sample of thirty-five households, the number we thought we could reasonably complete during the fieldwork period. Thirty-three surveys were

Table 9.1. Inclusion and Exclusion in Household Health Survey

Inclusion/Exclusion Criteria	Number
Participated	33
Refused	21
Unoccupied (seasonal use, abandoned, for sale, etc.)	14
Business (no residents)	11
Repeats (repeat numbers in random chart or utility list)	9
No dwelling (vacant slots in trailer park, poles/wells with attached meters)	7
No-shows	3
Too feeble to participate	3
Cancellations without opportunity to reschedule	2
Unapproachable (guard dogs and no trespassing signs)	2
Total	105

Table 9.2. Survey Completion Rate

	Number	Percent
Participant Households	33	54
Direct Refusal Households	21	34
Nonparticipant Eligible Households (unapproachable, cancellations, no-shows)	7	11

completed. We made multiple visits to verify addresses and contact residents, thoroughly investigating each of the 105 addresses to obtain the final sample size. To solicit participation in the research, we made a minimum of four attempts (during the day, evening, and weekends) at each resident address and spoke with neighbors to verify household occupancy. Inclusion and exclusion results from the 105 addresses drawn are shown in table 9.1. Sixty-one addresses were eligible for the project, and forty-four addresses were not eligible for the project (see table 9.2).

My assistant and I encountered many challenges and problems during this phase of research, some having to do with the unique physical circumstances of a rural community and others concerning the people who resided there. Locating addresses and verifying resident occupancy were no easy tasks. Many dwellings in Caliente did not have address numbers posted, and we discovered early in the fieldwork phase that some streets were not identified on maps or signposts, and some different streets had the same name. Residents of Caliente receive their mail at post office boxes, so sometimes residents themselves did not know their house numbers or street names, and they did not find this unusual. The general sentiment was that "those who need to know knew where they lived, and others didn't need to know." Caliente had more "seasonal" housing than we expected, and it was time-consuming to verify this status. We also found abandoned houses. NO TRESPASSING and KEEP OUT signs and dogs enclosed in yard fencing also presented challenges, but persistence through repeated visits to the fence line often paid off in these cases.

In addition to the challenges of locating addresses, on several occasions people assumed we were from Child Protective Services, religious solicitors, or census takers and tried to turn us away before we could identify ourselves. Representatives from all three of these groups were also in the community making household calls, and on the first field trip we drove university vehicles with the Nevada state seal on the side. To overcome this challenge, we made formal presentations at the senior center and posted fliers; the newspaper printed articles about the Community Health Assessment Project; and we switched to private cars. In addition, we introduced the project to the managers of a subsidized apartment complex and a trailer park, and they sometimes acted as our spokespeople.

Another major challenge in this phase of work again had to do with the political climate of the community. Researchers encountered residents both for and against transportation and storage of high-level nuclear waste at Yucca Mountain. We were often put on the spot during our formal interviews and in the general community as to our personal ideas and beliefs concerning this issue. We consistently maintained a neutral attitude and always attempted to refocus the discussion back to the purpose of the pilot study, but political awareness was essential to our fieldwork.

Since we were very visible within the community, many residents who were not eligible—that is, their households had not been drawn in the random sample—requested to be in the study. We spent considerable time with these individuals, explaining the purpose of the pilot study and why they were not eligible for participation. However, many of these individuals were long-term Lincoln County residents, and they expressed concern and sometimes anger over health problems and radiation exposures from past weapons testing at the NTS. They argued that they, as downwinders, should have been the focus of our study instead of planning for Yucca Mountain.

In our random sample, twenty-one eligible households directly refused to participate in the project. Some people refused because of the time involved in completing the questionnaire, about two hours, or because they were new to the community and knew little to nothing about Yucca Mountain. The majority who refused, however, did so because of their past experiences with the federal government in regard to fallout from the NTS. Some who had participated in earlier government-funded epidemiological studies on thyroid disease and leukemia were never given the results of the studies, even though researchers had promised them. Others knew the results but were disturbed that they were not more conclusive and that no medical benefits were offered to study participants; they saw no reason to participate in any more so-called health studies. Others refused to participate because they thought they were eligible under

RECA but had been denied compensation, and they generally expressed the sentiment that "even if baseline health data were collected and there was radiation exposure from Yucca Mountain activities, the government wouldn't pay anyway." They saw participation in the household survey as a waste of time. As one man said, "You don't need to know about my health 'cause nothing is going to come of it anyway."

Following fieldwork and data analysis, we pointed out in our report to the NWPO that multiple indicators of health are needed in any one specific community for good baseline health data. That is, no one indicator will stand alone as an assessment tool, no matter how well that tool is designed. Thus we said that a community household survey ought to be considered as only one tool among many. We did, however, make a number of recommendations based upon an assessment of this pilot study.

In our assessment, the questionnaire used in the pilot study was too long, even though we had purposely designed it to be very inclusive since we wanted to capture as diverse a picture of health conditions within the household and community as possible. We recommended that the questionnaire for future studies be redesigned to focus exclusively on health profiles of household members, eliminating descriptive information about the general environment of the community and household and extended-family residential patterns. We also suggested a redesigned questionnaire that could be administered in approximately thirty minutes; one hour at the most for large families. During the pilot phase, all adult household members were interviewed separately; but we found that adult women were the most knowledgeable concerning the family's health, including the health of adult males and children. In many cases, adult men had to rely almost exclusively on their spouses or mates for their health profile information. Thus we recommended that whenever possible, the primary informant or respondent in future studies be the primary adult woman of the household. This change would entail getting permission from other adults in the household for her to serve in this role, but it would greatly expedite the interview process without necessarily sacrificing accuracy of data.

The methodology selected for the household survey guaranteed a random sample, but given the nature of the rural community, it was exceedingly time-consuming to locate and confirm eligible respondents. We recommended this method for assuring randomness. The number of households sampled in the pilot was purposely kept small, but we recommended that a larger number of households be included in future surveys in order to get a reliable statistical sample of the community based upon the total number of community households. It is possible that with advanced notice in the community, a phone survey could be conducted. That is, field investigators could make initial contact with respondents and then follow up by telephone interview to complete all or part of the questionnaire. It is essential, however, that field or phone researchers be skilled interviewers and generally knowledgeable about "rural" culture. We recommended that the interviewers be women, preferably from outside the study community, as several respondents reported they would be uneasy with "people they knew" taking their health information and protecting their confidentiality.

Consideration could also be given to identifying "index" families within the community that could stand as surrogates for the community over an extended period. The health data of these families could be more closely monitored than could a larger sample. The AEC-DOE used this research index family model during weapons testing at the Nevada Test Site, and the model should be explored as to its strengths and weaknesses. In addition to household health surveys, we recommended the use of other assessment tools as indicators of community health. For example, we recommended that local and county health data collections systems be strengthened. We also recommended that computer equipment, software, and technical assistance be given to local pharmacies to track trends and patterns in pharmaceutical prescriptions, to the local public health nurse to track trends and patterns in services and treatments given, to home health agencies and respiratory therapists to track changes in care provided, and to local physicians and clinics for trends in treatments. All this data should be supplemented through resources and funding from the federal government to the Nevada state health department for reinstituting annual and standardized community health profiles, perhaps as part of the Radiation Exposure Screening and Education Program.

Conclusion

The Community Health Assessment Project was meant to be only a pilot project to test the survey instrument and field methodology. In this regard, the project was a success in that we identified a number of problems with the instrument and experienced how challenging it is to conduct fieldwork in rural communities. However, what we learned about most is how the legacy of weapons testing at the NTS continues to place a shadow over the lives of downwinders. Much of the political controversy in Lincoln County—for example, regarding the transportation and storage of high-level nuclear waste at Yucca Mountain—is between those individuals and families who were residents of the county during the days of weapons testing at the NTS and have a history of dealing with the federal government on issues of radiation compensation, and those who have no such history. Those without a radiation history tend to see Yucca Mountain as an economic boost to a failing rural economy, while radiation downwinders see it as yet another government project that has no regard for the health and safety of rural residents. They see Yucca Mountain as a potential replay of what happened to them in the past and continue to feel a great mistrust toward the government. It was generally long-term residents who expressed the most dismay that our health assessment project focused on data collection in regard to Yucca Mountain instead of focusing on their health problems from past radiation exposure. As stated previously, many had participated in the epidemiology studies in the 1960s and later that looked at the incidence of thyroid disease and leukemia in downwinders; but they never saw the results of such studies, nor were they offered any health benefits as a result of their participation. These individuals were the most adamant in their position about not participating in any more health studies. "You don't need to know about my health 'cause nothing is going to come of it anyway" was the basic expressed sentiment. Before nuclear testing began in the early 1950s, there was no good baseline health data available, and there will not be good baseline health data should the Yucca Mountain project become operational or should weapons testing be resumed, unless major changes occur in both the mindset of rural communities and in Nevada's health and environmental agencies. I do not see this possibility as likely. However, it will be those along transportation routes and in proximity to Yucca Mountain and the NTS who will once again bear the burden of the nation's nuclear load and once again have both their physical and mental health assaulted in ways relatively unknown in the rest of the country.

Even though the Yucca Mountain project remains a controversial one among some residents of Nevada, Nevada's governor and its entire congressional delegation have consistently shown opposition to the project through resolutions and other explicit statements of policy. Nevada's governor, Kenny Guinn, has called the project "the single greatest threat to the health and safety of the people of this state," and in 2001 he proposed establishing a Nevada Protection Fund. The Nevada legislature in June 2001 appropriated $4 million for the protection fund, to be used to mount legal challenges against the project and to implement a public awareness campaign to make people in other states aware of the risks and impacts they will be facing from the transportation of high-level nuclear waste should the project be approved. Following the legislature's action, the Clark County Board of Commissioners indicated that Clark County would contribute $1 million to the fund (Governor Guinn's Nevada Protection Fund 2005). In September 2001, the Agency for Nuclear Projects, the administrative entity for the fund, signed a contract with the Washington, DC, law firm of Egan & Associates to provide legal services in the fight against Yucca Mountain. Several lawsuits have subsequently been filed. In April 2002, Governor Guinn officially issued to Congress a "Notice of Disapproval" of the proposed Yucca Mountain project. But in July 2002, Congress approved President Bush's recommendation of the Yucca Mountain site for development.

However, the DOE is having problems pushing the project forward. The agency filed a license application with the Nuclear Regulatory Commission (NRC) to construct the repository, but the NRC ruled that the application was incomplete and inadequate. More recently, in April 2005 Congressman Jon Porter, chairman of the Subcommittee on the Federal Workforce and Agency Organization (of the House Committee on Government Reform), announced, after reviewing documents from the DOE and Department of Interior, that congressional hearings would be held regarding allegations that federal scientists falsified data used to establish the safety of the Yucca Mountain nuclear waste repository. In a press release on April 1, 2005, Congressman Porter said, "After reviewing the first set of documents, I am appalled at the blatant misconduct by Federal employees. The information that I received is damning. The legitimacy of the science surrounding the storage of nuclear waste at this facility is indeed in question. I look forward to the hearing that my subcommittee will hold on this issue to get to the bottom of this misconduct, as well as obtaining additional documents from both Departments as they continue to respond to my earlier request. Nevadans, and all Americans, deserve to know the truth when it comes to safety issues of this magnitude" (Nuclear Waste Project Office 2005). There is no doubt that Nevadans who were downwinders during atomic testing wanted to know the truth about the dangers of radioactive fallout in the 1950s and 1960s, and they certainly want to know the truth about Yucca Mountain. It seems entirely reasonable that radiation downwinders see Yucca Mountain as yet another government endeavor with no regard for their health and safety and as a replay of what happened to them in the past. They have every right to feel a great mistrust toward the government.

Notes

1. This section draws heavily on the photojournalistic work of Carole Gallagher (*American Ground Zero*, 1993) and the interviews she carried out among downwinders, because she, more than anyone, has truly captured their lived experiences.

References

Ball, Howard
1986   Justice Downwind: America's Atomic Testing Program in the 1950s. New York: Oxford University Press.

Boutté, Marie I.
1994   Literature Review for Assessing and Monitoring Health Effects of Nuclear Waste Repository. Carson City, NV: Nuclear Waste Projects Office.
1997a Health Effects Studies: Epidemiology at Nevada Test Site—Thyroid Cohort Study. Carson City, NV: Nuclear Waste Projects Office.
1997b Health Effects Studies: Epidemiology at the Nevada Test Site Part II—Leukemia. Carson City, NV: Nuclear Waste Projects Office.
2002   Compensating for Health: The Acts and Outcomes of Atomic Testing. Human Organization 61(1):41–50.
2004   Advocacy for the Exposed: A Look at Radiation Compensation. Paper presented at the Annual Meeting of the Society for Applied Anthropology, Dallas, April 2.

Department of Energy
1991   Frequently Asked Questions about the Nevada Test Site. Las Vegas: Department of Energy.
1994   United States Nuclear Tests: July 1945 through September 1992. Las Vegas: Department of Energy.

1995   A Perspective on Atmospheric Nuclear Tests in Nevada: Fact Book. Las Vegas: Department of Energy.

DOE. *See* Department of Energy

Fradkin, Philip L.
1989   Fallout: An American Nuclear Tragedy. Tucson: University of Arizona Press.

Gallagher, Carole
1993   American Ground Zero: The Secret Nuclear War. Cambridge, MA: MIT Press.

Goin, Peter
1991   Nuclear Landscapes. Baltimore: Johns Hopkins University Press.

Governor Guinn's Nevada Protection Fund
2005   Governor Kenny Guinn's Nevada Protection Fund: Assuring Nevada's Victory over Yucca Mountain. Electronic document, http://www.state.nv.us/nucwaste/npf.htm, accessed May 20, 2005.

Heath, Clark W.
1966   Subject: Leukemia in Fredonia, Arizona. Washington, DC: US Public Health Service, Leukemia Unit, Epidemiology Branch.

Kerber, R. A., J. E. Till, S. L. Simon, J. L. Lyon, D. C. Thomas, S. Preston-Martin, M. L. Rallison, R. D. Lloyd, and W. Stevens
1993   A Cohort Study of Thyroid Disease in Relation to Fallout from Nuclear Weapons Testing. Journal of the American Medical Association 270:2076–82.

Kirk, Roger E.
1990   Statistics: An Introduction. 3rd ed. Fort Worth, TX: Holt, Rinehart and Winston, Inc.

Miller, Richard L.
1986   Under the Cloud: The Decades of Nuclear Testing. New York: Free Press.

Nuclear Waste Project Office
2005   Chairman Jon Porter's Initial Probe into Allegations That Federal Scientists Falsified Data Used to Establish the Safety of the Yucca Mountain Nuclear Waste Repository Reveals Disturbing Result. Electronic document, http://www.state.nv.us/nucwaste/news2005/pdf/porter050401probe.pdf, accessed May 20, 2005.

Titus, A. Costandina
1986   Bombs in the Backyard: Atomic Testing and American Politics. Reno: University of Nevada Press.

Udall, Stewart L.
1994   The Myths of August: A Personal Exploration of Our Tragic Cold War Affair with the Atom. New York: Pantheon Books.

US Congress. House of Representatives. Committee on Interstate and Foreign Commerce. Subcommittee on Oversight and Investigations

1979   Low-Level Radiation Effects on Health. Serial no. 96-129. 96th Cong. 1st sess. April 28, May 24, August 1. Washington, DC: US Government Printing Office.

1980   The Forgotten Guinea Pigs: A Report on Health Effects of Low Level Radiation Sustained as a Result of the Nuclear Weapons Testing Program. Report 96-96-IFC 53. 96th Cong. 2d sess. Washington, DC: US Government Printing Office.

US Congress. Senate. Committee on Labor and Human Resources

1982   Statement of Gloria Gregerson for Citizen's Call on S.1483, the Radiation Exposure Compensation Act of 1981. 97th Cong. 2d sess. April 8.

Wachholz, B. W.

1990   Overview of the National Cancer Institute's Activities Related to Exposure to the Public to Fallout from the Nevada Test Site. Health Physics 59:511–14.

Wasserman, Harvey, and Norman Solomon

1982   Killing Our Own: The Disaster of America's Experience with Atomic Radiation. New York: Delacorte Press.

t e n

From Analysis to Action
Efforts to Address the Nuclear Legacy
in the Marshall Islands

Holly M. Barker

The RMI [Republic of the Marshall Islands] is in a very precarious position. We have very significant radiological burdens in the RMI that we lack the resources, knowledge, or capacity to address. These radiological burdens—including the need to clean-up private property and return populations to their home islands, and the need to provide adequate healthcare and monitoring to all communities exposed to significant levels of radiation—are expensive. Despite the costs of remedies, we are simply asking the US government for the same assistance, services, and compensation that it extends to its own citizens exposed to radiation or whose private property is contaminated....

The RMI is extremely worried about the well-being of the people in the Marshall Islands who were exposed to radiation from the 67 atmospheric atomic and thermonuclear weapons tests in the RMI, as well as the populations resettled on contaminated islands, including children who were born and raised in environments laced with radiation from the US nuclear weapons tests....

More than ever, it is clear to us that the US government's position regarding radiation exposure in the RMI is antiquated, and needs to be updated. (US Congress, Senate Energy and Natural Resources Committee 2005)

America's nuclear history in the Marshall Islands has been colored with official denial, self-serving control of information, and abrogation of commitment to redress the shameful wrongs done to the Marshallese people.... Today, not only is the US government backpedaling on this issue but its official position as enunciated by the current administration is to flee its responsibilities to the Marshall Islands for the severe nuclear damages and injuries perpetrated upon them.

—Tony deBrum 2005

Most people in the world associate Hiroshima and Nagasaki with nuclear devastation. We can imagine the buildings that were leveled and the incineration of all living things—images we should never forget, as they are reminders of the destructive capacity of human nature.

Ten thousand immigrants from the Marshall Islands live in the United States, and fifty-five thousand Marshallese remain on their home islands; many of these Marshallese serve as living reminders that in the 1940s and 1950s nuclear bomb testing in the Pacific left a debt that the United States is still not willing to pay. For twelve years, the Marshall Islands experienced the equivalent of 1.6 Hiroshima-sized bombs every single day. Many people assume that the islands were deserted during the tests, but the Marshallese can tell you otherwise.

In radioactive iodine alone, 6.3 billion curies of iodine-131 were released into the atmosphere as a result of the nuclear testing in the Marshall Islands—an amount 42 times greater than the 150 million curies released by atmospheric testing in Nevada, 150 times greater than the estimated 40 million curies released as a result of the Chernobyl nuclear accident, and 8,500 times greater than the 739,000 curies released from Atomic Energy Commission (AEC) operations at the Hanford Nuclear Reservation (Centers for Disease Control 1998). While amounts of radionuclides released into the environment do not precisely correspond to amounts of radiation that enter the local food chain or cause illness, these figures do provide us with rough measures with which to compare degrees of radiation contamination for different areas.

After the deployment of atomic weapons during World War II, the United States needed to learn more about the capabilities of its newest weapon—more information than the destruction of Hiroshima and Nagaski provided. The United States decided to make a proving ground out of its small islands in Micronesia, acquired as a United Nations trust territory following the war. As the trust territory administrator, the United States promised to safeguard the well-being of the territory's inhabitants.

On the atolls of Bikini and Enewetak in the Marshall Islands, the United States detonated sixty-seven atmospheric, on the ground, and underwater atomic and thermonuclear weapons from 1946 to 1958. From nuclear weapons tests in the Marshall Islands, the United States learned how its naval fleet would survive a nuclear attack. In 1946 US researchers anchored navy vessels, including the *Nagato*, a Japanese flagship captured at the end of World War II, in Bikini's lagoon. Test Baker, an underwater shot, debilitated and sunk many vessels, which remain on the bottom of Bikini's lagoon today.

Also in the Marshall Islands, the United States detonated its largest weapon ever tested, the Bravo shot of March 1, 1954—the equivalent of one thousand Hiroshima-sized bombs. Bravo exposed the crew of a Japanese fishing boat near Bikini, Marshallese residents downwind from Bikini, and US servicemen to levels of radiation that caused death and lifelong illness. Following Bravo, US government researchers evacuated some of the islanders and enrolled them in a secret medical experiment, called Project 4.1, to study the effects of radiation on human beings. Later, the US government resettled the unwitting participants in this program on an island highly contaminated with radiation to learn firsthand how human beings ingest and absorb radiation from their environment.

During the Cold War, the United States made immeasurable political strides as nuclear superiority guaranteed status as a superpower and ushered in a period of nuclear deterrence. However, this political advancement did not come without a price for the Marshallese, whose health and environment continue to display the scars of US achievements.

Recently, the US National Cancer Institute (NCI) predicted that the Marshallese will experience hundreds of future cancer cases linked to the US nuclear weapons testing program. Radiological illnesses from the testing program continue to overwhelm the capabilities of the public health infrastructure in the Marshall Islands. Beyond the participants of Project 4.1 who receive medical care, the US government contributes only $7 per patient per month for the communities most affected by the testing program and for people with confirmed radiogenic illnesses, such as cancer.

There is no oncologist in the Marshall Islands, no chemotherapy, no cancer registry, and no nationwide screening program for early detection of cancer.

Part of the reason US assistance with the aftermath of the testing program remains so paltry is that the US government refuses to acknowledge the scope of the area affected by radiation. During the time of the trust territory, the US government maintained that the weapons tests created radiological contamination in only a very narrow area of the RMI, and the US government successfully codified its definition of the geographic scope of contamination in US law (Public Law 99-239). Despite a preponderance of US government documents that surfaced after Congress enacted this law, as well as new scientific information showing that lower levels of radiation cause more harm than previously understood, the US government refuses to acknowledge radiation-related needs beyond the scope of current US law.

The Marshall Islands currently has a petition before Congress for additional assistance, primarily to create the capacity to respond to the health care burdens resulting from the US nuclear weapons testing program and to provide adequate funding to compensate for personal injury and private property damage. The Senate Energy Committee, the House Resources Committee, and the Subcommittee on Asia and Pacific of the House International Relations Committee are the committees that must consider the petition by the Marshall Islands.

The people of the Marshall Islands deserve our appreciation for the monumental sacrifices they incurred during the Cold War, as well as our assistance in addressing the persistent problems caused by radiation exposure.

Getting Started

I grew up in a small university town in Rhode Island with a family and community that educated itself about the human and environmental impacts of nuclear energy and nuclear weapons. In high school I wrote to Dr. Helen Caldicott for help with a research paper. I devoured a package of materials she sent to me about the unsolved problems linked to nuclear power and the risks of nuclear power plants to people and the environment. Meanwhile, neighbors and parents of my friends drove from Rhode Island to Groton, Connecticut, to protest the production of Trident submarines armed with nuclear weapons. Political science classes at the University of Rhode Island that focused on the Cold War and Star Wars gave me what now seems like a scripted preparation for my adult journey, a journey that is inseparable from the Marshall Islands—the location the Peace Corps assigned me to and the focus of my employment and research as an anthropologist for the last eighteen years.

Even before I first set foot in the Republic of the Marshall Islands in 1988, I called the US State Department to ask about lingering radiation effects from the massive testing of US nuclear weapons there. From the time I began asking these questions until the present, virtually every US government representative I talked to maintained that there was nothing to worry about—that the islands, its residents, and its visitors (including Peace Corps volunteers) were safe. I strongly disagree with the US government position because it erases the sufferings and experiences of countless Marshallese, and I have spent my entire adult life trying to help the Marshall Islands seek redress from the US government for the lingering hardships that are the legacy of the US nuclear weapons testing program.

It was not until I got to the Marshall Islands that I learned the full extent of the testing program. Researchers designed the weapons to produce as much local fallout as possible, to create a laboratory in the Marshall Islands for studying the effects of radiation and to allay international criticism about atmospheric radiation. The total yield of the testing program was one hundred times the yield tested in Nevada (Nuclear Claims Tribunal 2003), yet the US government has been far more responsive to the needs of the people downwind from the Nevada tests than to the Marshallese, who face neglect and denial of responsibility by the US government (see Boutté, Dawson, and Madsen, this volume).

The Peace Corps director in the Marshall Islands responded to my concerns about radiation levels by agreeing to post me as far away from the ground zero sites as possible; the testing occurred in the northwest of the RMI, and the Peace Corps placed me on an island in the southeast. As I learned the Marshallese language, became part of a local community for my two years of service, and read about the US and RMI positions regarding the aftermath of US nuclear weapons testing, I could see the disconnect between Marshallese perceptions about radiation effects based on their first-hand experiences and a US government position that did not factor in Marshallese concerns.

The US government maintains that the nuclear weapons tests affected just four populations in the Marshall Islands—called the 4 Atolls—the people of Enewetak and Bikini, whom the US government relocated for the testing program while using their islands as ground zero locations for detonations, and the people of two inhabited atolls

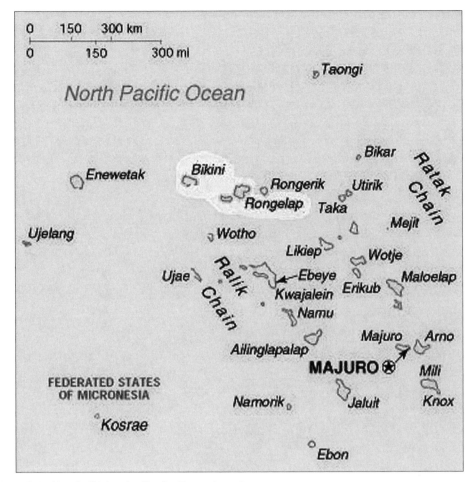

Map 10.1: Marshall Islands. Credit: Dame Jane Resture

directly downwind from the test sites, Rongelap and Utrik. Although the US government evacuated Marshallese downwind from the test sites for much smaller tests, it failed to relocate any islanders before detonating its largest thermonuclear device. Consequently, the people of Rongelap received near-lethal doses of radiation as a result of the Bravo test on March 1, 1954.

When I learned about nuclear issues in the RMI while serving as a Peace Corps volunteer, I felt compelled to speak out about them. The Peace Corps director in the RMI threatened to terminate my service for writing an article to the country's only newspaper, asking the paper to translate articles about nuclear issues into Marshallese so the people most affected by these issues could benefit from the articles. I survived, and even thrived, in the Peace Corps and upon completion of my service moved to Washington, DC, where I hoped to continue work in the international realm. I quickly found my niche at the RMI Embassy in Washington, DC, my only employer since 1990.

Before I arrived at the embassy, an effort was under way in the United States to open US government documents—particularly at the Department of Energy (DOE)—pertaining to radiation exposure during the Cold War. In 1993 dozens of boxes containing thousands of declassified documents about the US nuclear weapons testing program in the RMI began to arrive on the embassy doorstep. I began to read through these documents, one by one. It was clear from the first day I sifted through these documents that damages, injuries, and radiological contamination related to the testing program were much more widespread than previously acknowledged by the US government and understood by the RMI government.

After the RMI government understood that US government documents detailed exposures beyond the limited parameters of the US position, the RMI government wanted to talk to the people who received the significant radiation exposures noted in the documents to determine whether they experienced problems resulting from their exposures. No one in the RMI believes that radiation affected only four atolls; in 1994 the RMI government took steps to conduct its own research, the first government-sponsored effort to assemble this information. Former RMI ambassador to the United States Wilfred Kendall (now the minister of education) and former RMI senator Tony deBrum asked me to conduct extensive interviews with populations both included in and excluded from the area defined by the US government as affected by the tests. Working with local counterparts, I conducted more than two hundred interviews in 1994. The interviews overwhelmingly confirmed that the weapons testing program created profound medical, environmental, social, political, and economic problems for many populations in the RMI, not just the four atolls acknowledged by the United States (Barker 2004). Furthermore, the interviews demonstrated how the nuclear weapons testing program affected the lived experiences of the Marshallese on even the smallest and most intimate levels: horrific birthing abnormalities experienced by women; families trying to cope with and find treatment for cancers, retardation, and thyroid disorders; the anguish of a soaring suicide rate in young males who cannot live on their home islands because of lingering contamination but do not have the skills or opportunities to find employment in urban areas.

In 1994 the RMI government coupled the declassified documents demonstrating greater damage and injuries than previously acknowledged with ethnographic data detailing the human consequences of the radiation experienced by the Marshallese. The RMI government presented this information—along with evidence about why it believes the US government exposed Marshallese citizens to radiation for experimental purposes—to the White House Advisory Committee on Human Radiation Experiments (ACHRE). In its final report, issued in 1995, ACHRE confirmed two known experiments during which US government researchers purposefully exposed Marshallese citizens to radiation, not for the well-being of the subjects but to advance the research agenda of the US government (ACHRE 1995; Johnston, this volume).

What the RMI presented to ACHRE is just part of the story. There is much information about the testing program in the 1940s and 1950s that the US government still deems too critical to current national security interests to release. The boxes of declassified documents contain thousands of pages that are blacked out and stamped "deleted." As just one example of the missing information, the US government has yet to provide radiation exposure data for all of the sixty-seven tests. It is impossible, therefore, to understand the cumulative impact of the entire weapons testing program on the people and environment in the RMI, but scientists are able to make predictions. There is enough information to challenge the US government position regarding assistance for communities affected by the testing program and to help shape research questions that produce better understandings about the Marshallese experiences as a result of the intersection of their history with the US Cold War agenda.

History of the US Nuclear Weapons Testing Program in the RMI

During World War II, the United States wrested control of the Marshall Islands from a brutal Japanese military regime,[1] and the US Navy became the administering authority for the Marshall Islands in 1945. At the end of the war, the United States dropped atomic weapons on the cities of Hiroshima and Nagasaki—some historians believe to test atomic weapons in a real-life context rather than to end the war as is commonly believed.[2]

From the Trinity test in the New Mexico desert and the weapons dropped on Hiroshima and Nagasaki, the United States had some understanding of the strength, capacity, and damages resulting from nuclear weapons, but it needed to more fully explore the destructive capacities of the bomb. The US Navy determined that its newly acquired possession in the central Pacific was the perfect venue in which to expand on the US government's understanding of its newest technology.[3] Because of the geographic isolation of the Marshall Islands, the United States could conduct its scientific studies of the effects of the weapons tests in secret, without the scrutiny of the American public or the international community, and without the watchful eye of the Russians as the Cold War gained momentum.

In 1946 the US Navy launched its first nuclear weapons tests in the Marshall Islands as part of Operation Crossroads—the literal crossroads in US weapons technology as the United States took bold steps into the nuclear age. Operation Crossroads consisted of tests Able and Baker at Bikini Atoll.[4] Able was an airdrop, and Baker was an underwater detonation to determine how naval ships would endure a nuclear attack. Animals left on the decks for purposeful exposure to the blast lost their hair, became ill, and sometimes died. Similarly, US military personnel sent to inspect or clean the ships after the tests received high doses of radiation, and many of these servicemen became sick or died.[5]

In 1947 the United Nations transferred administration of the Marshall Islands from the US Navy to the U.S government. The Marshall Islands became part of the United Nations Trust Territory of the Pacific Islands.

Of the arsenal of sixty-seven weapons, eighteen were in the megaton range (a measure of explosive power equivalent to 1 million tons of TNT). The fifteen-megaton Bravo test created a mushroom cloud that rose 25 miles into the air. The force from the weapon pulverized coral, coconut trees, and any objects in its path, and the unleashed energy pulled these materials into the mushroom cloud, where they mixed with radioactive materials. When the force of the weapon subsided and the materials that had gathered and blended with the radiation inside the cloud fell to the ground—commonly called radioactive fallout—it coated the waters, islands, food crops, water catchments, houses, animals, and people near the test sites.

The "Control" Population

Marshallese encounters with the bombs did not end with the detonations themselves. They experienced both direct problems linked to the testing program, such as health and environmental issues, and indirect problems, such as changes in diet, resettlement issues, and abrupt changes to their culture, economy, and politics. Many RMI government officials conclude that the US government purposefully exposed Marshallese citizens to radiation from nuclear weapons to study the effects of radiation on human beings (Anjain-Maddison 2005). Prior to the Bravo test in 1954, the US government evacuated inhabited communities downwind from the ground zero locations—on Rongelap, Ailinginae, Rongerik, Wotho, and Enewetak—as a precaution. As stated earlier, when the United States detonated its largest thermonuclear weapon, it decided not to evacuate communities directly downwind from the proving ground, and it redrew maps of the evacuation area to fall just outside the inhabited islands of Rongelap (Thomas 1953). During the Bravo detonation, a US naval ship was anchored off the reef of Rongelap. When radioactive fallout from Bravo moved toward Rongelap, the boat chugged off, taking the US servicemen to safety but leaving the Marshallese behind in their highly contaminated environment, where they continued to ingest and breathe radiation. The people were given no instructions about how to reduce their radiation exposure by staying indoors, covering their food and water, and wearing long-sleeved clothing.

US personnel did not return to evacuate the Rongelapese until more than two days after the United States knew that radiation coated the atoll. After evacuation, the United States placed the exposed people of Rongelap and Utrik into a secret medical study, called Project 4.1, to understand the effects of radiation on human beings. According to Isao Eknilang (interview with author, September 30, 2004), the US government brought the study subjects to Kwajalein Atoll:

> We were headed into a tiny tent town in Kwajalein, presently a United States missile test site, where white-gowned American doctors and nurses began their program called, "A Study of Human Beings Exposed to Radiation," the infamous Project 4.1. In Kwajalein we were subjected to the most extraordinary and humiliating examinations we have ever known. And as if that was not

Figure 10.1. Examination of burns suffered by a Rongelap boy during Bravo fallout. Source: Project 4.1 photo, US Navy. Republic of the Marshall Islands Embassy photo archive

> enough, other people living in the vicinity began visiting the tent compound
> to gawk at our unnatural conditions.

A notation for the Project 4.1 study appeared in a 1953 document on planning the scientific tests in conjunction with the Bravo test the next year (DOD 1953). The US government also chose a "control" population as part of its study. According to current US law, the control population is not considered exposed to or affected by radiation because they were not present on Rongelap or Utrik on March 1, 1954.

Many individuals who received near-lethal doses of radiation were related to or close friends with those in the control population, and US government representatives told members of the control population that they needed to take part in the medical studies to help their fellow citizens. The control members felt sorry for people who experienced burns down to their bones, hair falling off their heads, and severe flulike symptoms that rendered them unable to care for their own children immediately after the Bravo event. Not surprisingly, the people selected to participate as control subjects wanted to help their suffering family and friends in some manner, since taking care of others, and particularly taking care of family, is a central tenet of Pacific Island cultures. As stated by the brother of the woman quoted above (Lijohn Eknilang, interview with author, March 1, 2004):

> I was living on Ebeye for the Bravo test so I wasn't on Rongelap with the rest of my family. They [US doctors] never asked us for permission to take part in the program [after the Bravo test], but they told us that we could help the people who were on Rongelap. A lot of those people were my relatives—who could ever refuse to help? When the people were brought from Rongelap to Majuro they were kept in the military area, and they were suffering a lot. We felt so sad for them.... I believed the doctors when they told me that I was helping the people, but maybe I was only helping the doctors get information.

What many members of the control group did not anticipate was that US government researchers would insist that they participate in every medical examination. Helena Alik recalls (interview with author, March 13, 1994) that in more than one case trust territory police chased down control group members, sometimes pulling children in the control group out of classrooms when they failed to appear for scheduled medical examinations—exams that often included painful procedures such as bone marrow extraction or the injection or drinking of radioactive substances without patient knowledge or consent (ACHRE 1995; Seligman 1999).

Between the Bravo incident in 1954 and the time the US government returned people to Rongelap Atoll, US government researchers documented high levels of radiation in the environment and the foods people consumed: "Edible plants other than coconuts, such as pandanus, papaya, and squash, have been found to contain levels of Sr 90 which are above the tolerance level as defined in the Radiological Health Handbook" (Donaldson 1955:32). The US government resettled both the "exposed" and "control" populations on islands highly contaminated to study the human uptake of radiation from the environment (Barker 2004; Johnston and Barker 1999, 2001). Although the control population did not receive the high exposure of radiation from the Bravo test, after they resettled Rongelap with the initially exposed group, they began to exhibit the same types of radiation-related health problems as the exposed group. Catherine Jibas (interview with author, August 23, 1994) relates:

> I was not on Rongelap for the Bravo test, but I returned later in 1957.... It was around this time that I had my first pregnancy. My baby had a very high fever when he was delivered, and the attending health assistant told me my son wouldn't survive the night. He was so dehydrated from the fever that his skin actually peeled as I clasped him to me to nurse. The only thing we knew

to do was to wrap him in wet towels. And so it was that I held him to my body throughout the night, changing the towels and willing him to fight for his life. He lost the fight just as dawn broke....

My second son, born in 1960, was delivered live but missing the whole back of his skull—as if it had been sawed off. So the back part of the brain and the spinal cord were fully exposed. After a week, the spinal cord became detached and he, too, developed a high fever and died the following day. Aside from the cranial deformity, my son was also missing his testicles and penis. He urinated through a stump-like thing measuring less than an inch. The doctors who examined him told me that he would not survive. And sure enough, he was dead within a week.... You know, it was heartbreaking having to nurse my son, all the while taking care that his brain didn't fall into my lap. For in spite of his severe handicaps, he was healthy in every respect. It was good he died because I do not think he would have wanted to live a life as something less than human.... If it were not for the bomb testing, I would not have to watch helplessly as two of my children were taken from me.

Throughout the time that the exposed and control groups participated in Project 4.1, US government researchers told the participants that the purpose of the program was to provide medical care. In ethnographic interviews, many Marshallese enrolled in this program indicate that they felt like guinea pigs for US doctors, not like patients. According to Kalemen Gideon, a Marshallese health assistant on Likiep Atoll (interview with author, September 2, 1994):

From discussions I had with numerous people...[t]hey all wanted to know why they were not being told anything when it was their life's blood that the DOE doctors were taking to conduct their tests and experiments. Therefore, they questioned whether the doctors were truly concerned for their well-being or just for the success of their damned experiments.

Recently declassified documents corroborate Marshallese suspicions about experimentation; US government documents discuss topics such as the pulling of both decayed and healthy teeth from subjects for the purpose of study (Brookhaven National Laboratory n.d.)[6] and the need to provide placebo pills to patients so subjects would stop complaining about feeling like study subjects (Conard 1958).

For decades, the Marshallese study subjects complained about medical problems that emerged after their radiation exposures, but the US government always denied any link between these conditions and radiation exposure and instead retaliated with "slick mathematical and statistical representations to dismiss the occurrence of exotic anomalies, including malformed fetuses, and abnormal occurrences of diseases in so-called 'unexposed areas,' as coincidental and not attributable to radiation exposure" (deBrum 2005). DeBrum, a lifetime public servant in the RMI and often point person for the RMI government in dealings with the DOE, noted:

> We have been told repeatedly…that our birthing anomalies are the result of
> incest or a gene pool that is too small—anything but the radiation. These
> explanations are offensive and obviously wrong since these abnormalities cer-
> tainly did not occur before we became the proving ground for US nuclear
> weapons. Selective referral of Marshallese patients to different military hospi-
> tals in the United States and its territories also made it easier for the US gov-
> ernment to dismiss linkages between medical problems and radiation
> exposure. The unexplained and multiple fires that led to the destruction of
> numerous records and medical charts for the patients with the most acute radi-
> ation illnesses further underscores this point. In spite of all these studies and
> findings, we were told that a positive linkage was still impossible because of
> what they called "statistical insignificance." [7,8] (deBrum 2005)

For many decades after the Bravo incident, the US government kept the control population enrolled in Project 4.1 so that the United States could benefit from medical research. When the US government officially terminated the research program and switched to a strictly medical care program in 1998, the control population found itself outside any US public law language authorizing its inclusion in medical care programs. Therefore, it is up to political appointees at the DOE to determine whether to include the control population in the current medical monitoring and care program. Some DOE Office of Health Services directors who have responsibility for the DOE's programs in the RMI want to include members of the control population; others have sought to remove them. According to Alfonso Jebtak, a control subject (interview with author, September 18, 2004):

> They [DOE doctors] sure had no problems using us when they needed us. For
> most of my life they stuck me with needles, told me to take pills, and did
> whatever they wanted to me. Now that I'm old and need medical care for all
> I've been through they might stop caring for me! I don't have enough money
> to even purchase the medication they currently have me on.

Given the control group's involvement in confirmed human radiation experiments and their resettlement on highly contaminated lands, it is clear that the group has ongoing health care needs—needs that the RMI government does not have the capacity or the responsibility to address, and needs that the US government continues to deny responsibility for.

Marshallese Songs and the US Nuclear Weapons Testing Program

One way the Marshallese affected by the US nuclear weapons testing program give voice to the emotions they feel, and the problems they endure, is through song. Singing is a vital part of the culture, as it imparts oral history to younger generations and binds communities at all important events (religious, social, and political).

After the US government returned the people of Rongelap to contaminated islands in 1957, they began to experience extreme medical problems, and they witnessed changes to their environment, including changes to crops and animals. In 1985 the community made the decision to relocate to the island of Mejatto on Kwajalein Atoll—an island never occupied and difficult to live on because of the lack of cultivated foods—rather than continue to put the health of themselves and their children at risk on Rongelap. The move and the medical ailments of the people created much sorrow and suffering and became the subject of a song written around 1985 by Tarines Abon, a member of the control population:

> I wrote the song while we were living on Mejatto. Life was very difficult there.
> I saw suffering and sadness. Those are the feelings I had because of the experiences with my own body [health], and the experiences of the Rongelapese when we had to leave our home islands. (Interview with author, September 30, 2004)

The song Tarines Abon wrote on Mejatto Island, "177 Song" (Barker 2004), refers to Section 177 of the Compact of Free Association and the medical program for the four atolls and people acknowledged by the Nuclear Claims Tribunal in the Marshall Islands to have a radiogenic illness (discussed later in this chapter). Recently, the US Congress directed the 177 Health Care Program (HCP) to concentrate on preventive care. Therefore, the program lacks the ability to treat tertiary illnesses such as cancers, and the recipients of the program feel frustrated by the inadequacy of resources to support the type of health care they need.

"Al in 177" ("177 Song")

Naat inaaj ella lok jen entan kein ko ijaje kio?
Komaron ke juon ao ri-jinet im ao marin ko?

Ne ij ped ilo ao radiation en bwe imojino kon tyroit im ao jojolair,
Konan eo in bwe in wiwa wot ion juon ao jikin aeneman.
Im jab na wot ak ro ilo nomba en 177.

Aolepen lomnak eo ao ij liwoj rej nan kom kio.
Kon wewin ko ij lo ilo an raan jabe kein ad.

[When will I be released from my sufferings that I still do not understand?
Would you guide me and give me strength?

I am irradiated because I am weak from thyroid disease and despair,
I only want to live in peace.
This is not only my wish but all those who belong to the number 177.

All these thoughts of mine I give to you.
These are the experiences I see in these days that no longer belong to us.]

It is clear from Abon's song that radiation is synonymous with the loss of health and a diminished quality of life for people in the 177 HCP because of health problems linked to the testing program. The suffering and despair is ongoing for communities affected by the testing program, and their unyielding desire is to once again live in peace, yet they recognize that this is difficult. The "days no longer belong to" the people because the US government continues to exert its power and ability to minimize its responsibility for the needs of the affected communities. As control group member Alfonso Jebtak noted in an interview, "Jej ped ilo jaje" ("We are in a state of unknowing" or "We don't know what will happen"). The affected communities do not know what sufferings they still must endure or if the US government will address their problems.

A 2004 song also conveys, in culturally appropriate terms, sentiments about Marshallese experiences in the aftermath of the testing program. ERUB, a nonprofit Marshallese group named for the first letters of Enewetak, Rongelap, Utrik, and Bikini, wrote and performed the song for RMI's government ceremony marking the fiftieth anniversary of the Bravo test. The name of the organization is a play on words, as the Marshallese word *erub* means to explode, blow up, or be broken and certainly refers to the aftermath of the testing program for the four atolls comprising the name.

"Al en ERUB" ("ERUB Song")

Ilo 1954 eo ilo March juon raan.
4 atoll ear joraan, jen bom im kin radiation

Anij in jouj im iakwe
Onake ailin kein am jen joraan in elap rainin,
Kwon kalikar iman mejen lolin rainin
Einwot rose ko rej ebebe I-ion lometo.

4-atoll, 4-atoll, 4-atoll, 4-atoll
4-atoll, 4-atoll...ERUB!

[In 1954 on the first day of March
4 atolls were damaged, from the bomb and the radiation

God who is kind and loving
Provide for these islands of yours that are still so damaged today,
Please show us the face of this world today
Like roses that just float away on the ocean.

4-atoll, 4-atoll, 4-atoll, 4-atoll
4-atoll, 4- atoll...ERUB!]

Linguistically, it is evident from this song that the term *4 atoll* was created and disseminated by the US government, seeking to confine its responsibility for damages and injuries linked to the testing program to just four atolls. If the Marshallese defined for themselves the area "exposed" to radiation as just four atolls, then Marshallese would undoubtedly use the Marshallese term for the number four, *emen*, to define this area. In the Marshallese version of the ERUB song, even the term *4 atoll* is said in English. Marshallese who do not speak English use the English term for the designation. The use of the English term, and not pidgin, shows that the United States introduced the words abruptly, because the words did not work their way into the language and become mixed with the Marshallese language—they stand on their own as English words that do not get translated into Marshallese, which is also the case with the words *radiation, poison, cancer, tumor,* and *thyroid* (Barker 2004).

Compact and 177 Agreement

In the 1970s, Micronesians began to push for an end to the US colonization of their islands. In 1979 the Marshallese people split off from the rest of the trust territory to become a self-governing nation, but still under the auspices of the US trust territory. After fifteen years of negotiations, the Compact of Free Association came into effect in 1986. The compact gave the Marshall Islands independence and allowed the United States to maintain vital defense rights in the geopolitically important area in the mid-Pacific.

The compact also addressed the radiological problems resulting from weapons testing. In Section 177 of the compact, the United States "accepts responsibility for compensation owing to citizens of the Marshall Islands…for loss or damage to property and person…resulting from the nuclear testing program" (Compact of Free Association 1986). The compact provided $150 million in assistance for all past, present, and future damages related to the testing program and allowed Congress to provide ex gratia assistance on an as-needed basis. The $150 million appropriation was recognized as a "down payment" and was not intended to represent a comprehensive assessment of damages, a legally adjudicated settlement, or a monetary damages award (US Congress, House Resources Committee 1999). If the RMI can demonstrate new information, not known when the United States and the RMI agreed to the $150 million settlement, that renders this amount manifestly inadequate, then the "changed-circumstances" provision of the compact gives the RMI the right to petition Congress for additional assistance.

Since 1985, new information makes it clear that the cumulative levels of radiation caused substantially greater injury to people and property (land, reefs, and so forth) than was previously known or made public. The Nuclear Claims Tribunal, created as part of the 177 agreement as an alternative to the US courts,[9] adjudicates claims for personal injury and property damage. Although the tribunal does not have adequate funding to pay for its awards, tribunal awards include $72.6 million in personal injury claims, as well as more than $386 million to the inhabitants of Enewetak Atoll and more than $563 million to the people of Bikini to compensate for the loss of their land, restoration of the atolls, and hardship endured during decades of forced resettlement. Tribunal funding is almost gone, which means the tribunal cannot compensate awardees for the claims they received; the current shortfall in funds is more than $17 million for personal injury claims and $1.1 billion for the two property claims. The communities of Bikini and Enewetak now have cases pending in US federal courts, seeking payment on property damage awards that the tribunal lacks the funding to honor. Unlike downwinders in the United States, who receive the full amount of their awards six weeks after a successful claim, the tribunal makes pro rata payments, and to date 45 percent of claimants have died without receiving full compensation for their medical ailments linked to the testing program (US Congress, Senate Energy and Natural Resources Committee 2005). The tribunal also lacks funding for future personal or property claims—including pending land claims from a dozen communities, including Rongelap, Utrik, and other atolls outside of the US government's official area of responsibility—and future cancers predicted by the NCI.

New Information about the Consequences of the Testing Program

The RMI government does not have the capacity to respond to the health care needs of its citizens related to the US nuclear weapons testing program. Nor does it have the ability to clean up contaminated environments and safely resettle communities on islands that remain uninhabited. The RMI government put together a team of independent policy, scientific, legal, and medical advisers, as well as representatives from communities most affected by the testing program, to consider information from declassified data pertaining to the testing program and new scientific understandings about the effects of radiation exposure. This advisory group, called the Advisory Committee on Changed Circumstances (ACCC), helps the RMI government develop policies for working with the US government to address needs linked to the testing program. Examples of information analyzed by this group—information that was not available to the negotiators of the compact—include:

Biological Effects of Ionizing Radiation (BEIR)

The National Academy of Sciences (NAS) established a committee to report on the biological effects of ionizing radiation (BEIR). This committee produces reports, called BEIR studies, that periodically update scientific understanding about radiation. The BEIR V Committee (1990) asserted that since 1986, when the compact came into effect, radiation had been almost nine times as damaging as had been estimated by the 1972 BEIR I Committee, which informed radiation standards during compact negotiations. As a result of this new understanding, BEIR substantially upgraded the health detriment resulting from radiation. A 1982 DOE publication of a radiological survey of the fourteen northernmost atolls in the RMI stated that the total number of cancers anticipated for the 233 people residing on Rongelap on March 1, 1954, was 0.6 (DOE 1982); the current figure is approximately 56, based on the findings of BEIR V.

In addition to the BEIR V report, the BEIR VII report, sponsored by the departments of Defense, Energy, and Homeland Security; the US Nuclear Regulatory Commission; and the US Environmental Protection Agency (EPA), concluded that low levels of exposure to ionizing radiation may cause harm in human beings and are likely to pose some risk of adverse health effects. The report specifically focused on low-dose, low-LET (linear energy transfer) ionizing radiation that can cause DNA damage and eventually lead to cancers. The report called for further research to determine whether low doses of radiation may cause other health problems, such as heart disease and stroke, which can occur with high doses of low-LET radiation. What is most clear from the review of available data is that the smallest dose of low-level ionizing radiation can increase health risks to humans. As stated by the chairman for the report, Richard R. Monson, associate dean for professional education and a professor of epidemiology at the Harvard School of Public Health:

> The scientific research base shows that there is no threshold of exposure below which low levels of ionizing radiation can be demonstrated to be harmless or beneficial.... The health risks—particularly the development of solid cancers in organs—rise proportionally with exposure. At low doses of radiation, the risk of inducing solid cancers is very small. As the overall lifetime exposure increases, so does the risk. (Monson 2005)

This finding is significant to the RMI, since cumulative radiation from each of the sixty-seven atmospheric tests exposed everyone alive during the testing program to some level of radiation—much higher levels in the north, where the testing occurred, and proportionally smaller yet not insignificant amounts farther south. Furthermore, many people received chronic exposure from being born and raised on islands with residual radiological contamination. Regardless of location in the Marshall Islands, exposure doses to individuals are substantial, despite the fact that the US government historically labels any groups except the residents of Rongelap and Utrik on March 1, 1954, as "unexposed populations" (Behling et al. 2002).

The BEIR VII Committee reported that studies of mice and other organisms produced extensive data showing that radiation-induced cell mutations in sperm and eggs can pass on to offspring; there is no reason to believe that such mutations could not pass on to human offspring. At multiple bilateral meetings with the US government, Marshallese expressed their concerns about reproductive abnormalities, but the US government maintains that radiation does not affect subsequent generations.

Also of concern to the RMI is the portion of the BEIR VII report updating the risk of dying from cancer for women and men, and for children compared to adults.

According to the 1990 report, the risk of dying from cancer due to radiation exposure was 5 percent higher for women than for men; the latest report updates the risk to 37.5 percent higher for women than for men. The report estimates that the differential risk for children is even greater. For instance, the same radiation in the first year of life for boys produces three to four times the cancer risk as does exposure between the ages of twenty and fifty. Female infants have almost double the risk of male infants. There has never been an attempt to consider the different health risks for women and children as a result of radiation exposure in the RMI.

Radiation Protection Standards and Cumulative Doses

At the time of the 177 agreement, the upper limit on radiation to a member of the public was 500 millirems per year. The current dose limit and cleanup criteria specified by the EPA is 15 mrems per year. The lowering of acceptable exposure levels affects cleanup and resettlement activities presently under way on many atolls in the Marshall Islands, both in the scope of the cleanup activities required and the additional cost of more stringent cleanup operations.

It is important to compare the current EPA standard of radiological safety to dose information in recently declassified documents not available to negotiators of the compact. Included in declassified DOE documents (which the RMI received for the first time in the 1990s) was a 1955 US government document tallying the cumulative exposures from all six tests in the Castle series, including Bravo (Breslin and Cassidy 1955). The document lists exposure levels well above a 15 mrem standard, including on many atolls beyond the four atolls:

Atoll	Exposure Level
Rongelap	202,000 mrems
Ailinginae	67,000 mrems
Utrik	24,000 mrems
Ailuk	6,140 mrems
Likiep	2,196 mrems
Jemo	1,978 mrems
Wotho	784 mrems

This new dose information is important to scientists trying to establish doses from fallout received by the Marshallese during the testing program. New research indicates that the US government grossly underestimated radiation doses for people exposed to the Bravo test. In the case of thyroid doses to the residents of Rongelap and Utrik, independent researchers hired by the Nuclear Claims Tribunal believe that the United States underestimated doses by ten- to twentyfold; that whole-body doses from external radiation were more than twofold higher than previously estimated; and that internal exposure to tissues other than the thyroid, previously dismissed as "insignificant," resulted in doses of hundreds of rads (hundreds of thousands of mrems) (Behling et al. 2000).

During the negotiations of the 177 agreement, the US government limited discussions about the testing program to the effects of the Bravo event. There were no independent researchers or Marshallese doctors collecting data during the testing time to refute data brought to the table by US negotiators. Information declassified by the US government decades later provides yields for the remaining sixty-six weapons tested in the Marshall Islands. It is now known that thirty-three of the nuclear weapons detonated in the RMI were larger than the biggest weapon detonated in the continental United States. Furthermore, recently declassified information demonstrates the use of toxic tracer chemicals (such as arsenic) in weapons, which served as "thumbprints" for researchers to identify which weapons contaminated the ecosystems under study; the RMI still does not know the potential adverse effects of these tracers on human health and the environment (past and present), as the US government never undertook a comprehensive environmental survey to detail the presence of nonradiogenic contaminants in the environment and maintains that they pose no risk. It also bears mentioning that the US government currently tests missiles at Kwajalein Atoll in the Marshall Islands; that the missile testing program adds subsequent toxins to the environment, including small amounts of radioactive materials used in the noses of the missiles for ballast; and that existing military weapons tests need to be included in discussions about cumulative US government impacts.

US National Cancer Institute Information

In a September 2004 report prepared for the US Senate Energy and Natural Resources Committee, the NCI predicted that the Marshall Islands will experience a 9 percent cancer increase in the population that was alive during the testing program, from 1946 to 1958. This 9 percent increase represents more than five hundred additional cancer cases that will develop as a direct result of the US weapons testing program and independent from the naturally occurring level of cancer in Marshallese. In 2004 the NCI estimated that several hundred testing-related cancers in the RMI—including 85 percent of stomach cancers and 80 percent of colon cancers—had yet to develop or be diagnosed (NCI 2004). The NCI report also estimated future cancers in populations throughout the RMI, not just the communities of Rongelap and Utrik:

> [T]he National Cancer Institute…told us that the RMI should anticipate hundreds more radiation-related cancers in the future—these are cancers that would not exist in the RMI if the US nuclear weapons testing program did not take place…. [T]his news is devastating to the RMI as we lack the infrastructure, and the human and financial resources to respond to these cancers. Every family in the RMI has a first-hand understanding of the pain and suffering cancer patients and their loved ones endure, so it is difficult for us—even from

an emotional standpoint—to anticipate several hundred more cancers linked to the testing program. We thought most of the healthcare burdens were behind us, but it is clear that we now need to adjust our thinking and plan for the future. The NCI also tells us that these cancers will not be limited to just the 4 atolls, yet the 4 atolls are the only populations in the RMI that receive any radiation-related healthcare. All of our citizens who contract cancers will need healthcare—healthcare that we are currently unable to provide. (US Congress, Senate Energy and Natural Resources Committee 2005)

Shortcomings in Health Care

As discussed earlier, the control population is just one example of a community outside the four atolls not eligible for US assistance for problems linked to the testing program. The US government did not evacuate other groups of people, such as the Ailuk community, after the Bravo event. Like the people of Utrik, the population of Ailuk received doses of radiation to warrant removal from their home islands. But the US government considered the atoll's population of 401 people in 1954 too large and cumbersome to evacuate:

> Based upon the estimate of the fallout time it was calculated that a dose... would reach 20 roentgens. Balancing the effort required to move the 400 inhabitants against the fact that such a dose would not be a medical problem it was decided not to evacuate the atoll. (House 1954)

Consequently, the residents of Ailuk remained in their radiation-laced environment without medical monitoring or care and remain ineligible for US government–provided health care. Ethnographic data collected on Ailuk demonstrates pervasive health problems that began to appear after the testing program. According to Rine Sneid (interview with author, September 5, 1994):

> Four [of my] children were born prematurely..... One of them died after his first birthday. Another was stillborn.... I have yet to see any doctor.

The US government ignored several other atolls just outside the four-atoll parameter, including Likiep, Mejit, Wotho, Kwajalein, Ujelang, and Wotje, because the radiation doses received by residents were not perceived as problematic in earlier decades.

The US government's efforts to define communities exposed to radiation as static in time (during just the twelve years of the testing program) and geographically based fail to consider the needs of individuals such as cleanup workers or a church leader sent to Rongelap when the atoll was highly contaminated. In the 1970s and 1980s, DOE contracted laborers from the Marshall Islands and other areas in the trust territory to assist with cleanup of the ground zero locations of Bikini and Enewetak. Some of these workers and their families moved to former test sites, where they lived in a highly contaminated environment, ate local foods, drank the water, and raised their children.

Table 10.1. Per-Patient Per-Month Health Care Expenditures (1997)

United States	$PPPM
Commercial population	$135
Medicare (Nebraska)	$221
Medicare (New York)	$767
Medicaid (Michigan)	$120
Pacific region	
Commonwealth of the Northern Marianas	$60
Guam	$40
American Samoa	$30
Republic of Palau	$26
RMI	
National health care system	$11
Section 177	$13.60*

*The PPPM for Section 177 is calculated as follows: $2 million annually, divided by 12,259 patients, divided by twelve months equals $13.60 PPPM.

The funding for the 177 program has dropped from $2 million annually to $1 million annually. In 2003, the program operated on only $500,000. Each fiscal year the tertiary care budget for 177 patients was consumed within the first three months. Congress, therefore, decided to limit the 177 HCP to primary health care, despite the fact that many of its patients have tertiary illnesses, such as cancer. Source: Palafox 2000

These workers received exposure produced by the weapons tests, but their exposure occurred after the twelve years of testing recognized by US public law. If any of these workers were alive during the testing program and contracted a radiological illness recognized by the Nuclear Claims Tribunal, they are eligible for whatever portion of a claim the tribunal can award and the US contribution of $7 per patient per month in the 177 HCP. In comparison, the average US expenditure is $230 per patient per month for similar services (see table 10.1).

The table above illustrates the cost per person per month to achieve basic levels of primary, secondary, and tertiary health care in the United States and the Pacific region, as compared to the 177 Health Care Program and the RMI national health care budget. These figures are based on 1997 health care dollars and do not reflect increased health care costs since that time.

As in Ailuk, Likiep, and other communities outside the four atolls, there is no US government program to monitor the health of cleanup workers so that doctors can detect illnesses in early stages and hopefully prolong the lives and reduce the pain and suffering of sick people. In addition, Micronesian contractors to the DOE are ineligible to participate in a US Department of Labor (DOL) compensation program for DOE workers exposed to radiation because they are not US citizens (although they were citizens of the US trust territory when the DOE employed them). US citizens eligible for this program receive $150,000 in compensation, plus future medical coverage, including doctor and hospital visits, medical treatments, diagnostic laboratory testing, prescription drugs, and other benefits.

One of the workers sent to Bikini as a carpenter from 1971 to 1973, John Milne, established the Marshall Islands Radiation Victims Association (MIRVA) to advocate for the needs of all workers exposed to radiation during employment for the AEC (the predecessor to the DOE) or the DOE. At a bilateral meeting between the RMI and the DOE in 1997, where representatives from the US Department of State and Department of Interior also participated, John Milne appealed to the US government to assist the workers:

> I am appealing to you participants to this bilateral meeting for help. We need immediate access to professional appropriate medical care. We need compensation for the families of those who succumbed to radiation sickness and for individuals who are now afflicted with it…. We need help in establishing an administrative entity to be in contact with members of our group and to collect more detailed information on who was exposed and to track the results. (Milne 1997)

Milne believed the US government knew that the workers' employment with the DOE had the potential to cause health problems, but no effort was made to protect or inform the workers about the risks of radiation exposures or ways to reduce their occupational exposures. Milne described his experiences with US government representatives during his employment on Bikini Atoll:

> While at Bikini the Atomic Energy Commission representatives took nose swabs and urine samples from us. When we invited them to share with us the local food we regularly ate, they refused, but put on rubber gloves and picked up lobster and fish with metal tongs and put them in plastic bags which they took away. When we were low on rain water for drinking, the AEC representatives advised us to drink the well water. We showered, cooked with and drank that water. We were never told of any restrictions nor advised or cautioned to not eat the local food we harvested from the land and the sea. We were never told the results of the urine and nose swab tests that were taken. (Milne 1997)

Sadly, Milne died in 2004 without realizing his hope of securing assistance for the test site workers.

When looking at the health problems related to the nuclear weapons testing program, people tend to focus attention on cancer or thyroid illnesses, but numerous other medical conditions warrant attention. Marshallese exposed to radiation contend with mental retardation, birth abnormalities, stunted growth, and psychological trauma, not to mention the numerous health consequences of forced relocation. The whole testing program, not just the radiation exposure, caused disruptions to the culture and complex health problems (Palafox 2005). For example, when an entire population is picked up and moved off its land, it loses the ability to provide for itself (Johnston and Barker 1999, 2001). Virtually overnight, the US government moved populations such as the Rongelapese, the Bikinians, and the Enewetakese from their own islands, where they had cultivated local foods and provided for themselves. The US government thrust these populations into urban areas or onto other people's land, where they did not have the same rights or ability to cultivate resources. In a good-faith effort to provide food for resettled populations, the US government extended US Department of Agriculture feeding programs to some populations. For many years this assistance consisted of canned and processed foods. The rapid shift to imported foods created many health problems indirectly related to the nuclear weapons testing program—illnesses such as diabetes and high blood pressure—and discouraged local cultivation.

Currently in the Marshall Islands, three levels of health care are available to certain segments of the population exposed to radiation. The DOE provides approximately $1.1 million a year for health care for radiogenic illnesses in the 119 people still alive who resided on Rongelap or Utrik during the Bravo event.[10] Because the congressional mandate authorizes the DOE to treat only radiological conditions, an elderly patient exposed to radiation must receive care for cancer or thyroid illnesses from one set of doctors and care for nonradiogenic illnesses from other doctors, who may not have access to their medical histories. The senator for Rongelap Atoll, Abacca Anjain-Maddison, told the DOE during bilateral meetings with the RMI that sometimes a patient is opened up for surgery to address a radiogenic condition, then sewed up and sent to another facility for care for nonradiogenic illnesses (Anjain-Maddison 2004). Numerous DOE patients with complications from nonradiogenic illnesses have died because the DOE could not or would not evacuate them to the mainland United States since the evacuation option is available for only a specific number of conditions that the DOE categorizes as radiogenic.

Beyond the DOE program, the US government currently provides $1 million a year on a discretionary basis for 177 HCP, a basic health care program for people from the four atolls most affected by the weapons testing program. Congress funded this program for the first fifteen years of the compact. In recent years, the RMI government drew down $2 million annually from the Nuclear Claims Trust Fund to continue the program. For fiscal year 2005, the program operated with bridge funding by the RMI government and a $1 million contribution from Congress.

Both the DOE and 177 HCP are discretionary by nature, which means they are subject to the whims of Congress and the executive branch. Each year the RMI devotes countless hours and resources to make sure these essential health care programs continue; unfortunately, securing these programs is always a battle, as the RMI competes for funding from committees and members with interests beyond the Marshall Islands. The discretionary approach also leads to inconsistent budget flows that can send the programs into chaos. When Congress zero outs or reduces funding for programs, administrators must fire doctors and disrupt services to patients, including elderly patients with complex medical problems requiring constant and regular medical attention (thyroid disorders and diabetes).

Beyond the DOE program for a select few and the underfunded 177 HCP, the only other health care option in the RMI is the national health care system, which lacks the financial and human resources, as well as the proper infrastructure, for routine needs let alone complex radiological illnesses. Marshallese workers employed by the DOE and the people of Ailuk are just two of many groups with radiological needs not covered by US government assistance.

In a remote nation with a limited ability to provide health care, it is ineffective to have three parallel programs of health care delivery (DOE care, 177 HCP, and RMI public health). This multitiered approach creates unequal health care delivery and unnecessarily duplicates medical services.

The Equity Argument

The geographic area defined by Congress as exposed to radiation from the Nevada tests and eligible to participate in the downwinders' program is significantly larger than the four-atoll area recognized as "exposed" in the Marshall Islands. The total yields in Nevada were 1 percent of the yields of the Marshall Islands (1,096 kilotons in Nevada compared to 108,496 kilotons in the Marshall Islands). A map that superimposes the entire Marshall Islands over the US downwinders' affected area underscores the discrepancies in geographic areas considered exposed (see map 10.2).

In May 2005, the NAS recommended expanding eligibility for the downwinders beyond the current geographic boundaries and called on Congress to move quickly to provide assistance to downwinders suffering from radiogenic conditions. The NAS also noted that Congress should apply new scientific information about radiation to extend coverage of the Radiation Exposure Compensation Act (RECA).[11]

While communities downwind from the Nevada Test Site provide a comparison for personal injury disparities between the United States and the RMI, cleanup activities at Hanford provide a similar comparison for the restoration of contaminated lands in the United States compared to those in the RMI. In response to the environmental contamination caused by Hanford, the US government appropriates $2 billion and employs approximately eleven thousand workers annually to assist with cleanup. From the fiscal year 2005 budget, the DOE estimates a total life-cycle cost of $56 billion and a completion date of 2035. Furthermore, the goal for cleanup at Hanford is 15 mrem; the US government maintains that the RMI should settle for the less-stringent international standard of 100 mrem, even though contamination took place when the RMI was a trust territory of the United States. The Nuclear Claims Tribunal does not have funding to make property awards that would allow the affected communities to reduce radiological contamination, revegetate islands, and someday return to their homelands.

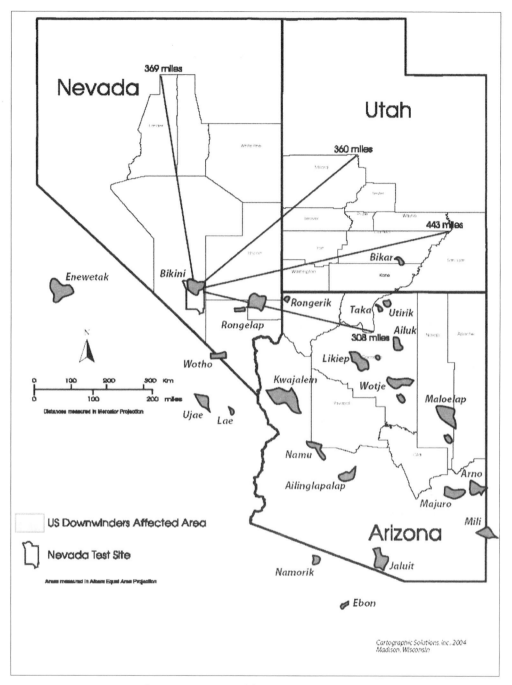

Map 10.2. Comparison of area contaminated by atmospheric weapons in the Marshall Islands and the downwinder area in the continental United States. Source: Republic of the Marshall Islands Nuclear Claims Tribunal

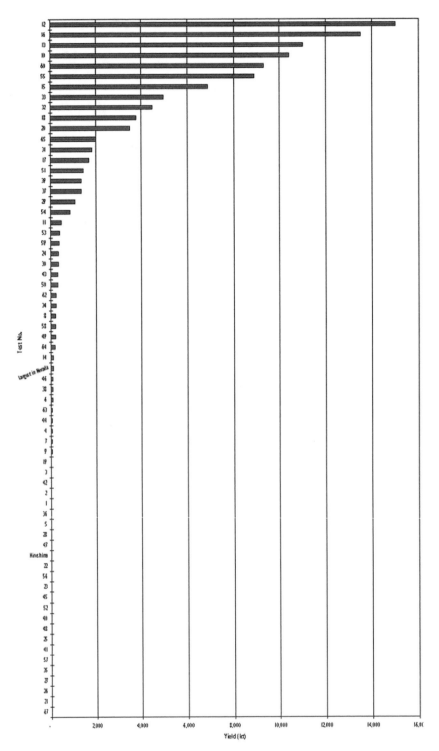

Figure 10.2. Comparison of costs to clean up contaminated lands associated with the nuclear weapons production facility at Hanford, Washington, and the nuclear weapons tests in the Marshall Islands. Source: Republic of the Marshall Islands Nuclear Claims Tribunal

The RMI's Changed-Circumstances Petition

The RMI government submitted a changed-circumstances petition to the US Congress in September 2000, detailing changes in radiation science, explaining the need to update US policy regarding radiation-related damages and injuries, and seeking assistance to build health care systems and replenish the Nuclear Claims Trust Fund so it could pay its awards. The position of the executive branch remains that there is no legal basis for changed circumstances. The RMI strongly contests this position and points to the issue of private property as just one example. The US government took private property belonging to Marshallese families for nuclear testing purposes. When the US government takes private property, landowners are entitled to just and adequate compensation, yet this payment cannot occur in the RMI because the Nuclear Claims Tribunal lacks funding to pay its property awards.

The RMI government will continue to push Congress and the executive branch to address radiological and other needs resulting from the US nuclear weapons testing program. Congress convened hearings in both the House and the Senate in 2005 to consider the nuclear legacy in the RMI and the adequacy of US programs. As the mayor of Rongelap, James Matayoshi, noted in his speech marking the fiftieth anniversary of the Bravo test, Marshallese will continue to press the United States for fair treatment for problems related to the testing program:

> For all these years under American guidance, we have learned principles of democracy and human rights under which all men aspire to live. Yet, when we seek to be treated with honor and dignity, we are denied the means to assure that fairness and justice is guaranteed to all. The United States continues to be less than forthcoming in its handling of information and dissemination of facts pertaining to the testing program....
>
> Here we are, fifty years after Bravo, and the people forcibly removed from their homes for the atomic [and thermonuclear] tests…have yet to return home. The question of exposure as it affects other atolls in the Marshalls has yet to be fully addressed. Many claims [to the Nuclear Claims Tribunal] are still being prepared. Adjudicated claims have not been paid in full as agreed upon by the United States. Medical and monitoring programs, promised by those who exposed us, have been severely curtailed or abandoned. Making "non-exposed" Marshallese responsible for the medical needs of "exposed" Marshallese is not a solution. America must own up to the problems it created. (Matayoshi 2004)

At the time of this writing, the president of the Marshall Islands, Kessai Note, continues to visit Washington, DC, to advance a bilateral effort for the RMI and representatives of Congress and the executive branch to review the adequacy of existing US assistance for problems stemming from the testing program and to make recommendations about specific remedies. The first task of the bilateral effort is to consider ways to address the health care needs of all populations exposed to radiation. Rather than having the US government establish the scope of problems related to the testing program and the assistance required, the Marshallese demand active participation in efforts to define the remedies needed now and in the future.

Conclusions

As the RMI and the US government continue to address the legacy of the US nuclear weapons testing program, there are several points to keep in mind:

- There was no form of government in the RMI during the testing program other than the United States.

- The $150 million settlement for the 177 agreement was an arbitrary, political figure. Congress expected and planned for changed circumstances as it was recognized at the time of the negotiations that complete information was not available.

- Smaller doses of radiation do more damage than was understood prior to 1986.

- The EPA standard for safe levels of exposure to human-made sources of radiation is 15 mrem per person per year, down from the standard of 500 mrem per person per year at the time the compact came into force.

- It was not just the Bravo shot that exposed Marshallese people to radiation. US government documents demonstrate that radiation from the other sixty-six tests conducted in the RMI exposed Marshallese people and their private property to radiation.

- It was not just the four atolls exposed to radiation from the US nuclear weapons testing program. US government documents acknowledge, for example, that the people of Ailuk received exposure to radiation levels that were high enough to warrant evacuation following the Bravo event. Other midrange atolls, such as Likiep, Mejit, and Wotje, received significant doses of radiation.

- Definitions of exposure to radiation confined by time or space ignore the needs of groups that do not fall into an atoll/geography-based definition of exposure, such as the Marshallese workers, and are not eligible for any US government health monitoring or care (such as a DOL compensation and medical monitoring program for US citizens employed by the DOE and exposed to occupational sources of radiation).

- The compact planned to provide adequate health care for communities with health problems linked to the US nuclear weapons testing program. Funding for radiation-related health care is manifestly inadequate, and the parallel, multi-tiered systems of health care in the RMI create inequity for patients.

- US citizens downwind from the Nevada Test Site receive full settlement for their personal injury claims, and the US Congress appropriates additional funds for compensation when funding for claims runs out.

- Standards of health care, environmental cleanup, and public safety are different for Marshallese than for Americans.

- Marshallese members of the control population have health care needs related to their participation in US medical experimentation that the United States must address.

- The US government pays $2 billion annually for the cleanup of Hanford. The Nuclear Claims Tribunal has paid only $4 million of $1.1 billion in property claims due to a manifest inadequacy of funding and has no funding to pay future property awards.

No matter the outcome of the RMI's efforts to seek further redress under the changed-circumstances provision, the process of getting the United States to recognize the shortcomings in current US assistance and the need to take measures to address the burdens of the testing program will continue for years to come. We still do not understand all there is to know about radiation, but the US government needs to update its antiquated policies regarding exposure in the RMI and will need to continue to update its policies in the future as we learn more about radiation and its effects and in response to information contained in recently declassified US government documents.

The one asset the US government wants to secure from the RMI in exchange for any additional assistance is closure. The RMI government cannot offer the US government closure on the nuclear legacy or promise that it will not petition Congress for future assistance. It is likely that new damages and injuries will become known in the future because the US government has not been forthcoming with all information about the testing program, and our knowledge about radiation and its effects continues to develop.

In addition to changes in information about the testing program, there is a change in how communities and elected officials in the RMI engage in these issues. During compact negotiations, RMI representatives depended on a good-faith effort by the US government to detail the extent of damages and injuries related to the testing program. The United States chose to limit the damage area to just four atolls. Since that time, Marshallese communities and their elected leaders have found productive ways to challenge US government efforts to minimize the US scope of responsibility. The RMI challenges US government policies at annual meetings with the DOE and every time it appears before Congress.

Marshallese leaders, and even patients enrolled in medical programs for radiation-related illnesses, are demanding to have a say in how medical care is designed and delivered. Marshallese have become actively engaged in developing and implementing their own remedies, such as redesigning medical programs rather than accepting US programs imposed upon them. The goal of the compact is to increase the self-reliance of the Marshall Islands. With this goal in mind, it makes sense to build a sustainable health care system in the RMI so the RMI can diagnose and treat all illnesses linked to the testing program.

It will be impossible to provide adequate health services to the affected population without improving existing hospitals, health facilities, and health care infrastructure in the RMI. Provision of health programs for affected people outside the RMI medical system is not cost-effective, is unsustainable, and leaves affected populations with no or substandard health care services. Future planning and funding must develop and sustain the RMI health care system's efforts to deliver comprehensive and culturally tailored health care services to affected populations, as envisioned in the compact, and must include affected communities during every phase.

The cost involved in establishing an adequate health care program to address health care needs from the testing program is significantly less than the cost of pursuing the same level of care in the United States. An economy of scale would result in the system being able to care for a greater number of affected people, onsite, and at a lesser cost and would ensure the participation of affected communities. All present and future generations affected by the US nuclear weapons testing program and living in the RMI would receive appropriate health care within the local infrastructure. Improvements in the public health infrastructure that delivers care to populations affected by the US nuclear weapons testing program would also improve health care delivery to all people living in the RMI.

The obligation to provide medical care for the adverse consequences of the US nuclear weapons testing program cannot be met without comprehensive medical monitoring of populations previously exposed to ionizing radiation. A lack of medical monitoring has precluded the opportunity for early diagnosis and treatment of cancer and other radiogenic illnesses. Failure to detect and treat cancers and other radiogenic illnesses in their early stages results in more pain and suffering for patients and a larger cost of care for health care institutions.

As for the Nuclear Claims Tribunal, the compact agreed that an independent tribunal would consider claims for personal injury and property damages. The tribunal fulfilled its mandate by determining personal injury claims based on similar US programs and by adjudicating property claims, yet it does not have adequate funds to fulfill its obligations.

Many factors need to fall into place to achieve desired political outcomes. The RMI government remains committed to advancing the interests of all Marshallese citizens affected by the testing program. The communities themselves are demanding that they be part of the process and receive the same consideration as US citizens:

> There was nuclear weapons testing in the United States and there was nuclear weapons testing in the Marshall Islands, but there is great disparity between healthcare and compensation programs for the people affected by both of these

testing programs, and in levels of funding available for clean-up activities. The Marshall Islands is not asking for a grandiose healthcare system or to make its people wealthy with compensation money, it is only asking for fairness. The US government conducted its nuclear weapons testing program in the Marshall Islands because it recognized the hazards of these activities for its own citizens and ecosystems. It seems only fair that the Marshall Islands receive equity in levels of care, funding, and protection to US citizens, particularly since they were wards of the US government when the testing activities took place. (Gerald M. Zackios, US Congress, Senate Energy and Natural Resources Committee 2005)

Notes

This chapter was written with support from the John D. and Catherine T. MacArthur Foundation. This work is dedicated to the many key informants I interviewed over the years who died prematurely—people such as Almira Matayoshi, Aruko Bobo, John Anjain, George Anjain, and John Milne—and to the several Marshallese who die every month from cancers that are treatable in the United States but are often death sentences in the RMI because of inadequate or nonexistent detection and treatment options.

1. Prior to World War II, the Japanese occupation of the Marshall Islands was civil. The Japanese government was committed to building schools and infrastructure and advancing the well-being of the Marshallese people. When the regime converted from civilian to military during the war, the Marshallese experienced murder, torture, and human rights abuses at the hands of Japanese soldiers, as well as extreme hunger in areas where US forces cut off supplies to Japanese troops.

2. For example, see Gar Alperovitz (1996). Many historians believe that the Truman administration knew that the Japanese were prepared to surrender before Hiroshima and Nagasaki were bombed.

3. For an excellent account of the roles that the various armed forces played in nuclear weapons testing in the RMI, see Jonathan Weisgall's *Operation Crossroads* (1994).

4. The name of the bikini bathing suit came from the atomic tests at Bikini Atoll, as the tests, like the avant-garde fashion, symbolized something explosive, hot, and new to the public (Boyer 1994).

5. For more information about the atomic veterans, see the National Association of Atomic Veterans' website: http://www.naav.com/.

6. The documents note the names and identification numbers of patients and whether the pulled teeth were decayed or healthy. Frances Qua, who participated in the dental exams as part of the Brookhaven team, provided the documents to the RMI Embassy in Washington, DC, with an explanation that Brookhaven pulled healthy teeth to analyze radiation levels for research purposes.

7. Curiously, all the medical files for the people most exposed to radiation in the Marshall Islands disappeared in a series of unexplained and uninvestigated fires in Cleveland, Majuro, and Ebeye and inside the locked safe of the high commissioner for the Trust Territory of the Pacific Islands. Also see Tony deBrum's 1994 testimony to ACHRE.

8. The contractor for the program changed from Brookhaven National Laboratory, a lab that does defense research for the US government, to an independent health care provider, Pacific Health Research Institute, and the University of Hawaii's John A. Burns School of Medicine, Department of Family Health.

9. The RMI had to dismiss cases pending in US courts to accept the compact and the Nuclear Claims Tribunal as an alternative judiciary.

10. The DOE has also extended this program to the control population, although this is not specified in congressional authorization and is subject to change depending on political leadership at the DOE.

11. RECA currently includes residents of parts of Nevada, southern Utah, and Arizona, as well as workers who handled uranium.

References

ACHRE. *See* Advisory Committee on Human Radiation Experiments

Advisory Committee on Human Radiation Experiments
1995   Final Report of the Advisory Committee on Human Radiation Experiments. Washington, DC: US Government Printing Office.

Alperovitz, Gar
1996   The Decision to Use the Atomic Bomb. London: Vintage.

Anjain-Maddison, Abacca
2004   Remarks to a bilateral US-RMI meeting on issues related to US nuclear weapons testing. Department of Interior, Washington, DC, November.
2005   Statement to the nongovernmental organizations meeting, Nuclear Nonproliferation Treaty Conference, New York, May 6.

Barker, Holly
2004   Bravo for the Marshallese: Regaining Control in a Post-Nuclear, Post-Colonial World. Belmont, CA: Wadsworth/Thomson Learning.

Behling, Hans, John Mauro, and Kathy Behling
2000   Reassessment of Acute Radiation Doses Associated with Bravo Fallout. McLean, VA: S. Cohen and Associates.
2002   Final Report: Radiation Exposures Associated with the US Nuclear Testing Program for Twenty-one Atolls/Islands in the Republic of the Marshall Islands. McLean, VA: S. Cohen and Associates.

Boyer, Paul
1994   By the Bomb's Early Light: American Thought and Culture at the Dawn of the Atomic Age. Chapel Hill: University of North Carolina Press.

Breslin, Alfred J., and Melvin E. Cassidy
1955   Radioactive Debris from Operation Castle: Islands of the Mid-Pacific. New York: Atomic Energy Commission, Health and Safety Laboratory.

Brookhaven National Laboratory
n.d.   "List of Teeth Samples from the Marshall Islands"; "Second List of Teeth Samples from the Marshall Islands." Undated memos.

Centers for Disease Control

1998   Thyroid Disease Study in the Marshall Islands. Update presented at RMI–DOE meeting, Honolulu, July 1.

Compact of Free Association

1986   Public Law 99-239, US Code 1681.

Conard, Robert A.

1958   Memorandum to Dr. Charles L. Dunham, director of the Division of Biology and Medicine of the Atomic Energy Commission regarding a medical mission on Rongelap Atoll. Upton, NY: Brookhaven National Laboratory.

deBrum, Tony

2005   Statement to the United Nations Nuclear Nonproliferation Treaty Conference on Behalf of All Indigenous People and Nongovernmental Organizations. New York, May 11.

Department of Defense

1953   J-21366(D). To: Distribution, From: Commander, Task Group 7.1, Subject: Outline of Scientific Programs—Operation Castle (Supersedes J-17930 dated 8 May 1953 and J-18603 dated 1 July 1953). Department of Energy, Marshall Islands Historical Documents Archive. Electronic document, http://worf.eh.doe.gov/data/ihp1d/400415f.pdf, accessed October 25, 2006.

Department of Energy

1982   The Meaning of Radiation for Those Atolls in the Northern Part of the Marshall Islands That Were Surveyed in 1978. Washington, DC: Department of Energy.

DOD. *See* **Department of Defense**

DOE. *See* **Department of Energy**

Donaldson, Lauren

1955   A Radiological Study of Rongelap Atoll, Marshall Islands, during 1954–1955. Seattle: Applied Fisheries Laboratory, University of Washington.

Graham, William

2004   Briefing to congressional staff regarding the RMI's Changed Circumstances Petition to Congress. Washington, DC, April 23.

House, R. A.

1954   Memorandum for Record Regarding the Bravo Shot, Discussion of Offsite Fallout. US Air Force. Declassified document filed with the Republic of the Marshall Islands Nuclear Claims Tribunal, Atoll of Ailuk Claim.

Johnston, Barbara Rose, and Holly M. Barker

1999   The Rongelap Property Damage Claims Study: Efforts to Seek Redress for Nuclear Contamination and Loss of a Way of Life. Majuro, RMI: Nuclear Claims Tribunal, Office of the Public Advocate.

2001   Hardships Endured by the People of Rongelap as a Result of the US Nuclear Weapons Testing Program and Related Biomedical Research. Majuro, RMI: Nuclear Claims Tribunal.

Matayoshi, James
2004   Statement at RMI ceremony honoring radiation victims, Majuro, RMI, March 1.

Milne, John Meliong
1997   Statement to a bilateral RMI–US meeting on the US nuclear weapons testing program in the RMI, Majuro, RMI, January 21.

Monson, Richard R.
2005   Low Levels of Ionizing Radiation May Cause Harm. Electronic document, http://hps.org/documents/BEIRVIIPressRelease.pdf, accessed July 7, 2006.

National Cancer Institute
2004   Estimation of the Baseline Number of Cancers among Marshallese and the Number of Cancers Attributable to Exposure to Fallout from Nuclear Weapons Testing Conducted in the Marshall Islands. Prepared for the Senate Committee on Energy and Natural Resources, Washington, DC: Division of Cancer Epidemiology and Genetics, National Institutes of Health.

NCI. *See* **National Cancer Institute**

Nuclear Claims Tribunal
2003   Annual Report to the Nitijela for the Calendar Year 2003. Majuro: Nuclear Claims Tribunal.

Palafox, Neal
2000   RMI Changed Circumstances Petition, chapter on health care needs, submitted to the US Congress. September 2000.
2005   Statement of Neal A. Palafox, MD MPH, Professor and Chair, Department of Family Medicine and Community Health, John A. Burns School of Medicine, University of Hawaii to the Senate Energy and Natural Resources Committee July 19, 2005. Electronic document, http://energy.senate.gov/public/index.cfm?FuseAction =Hearings.Testimony&Hearing_ID=1478&Witness_ID=4218, accessed November 9, 2006.

Seligman, Paul J.
1999   Letter from deputy assistant secretary for health studies, Department of Energy, to Nanmij Anjain, regarding the injection of patients and/or tritiated water clinical tests, June 28. Private correspondence shared with author by recipient.

Thomas, Elbert
1953   Letter from the high commissioner of the Trust Territory of the Pacific Islands to James P. Davis, director, Office of Territories, Department of Interior, February 5. Department of Energy, Marshall Islands Historical Documents Archive. Electronic document, http://worf.eh.doe.gov/data/ihp1b/4060_.pdf, accessed October 25, 2006.

US Congress. House of Representatives. Committee on Resources

1999   Testimony by Howard Hills regarding the political nature of the $150 million settlement figure. 106th Cong. 1st sess.

US Congress. Senate. Committee on Energy and Natural Resources

2005   Testimony of Gerald M. Zackios. 9th Cong. 1st sess. May 25.

Weisgall, Jonathan

1994   Operation Crossroads: The Atomic Tests at Bikini Atoll. Annapolis, MD: Naval Institute Press.

e l e v e n

Russia's Radiation Victims of Cold War Weapons Production Surviving in a Culture of Secrecy and Denial

Paula Garb

In April 1986 the Chernobyl nuclear power plant in the Soviet Union released from 50 to 80 million curies of radioactive debris into the atmosphere. This catastrophe commanded worldwide attention at the time, and to this day the Chernobyl accident remains a stark symbol of the hazards of nuclear power. What happened two and three decades before at a site in another part of the Soviet Union—Chelyabinsk—was a well-kept secret for decades. The nuclear disasters in Chelyabinsk resulted in far more environmental and human sacrifices than did Chernobyl but remained shrouded in secrecy throughout the Cold War, until a few years after the Chernobyl accident. Even today people inside and outside the former Soviet Union are more likely to know about Chernobyl than about the series of accidents from the early 1950s to the late 1960s at a secret weapons facility tucked away in a remote site in the Chelyabinsk region of the Russian Urals. The Chelyabinsk accidents released more than 146 million curies into the atmosphere, nearly double the release of Chernobyl.

Not only were the numbers of curies released in Chelyabinsk much higher than at Chernobyl but more people were affected and over a longer period of time (Komarova 2003). Furthermore, three generations have lived in the areas that were contaminated by the Chelyabinsk accidents, and many residents, having been exposed to high doses of radiation, were evacuated to places where they became victims once again several years later. In contrast, the Chernobyl disaster was a one-time event, and most evacuees have not returned to the most highly contaminated areas (Komarova 2003).

The purpose of this article is to (1) describe the consequences of the Chelyabinsk nuclear disasters for the people of the region and how they perceive and cope with their predicament; (2) illustrate the culture of secrecy and denial in the Russian nuclear weapons industry; and (3) provide glimpses into the processes of behind-the-scenes anthropological fieldwork in such nuclear landscapes.[1]

The chapter begins with an account of the accidents at Chelyabinsk and how secrecy was maintained, both inside and outside the Soviet Union. Next I explain how I came to study these issues and how I experienced the people and places affected by the nuclear disasters soon after some of the secrets were brought to light. Stories throughout the rest of the chapter are about the victims' lives yesterday and today, how they have coped, and how officials have responded to their plight. The stories are interspersed with insights from my own experiences in Chelyabinsk that mirrored those of the local population as we faced similar choices about how to evaluate the risks to our safety, protect our health, and approach officials to peel away the thick layers of secrecy.

What Happened at Chelyabinsk and Why the Secrecy?

The Chelyabinsk weapons facility, known as the Mayak Chemical Combine (*mayak* means "lighthouse"), stands in a city that was originally called Chelyabinsk-40, later renamed Chelyabinsk-65 (now Ozersk). It is a closed city of nuclear weapons employees in Russia, the largest successor country of the Soviet Union. Next door is another secret city, Snezhinsk (once called Chelyabinsk-70), which once housed a nuclear research facility and its employees. Neither city was on the map until 1989. Both are still closed cities that require special government permission to enter.

Mayak was the Soviet Union's first weapons-grade plutonium production center, similar to the US plant at Hanford, Washington. It also made bomb cores like those produced at Rocky Flats, Colorado, and perhaps continues to do so. According to Ann Imse, the author of a comprehensive series on Mayak and its victims published in the *Rocky Mountain News*, "Today, 14,500 employees [at Mayak] work on nuclear projects ranging from weapons to power plant fuel. In the super secret Plant 20 [in Mayak], US officials say, workers are manufacturing plutonium bomb cores—something the US stopped doing...or rebuilding existing cores that have decayed. But no one knows for sure" (Imse 2003a).

Most of the radioactive elements released from Mayak since 1949, when it opened, have been strontium-90 and cesium-137. These elements are the most dangerous radioisotopes to the environment because they can survive for hundreds of years. Cesium-137 can also be mistaken for potassium by living organisms and taken up as part of the fluid electrolytes, meaning it is passed on up the food chain and reconcentrated from the environment by that process. Strontium-90 can be mistaken for calcium and is also taken up by living organisms and made a part of their electrolytes, as well as deposited in bones. As a part of the bones, it is not subsequently excreted like cesium-137. It has the potential for causing cancer or damaging the rapidly reproducing bone marrow cells (Nave 2005).

About 120 million curies of radioactive elements are trapped in Lake Karachay inside the closed city; some 20 million were released in a storage tank explosion—the Kyshtym explosion (named after the nearest town)—in 1957; 3 million are in Lake Staroe Boloto; 1.75 million were dumped into the Techa River between 1949 and 1956; 600 were disbursed by a 1967 dust storm; and 6,000 are in groundwater creeping from the complex toward the city of Chelyabinsk, the region's administrative center with a population of more than 1 million (Cochran et al. 1993).

The victims of the Chelyabinsk disasters consider themselves the unknown targets of the nuclear weapons built in their backyards. They bitterly declare that throughout the Cold War no bomb was ever dropped on enemy territory; they were the only victims. They were the hidden casualties of the Cold War, essentially victims of friendly fire. The Soviet government officially told the world about the accidents in Chelyabinsk after the Chernobyl disaster, but the US military establishment and government were apparently aware of the 1957 explosion around the time it occurred, three decades before Soviet acknowledgment. Francis Gary Powers, a US pilot shot down over the Urals in a U-2 spy plane on May 5, 1960, had been taking photos to assess the impact of the accident. This information only came out decades later.

Why the conspiracy of silence? The Soviet Union certainly had reason to conceal the accident, but why would the United States not make it public at the time? Perhaps no nuclear nation wanted to point a finger at the Soviet Union for this environmental disaster because similar incidents were occurring around the same time in the United States and England (Dalton et al. 1999). Perhaps Western leaders feared that if they drew the world's attention to the Soviet accident, they would open the door to investigations of their own dangerous activities. In democratic societies such as the United States and England, undoubtedly public interest groups would have probed for more information about these developments in the neighborhood. Chelyabinsk antinuclear activists maintain that had the 1957 Kyshtym explosion become public knowledge at the time, antinuclear movements might have been launched earlier, and perhaps international public pressure for more stringent safety measures could have prevented many subsequent accidents, including Chernobyl.

The Journey to Chelyabinsk Begins

In the early 1990s, I undertook anthropological research in Chelyabinsk, Russia, looking through the lens of an American child of the Cold War, raised by parents with roots in the pre-Soviet Russian Empire,[2] and an American adult who raised a family in the Soviet Union. In the late 1960s I had gone to live in the USSR, compelled by a need to understand the mysteries behind the Iron Curtain. I spent nearly twenty years of my adult life in the Soviet Union before it collapsed into fifteen different pieces. I married a Russian, became near-native fluent in Russian, and completed all my higher education in the Soviet Union. As someone with deep attachments to the country of my birth (the United States) and the country of my heritage (Russia), which for most of my formative years raced to build weapons of mass destruction in defense against one another, it grieved me to hear stories about environmental disasters and the resulting human tragedies around the weapons-grade plutonium facilities in both countries.

Chelyabinsk became the subject of my first research and fieldwork project after I received my PhD in anthropology in the Soviet Union in 1990.[3] My task was to interview people who lived near the weapons facilities; the scientists, officials, and employees who worked inside the closed cities; and government officials in Moscow (the Russian capital) and Chelyabinsk (the capital of the Chelyabinsk region). The purpose was to learn the wide range of opinions about the environmental consequences of nuclear weapons production.

After establishing contacts with Russian environmentalists who could help me make the connections I needed in the diverse communities I wanted to study, on December 11, 1991, just a few days after the breakup of the Soviet Union, I set off for the city of Chelyabinsk with a few Moscow-based environmentalists. We arrived at 5:00 a.m. on a fully booked and cramped red-eye Aeroflot flight that reeked of sweat, garlic, and vodka from the weary Russian passengers. We were greeted in this city of 1 million by freezing weather, minus 30 degrees Celsius. We were miserably cold, but the upside was the crisp fresh air and the glimmering snowflakes covering the trees and ground. It was a genuine Siberian winter. As we rode into town in a taxi, we saw twenty or thirty people huddled around a fire made of wooden boxes, waiting for a grocery store to open at 8:00 a.m. so they could secure basic food items in catastrophically short supply. This was a typical scene across the country, which was plagued by basic food shortages.

My first stop was the home of a local environmentalist who was hosting our visit. It was a tiny apartment with one bedroom for the whole family—both parents and two children. I slept on the couch in the adjoining living room. The apartment was clean and cozy, the walls lined with good books, and the household equipped with a microwave oven, VCR, TV, computer, hot water, and warm heaters. The hostess was kind and generous. This was my home for the duration of that visit. Chelyabinsk had only recently opened up to foreign visitors. The hotels were still wary of taking foreign guests, did not yet have procedures in place for that, so it was easier for me to live in someone's home than to postpone my trip endlessly waiting for a hotel reservation. On all subsequent visits I stayed in an adequately comfortable hotel in Chelyabinsk and made day trips to the villages near the weapons plant.

My hostess was an ethnic Russian who had grown up in Chelyabinsk. Although Russians constitute the majority ethnic group in the larger Chelyabinsk region, Tatars and Bashkirs represent a large minority. Of the nearly twelve thousand residents in the villages most affected by the nuclear accidents, around 51 percent are Turkic-speaking Tatars and Bashkirs of Muslim religious heritage. Around 46 percent are Russians (Komarova 2003).

Of these groups, the earliest settlers were the Bashkirs, whose history in the region dates to the fourteenth century. Traditionally they were nomads, and many aspects of this heritage are still evident today, even though they have been sedentary agriculturalists since the early eighteenth century. Tatars, who speak a related Turkic language, appeared in the region in the late seventeenth century. Historically they were farmers and urban dwellers. Tatars did not settle in compact communities but were dispersed throughout Chelyabinsk. Despite the cultural differences between Bashkirs and Tatars, due mainly to the differences in their nomadic and farming backgrounds, they share more with each other than with neighboring non-Turkic and non-Muslim ethnic groups. Intermarriage between the two groups is much more common than it is with non-Muslim nationalities.

Of the towns and villages where I interviewed residents, Muslyumovo has the largest percentage of Tatars and Bashkirs. The village is situated along the Techa River, approximately 30 miles from Mayak. It is on a site that is acknowledged to be contaminated from both the dumping of plutonium waste from Mayak in the early 1950s and the 1957 explosion. In the early 1990s Muslyumovo had a total population of 4,022. Tatars numbered 3,302; Bashkirs 379; and Russians 341.

The main occupations in Muslyumovo are stockbreeding, grain growing, and servicing the railway station. Most villagers live in small and rundown three- to four-room log cabins with minimal furniture. Their homes overlook dirt roads that become hard to travel on when muddy from rain or slippery from snow.

Victims of Environmental Disasters

In the early 1950s, after Mayak had been dumping plutonium into the Techa River for a few years, doctors observed a marked increase in disease and deaths among the inhabitants of the many villages along the river. Scientists did not yet know that plutonium would not dissolve in water and lose its lethal power. As a result of the obvious dramatic health problems created by the dumping, twenty-two villages along the river in its most contaminated areas were evacuated.

By 1952–53, signs began appearing along the Techa River warning the remaining residents that it was dangerous to use the water. Muslyumovo was not evacuated, even though it was in the middle of the other twenty-two villages that were moved. Officials usually cite two reasons—the village was too big, and the train crossroads at Muslyumovo was too important for regional transportation to abandon. People in Muslyumovo periodically noticed pink pieces of fluff floating in the water. Anglers brought home three-foot-long fish that were blind. Officials warned people not to swim in or use the water in the river, but they did not explain why it was dangerous. Rumors began to circulate about radiation contamination. But if people knew the word *radiation* they understood it in simplistic terms, equating its effects with those of an X-ray. Inhabitants claim that officials never clarified either the scope of the radiation contamination or its health and environmental consequences. About twenty-eight thousand people along the Techa depended on the river for drinking and irrigation water.

In the late afternoon of September 29, 1957, one of Mayak's 80,000-gallon storage tanks exploded after its cooling system failed. The explosion released about 20 million curies of radioactive debris over a territory of 6,000 square miles with a population of around 270,000. Plant and local government officials evacuated approximately 10,700 people permanently. More than half of these people were evacuated eight months after the incident, which means they consumed contaminated food for three to six months unrestricted and continued to eat some contaminated food until evacuation. The entire population of the region consumed the 1957 harvest, which was contaminated with radionuclides (Cochran et al. 1993).

This is how Mikhail Gladyshev, formerly the director of Mayak's plutonium facility, recalled the events:

> The day after the explosion it was clear that northeast winds were spreading radioactive materials over population centers and waterways, so we began evacuating the people from their native villages. We had to issue new clothes and other necessities to the evacuees, arrange for their decontamination in showers, and resettlement. It took major organizational efforts and expenditures. The overwhelming majority of the evacuees were Bashkirs. It's amazing that the whole evacuation was completed in a relatively short period and without any resistance from the population. The job was finished so rapidly that very soon the people adapted to their new conditions and new life. (Gladyshev 1990)

Evacuees interviewed for this study confirm that the population did not put up any resistance. They explained that people were conditioned by the Soviet government to obey orders and to believe that their leaders knew what was best for them. Even though the evacuation went more smoothly than officials expected, the evacuees suffered deep emotional trauma from this sudden uprooting from ancestral villages. I talked to people who worked at one of the health resorts where evacuees were housed from October 1957 to May 1958. They recall caring solely for evacuees from neighboring villages and doing this job without the assistance of Mayak officials and physicians. Aleftina Fisko, a Russian woman who worked in the cafeteria of a resort for Mayak employees, told me (interview with author, April 1993) that throughout the period when evacuees were at her resort, no doctors or managers from Mayak even visited the site, "as if they were afraid of being contaminated." She recalled that in early October 1957 several hundred Bashkirs and Tatars, whole families with children and elders, were brought to the resort:

> Most of them did not speak any Russian; they talked to each other in their own language. They lived in buildings that were only used in summer so they weren't heated, and were given free food for only two months. Afterwards they had to find their own food until they left in May, I have no idea where to. All the belongings they brought with them from home were confiscated and

burned. The Bashkir women tried to sneak into the building where they had been forced to leave all their clothing, including their ethnic attire. As soon as they were seen in these clothes they were made to give them up for burning. Some were so desperate they even managed to return to their villages before they were burned down in order to retrieve food and clothing. The women did all the housekeeping and hunting for food, while the men roamed around town and drank vodka.

An evacuee from the 1957 disaster told me that when soldiers came from Mayak to inform his fellow villagers that they had to leave their homes forever the very next morning, they advised the men to drink up whatever vodka they had in stock to protect themselves from the exposure: "The male villagers did as told. We took all the alcohol out of storage in the village store and homes and drank as much as we could. We had a great time." Some men were apparently delighted by this officially sanctioned drinking spree. Some informants speculated that this binging had increased alcoholism among the population.

Men and women recalled their resettlement with tears filling their eyes as they described how they had to slaughter their animals the night before they left, prepare their homes for burning, and part with family heirlooms. Then they were loaded onto army trucks that took them to barracks or unheated resort facilities, herded into showers, issued military clothing, and left to their own resources to gradually recover their lives. Some were eventually offered other housing, but many were forced to find shelter and jobs on their own. One major obstacle to finding work was that when they were forced to leave their homes, they also had to sign a paper promising not to tell anyone why they had moved. When they came to a new place looking for work, they were not able to give a previous reference because they could not say where they were from.

People could not hold back their tears as they told me that for years they pushed all thoughts about their past from memory, except in their dreams, and they refrained from talking to anyone, even their loved ones, about what had happened. Some said they were telling their stories for the first time. It was cathartic for them to speak openly about this pain. Around that same period, for another study, I interviewed survivors of one of the several ethnic wars that developed in the region after the breakup of the Soviet Union. Many of these war victims had clear symptoms of post-traumatic stress disorder—depression and crying triggered suddenly by a bad memory. The victims of the 1957 Kyshtym explosion had the same symptoms decades after the actual traumatic events.

Research about environmental-disaster victims (Erikson 1991; Vyner 1988) shows that psychological trauma is caused when victims cannot see, smell, or feel the environmental problem that they fear is causing them health problems. Trauma is also heightened because the disaster has no clear ending. Hanford, Washington, was home to a facility like Mayak, where similar contamination occurred throughout the Cold War, although with much less severe consequences. Nevertheless, the population around Hanford has suffered trauma from the experience of living near such a site. A

Figure 11.1. A Geiger counter near one of Mayak's Techa reservoir systems shows 785 micro-roentgens, some fifty to seventy-five times the normal background radiation. Source: Bellona

paper published in 1995 by the Hanford Health Information Network, organized by the Washington State Department of Health, indicates how post-traumatic stress disorder applies to Hanford's downwinders:

> Exposure to radiation may lead to a range of feelings and emotions. Concerns about exposure may be likened to a large, dark cloud that hangs above your head. This cloud contains the many emotions that you, as a downwinder, might experience: fear, anger, frustration, anxiety, distrust, uncertainty and grief. All together, these feelings may seem overwhelming and unmanageable. (Hanford Health Information Network 1995)

As information was released after the 1986 Chernobyl disaster, people gradually began to understand the effects of radiation on the environment and health. However, it was not until 1989, when the Soviet government officially acknowledged the Mayak disasters, that the Chelyabinsk population became fully aware of the implications of their proximity to the nuclear weapons facility.

They knew of their own health problems but did not relate them to Mayak until the post-Chernobyl revelations. For instance, since 1953 officials in Muslyumovo had been telling the community that the river was dirty, but not that the source of the dirt was Mayak. The local residents called their strange illnesses the river disease. The

Figure 11.2. Girls rest on the banks of the contaminated Techa River near Mayak. Source: Thomas Nilsen

symptoms—numbness in the extremities, aching joints, frequent and severe headaches, bleeding of the nose and gums, and fatigue—were periodic and in some cases constant. Some people even died of the river disease. Physicians who identified and studied this phenomenon named it the Muslyumovo syndrome (Komarova 2003).

After 1989, when people in Muslyumovo learned that the dirt in the river was radiation and how dangerous it was, the young people of the village renamed the Techa the *atomka*—a slang derivative from the Russian word for *atomic*.

Earlier, however, people did not draw the connection between Mayak and their illnesses—for one because Mayak was not allowed to be part of the people's consciousness. The situation was also a function of the Soviet infrastructure, which isolated one village from another via bad roads, no phones, and so forth. So people did not and still do not know much about what is happening outside their village or town. More than isolation, the main reason people did not make the connection was government policies of secrecy regarding the defense industry. People pretended such places did not exist for fear of thinking or saying something that would get them in trouble. It was as if Mayak and the closed cities were invisible.

Some people outside the closed cities knew that the facilities were connected to the defense industry. They spoke with pride about their country's accomplishments in defending itself against the enemy and believed the costs of having such a dangerous neighbor were well worth the benefits. During my fieldwork in the 1990s, I heard some antinuclear environmental activists speak with pride about the accomplishments of the defense industry while at the same time criticizing it. Residents living close to Mayak told me they regarded the facility as a potential source of privileged employment and therefore generally looked upon it favorably as a place that benefited the neighboring area economically. If Mayak hired a son or daughter, who then moved to the closed city, he or she could share the benefits of the high standard of living with relatives who remained on the outside.

Lifestyle Adaptation in Contaminated Territories

The first published comprehensive information about the health effects caused by Mayak was released in December 1991. The results had the impact of a bombshell on the entire population. The article summed up a study done by a government commission that revealed that since 1950 the incidence of leukemia among the population exposed to radiation along the Techa River had increased by 41 percent. From 1980 to 1990, all cancers among this population had risen by 21 percent and all diseases of the circulatory system by 31 percent (*Zelyony mir* 1992).

Local doctors then and now say it is impossible to obtain completely dependable health data because physicians were supposed to limit the number of death certificates they issued with diagnoses of cancer and other radiation-related illnesses. This restriction was part of the general Soviet practice of controlling health statistics so that rates of certain illnesses would not be embarrassingly high. Once a certain number of illnesses had been reached, no more were to be reported.

Another problem is that the Bashkirs and Tatars, due to Muslim religious considerations, would rarely permit an autopsy to establish cause of death. When they did allow an autopsy, they were angered when they saw a whole team of physicians at the side of the deceased within hours after death, whereas during the illness the doctors had not appeared once to offer the patient aid.

Galina Komarova, a Russian anthropologist, is one of few academics who have collected data about the social, cultural, ethnic, and confessional aspects of populations in areas contaminated by radiation. Between 1993 and 1998, in the most polluted areas of Chelyabinsk, with a population of around twelve thousand in four villages, she identified occupation, farming techniques, nutrition, personal hygiene, medical practices, religious beliefs, and ethnic identification as factors leading to greater or less exposure to the harmful effects of living in contaminated communities. She looked at behavioral differences according to age, educational level, economic status, and cultural and religious norms. What follows in this section draws entirely on her findings (Komarova 2003).

Ninety-five percent of the residents Komarova questioned in the most contaminated inhabited areas of Chelyabinsk regarded their exposure to radiation contamination as a health hazard, and almost all of them attributed their own illnesses to the Techa River. Fewer than 5 percent considered themselves relatively healthy. As mentioned earlier, they commonly referred to their poor health as the river disease. Even though people believed the Techa River was the cause of their ailments, they still used the river and its banks extensively in their daily lives.

Komarova looked at lifestyle adaptation among the Muslim and non-Muslim residents in these areas to understand how the people were coping with their knowledge about the contamination and how they might be lessening or increasing their exposure as they went about their daily lives, either following traditional norms or consciously developing new habits. She found that the significant rise in Islamic daily religious practices among the Tatars and Bashkirs affected their exposure in both negative and positive ways. For instance, the sharia hygienic rules prescribing rinsing of the mouth and throat and washing five times a day can be a health hazard in an area where the water is contaminated. Muslim women are reluctant to go to non-Muslim doctors, especially for gynecological problems, so they are less likely than non-Muslim women to receive treatment for illnesses in their early stages or to get treatment at all. The result is that the rate of gynecological diseases among religious Muslim women in the Techa area is significantly higher than that of non-Muslim women.

Exposure to radiation through food and water consumption also differs between the Muslim and non-Muslim inhabitants of the Techa region. The main source of radiation through food is from milk and beef from local animals that graze along the banks of the Techa River. Muslims and non-Muslims alike eat mostly their own garden-grown produce and their own livestock. Beef, mutton, fowl, and horsemeat are the traditional foods of the Bashkirs and Tatars and are considered by the local people to be the most contaminated. Pigs are regarded as the least contaminated because they are raised in farmyards and are not allowed to roam along the banks of the Techa. Even though pork is forbidden food among Muslims, in the Techa region Muslim religious leaders allow its consumption as a way to decrease health risks. They give the same dispensation when it comes to the consumption of fermented dairy products, such as cheese, cottage cheese, sour cream, buttermilk, and whey. Using household dosimeters, Techa residents have discovered that these fermented products have much less radioactivity than fresh milk. Although the sharia recommends whole milk for devout Muslims, religious Bashkirs and Tatars consume fermented dairy products instead.

As is evident from these examples of conscious changes in traditional diet, the Muslim inhabitants of the region are partially adapting the dietary habits of their non-Muslim Russian neighbors. In some ways Russians are also adapting the dietary habits of their Tatar and Bashkir neighbors. For instance, Russians have come to drink green tea like their Muslim neighbors, and even when they brew black tea, they follow the Muslim practice of throwing out the leaves within a few minutes. They have made these changes because they have heard that green tea and short brewing times decrease the carcinogenic elements of tea. Both Muslims and non-Muslims have cut back on their consumption of mushrooms, which they regard as among the most contaminated food in the area. To avoid river water, both groups also tend to use water from wells or pumps to prepare food, even though they prefer the taste of river water.

Listening to horror stories told by the inhabitants of Muslyumovo and other villages along the Techa River, who attributed sterility, congenital deformities, stillbirths, and strange chronic illnesses to local radiation contamination, made me anxious about my visits to the region, especially to contaminated rural areas. For instance, drinking tea is an obligatory ritual of hospitality throughout Russia. It is one of my favorite rituals, but in the village of Muslyumovo, regarded as one of the most contaminated villages, I dreaded each invitation to have tea and food with the villagers. At the same time I felt guilty about hesitating to share the same potential fate as these kind and friendly people, who had opened up their homes and hearts to me and my other American colleagues on this project.

It was easy for me to sympathize with the plight of these people, who knew of their radiation exposure but had no consistent or reliable information about the health effects, and therefore had no way to make informed decisions about preventive lifestyle measures. After taking several trips to the region, my anxieties about health risks from eating food, drinking water, and breathing air in a place that was often referred to as the most contaminated on earth continued to rise.

Looking back on those years of fieldwork in Chelyabinsk, I can't help but wonder if the death of Dr. Nina Solovyova from breast cancer, a year after she spent several months in Muslyumovo, living in villagers' homes as she studied Muslyumovo syndrome, was directly due to her research. As I was writing this chapter and consulting with my colleague Galina Komarova, we discussed our perceptions of the risks we took doing these studies in the 1990s. I learned from her that another physician who had worked with Dr. Solovyova had also died of cancer a few years later. Komarova told me that the husband of the third researcher on the team forbade his wife to continue research in Muslyumovo after the deaths of her two colleagues. Komarova revealed to me for the first time how the knowledge of the deaths of these women she had also worked with compelled her to deliberately avoid visiting those areas of Muslyumovo where the radiation levels were highest.

These kinds of anxieties are the type of behind-the-scenes information that researchers rarely reveal in their academic articles or even in informal conversations with colleagues. In all the years Komarova and I had known each other and worked together in the field, we had not discussed our fears about radiation exposure until I told her about wanting to write about this aspect of our work.

The Perspective of Chelyabinsk Officials

How do plant officials respond to accusations against them that their policies led to nuclear disasters and that they withhold from the public crucial information about their safety? Yevgeny Ryzhkov has been Mayak's director of public relations ever since

I met him in the early 1990s. When I first interviewed him about the nuclear accidents (December 1992), he focused all the blame on past production procedures and past policies of not informing the public. He told me, "My policy is to answer any questions from the public to prevent wild rumors." He claimed that mistakes had been made in the past but that they had become much less likely because of knowledge and experience accumulated over the years. The population outside the plant, however, continued to mistrust him and other officials. He said he could not blame them, because they had been lied to so many times before. He said his goal was to regain the people's trust by always being forthright in responding to their concerns about safety and the facility's activities.

Officials, scientists, and members of their families who lived inside the closed cities of Snezhinsk and Ozersk, even before the 1957 explosion, commonly told me they were healthy and therefore were living proof that the accidents of the 1950s and 1960s were not as damaging to people's health as claimed. Some of these informants appeared to genuinely believe what they said. However, a couple of them, speaking to me off the record and away from their fellow residents, said just the opposite. This latter view was also reflected in the results of a University of California–Irvine public opinion survey conducted in 1993 inside Snezhinsk, where roughly half the population claimed their families' health was affected by operations at the facilities in nearby Ozersk (Dalton et al. 1999). Reliable health data are next to impossible to obtain, so none of these claims can be proven right or wrong.

Officials in local government seemed to talk out of two sides of their mouths. On one hand, they fought hard for the Chernobyl law, which ensures generous government allocations to areas affected by the Chernobyl accident, to be applied to the Chelyabinsk region. In so doing, they cited the tremendous health and related social problems caused by the 1957 accident. On the other hand, when they talked to their own constituents and to inquiring guests like me, they usually maintained that environmentalists should focus on industrial pollutants and low living standards as the main culprits in the region's health problems, not on the military complex.

At a meeting of several regional leaders in September 1992, one of them maintained that environmental activists had done more damage to the country than Chernobyl because they generated "radiophobia," the term used in Russia to denote excessive fear of radiation among the population. They claimed radiophobia was far more debilitating than the purported health problems. Furthermore, they charged that visiting foreigners worsened the situation by asking people questions about how radiation affected them and thus stirring up unnecessary thoughts and feelings. Another official at the same meeting, a physician, claimed that when he went door to door in communities such as Muslyumovo, where people were convinced that all their ailments were due to radiation, he became convinced that their illnesses were caused by their low standard of living, not radiation. Not one official at this meeting expressed a dissenting opinion.

In 1992 it was a remarkable experience for me as a foreigner to sit at a roundtable of local officials and environmentalists and take notes on their heated discussion about what for so many decades, up until 1989, had been a taboo topic. As the victims of the 1957 Kyshtym explosion had told me, they had not raised this subject even in their own homes, let alone in a public forum where an American could listen and take notes. Since the aftermath of Chernobyl in late 1986, the Soviet Union and its successor country, Russia, had been transformed dramatically. I was now taking for granted the openness of the system.

Thus, without hesitation, at that meeting I approached an official from the closed city of Ozersk to request a visit to the facility to interview employees and residents for a book my colleagues and I were writing about the environmental and sociocultural issues in Chelyabinsk (Dalton et al. 1999). I knew that Americans from US nuclear weapons facilities had already been to Mayak. The official told me that the authorities in Ozersk could not grant such permission; I had to make a formal request for the visit to the Ministry of Atomic Energy in Moscow. The ministry would take care of all the formalities required.

A few months later, after making the formal request to the ministry, providing a detailed explanation about the purpose of the visit and a copy of the interview questionnaire, I was notified that my colleagues and I could go to Ozersk in December. We would be accompanied by a sociologist who worked for the ministry and would be met in Chelyabinsk by someone from Ozersk, who would drive us to the site.

On a very cold winter day in December 1992, John Whiteley and I (both from UC-Irvine), together with our Ozersk escort and our escort from the Sociology Department at the Ministry of Atomic Energy, set off from our Chelyabinsk hotel to the once virtually invisible town. An hour or so later, when we arrived at the heavily guarded closed gates to the city, hidden behind a dense forest, two young security officers asked each of us for our passports to check them against the guest list. The security officers exchanged a few words that we could not hear, looked at the list, and looked at our passports a few times. There was a moment of uncertainty about our status. Finally, they saw all our names on the list and returned our passports. The officers cleared us to enter the city gates.

Our host drove us to a municipal building, where we were to meet the director of the Mayak facility. We waited for more than an hour. Instead of the director, two other men appeared. One was the official who had told me a few months earlier, in vast detail, all the procedures I had to follow to get permission to visit. He and the other man astonished us with their news. They claimed we had not followed all the proper procedures, that we actually did not have permission to enter the city, and that we must leave as soon as possible. He said we had skipped a step in the process, but he did not clarify which step.

It did not make sense to any of us, least of all to the Moscow and Chelyabinsk escorts. We were dumbfounded. I explained to the official who had originally instructed me that I had, indeed, followed every procedure he recommended. In addition I pointed out what I thought was already obvious: that if we did not have proper permission to be there, we would not have been accompanied by a Moscow official and the facility's own official and would never have been allowed through the gates.

When pressed about what specific step in the process we had skipped, the officials finally told us that the visit had not been cleared with the Chelyabinsk FSB, the security services formerly known as the KGB. "How was I supposed to do that?" I asked in astonishment. Was that not the responsibility of the Ministry of Atomic Energy? That is how it had always worked in the Soviet era. Later, when I talked about this strange turn of events with our Moscow host from the Ministry of Atomic Energy, we concluded that the timing of our visit had been unfortunate. We learned later that the day we had gone to Ozersk marked a major turning point in Russian politics—that morning, Russian president Boris Yeltsin had shifted many decision-making functions of Moscow to local governments and authorities. This change may have given a green light to the local FSB to say to the Moscow authorities, "Hey, you didn't clear this visit with us." Perhaps the local FSB was flexing its muscles, showing Moscow it would no longer take orders and instead would decide itself who would come and go in Chelyabinsk. I will probably never know the real reason, but this one makes the most sense to me.[4]

This experience marked the end of a roughly three-year period, from 1989 to 1993, when officials appeared to be open to efforts my colleagues and I, working inside and outside the country, were making to unravel the mysteries of the Soviet and post-Soviet nuclear weapons industry and its environmental consequences. During the period of openness, officials were predictably cooperative in sharing information and opening doors to more data. Afterward, it became impossible for me and others to predict official responses to fact-finding research in this area. The search for truth by locals and foreigners became increasingly frustrating and more often than not futile.

A Chance Meeting with a Defense Industry Employee

Also in 1992, a conversation I had with a fellow passenger on a flight from Chelyabinsk to Moscow gave me an uncensored view of the political views of someone who had spent his whole career in the Soviet defense industry—and apparently most of it in one of Chelyabinsk's closed cities. Igor talked about his nostalgia for life in the former Soviet Union, his support for the Russian chauvinistic and anti-Semitic political forces emerging in post-Soviet Russia, and the environmental consequences of nuclear weapons production. He represented the kind of attitudes of suspicion that led to the clampdown on openness. Ryzhkov and the other officials I met in Ozersk struck me as having more progressive views than Igor. I think they would have preferred a continuation of openness and truth telling, but long years of Soviet conditioning made them able to go with the ebb and flow of openness.

Igor, who had not gone through the regular security checks in the terminal and just showed up on the tarmac separately from the rest of us, had evidently either bribed his way onto the plane or used his connection with the flight crew to secure a ticket. When he boarded, he sat next to me. He was a man in his fifties. He had done some heavy drinking just before the flight, making him more talkative than he might have been otherwise.

As I mentioned earlier, my Russian was near-native fluent. Rarely would Russians detect an accent in casual conversations. And if they did, they usually thought I was from one of the Soviet Baltic republics—certainly not from the United States or any other Western country. At first Igor clearly assumed he was sitting next to a Russian woman. He was so busy lamenting how awful life had become with the collapse of the Soviet Union that I did not have a chance to identify myself. When he asked why I was in Chelyabinsk, I simply said I was an anthropologist doing fieldwork there, without mentioning the subject of the fieldwork or my nationality. Igor boasted that he was returning from important business connected with the defense industry. He would not have shared with me his disgust with the new Russia or his line of work if he had had any clue that I was a foreigner. My hunch was confirmed later.

Meanwhile, as Igor lamented the corruption that had forced him to go through the back door to get on the flight and the drastic decline in living standards that had affected most of the population, he was eager to find blame with "those who never worked in the factories, in the fields, who never created anything—the Zionists. Russia is the last outpost against Zionists," he declared. In the Soviet Union, using the term Zionist was the politically correct way to express anti-Semitism. He ranted on, saying, "The Zionists have taken over America and all other countries. The Gulf War against helpless Iraq was intended to defend Israel. The whole world is working for Israel." He explained that he knew what he was talking about because he had worked with Jews for thirty years in the defense industry, where he claimed he saw them engage in sabotage. Ethnic Russians, on the contrary, only tried to make life good for everyone but were unappreciated by the other ethnic groups that had broken away from the Soviet Union, he complained.

By this time I realized I was sitting next to what in those days the Russians called a Red-Brown—that is, someone with a mix of communist (Red) and fascist (Brown) ideology. The situation gave me an opportunity to learn more about a political trend that was still a mystery to me and about someone who worked in the weapons industry. So I cautiously began to guide his monologue into a dialogue by asking him questions about his life.

At some point he detected my slight accent and asked the question I had dreaded: "Where are you from? The Baltics?" After a brief pause I told him the truth—that I was from the United States. He was visibly surprised but not immediately hostile, as I had expected he might be given all he had said before about the negative role of Americans in the world. Instead he proceeded to tell me how much he respected CIA and FSB counterintelligence officers: "They are people like me and my friends who live to defend their countries. My friends and I have always spoken the truth."

The conversation did not progress in a logical way. My recounting of what we talked about has been reorganized to make it easier for the reader to follow. The conversation zigzagged in and out of the history of Igor's life; his simplistic and contradictory views about history, contemporary Russia, and the world; and how unfair the accusations were about the nuclear environmental damage caused by Mayak. To prove his point, he boasted that he swam in Lake Karachay next to Mayak. I could not conceal my astonishment, because I knew levels of radiation were so high at the lake that just standing on its shores for five minutes could be lethal (Cochran et al. 1993). I said as much to him, expressing my skepticism about his heroic feat. Abruptly he became hostile and suspicious. My knowledge about Lake Karachay and the radiation levels in the closed region marked the turning point in his attitude toward me, from good-natured to outright belligerent.

His whole body stiffened and his eyebrows furled as he pointed his finger at me judgmentally and spoke angrily: "You're not an anthropologist. I know what you really are," implying that I was working for the same US intelligence service that he had so highly praised just a few minutes earlier. The tirade continued: "You are from a so-called civilized country, but you don't know anything I know. So it means that country is not as highly developed as you claim. On September 7 Americans said on television that Russians are pigs." I had no idea what statement he was talking about. But I could see his anger rapidly turn to rage. We both fell silent for a few minutes. Then he spoke again with hostility, the volume of his voice rising as he continued his accusations against me. My fears rose. I could not hear him anymore. I told him the conversation was over. Thankfully, Igor did not speak to me for the rest of the flight.

I cannot say that Igor was a typical product of Russia's defense industry, although I suppose there are more people with views like his than I had suspected. His tongue was loosened by liquor, whereas some of the officials, scientists, and local people I had met might have been in better control of such extremist views. Furthermore, Igor did not have the self-censorship that I frequently encountered when formally gathering data with my US identity revealed in this xenophobic culture. The kind of chauvinistic extremism Igor expressed was a minority view of the world in Russia at that time. However, the venom of his anger toward the West in general, and with regard to the humiliating economic decline of the former superpower, represented a common enough phenomenon in post-Soviet Russia.

The final two sections of this chapter illustrate the trend back to secrecy, in part due to the mentality of people like Igor and the willingness to acquiesce to the powers that be by people like Ryzhkov.

My Final Visit to Chelyabinsk

As I was reading all my old fieldwork notes from that period in preparation for writing this chapter, several journal entries reminded me that various people I talked to in Chelyabinsk had remarked that so and so said this or that American visitor was interested in the region in order to gather intelligence information about the defense industry. It must have been hard for ordinary people and officials to believe that outsiders were coming to these godforsaken sites motivated by scholarly curiosity, let alone an altruistic desire to help people. On every research visit, Whiteley and I arrived with huge boxes full of medicine and clothes, which were badly needed by the people we met in the villages. The villagers were grateful, but I noticed that many people were suspicious of us.

By 1994 I was not enjoying the work in Chelyabinsk because of the increasing roadblocks to gathering information and because of my concerns about the health risks. No matter how hard I have tried to enjoy this particular journey of discovery, I ultimately failed. No matter how deliberately I sought beauty in the nuclear landscapes I visited, I could not see much beyond the bleak and insidiously sinister natural and industrial terrain. Whether I was visiting the Hanford nuclear reservation in the desert of southeastern Washington or the Chelyabinsk nuclear site in the thick pine and birch forest areas of the southern Urals, my whole body protested my presence in these places.

A good reason to discontinue my fieldwork in Chelyabinsk presented itself in the summer of 1994. False accusations against me were published in a local Chelyabinsk newspaper and later in a national newspaper in Moscow. The pieces claimed I was a CIA agent working undercover as an academic.

This is what happened: On the last day I interviewed people in Muslyumovo before I was to return to Moscow that afternoon, a local friend told me that an FSB agent from Ozersk was asking people if they had seen an American in the village collecting blood samples from villagers. Indeed, many of the villagers had asked me to take their blood samples back to the United States to be tested for the presence of strontium-90 or some other component of radiation. The villagers did not trust their Russian labs and wanted to know how much radiation exposure showed up in their bloodstreams. This information was not the subject of my work, but I agreed to help them, figuring it would do no harm.

My Chelyabinsk colleagues were visibly upset about the sudden appearance of the man from the FSB. Their anxiety led me to decide that it would be better for all of us if I cut my day trip to Muslyumovo short, went back to Chelyabinsk without any blood samples, packed my suitcase, and got an early start to the airport. I did not want to get engaged in a conversation with a security agent in a provincial town. I figured it would be better to have such a conversation in Moscow, where officials were more open-minded than those in Chelyabinsk.

On the way back to Chelyabinsk, a Russian colleague who lived in the region recalled the reaction of a biologist, a research professor, to his question about the rumor that Americans could use Russian blood samples to discover Russians' genetic code and develop a genetic weapon against Russia. My colleague thought the professor would laugh at the idea. Instead, he said, "Oh yes, we have messed up our gene pool so much that we can be a terrible weapon." That story convinced me all the more that I had made the right decision to leave Muslyumovo, and without any blood samples.

At the airport check-in counter I saw a few militiamen engaged in a serious conversation with a tall, well-built man in his thirties. This tall man had a short haircut, was in terrific shape, wore a gray suit, and looked like the typical FSB agent portrayed in movies. I remembered how one of my friends in Moscow had said that "all FSB agents look alike, as though they are poured from the same mold, wear the same shoes and suits, and get the same haircuts." While I went to the next counter to pay for my overweight luggage, I watched out of the corner of my eye how several men, looking like they were from the same mold, hovered over my checked suitcases as though they were certain they contained an explosive. I had departed from that airport many times but had never seen such an entourage at the check-in counter, or anywhere else in the airport.

When I approached the line leading to the waiting room for the flight, I saw the man in the gray suit from the check-in counter. When I handed my ticket to the militiawoman at the entrance, she told the man in the gray suit that number 112 had arrived. How much more obvious could they be? While my purse and computer were still in the X-ray machine, a militiaman asked me to show him what was inside. I said cheerfully, "Gladly, but only after my things come out of the X-ray machine." He nervously apologized, embarrassed by having asked the impossible of me in his anxiety.

After the militiaman had gone through my hand luggage and found nothing, the man in the gray suit, who had been silently watching, asked me to open up my coffee cup. He was disappointed to see it empty, and I was secretly gleeful to see his frustration. Then the agents asked me to open my suitcases, which had been brought there especially for examination in my presence, instead of being loaded on the plane as was the usual procedure. They asked me to identify a large cylindrical object they detected inside the suitcase. It turned out to be my flashlight, which I take everywhere for field-work—you never know when the lights will go out! I had forgotten about it and thought they had seen my Swiss Army knife, another necessary item for fieldwork in dicey places. Actually, the knife was in my purse, but I had forgotten that.

Disappointed again, they were no longer interested in my suitcase. The militiaman told me in parting that I should always know what's in my suitcase—as if that was my real problem. He apologized for holding me up and assured me that my suitcases would make it to the plane on time. When I asked him what they were searching for, he said contraband. I dropped the subject, not wanting to hear more.

An article in a Chelyabinsk newspaper published a couple of weeks after my visit claimed that the activities of foreign researchers, working independently with local environmental activists to collect people's blood samples for testing in laboratories abroad, had been initiated by foreign intelligence agencies (*Rabochaya gazeta* 1994). More worrisome than that was an article in a national newspaper published in Moscow; it named me as the person collecting blood samples to obtain secrets about Russian nuclear weapons production and accused me of being a foreign agent, using a university as my cover.

A Chelyabinsk environmentalist later told me that he and a few others were called into the FSB for questioning about my last visit. He claimed that the agent seemed most indignant about the possibility of a foreigner taking blood samples from the local population and not paying the authorities for the access. "After all," he explained, "these blood samples and the information they reveal are worth millions of dollars." It was difficult to know to what extent the concerns were really about security or financial issues. This was a time in the young capitalist country when privatization of state industries was going ahead full speed, the commercialization of the nuclear industry was under discussion, and suddenly everything was for sale.

For awhile I thought I might return to Chelyabinsk once the dust had settled, but each time I considered the possibility, I decided the risks were too great. I feared that if I resumed the fieldwork, at best some very unpleasant and unreasonable questioning awaited me. Since that time, I have followed developments from a distance.

Chelyabinsk Radiation Victims Today

On my first visit to Chelyabinsk, in December 1991, just a few hours after I saw that long line of people waiting at 5:00 a.m. to get groceries at 8:00 a.m., a television journalist who had covered environmental stories for twenty years made this prophetic comment: "It will take more than one generation to improve the environment. We will have ample food and clothing long before the environment is cleaned up." Indeed, economic conditions in Russia have improved dramatically since the early nineties when I began this research. Russians no longer wait in long lines for goods in short supply. Unfortunately, the same kind of progress has not taken place in terms of environmental cleanup, financial compensation to radiation victims, and improved living conditions, economic status, and medical care in the contaminated areas of Chelyabinsk. This situation is largely due to Russia's lack of resources and lack of determination to right the wrongs committed by the nuclear weapons industry against its own people during the Cold War. The resistance of local and national officials to face these daunting issues has not changed in the past decade.

In recent years, some of the region's villagers have sued the Russian government for damage to their health. An account in the *Seattle Times* by Mark McDonald describes a conversation he had with one such defendant, an ethnic Tatar named Glasha Ismagilova. She was eleven at the time of the 1957 Kyshtym explosion, and like hundreds of other children her age, she was taken by her school into the fields to dig up and dispose of contaminated crops. McDonald writes: "Week after week they dug up contaminated potatoes and carrots with their bare hands, then buried them in pits. They filled poisoned wells, cleaned bricks covered in radioactive soot, buried dead cattle, dismantled houses" (2004). It was not until the mid-1980s that she and others were told the nature of the contamination.

Ismagilova, according to McDonald, "spoke calmly about her own illnesses—about the new three-inch tumor on her liver, the painful crumbling of her knees and hips. Tears started to come only when she remembered borrowing her mother's orange sun dress on that morning 47 years ago when the Mayak Cleanup began. She wanted to look nice because she thought her fourth-grade class was headed off on a field trip" (2004).

The ethnic Tatars and Bashkirs who constitute the majority of villagers most affected by the Mayak disasters also charge environmental racism. Controversy still rages about why the ethnic Russian side of the village that Ismagilova comes from was evacuated and the ethnic Tatar and Bashkir side was not. McDonald cites an official who claims that no one knows why some were resettled and others were not. According to McDonald,

> Ismagilova does not accept the government's explanation that the Tatar side of her village was safe enough while the Russian side had been contaminated. She said this was genocide.... "[O]ur families were not well-educated, so it was eas- ier for the authorities to keep us in the dark.... Almost all the people here were liquidators, but they're too old and sick to press their claims," Ismagilova said, the tears coming again. "They did the state's dirty work 45 years ago, and now they have no money. Not even enough for bread. They have no future." (2004)

There are indications that the minority Bashkir and Tatar populations in the Chelyabinsk region may have been a target of selective human rights violations, mainly because Muslyumovo and a few other predominantly Bashkir-Tatar villages were not evacuated from the Techa River, perhaps deliberately so the people could be used as guinea pigs to study the long-term effects of low-dose radiation. However, no such minority populations exist at nuclear weapons facilities in Krasnoyarsk and Tomsk, where Russian and other Slavic villagers were subjected to similar nuclear vic- timization. This fact makes it more difficult to assert unequivocal claims of environ- mental racism, because it appears as though the leaders of the Soviet defense industry showed a general disregard for the health of all people, no matter what ethnic back- ground, including employees at the plants.

For the reasons stated above, activists in the White Mice (the Russian equivalent of "guinea pigs"), Muslyumovo's antinuclear organization, hesitate to charge officials with environmental racism. But they do charge human rights violations because the government has not taken adequate measures to move the villagers to a site farther from the river. They have written to international human rights organizations about their grievances over environmental injustice but have not framed their complaints as charges of environmental racism.

In any case, medical evidence abounds that these villagers are at a very high risk for lethal exposure to radiation. Svetlana Kostina, a researcher at the Chelyabinsk regional government's department for environment and radiation, reports that "the current dose of radiation absorbed by Muslyumovo residents is 10 times higher than internationally acceptable levels.... Only 18 percent of the village children aged 6 to 14 can be called healthy, while the rest of the children suffer from acute memory loss, attention deficit disorders, and exhaustion" (Badkhen 2001).

Galina Komarova observed in the four most contaminated villages along the Techa River that households that let their cattle graze on the banks of the Techa were polluted with radionuclides to a significant degree. Her onsite surveys showed that children spent an average of half an hour a day by the river and teenagers about an hour and a half a day. In spite of prohibitions issued by adults, and even though all residents knew that proximity to the river was directly related to higher exposure to radiation, Komarova saw children and teenagers daily playing by and in the Techa. Village shepherds spent up to eleven hours a day by the river. Komarova found that over the five years she studied lifestyles in Muslyumovo, from 1993 to 1998, use of the Techa grew more intensive, and not simply for leisure-time activities. Having lost their former sources of income due to the collapse of the collective-farm system and local industry, the Techa villagers had to resort to using natural resources for their livelihoods more than in the past (Komarova 2003).

Ann Imse interviewed several patients at the Urals Center for Radiation Medicine in Chelyabinsk and observed the same ailments and psychological trauma that I had encountered ten years earlier. For instance, fifty-six-year-old Nadezhda Nikolskaya, who grew up along the Techa River near Muslyumovo and was hospitalized for radiation sickness, told Imse that she had lost two of her three sons to what she believes was radiation illness. She complained to Imse, "People still live there, and they don't do anything!" According to Imse, "Ivanov [the doctor in the hospital where Nikolskaya was interviewed] enters to give her a sedative. She meekly drinks it down." Vera Kazantseva, seventy-six, another patient, said, "Our children are sick, our grandchildren are sick." Her four children and two grandchildren have ulcers, and Kazantseva is sure they come from radiation exposure (Imse 2003b).

Nurislan Gubaidullin, sixty-two, said his wife had died of stomach cancer several years earlier; his wife's mother, brother, sister, and niece had also died of cancer. He was told that the constant pain in his legs was caused by the high dose of radiation he received during cleanup after the 1957 Kyshtym explosion, when he plowed polluted lands on his tractor. "We've got a bad environment here. That's why we are all ill," he asserted (Badkhen 2001).

Officials at Mayak continue to deny the validity of accusations that link the serious health problems in the region to the activities of Mayak. Their quotes in articles by more recent visitors are nearly identical to those I heard from officials ten years earlier. Here is an excerpt from Ann Imse's conversation with Yevgeny Ryzhkov (who was still Mayak's spokesman a decade after my own interviews with him) and another Ozersk employee:

> Mayak spokesman Ryzhkov insists the bad health among the plant's neighbors
> has nothing to do with radiation. He and fellow Mayak worker Vadim
> Borodin, now 75, cite themselves as proof, saying they're not suffering from
> radiation, despite higher contamination than these complaining civilians. "I'm
> 64 years old, and of course I have illnesses," Ryzhkov said. But he blames
> them on his genes, on smoking, on drinking. "The civilians should be blaming

their unhealthy lifestyle, not radiation," he said. "People think they are receiving high doses, but it's stress. They think they are victims, and they need medical and psychological care." (Imse 2003a)

Not all of Russian officialdom has denied the terrible predicament of the Chelyabinsk radiation victims. The Chernobyl law, which mandated the relocation of all victims of the Chernobyl accident, as well as monetary compensation, applies also to all victims of the Chelyabinsk disasters, thanks to many years of tireless efforts by Chelyabinsk environmental activists. Implementation of that law in regard to Chelyabinsk victims, however, has required the environmentalists' constant vigilance and struggle, but without much success. In 1994, in the spirit of the law, the administration of the Chelyabinsk region passed a resolution to build a new village farther away from the Techa River, where Muslyumovo victims living in the most contaminated areas of the village could relocate. However, eleven years later the resolution still has not been implemented fully. For instance, as of February 2006, at the time of this writing, the 444 families in Muslyumovo who lived in the most contaminated areas of the village and who agreed to move to safer territory still awaited the necessary funding.

In December 2003, Grigory Yavlinsky and Sergei Mitrokhin, leaders of the opposition political party most closely associated with Russia's environmental activists, brought this issue to the attention of the highest authority in Russia, President Vladimir Putin, in a private meeting. As a result, Putin delegated the minister of atomic energy, Alexander Rumyantsev, to allocate funding for relocation. The problem is that ultimately relocation is contingent upon the Chelyabinsk regional government developing and implementing a plan of action, which it has not done so far (Yabloko News Agency 2005).

In Russia today we hear controversy over the prospect of further contamination from the importation of foreign nuclear waste for reprocessing and storage. Arguments abound for and against this new trend: a potential source of huge revenues as well as further contamination. This is a major issue for environmental activists, who refer to this trend as "transforming plutonium bombs into a plutonium economy" (Mironova 2000). On this issue, according to opinion polls conducted by ROMIR Monitoring, a market research company, 90 percent of the Russian population supports the environmentalists and opposes the import of foreign nuclear waste (*Pravda* 2003).

The importation of nuclear waste attracts billions of dollars to Russia's nuclear weapons sites and their closed townships, once enclaves of prosperity but now financially struggling communities, not much better off than the nearby historically poor towns and villages. Vladimir Slivyak, cochair of Ecoprotection in Russia, maintains that the importation of nuclear waste is "for the benefit of a small group in the nuclear power industry to the detriment of future Russian generations" (*Pravda* 2003).

This is how the spokesman for Ozersk's nuclear facilities, Yevgeny Ryzhkov, frames the issue: "'Our reprocessing techniques have been polished to perfection.... We have been doing this for 30 years with no negative effect on the environment.' Besides, he says that Mayak can afford the costly procedures of environmental cleanup only by reprocessing more spent nuclear fuel. 'As soon as we get more spent nuclear fuel to reprocess, we will thrive'" (Badkhen 2001). Furthermore, Ryzhkov claims that Mayak will never completely shut down. It is the only Russian factory making "certain nuclear parts for the military," making radioactive isotopes, reprocessing spent nuclear fuel, and "diluting uranium from Russian bombs to less-enriched uranium for power plants" (Imse 2003c).

Some locals believe they see evidence that Mayak continues to contaminate the area. Imse quotes Garifulle Khabibullin, an ailing villager from the Techa and a tractor driver at the time of the 1957 explosion who helped with the cleanup. He claims: "Sometimes, the river rises in the morning even when it has not rained, and by noon, it's back to normal level.... I'm sure they're dumping" (Imse 2003a).

In Russia's contemporary political climate it is much harder than it was more than a decade ago to investigate such claims. As Imse notes, "Reports of the death toll have disappeared. Doctors who spoke openly during the 1990s have stopped talking. Mayak officials deny that the plant's neighbors are being contaminated" (Imse 2003a). A Tatar village mullah reflects the sentiments of those in Chelyabinsk, who have no reliable source of accurate information about their health risks as the neighbors of nuclear weapons facilities but have deduced from their life experiences that they are victims: "The government and authorities of the Chelyabinsk region are trying to forget this. But we in the villages will never forget this hell. Our sicknesses and daily funerals don't let us forget it!" (Imse 2003a).

Conclusion

There are no hopeful signs that anytime soon the people of Chelyabinsk will penetrate the culture of secrecy and denial in Russia's nuclear weapons industry to understand the full extent of the environmental and health consequences of the arms race, let alone mitigate the damage.

During the brief period of unprecedented openness about these problems right before and after the breakup of the Soviet Union, we learned that huge nuclear accidents had taken place in the 1950s and 1960s, that they were far bigger than the Chernobyl explosion in 1986, and that they impacted a much larger population. When that secret was exposed, people began thinking of themselves as the victims of friendly fire—of Soviet bombs meant for the enemy but turned on the nation's own citizens. When they realized that other nuclear powers knew about the 1957 Kyshtym explosion long before it was revealed to the Soviet people, antinuclear environmental activists lamented that, if not for the culture of secrecy maintained by all nuclear powers, international pressure might have prevented subsequent accidents, including Chernobyl. In the period of openness, officials were cooperative in sharing information and opening doors to more data.

Just a few years later it became impossible for me and others to predict official responses to fact-finding research in this area. One day you thought you had permission for research, but by the end of the day you did not. One day you were welcomed as a legitimate academic, but by the end of the day you were accused of being a CIA agent. My careful yet futile efforts to get into and stay in the closed nuclear city of Ozersk, home of Mayak, long enough to conduct an opinion poll about environmental values illustrate the obstacles to information gathering for people inside and outside post-Soviet Russia. The stories about my chance encounter with a nuclear weapons employee and my near brush with the Chelyabinsk FSB also show how deeply ingrained is the culture of secrecy in the nuclear weapons industry and in its citadels that are still closed to the public.

In the past decade, the anti-Western sentiments illustrated in these stories have increased and become a significant aspect of the political terrain in Russia, especially in relation to the issues covered in this chapter. I do not predict that the secrecy will return to what it was in the Soviet era, at least not as long as it is possible to take officials to court for violating safety rules. For instance, in March 2006 a Russian court ordered the dismissal of the director of Mayak, Vitaly Sadovnikov, for having authorized the dumping of "tens of millions of cubic meters of liquid radioactive waste into the Techa river in 2001–2004, even though the facility had enough money to prevent it.… Instead of preventing the damage to the environment, Sadovnikov had spent the money on maintaining a representative office in the Russian capital and lump payments to himself" (Bellona 2006). I see no signs, however, of a return to the openness that Gorbachev promoted just before the fall of the USSR.

As long as secrecy and denial prevail, it will be extremely difficult to conduct independent studies to verify the extent of health hazards that can be directly related to past and current activities at the Chelyabinsk nuclear facilities. What we do know, however, is that the attitudes of survivors with regard to their predicament range from complete denial of any health risks to a heightened state of anxiety that all health problems they and their families suffer are due to significant radiation doses in the water and food chain over long periods of time. This level of anxiety, illustrated in the poignant statements conveyed in this chapter, is sufficient to warrant further research and action that can give the population credible information to help them make better choices about where to live and how to adapt their lifestyles.

Notes

1. The research presented in this chapter resulted in part from a larger multidisciplinary project, conducted jointly with colleagues at the University of California–Irvine and Washington State University, about the environmental consequences of nuclear weapons production in Russia and the United States (Dalton et al. 1999). Some data about Chelyabinsk come from survey data and in-depth interviews that I conducted during seven months of fieldwork over twelve research visits to Russia from June 1991 to July 1999, including seven trips to the Chelyabinsk region from December 1991 to August 1994. I came to know people quite well by working with, observing, and interviewing environmental activists, nuclear sci-

entists, and officials in various Moscow-based and Chelyabinsk environmental organizations, in towns and villages from 3 to 30 miles away from the Mayak facility. After 1994 I gleaned additional insights from US and Russian media and from phone and e-mail conversations with people living near the sites, environmental activists, scientists, and officials.

2. The last czar of the Russian Empire was overthrown by the Bolshevik revolution on November 7, 1917. This date marks the beginning of Soviet government in most of the territory of the former Russian Empire. The USSR collapsed in December 1991, breaking up into fifteen successor countries, the largest of which is Russia.

3. I received my BA in history from Moscow State University in 1980, my MA in anthropology from the same university in 1982, and my PhD in anthropology from what was then called the USSR Academy of Sciences Institute of Ethnology and Anthropology in 1990.

4. Eventually the pendulum in Russia went in the other direction, giving Moscow back its former powers.

References

Badkhen, Anna
2001   Wasting Away. Electronic document, http://www.eng.yabloko.ru/Publ/2001/ Agency/tol-waste.html, accessed May 12, 2006.

Bellona
2006   Mayak Plant's General Director Dismissed from His Post. March 20. Electronic document, http://bellona.org/news/Mayak_plant_%20general_director_dismissed _from_his_post, accessed December 19, 2006.

Cochran, Thomas B., Robert Standish Norris, and Kristen L. Suokko
1993   Radioactive Contamination at Chelyabinsk-65, Russia. Annual Review of Energy Environment 18:507–28.

Dalton, Russell J., Paula Garb, Nicholas P. Lovrich, John C. Pierce, and John M. Whiteley
1999   Critical Masses: Nuclear Weapons Production and Environmental Destruction in the United States and Russia. Boston: MIT Press.

Erikson, Kai T.
1991   Radiation's Lingering Dread. Bulletin of the Atomic Scientists 47(2):34–39.

Gladyshev, Mikhail
1990   Unpublished memoirs, recorded by Pyotr Tryakin.

Hanford Health Information Network
1995   Environmental Health Programs. Electronic document, http://www.doh.wa.gov/ hanford/publications/coping/coping.html, accessed October 22, 2006.

Imse, Ann
2003a   Radiation Hell. Electronic document, http://www.rockymountainnews.com/drmn/ world/article/0,1299,DRMN_32_1761420,00.html, accessed April 15, 2005.

2003b Legacy of Agony, Disability. Electronic document, http://rockymountainnews.com/ drmn/world/article/0,1299,DRMN_32_1768363,00.html, accessed April 15, 2005.

2003c Nuclear Cesspool. Electronic document, http://rockymountainnews.com/drmn/ world/article/0,1299,DRMN_32_1768364,00.html, accessed April 15, 2005.

Komarova, Galina

2003 Ethnic and Confessional Aspects of the "Maiak" Accident. *In* CIS Environment and Disarmament Yearbook. Pp. 1–33. Jerusalem: Marjorie Mayrock Center for Russian, Eurasian, and East European Research, Hebrew University of Jerusalem.

McDonald, Mark

2004 Russia Finally Acknowledging '57 Nuclear Disaster. Seattle Times, April 7.

Mironova, Natalia

2000 Danger Links between Plutonium Bombs and Plutonium Economy: Transparency and Openness Help Society to Make a Choice. Paper presented at the World Conference against the Atomic and Hydrogen Bombs, Nagasaki, August 9.

Nave, C. R.

2005 Nuclear Fission Fragments. Electronic document, http://hyperphysics.phy-astr.gsu.edu/Hbase/nucene/fisfrag.html, accessed October 25, 2006.

Pravda

2003 Hungary to Export Spent Fuel to Russia Illegally. Electronic document, http:// english.pravda.ru/russia/economics/11-09-2003/3699-spent-0, accessed October 26, 2006.

Rabochaya gazeta

1994 People Don't Investigate Radiation Alone. Electronic document, http://hyperphysics. phy-astr.gsu.edu/hbase/nucene/fisfrag.html, accessed March 12, 2005.

Vyner, Henry M.

1988 Invisible Trauma: The Psychological Effects of Invisible Environmental Contaminants. Lexington, MA: Lexington Books.

Yabloko News Agency

2005 The Issue of Muslyumovo Discussed in the Ministry of Atomic Energy. Electronic document, http://www.chel.yabloko.ru/news/print.phtml?id=470, accessed October 25, 2006.

Zelyony mir

1992 Government Report on the Health of the Population of Russia in 1991. Zelyony mir 48.

t w e l v e

Unraveling the Secrets of the Past

Contested Versions of Nuclear Testing in the Soviet Republic of Kazakhstan

Cynthia Werner and Kathleen Purvis-Roberts

The military team never once asked the opinion of the population, did not let them know of the possibility of expected dangers, kept secret and still keep secret the actual situation. Undoubtedly, the population in the region are worried, disturbed and are demanding, but people can only be calmed by the truth, and not half-truths and unfounded confirmations. (Balmukhanov et al. 2002:36)

—*Saim Balmukhanov, medical researcher*

We can now state for certain that our society is quite familiar with the word "radiation." However, this term usually has negative, fearful association. Radiophobia, which has been over-dramatized in the mass media since the declassification of the Semipalatinsk Test Site, has gotten into everyone's flesh and blood. (Shkolnik 2002:346)

—*Saule Ryskulova, biologist*

The people of Kazakhstan have been grappling with the legacy of nuclear testing for more than a decade.[1] Until Gorbachev's glasnost policy emerged in the late 1980s, the Soviet government kept all information concerning the Soviet nuclear testing program highly classified. With freedom of expression under Gorbachev, political activists introduced new "truths" about the evils of nuclear testing and unleashed a wave of opposition that eventually led to the closure of the Semipalatinsk Nuclear Test Site (SNTS) in 1991. In an attempt to dispel the influence of these emotional narratives and to vindicate their careers, nuclear scientists have countered with their own versions of the "truth," which they claim are based on scientific objectivity. The different versions of the past are hotly contested when it comes to issues of the Soviet government's culpability: Did the government take proper precautions to limit radiation dose exposures or did it knowingly expose its own citizens to harmful levels of radiation? If tests exposed people to dangerous levels, did the government do this intentionally to test the effects of radiation on human health? And did it do so covertly in a way that limited people's knowledge of nuclear testing and the risk of radiation?

In this paper, we plan to address these questions from three different perspectives. First, we describe the perspective of nuclear scientists who designed and executed nuclear tests in Kazakhstan. In recent publications and personal interviews, these scientists have defended their actions in the name of national security and have claimed that certain precautions accompanied the tests to limit impacts to the health and environment. Second, we present arguments made by medical researchers in Kazakhstan who stress the harmful health impacts of nuclear testing. Finally, we describe the perspective of Kazakh and Russian villagers who lived near the test site. Although the individual stories vary, most villagers do not feel that the government adequately protected them, and many believe it used them as guinea pigs. These different perspectives of the past coexist in a highly politicized present where victims are struggling to receive greater compensation for their suffering and nuclear scientists are striving to redefine their jobs in a post-testing context. Though their efforts are limited by weak organization and low funding, the victims use their own experiences and the scientific data of medical researchers to make their case to the government, as well as to international organizations. In a similar vein, the scientists present their version of the past to the international scientific community in an effort to demonstrate their willingness to cooperate in exchange for funding.[2]

The Semipalatinsk Nuclear Test Site

For nearly half a century (1945–91), the United States and the Union of Soviet Socialist Republics waged a cold war of unprecedented nature. Justified by the mutual incompatibility of capitalist and Marxist ideologies and the perceived likelihood of a third world war, the two superpowers engaged in an intensive arms race. Although commentators often characterize the Cold War as a war without direct conflict, it was certainly not a war without victims. In addition to those who perished in the proxy wars fought in Korea, Vietnam, Afghanistan, and elsewhere, hundreds of thousands of US and Soviet citizens suffered exposure to dangerous levels of radiation as their governments produced and tested nuclear weapons that could be used if international tensions escalated into a "hot war." In both countries, the majority of the radiation victims lived in relatively remote areas and belonged to economically and politically disadvantaged social groups. Among the victims were the Kazakh pastoralists and the Russian peasants who lived dangerously close to the SNTS in what is now northeastern Kazakhstan.[3]

In August 1947, just two years after the United States tested the infamous Trinity bomb in Alamogordo, New Mexico, the leaders of the Soviet Union passed a special resolution to build a secret military city in the Kazakh Republic. They designed the new city, named Semipalatinsk-21, to be the headquarters for the Soviet nuclear testing program (Nazarbaev 2001). Because they lived in a "special city," all residents had to have security clearances. The city's entrances were carefully guarded with barbed wire and three checkpoints, and stores offered consumer goods that could not be found in most Soviet cities. Like other special cities in the Soviet Union's military-industrial complex, Semipalatinsk-21 did not appear on maps until it was renamed Kurchatov in the 1990s in honor of the nuclear physicist Igor Kurchatov.[4] The government instructed the forty thousand residents of Semipalatinsk-21 to tell people they lived in Semipalatinsk, a larger city 87 miles to the east. The Soviet military censored all letters leaving or entering the city. Just as the state hid the residents' real existence from the outside world, the state concealed their deaths: those who died in the secret city were buried elsewhere (Balmukhanov et al. 2002:10–11; Shkolnik 2002:14). Health and mortality statistics for residents of Kurchatov are still difficult to obtain, making it difficult to assess the impact of nuclear testing on these citizens.[5]

Between 1949 and 1989, the Soviet military conducted 456 nuclear tests, including 30 surface tests and 86 atmospheric tests, at the SNTS, also known as the Polygon.[6] Semipalatinsk-21 was located on the northeastern corner of the 7,000-square-mile test site. The Ministry of Armed Forces, in collaboration with the USSR Cabinet of Ministers and the Central Committee of the Communist Party of the Soviet Union, chose the test site location for several practical reasons. The nearby city of Semipalatinsk had a functional airport, which was important for ferrying supplies, military personnel, and scientists to the new testing facility. The military constructed an additional airport in Semipalatinsk-21 for cargo planes. Supplies could also be shipped to Semipalatinsk-21 along the Irtysh River from Russia or Semipalatinsk, except when the river was frozen over during the long Siberian winter. Finally, the military built a special railway from Semipalatinsk to Semipalatinsk-21. Geologically, the land in this area was stable enough to withstand many nuclear blasts, and the varied topography included the Degelen mountain range in the south and a flat steppe zone in the north. These variations would enable the military to test the weapons under different geological conditions and to investigate the impact of nuclear blasts in different environmental conditions (Balmukhanov 2002; Shkolnik 2002:6–8).

The Ministry of Armed Forces selected the location also because of its relatively low population density. However, more than twenty thousand residents lived in more than a dozen villages situated along the border of the test site, and the Polygon displaced several more villages.[7] The population in the affected area quadrupled between 1949 and 1989 (Nazarbaev 2001). Some researchers estimate that approximately 1.5 million people living in nearby villages and cities may have received significant doses of radiation from Polygon tests (Balmukhanov et al. 2002:2).[8] The test site encompassed land in three different oblasts, or provinces, of the Kazakh Republic: Semipalatinsk, Pavlodar, and Karaganda.[9] The highest levels of radioactive fallout

Table 12.1. Villages and Cities near the Semipalatinsk Nuclear Test Site and Their Populations, 1960

Village/City	Population
Dolon	906
Kara-Aul	2,335
Kanonerka	1227
Mostik	637
Sarzhal	832
Semipalatinsk	163,000

Source: Bouville et al. 2000:149

have been found in the former Semipalatinsk Oblast (now the western half of East-Kazakhstan Oblast). Radioactive fallout has also affected people living north of the test site in the Altai Oblast of Russia. Table 12.1 shows 1960 population figures for key villages and cities affected by nuclear testing.

Most people who live near the test site are ethnically Kazakh or Russian. There are also smaller populations of Germans and Ukrainians. The Kazakhs have been indigenous to this region for centuries. Traditionally, their livelihood was based on nomadic pastoralism, with mixed flocks of sheep, goats, horses, and camels. Russian peasant migrations (1865–1900), World War I (1914–18), the Russian Revolution and Civil War (1917–21), and Soviet collectivization efforts (1928–38) disrupted this nomadic lifestyle. Russian and Ukrainian peasants migrated to the region in the nineteenth century after the Russian czar liberated serfs and encouraged them to settle in the less populated regions of Siberia and northern Central Asia. The ethnic Germans in the region are the descendents of those Stalin deported from Russia during the Second World War. Geographically, the Russians, Ukrainians, and Germans live in the villages north of the Polygon, and the Kazakhs are concentrated in the villages on the southern, western, and eastern sides of the Polygon. By the time the first nuclear test was conducted, the majority of rural adults worked either on a collective farm or in service jobs that supported the collective-farm system.

The SNTS had four regions for testing three different types of nuclear explosions (see map 12.1). The initial testing took place on the Experimental Field, or ground zero, located in the northern part of the test site, approximately 43 miles from Semipalatinsk-21. Underground testing was conducted in the other three regions: Balapan, Degelen, and Sary-Uzen. All the tests conducted at the Experimental Field were aboveground, meaning they offered the maximum potential exposure to the populations surrounding the Polygon. Between 1949 and 1962, the military detonated thirty surface and eighty-six atmospheric tests (Shkolnik 2002). For surface tests, the military placed the nuclear weapons on a tower and discharged them. Atmospheric

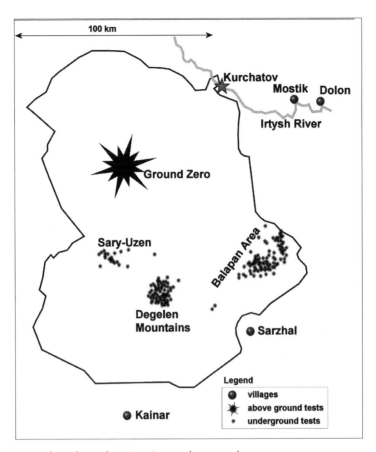

Map 12.1. Semipalatinsk Nuclear Test Site and surrounding environs.

tests involved airplanes dropping the weapons. During the first several years of testing, the military neither had much experience predicting radioactive fallout patterns nor much concern about protecting local populations from radioactive fallout (Shkolnik 2002:70–71). As a result, several large explosions occurred when the wind was blowing directly toward villages and cities adjacent to the test site. For example, the first atomic test, which took place on August 29, 1949, was one of the most devastating for human exposure because powerful winds thrust the radioactive cloud directly over the villages of Dolon and Mostik (Hille 1998). Several other tests, including ground tests conducted on September 24, 1951; August 12, 1953; and August 24, 1956, also led to significant levels of radioactive exposure (Shkolnik 2002:39).

Initially, Soviet military leaders did not know how the shock wave and radioactive fallout from a nuclear explosion would affect potential targets. So in addition to testing the explosive device, they devised experiments to study how nuclear weapons would affect military hardware, human-made structures, and domestic animals. At various distances from ground zero, the military positioned airplanes and tanks and built houses, apartment buildings, railway tracks and bridges, and a subway station.

The military also placed different types of animals (rabbits, sheep, goats, pigs, dogs, guinea pigs, rats, and mice) at various distances from the center to study the consequences of radiation exposure. It put some animals inside buildings constructed of various materials to gauge their protective qualities; it left others outdoors (Shkolnik 2002). Newspaper accounts suggest that Soviet soldiers were also intentionally exposed to assess the impacts of radiation on their fighting ability (Walsh 2002:135–43).

In 1963 the United States, United Kingdom, and USSR signed the Limited Test Ban Treaty, which limited nuclear tests to underground areas. Between 1961 and 1989, Soviet officials conducted 340 underground nuclear tests in the southern part of the Polygon. Many of these tests involved as many as five explosions at the same time, for a total of five hundred explosions (Shkolnik 2002). In the Degelen mountain range, the military inserted nuclear explosives into the ends of tunnels drilled horizontally into the mountains. In the relatively flat Shagan River basin (also known as the Balapan area), it bored holes into the ground to hold the explosive devices. Finally, the military conducted twenty-one tests in vertical holes in the Sary-Uzen area in the southwestern portion of the test site (Shkolnik 2002). Although the conversion to underground testing did limit human exposure to radiation, 45 percent of the underground tests leaked small amounts of radioactive gases into the atmosphere, as scientists expected they would. In addition, thirteen of the tests involved accidental leakages of more significant amounts of radiation, and four of the tests involved the intentional release of radioactive gases and aerosols from "peaceful," "excavating" explosions (Shkolnik 2002:53). (Several "peaceful" tests were conducted to see if small nuclear explosions could be used for nonmilitary purposes, such as the creation of a lake.)

The Semipalatinsk site saw its final underground test on October 19, 1989. Earlier in the same year, a powerful antinuclear social movement had emerged in Kazakhstan. In February, the first secretary of the Semipalatinsk Regional Committee of the Communist Party, Keshirim Boztayev, sent a telegram to the Central Committee of the Communist Party of the Soviet Union in Moscow, requesting a temporary suspension of nuclear explosions because of public concerns. Although Moscow's initial response was negative, another powerful voice of protest was soon heard. On February 26, the popular Kazakh poet Olzhas Suleimenov gave an emotional speech on television calling for the end of nuclear testing in Kazakhstan and invited people to a public rally on February 28. By the end of March, the newly formed Nevada-Semipalatinsk Antinuclear Movement had more than a million signatures of support. From the outset, the founders viewed the organization as an international antinuclear organization, with cosignatories and protestors from other regions of the world affected by nuclear testing. The organization's emblem signified the connection between Nevada and Semipalatinsk by displaying a Native American chief sitting next to a Kazakh elder. As the popular movement gained momentum, Kazakh politicians, including Nursultan Nazarbaev (chairman of the Kazakh Republic's Central Committee and now Kazakhstan's president), began to push harder for their demands.

Meanwhile, the Nevada-Semipalatinsk Movement scheduled a series of public protests. By criticizing the government's nuclear testing program, both the movement and local party leaders tested the limits of Gorbachev's glasnost policy. Rather than being punished for such disobedience, the antinuclear movement received several concessions, beginning with a reduction in the scheduled number of tests and promises for socioeconomic development in the region. A 1990 decision to temporarily suspend nuclear testing was followed by a landmark decision to close the test site on August 29, 1991, forty-two years to the day after the first nuclear test (Nazarbaev 2001; Shkolnik 2002).

Although closed, the former test site still poses a threat to nearby residents. Unlike before, the test site is now unguarded. There is no longer a fence or barrier to keep people out of the Polygon, and there are no signs indicating areas with high concentrations of radiation. Villagers who live in the area sometimes travel through the Polygon to reach other villages and cities. A more serious concern stems from risks associated with collecting and using contaminated materials from the test site. In particular, people have gathered scrap metal (from discarded military hardware) and copper cables (from the underground test tunnels) to sell for profit. (Each underground test involved large amounts of cable to provide both the electrical charge to detonate the bomb and the ability to take measurements about the device's yield and other characteristics.) In addition, residents of local villages have recycled quality cable and wood from the former military bases within the test site for use within their homes. Such activities further increase dose levels of nearby residents, who are already suffering the consequences of radiation exposure.

The SNTS is not the only place where people were knowingly exposed to radioactive material in the USSR during the Cold War. For example, the Mayak facility in the southern Ural Mountains of Russia was once home to a radiochemical processing facility for the production of plutonium for nuclear weapons. From 1949 to 1956, radioactive waste was dumped into the Techa River, which is used as a source of water for many villages, potentially exposing at least thirty thousand people (Garb, this volume; Kossenko 1997). People living in the villages use the water primarily for drinking and washing, thus receiving both internal and external doses (Degteva 2000). In 1957 an explosion at the Mayak facility released about 20 million curies of radioactive debris into the atmosphere, exposing up to 270,000 people in the region (Garb, this volume). Today, an analysis of the number of deaths and illnesses due to radiation exposure versus the proximity of villages to the processing facility displays a perfect dose-response curve. The closer to the Mayak processing facility one lived, the greater the chance of obtaining a radiation-related illness.

Such human rights abuses were not limited to the former Soviet Union. In *Plutonium Files*, Eileen Welsome details experiments the US government did on both soldiers and civilians to better understand how radiation affects human health. During several tests, thousands of military personnel were positioned less than 3 miles from atmospheric explosions at the Nevada Test Site. Soldiers were then asked to perform military exercises immediately after aboveground nuclear tests, in the guise of practicing maneuvers in the midst of a nuclear war (Welsome 1999:261–69). US Air Force pilots also flew directly through mushroom clouds to take radiation measurements (272–84). The impact of nuclear testing was not limited to military personnel. Several Native American groups, including the Western Shoshone, have been exposed to significant levels of radiation from the Nevada Test Site, similar to villagers in Kazakhstan who lived adjacent to the SNTS. The doses they received were greatly miscalculated, due to the failure of scientists to understand the culture and eating habits of these people. For example, the Western Shoshone increase their exposure to radiation by consuming the thyroids of small game animals, such as rabbit (Frohmberg et al. 2000). Residents of the Marshall Islands have been exposed to even greater levels of radiation from the US nuclear testing program. Marshallese from Rongelap Atoll were exposed to near-lethal doses of radiation and then were involuntarily enrolled in medical experiments that involved intensive examinations by medical researchers. After the Bravo test, residents were evacuated from Rongelap for several years due to radiation contamination, then later resettled there, even though the US government knew that radiation levels were still dangerous (Barker 2004; Barker, this volume). In addition to studying the impacts of radiation exposure from nuclear testing, the US government has learned about the impacts of radiation exposure from various medical experiments. Some of the most insidious experiments have been performed on prisoners (Welsome 1999:362–83) and pregnant mothers (219–28) without their knowledge of potential health impacts. In addition to exposure from nuclear testing, some populations in the Marshall Islands were used for medical experiments that involved radioisotopes (Johnston 1994; Johnston, this volume).

Nuclear Scientists Defend Their Actions

In response to the popular reaction against nuclear testing, nuclear scientists from Kurchatov and elsewhere have attempted to defend their actions during the years of nuclear testing. Throughout the Cold War, physicists dominated the research institutes at Semipalatinsk-21, as they were required to design the nuclear bombs, carry out the test explosions, and analyze data from the tests to design better weapons. Most were Russian scientists trained in Moscow. While only a fraction of these scientists have remained in the city since 1991, those who remain are rarely apologetic about the impact of their tests on local populations. On the contrary, they maintain that the nuclear tests were vital for national security interests and that adequate precautions were taken to limit radiation exposure to innocent populations.

One of the best sources for understanding these scientists' perspective is a book entitled *The Semipalatinsk Test Site: Creation, Operation, and Conversion*. This book was jointly prepared and published by the Cooperative Monitoring Center of Sandia National Laboratories and the Republic of Kazakhstan Institute of Nonproliferation in 2002. While the lead editor was Vladimir Shkolnik, Kazakhstan's minister of energy and material resources, the editorial board included the leading directors and deputy directors of the various research institutes associated with the National Nuclear Center in Kurchatov. Most of these researchers were associated with the nuclear test site during its operative phase and have been employed by the National Nuclear Center of Kazakhstan since its formation in 1993. Although individual views vary among scientists, the general ideas presented in this book echo the stories we collected during interviews with several scientists in Kurchatov. The book strives to provide what the authors consider to be an objective and scientific account of "the Test Site's military and scientific activities from the cold-war period through the present day" (Shkolnik 2002:iii). Distancing themselves from "emotional assessments of various events, which usually entail classification of these events as 'right' or 'wrong,'" the authors of the book claim to rely on "*unbiased witnesses*—official documents, research reports, and the assessments of professionals" (iii).

The scientists frame the issue of nuclear testing as a national security issue rather than a human rights issue. From their perspective, the primary goal was to design effective and powerful nuclear weapons, not to protect the environment or human health. As the authors state, "For the USSR, nuclear weapons were a military technological guarantee of the country's national security. Their power could practically rule out the possibility of foreign aggression both against the USSR and against its former allies" (Shkolnik 2002:25). This perspective was shared by nuclear scientists who developed nuclear bombs in the United States (Gusterson 1996). The Soviet scientists acknowledge that the first nuclear test in 1949 was "considered such an important military and political event at the time that the testers were permitted to disregard unfavorable weather conditions and conduct the test on a rainy day with strong wind gusts" (Shkolnik 2002:70). With such an urgent task at hand, it was easy to discount the needs of the local population. The authors refer to the surrounding areas as "poorly developed," with "small agricultural villages along the Irtysh and Shagan River valleys" and "practically barren steppe" with "temporary summer and winter camps" of Kazakh nomads (7). The authors continue to describe how construction workers arrived on the "uninhabited steppe" to build the test site (8). This depiction overlooks the fact that the government forced small settlements of pastoralists to resettle.

The scientists explain that national security interests ensured that the public could not be informed of any details associated with nuclear testing:

> The secrecy of all construction and equipping of the test site, nuclear weapon
> development, and reports containing the test results was protected by the
> USSR Ministry of Internal Affairs (MVD).... Secrecy was imposed on the
> results of exposure to harmful effects of nuclear explosions with various yields
> or the physical characteristics of nuclear physics packages, the degree of
> radioactive contamination of environmental systems and the terrain outside the
> grounds of the test site, possible outdoor and indoor public exposure doses,
> and the effect of radiation and other factors, such as seismic ones, on the health
> of residents of areas adjacent to the test site. (Shkolnik 2002:32–33)

One way to ensure secrecy was to limit public access to the test site. According to the scientists, the Experimental Field was fenced off with barbed wire and heavily guarded with military personnel at twelve different outposts (Shkolnik 2002:20). In his ethnography of nuclear scientists at the Lawrence Livermore National Laboratory in California, Hugh Gusterson describes the daily practices that maintain a culture of secrecy in the facility. For example, the facility is divided into different areas that require different levels of security clearances to enter, and lab employees are socialized to believe that they are under constant surveillance (1996:68–100).

Although secrecy was imperative, the scientists portray a picture in which the military, in cooperation with test site scientists, treated the surrounding population in a paternalistic rather than an indifferent manner. After acknowledging that national security was the dominant concern during the first test, the scientists stressed that various safety precautions were taken during subsequent tests, especially as more information became available about the harmful impacts of radiation exposure. As early as 1951, the government created the Radiation Safety Service to predict radiation levels in the plumes of nuclear explosions, determine allowable dose levels, and create evacuation plans when necessary (Shkolnik 2002:74). To limit public exposure to radiation, the scientists argue, wind conditions were carefully monitored such that new radioactive plumes were unlikely to overlap with previous plumes (41). For each nuclear test, the military included a representative from the Ministry of Health and the highest-ranking officials from the regional communist party in discussions related to public safety (32, 39). Though privy to some knowledge regarding the tests, these government officials were also sworn to secrecy.

In some special circumstances, local populations were temporarily evacuated before a test was conducted. Further, the military was often prepared to evacuate certain areas in case of unexpected events. The largest series of evacuations took place before the 1953 explosion of the first thermonuclear device. Approximately 2,250 villagers and nearly 450,000 heads of livestock were evacuated to temporary campsites at least 75 miles from ground zero. The villagers were compensated for their inconvenience with five hundred rubles per person, and they were allowed to return home ten to fourteen days after the explosion (Shkolnik 2002:76). The scientists fail to mention that not all villagers were allowed to evacuate, and they fail to describe what the villagers witnessed upon their return home.

During tests that did not require evacuation, military officials instructed local populations to stay outside of their homes. The scientists suggest that the shock waves associated with atmospheric testing created more of a risk than exposure to radioactive fallout. They note that structural damage from shock waves (including broken windows, broken door frames, and collapsed structures) occurred in fifty-nine villages and towns around the test site, resulting in numerous injuries and several deaths (Shkolnik 2002:48). However, the scientists fail to discuss whether radiation exposure rates might have been lower if the villagers had stayed inside their homes during periods of radioactive fallout.

Although the Kurchatov scientists attempt to portray the government as a benevolent protector of the public, they hint that preferential treatment was given to the residents of Semipalatinsk-21. For example, when radioactive plumes were heading toward Semipalatinsk-21, residents were "completely sheltered in specially equipped hard rooms in accordance with safety instructions" while villagers were "evacuated to open areas" (Shkolnik 2002:46). In addition, the military gave "individual protective devices" to and performed "dosimetric monitoring" on test personnel, but not ordinary citizens (84). Preferential treatment also extended to diets. Our interviews suggest that the diet of Semipalatinsk-21 residents included a higher percentage of foods imported from other regions. Despite these privileges, one scientist we interviewed suggested that radiation is just a small factor affecting public health. From his perspective, local health patterns in the villages were best explained by poor diets and psychological stress associated with "radiophobia." He added that he himself had been exposed to more radiation than most villagers, without any harmful impacts on his health. This perspective echoes that of officials and scientists associated with the Mayak facility in Russia, as described by Paula Garb in this volume. As in the case of Mayak, it is impossible to acquire health data for the residents of Kurchatov, and thus it is difficult to assess the extent to which this population has also experienced health problems associated with radiation exposure.

The Kurchatov scientists are even more ambivalent when they describe how the Soviet government carefully monitored the health of local residents. In 1957 the Soviet government opened Dispensary No. 4 in Semipalatinsk for the "continuous observation of the health status of residents of contaminated districts" (Shkolnik 2002:78). To protect the secret mission of the clinic, a sign identified it as Anti-Brucellosis Dispensary No. 4.[10] The Institute of Biophysics within the USSR Ministry of Health supervised the research conducted at Dispensary No. 4. Recruited from the military hospital in Semipalatinsk, the clinic staff had access to top-quality equipment and laboratories. Over the course of several decades, they studied the long-term impacts of radiation on approximately twenty thousand people from three districts in the Semipalatinsk region (Abay, Beskaragay, and Zhana-Semey). Researchers studied blood, urine, and stool samples for traces of radiation and prepared reports based on their findings. Their "patients" were divided into a test group (whose members had received doses ranging from 20 to 150 cSv) and a control group (whose members lived in the same towns but had moved there later in life). Approximately two thousand children were included in the study. Dispensary No. 4 was also charged with taking environmental samples. Air, soil, food, and water samples from the villages were collected and analyzed before, during, and after nuclear blasts (Grosche 2002; Shkolnik 2002:100–14).

In addition to Dispensary No. 4, the Ministry of Health collected data through a series of medical expeditions to villages surrounding the test site (Shkolnik 2002:100–14). With all this data, doctors and scientists investigated the correlation between radiation exposure and certain health problems, including cancer and birth defects. Due to the need for secrecy, however, patients could not be told that their doctors were studying the impacts of radiation exposure. The scientists who prepared the Shkolnik volume indicate that the Soviet government was very interested in monitoring the health of the local population, but they fail to indicate the extent to which the government provided effective treatments for this population.

From the scientists' perspective, the health impacts on local populations were minimal. In response to data suggesting that local populations have experienced changes in their cardiovascular and gastrointestinal systems, the scientists often attribute these changes to nonradiation-related factors, such as vitamin deficiency, industrial pollution, and poor sanitation (Shkolnik 2002:115–19). In general, the scientists support their arguments with data presented in a 1990 medical report submitted by Dispensary No. 4. According to this report, "The health status of people exposed to ionizing radiation in the past in doses up to 100 rems over the entire 30-year observation period does not differ from that of control groups" (328). The report also found no significant differences in the morbidity of children exposed to radiation compared to children in the control group. However, the report does suggest that radiation exposure has negatively affected the health of a "small group of the population" exposed to doses up to 150 rems. Among this population, there are "[p]oorly marked disturbances of natural immunity, cytogenetic effects, accelerated aging processes and excess cancer mortality" (328). Similar attempts to use scientific studies in ways that limit the number of radiation victims have been described in other settings, such as the Marshall Islands. Barker (2004), for example, discusses how scientists minimize the illnesses associated with radiation exposure in the Marshall Islands by comparing the illnesses found in an exposed group with the illnesses found in a control group. By denying that the control group was also exposed to significant levels of radiation, scientists are able to downplay the impact of radiation exposure on these populations.

Today, now that the SNTS is closed, many of these same scientists (and their successors) are applying their knowledge in ways that help the people who live around the site. For instance, the Institute of Radiation Safety and Ecology, affiliated with the National Nuclear Center in Kurchatov, is working to identify contaminated sites on the test site and restore them to their natural conditions. In addition, the Institute for Radiation Medicine and Ecology, formerly Dispensary No. 4, is using its knowledge to develop better treatments for radiation-related illnesses. The institute is closely affiliated with a neighboring institution, the Semipalatinsk Oncological Hospital.

Medical Researchers Offer a Different Perspective

Not all scientists in Kazakhstan have defended the Soviet nuclear testing program in the name of national security. Several medical researchers, in particular, have taken an active role in providing alternative scientific interpretations of existing data. One noteworthy medical researcher, Saim Balmukhanov, has been collecting medical data in the Semipalatinsk region since the 1950s. He first became interested in the region's health during casual conversations with doctors in Semipalatinsk in 1952 and 1953. He realized that the symptoms they described seemed identical to symptoms found among the Japanese populations in Hiroshima and Nagasaki. Initially, test site officials refused contact with Balmukhanov, who proceeded to collect data in the Semipalatinsk region for two summers with just a handful of colleagues. By the late 1950s, Balmukhanov had received more funding and support for his research from his home institution, and he was included on joint expeditions with the Institute of Biophysics of the Ministry of Health. His research took him to several key villages surrounding the test site, including Kainar, Dolon, and Sarzhal. He listened to local doctors as they described patients suffering from blotchy bald spots, skin with unusual burns, and extremely high blood pressure. Women were suffering from vulval bleeding and extremely long menstrual periods (Balmukhanov et al. 2002:133). Balmukhanov also discovered that the food and soil in the region were heavily contaminated with strontium-90, a radioactive element known to have adverse effects on biological organisms (19). He had little doubt that the medical findings were linked to radiation exposure, especially since disease rates were more than two to three times higher in areas close to the test site.

Although it was a risky move, Balmukhanov and his colleagues shared these disturbing findings with test site officials. In his recent memoirs, Balmukhanov describes how Colonel S. L. Turapin, the military official in charge of radiation surveys, reacted to this news:

> Turapin does not agree with the results of our radiological investigation, and simply pays no attention at all to the data concerning the health of the population. Most important was the radiation dose! At first the possibility of irradiation with high doses was completely repudiated. He argued for a long time about the level of radiation contamination in the village of Sarzhal...when we showed the results of our radioactivity measurements and a correspondingly high level of illness which was confirmed by several measurements, Turapin brings out another map of regional pollution with another dose rate. We argue as one does at the bazaar, and we do not agree with our figures. So, we fight over each population point: Kainar, Karaul. (Balmukhanov et al. 2002:20)

Balmukhanov was pressured to sign agreements stating that radiation doses did not exceed permitted levels. And test site officials repeatedly tried to convince him that the health problems he witnessed were due to other factors, such as vitamin deficiency, protein deficiency, tuberculosis, and brucellosis. After heated discussions, Balmukhanov received several warnings from leading officials in the Ministry of Health, the Ministry of Defense, and the KGB. Friends warned him to be careful or he might lose not only his career but also his life (Balmukhanov et al. 2002:21, 25). Like so many Soviet citizens, he practiced self-censorship until the late 1980s, when it became safe to talk about these issues. In 1989 he was finally allowed to return to the test site to continue his research (Walsh 2002:140).

Although the test site is now closed, nuclear scientists and medical scientists continue to intensely debate the extent to which radiation levels exceeded safe levels and the extent to which radiation can be blamed for local health problems. On the one hand, Balmukhanov and others argue that acceptable dose levels were regularly and knowingly exceeded (Balmukhanov et al. 2002:12–15). On the other hand, scientists from Kurchatov attempt to discredit medical scientists such as Balmukhanov by arguing that their research is methodologically weak and emotionally biased. For example, in the introduction to *The Semipalatinsk Test Site: Creation, Operation, and Conversion*, the authors start off by stating:

> Various publications have appeared in recent years on the history of the development of Soviet nuclear weapons, the possible scale of environmental radiation contamination, and the effect of nuclear testing on human health. Unfortunately, most of these publications, in addition to truth and a scientific presentation of information on the problem, contain many conjectures, inaccuracies, and uneducated guesses. These are especially common in publications containing information on the extent of radiation's effects on the health of residents of the inhabited areas that were contaminated by radioactive substances during atmospheric nuclear testing. (Shkolnik 2002:1)

There is no doubt that these comments are directed toward Balmukhanov, whose status has reached heroic proportions among the populations surrounding the test site.

Villagers Describe Their Memories of Nuclear Testing

The subjects of the scientific debates are real human beings who have their own stories to tell. Since 1989 the Kazakhs and Russians who live in the villages surrounding the test site have been able to speak openly about their experiences with nuclear testing. Many of these villagers have participated in political protests organized by the Nevada-Semipalatinsk Antinuclear Movement. Others have had their stories told in local newspapers. In this section, we will describe some of the information we have gathered about nuclear testing from those who lived near the test site.

All villagers who were alive during the tests have vivid memories of military personnel showing up in a village by helicopter the day before a test to warn them of upcoming "military exercises." The military personnel communicated with village leaders, who then communicated all necessary information to village residents. The explosions were never described as "nuclear tests" or "atomic bombs." After each test, military personnel would return to the village to monitor the situation and gather samples with their equipment.

Before each test, the military provided specific instructions. Mothers remember being told to close the windows to their homes, cover their water sources, and leave their homes during tests. Herders remember being told not to drink the water at certain places. And, those who were children during the tests remember soldiers telling

Figure 12.1. Researchers Cynthia Werner, Kathleen Purvis-Roberts, and Nurlan Ibraev stand near the spot where the first nuclear test was conducted at the Semipalatinsk Nuclear Test Site. Although radiation levels are dangerously high at "ground zero," there are no warning signs or fences to prevent local residents from visiting such spots. Credit: Cynthia Werner

them to leave school buildings so they would not be harmed by the earthquakelike shaking. They also remember being told to lie down on the ground and to avoid looking at the bright clouds in the sky. In Dolon, soldiers instructed people to lie down in low-lying areas.

As they retell their experiences, many villagers note that when they were young, they thought the tests were fun and exciting, and they rarely listened to the instructions. One middle-aged Kazakh man wonders whether he would not have eye problems now had he followed the instructions. He and others found it very thrilling to watch the emergence, development, and passing of mushroom clouds. It was similar to watching a fireworks display. The colors and shapes were constantly changing. Villagers remember children competing to be the first one to spot the emergence of a mushroom cloud. They also remember the excitement of having soldiers arrive in helicopters. One Kazakh woman recalls how she used to feel lucky to live in a secret military zone. Although she did not understand the purpose of the exercises, she knew they were significant, and she thought it was wonderful to live in a place where such important things happened. Today, the villagers admit that they did not realize the explosions were poisoning their bodies and endangering their health. One Kazakh woman in Dolon remembers soldiers telling villagers that the tests were good for their health. Officials may have warned them to take certain precautions, but they never explained the health consequences of not following the directions. And it is unclear that it would have made a difference if they had listened.

Older people living in the village of Kainar remember when they were evacuated in 1953 during a very large test. The military came to the village a few days before and helped them move their livestock away from the village. Most families left behind smaller animals, including cats, dogs, and poultry. For nearly two weeks, the villagers stayed at a temporary camp. After the military allowed them to return home, they found unusual things: many of their chickens were dead; some baby chicks were deformed; their dogs and cats were losing their fur, and some were covered with scabs. Several people described dogs and cats dying before their eyes in the first few days after their return.

Dogs and cats were not the only ones left behind in 1953. Kainar residents repeatedly told us that the military forced forty village men to stay behind, allegedly to maintain the village infrastructure. We interviewed one of the two survivors, a Kazakh man in his seventies by the name of Nurzhan Mukhanov.[11] At the time of the evacuation, he was in his early twenties, and he worked for the local radio station. He did not want to stay behind. As he describes the story, it was clear that people knew it would be dangerous to stay in the village. He wanted to help his widowed mother with the evacuation, but his supervisor said he had no choice but to stay. The brutalities of Stalin's collectivization drive and his father's disappearance during the subsequent repression in the 1930s were etched in his memory, so he obeyed his supervisor. According to his story, on the day of the explosion, military personnel took the forty men to a beautiful area a few kilometers from the village. The soldiers gave the men food and alcohol and instructed them to relax and enjoy the day. Before leaving, the soldiers provided Mukhanov and a coworker with some radio equipment and told them that further instructions regarding the exercise would be sent via radio. Mukhanov and his coworker waited for the instructions, but before they arrived, there was a massive explosion, followed by a mushroom cloud. The other men were very worried that something might be terribly wrong and were angry that Mukhanov did not provide them with any information. Mukhanov and his coworker insisted that they had not received any radio transmissions. A few hours later, military personnel, covered in white protective clothing from head to toe, returned to the scene to see how the men were doing. The men were still angry. They felt they were in danger and demanded to know why they had never been contacted with further instructions. The soldiers responded by saying that the radio operator on the other end had been drunk and had failed to do his job properly. Mukhanov now feels that he and the others were intentionally used as guinea pigs. He remembers how the soldiers took blood and urine samples from him and the others on a regular basis.

In some villages, such as Dolon and Mostik, residents were never evacuated. However, one Kazakh man remembers that soldiers came to his natal village, Bodene, in the early 1950s and gave people the opportunity to move to new homes in Kyzyl-Orda Province (more than 600 miles away). The soldiers explained that they were building a new military city (Semipalatinsk-21) nearby. The man believes that people would have moved had they known the military planned to test nuclear weapons nearby and that these tests would endanger their health. Without this information, the villagers chose to stay.

We have asked villagers whether they sensed that the military exercises were dangerous. Their answers vary. Only a few claim they did not know anything until the glasnost period, when it was safe for people to talk about these issues. Most were suspicious that their health problems might be related to the military exercises, but they did not know for sure. Many people remember experiencing headaches, toothaches, and nausea shortly after tests. Some women recall awful experiences with childbirth. The government wanted to conceal health problems, so doctors were not allowed to show deformed and stillborn babies to their parents. As one woman who lost a child told us, "I still don't know whether or not I gave birth to a monster." Besides health problems, several people remember particular experiences that made them wonder whether, or made them certain that, the tests were harming people's health. For example, one woman remembers people's horrified reactions when she entered a sports competition in Lithuania and the other children found out she was from the Semipalatinsk region.

In Kainar in the 1970s, a local schoolteacher named Bolat Zhakishev tried to convince village leaders that the explosions were dangerous. Zhakishev was a physics teacher. He said the explosions were nuclear tests and would have harmful effects on their health. Zhakishev lost his job for being so vocal.

Villagers today realize that many of their activities increased their exposure to radiation. For example, we interviewed many men who herded collective-farm livestock on territory within the Polygon. (See map 12.1.) According to several villagers in Kainar, collective-farm directors, under pressure to fulfill their annual production plans, made agreements with the military to allow herders to enter the Polygon to gather hay and herd animals. One elderly Kazakh man from Dolon remembers how members of his brigade, while herding sheep, visited ground zero and a small lake created by a nuclear explosion. For them, it was interesting to look at the airplanes and cars that had been used in the tests. The security guards allowed them to go close to these radioactive objects, although they were warned not to touch them.

Although some villagers suspected that the tests were dangerous, they did not have the political freedom to express their concerns until 1989. As Paula Garb describes in this volume, people were afraid to question the Soviet state, and this fear helped contain state secrets regarding the defense industry. It was not until the late 1980s that the villagers' trust in the government was totally shattered, as the Nevada-Semipalatinsk Movement exposed government secrets about nuclear testing and called for a ban on all future tests. The media accounts of nuclear testing that emerged in 1989 led many villagers to reinterpret their life experiences. They now have an explanation for illnesses that killed their relatives at young ages. They now have an explanation for the flulike symptoms and toothaches they experienced on the days of testing. And they now have an explanation for why the nightingales that used to sing during their childhoods are now a rare sight.

Conclusion

From 1949 to 1991, the Soviet military conducted more than 450 nuclear tests at the Semipalatinsk Nuclear Test Site. Until the late 1980s, the authoritarian nature of the Soviet government prevented any public discussions about the harmful effects of nuclear testing. Things changed radically in 1989 when the Nevada–Semipalatinsk Antinuclear Movement developed in the wake of Gorbachev's glasnost policies. In a matter of months, the issue of nuclear testing became a hotly debated topic in Kazakhstan. The ability to discuss events publicly led to increasing distrust of the Soviet government and its role in nuclear testing. As the antinuclear movement gained momentum and support, leading Kazakh politicians, including President Nursultan Nazarbaev, joined the struggle and pressured the central government to close the test site. At the end of 1991, the test site was closed, and Kazakhstan became an independent nation.

In this paper, we have looked at how three different groups are coming to terms with the past in the post-Soviet period. Nuclear scientists, medical researchers, and local villagers have different interpretations of the Soviet government's culpability during the forty years of nuclear testing. The interpretations of each group are shaped by its lived experiences with nuclear testing. First there are the nuclear scientists, who believe that radiophobia has exaggerated public understandings of the health risks caused by nuclear testing. These scientists argue that the health impacts were minimal, and they defend the state's actions in the name of national security. Next there are the medical researchers such as Saim Balmukhanov, who told government officials that the tests were having harmful effects on human health. The state silenced these medical researchers, and thus they were powerless to stop the tests. Finally, there are the Kazakh and Russian villagers who live near the test site. They now have answers to questions about their experiences and their health, yet their answers do not resemble those of the research scientists. Villagers portray themselves as victims of a state that placed national security interests above the health of its people.

These three different versions of the past coexist in a post-Soviet setting where the government responsible for nuclear testing no longer exists. Further, the Kazakhstani government, which inherited this problem, has limited resources and numerous other social and economic problems to resolve. As in other contexts, debates about the past are used to achieve political goals in the present. For domestic audiences, nuclear scientists provide their interpretation of the past as a way to justify their actions and to minimize their blame. It is interesting to note, however, that their message is not targeted to the victims of nuclear testing. Villagers frequently told us that the Soviet government and the Kurchatov scientists whom they associate with the former Soviet government never offered them any direct or indirect apologies or explanations. Instead, the scientists primarily publish their versions of the past for other scientists, especially international scientists. After the test site closed and the Soviet Union dissolved, these nuclear scientists needed to repackage their talents for new positions. The city of Kurchatov has declined to one-fourth its former size, yet many scientists still work there for the newly constituted National Nuclear Center of Kazakhstan. Although the center is funded by the Kazakhstani government, many of its projects involve international collaboration and international funding. Scientists in Kurchatov often compete for grants from international agencies such as the International Science and Technology Center, founded in 1992 to foster collaboration between "weapons scientists" of the former Soviet Union and Western countries. In this context, the nuclear scientists offer their version of the past to international scientists who are interested in learning as much as they can from the Soviet experience.

Just as the scientists use their knowledge of the past to gain international funding for their research, the villagers use their past experiences to gain domestic and international funding to alleviate their suffering. The villagers have benefited from media coverage. Throughout the 1990s, Kazakhstani newspapers were filled with stories about the victims of nuclear testing and reports from medical researchers (who confirmed that nuclear testing negatively affected villagers' health). The stories have also received some international coverage, including several articles in the *New York Times* and *National Geographic*. Although the stories have been told numerous times, the victims of nuclear testing have yet to receive much in terms of compensation or medical services. After the test site was officially closed, the Nevada-Semipalatinsk Antinuclear Movement attempted to redirect its focus toward compensation for victims. However, the movement lost its momentum in the mid-1990s amid accusations of corruption. In an alleged attempt to do away with his greatest opposition, the president of Kazakhstan offered Olzhas Suleimenov, the charismatic leader of the movement, a post as the ambassador to Italy. Although a handful of smaller nongovernmental organizations are devoted to victims' rights, none have the organization or power that the Nevada-Semipalatinsk Movement once held. Gone are the days when large and effective political protests are organized on behalf of victims. To date, financial compensation has been given to some but not all the defined victims, yet the amounts are very small, as the rates were established just before a significant increase in inflation. Some victims have received disability pensions, although other worthy victims have not, due to bureaucracy. Villagers who work for the state receive "ecological supplements" to their salaries, but many villagers lost state jobs when the government liberalized the economy. International organizations, including the United Nations, have studied the problem and provided some $1.1 million in development assistance, mostly financed by contributions from the government of Japan (United Nations Development Program 2006). A lot of international funding has gone to improve health care facilities, such as the oncological hospital in the city of

Semipalatinsk. Most villages provide some medical care, ranging from a single nurse or feldsher to a limited-care hospital. Some villages have received funding for local health care, while others have witnessed cutbacks. International attention to the victims of nuclear testing in Kazakhstan, however, faltered in the wake of 9/11. In a world filled with social and environmental problems, it seems that the victims of nuclear testing in Kazakhstan may soon be forgotten by the international community of donors.

Notes

1. Kazakhstan has been an independent nation since the dissolution of the Soviet Union in December 1991. From 1921 to 1991, the territory of Kazakhstan was part of the Soviet Union, and for most of that time it was known as the Kazakh Soviet Socialist Republic or the Kazakh Republic.

2. This research was supported by grants from the National Science Foundation (grant number BCS-0214406) and the National Council for Eurasian and East European Research (grant number 818-16). Additional support for preliminary research was provided by the American Association for the Advancement of Science (Women in International Science Collaboration Program), the National Research Council (Young Investigator Program), and Texas A&M University. We would like to thank our Kazakh collaborator, Nurlan Ibraev, who helped with local arrangements and logistics. This work would not have been possible without the support of the many Kazakhs and Russians who answered our questions and provided various kinds of assistance. This paper is based on approximately six months of fieldwork in northern Kazakhstan during the summers of 2000, 2001, 2003, and 2004. The research includes surveys of more than eight hundred villagers, doctors, and research scientists. In-depth and focus-group interviews were also conducted with these three populations, with special focus on villagers living in Kainar and Dolon. This work is dedicated to the victims of nuclear testing in Kazakhstan.

3. In addition to those living near the SNTS and the Novaya Zemlya test site in the Arctic, the Soviet nuclear program impacted the health of those living near plutonium and uranium production facilities, such as Chelyabinsk-65 in the Urals, Krasnoyarsk-26 in Siberia, and Tomsk-7 in Siberia (Donnay et al. 1995; Pierce et al. 1999).

4. Occasionally, the city has been called additional names, such as Town M, Konechnaya, Moscow-400, and Atom City (Balmukhanov 2002; Kuidin 1997; Shkolnik 2002). In this paper, we use the names Semipalatinsk-21 and Kurchatov.

5. We gathered current and historical health data for each of the villages where we conducted surveys and interviews. We attempted to gather comparable data for the city of Kurchatov but were told that this was impossible.

6. The total number of nuclear tests varies slightly from one reference to the next. Some of the variation can be explained by the fact that the number of tests does not equal the number of nuclear physics packages that were detonated (Shkolnik 2002:37). Variation can also be explained by the fact that "unsuccessful" and "nonmilitary" tests are sometimes not included in the figures.

7. It is difficult to acquire statistics on village populations during the testing period. We do know, however, that twenty thousand patients were observed at Dispensary No. 4 (Shkolnik 2002:324).

8. Estimates vary because scientists use different methods to calculate dose, and they do not agree on what constitutes a "significant" dose. Some scientists claim that as many as 1.7 million people have been exposed to radiation in Kazakhstan (Shkolnik 2002:145).

9. In the mid-1990s, the new government of Kazakhstan decreased the number of provinces (or oblasts)

by joining several together. During this time, Semipalatinsk and Ustkamen oblasts were joined together and renamed East-Kazakhstan Oblast; Karaganda and Zhezkazgan oblasts were joined together with the name Karaganda Oblast.

10. In 1992 Dispensary No. 4 was reconstituted as the Institute of Radiation Safety and Ecology. The institute still conducts research on radiation victims, yet the results are no longer classified information.

11. Pseudonyms are used to protect the identity of our interviewees.

References

Balmukhanov, Saim
2000   "Health and Social Impacts of Nuclear Testing in Kazakhstan." Lecture to National Research Council Young Investigator's Program, Kazakh Scientific Research Institute of Oncology and Radiology, Almaty, Kazakhstan, August 23.

Balmukhanov, S., G. Raissova, and T. Balmukhanov
2002   Three Generations of the Semipalatinsk Affected to the Radiation. Almaty, Kazakhstan: Sakshy Publications.

Barker, Holly
2004   Bravo for the Marshallese: Regaining Control in a Post-Nuclear, Post-Colonial World. Belmont, CA: Wadsworth/Thomson Learning.

Bouville, A., L. Anspaugh, M. I. Balonov, K. K. Gordeev, V. I. Kiselev, V. M. Loborev, N. K. Luckyanov, E. Pauli, W. L. Robinson, M. Savkin, V. V. Sudakov, and S. Zelentsov.
2000   Estimation of Doses. *In* Nuclear Test Explosions: Environmental and Human Impacts. Sir Frederick Warner and Rene J. C. Kirchmann, eds. Pp. 115–77. Chichester, UK: John Wiley and Sons.

Degteva, M. O. with M. I. Vorobiova, V. P. Kozheurov, E. I. Tolstykh, L. R. Anspaugh, and B. A. Napier
2000   Dose Reconstruction System for the Exposed Population Living along the Techa River. Health Physics 78(5):542–54.

Donnay, Martin Cherniack, Arjun Makhijani, and Amy Hopkins
1995   Russia and the Territories of the Former Soviet Union. *In* Nuclear Wastelands: A Global Guide to Nuclear Weapons Production and Its Health and Environmental Effects. Arjun Makijani, Howard Hu, and Katherine Yih, eds. Pp. 285–392. Cambridge, MA: MIT Press.

Frohmberg, Eric, Robert Goble, Virginia Sanchez, and Dianne Quigley
2000   The Assessment of Radiation Exposures in Native American Communities from Nuclear Weapons Testing in Nevada. Risk Analysis 20(1):101–11.

Grosche, B. with C. Land, S. Bauer, L. M. Pivina, Z. N. Abylkassimova, and B. I. Gusev
2002   Fallout from Nuclear Tests: Health Effects in Kazakhstan. Radiation and Environmental Biophysics 41:75–80.

Gusterson, Hugh

1996   Nuclear Rites: A Weapons Laboratory at the End of the Cold War. Berkeley: University of California Press.

Hille, R. with P. Hill, P. Bouisset, D. Calmet, J. Kluson, A. Seisebaev, and S. Smagulov

1998   Population Dose near the Semipalatinsk Test Site. Radiation and Environmental Biophysics 37:143–49.

Johnston, Barbara Rose

1994   Experimenting on Human Subjects: Nuclear Weapons Testing and Human Rights Abuses. *In* Who Pays the Price? The Sociocultural Context of Environmental Crises. Barbara Rose Johnston, ed. Pp. 131–41. Washington, DC: Island Press.

Kossenko, M. M. with M. O. Degteva, O. V. Vvushkova, D. L. Preston, K. Mabuchik, and V. P. Kozheurov

1997   Issues in the Comparison of Risk Estimates for the Population in the Techa River Region and Atomic Bomb Survivors. Radiation Research 148(1):54–63.

Kuidin, Yurii

1997   Kazakstan Nuclear Tragedy. Almaty, Kazakhstan: "Phoenix" Anti-Nuclear Ecological Fund.

Nazarbaev, Nursultan

2001   Epicenter of Peace. Antonina W. Bouis, trans. Hollis, NH: Puritan Press.

Pierce, John C., Russell J. Dalton, and Andrei Zaitsev

1999   Public Perceptions of Environmental Conditions. *In* Critical Masses: Nuclear Weapons Production and Environmental Destruction in the United States and Russia. Boston: MIT Press.

Shkolnik, Vladimir S., ed.

2002   The Semipalatinsk Test Site: Creation, Operation, and Conversion. Albuquerque, NM: US Government Printing Office.

United Nations Development Program

2006   Semipalatinsk Area. Electronic document, http://www.undp.kz/script_site. html?id=184, accessed May 25, 2006.

Walsh, Nick Paton

2002   When the Wind Blows. *In* Three Generations of the Semipalatinsk Affected to the Radiation. S. Balmukhanov, G. Raissova, and T. Balmukhanov, eds. Almaty, Kazakhstan: Sakshy Publishers.

Welsome, Eileen

1999   The Plutonium Files: America's Secret Medical Experiments in the Cold War. New York: Dial Press.

thirteen
Nuclear Legacies
Arrogance, Secrecy, Ignorance, Lies, Silence, Suffering, Action

Laura Nader and Hugh Gusterson

Radiation-induced cancer was the first disease to add a new dimension to this problem of cause and effect. This new dimension [lengthy latency period] has been fiercely resisted in many quarters, even ridiculed, in the face of a mountain of evidence that the time period between insult and disease can be measured in decades, not days, weeks, or months. (Gofman 1981:107)

After 15 years of investigating, I have concluded that the US government's atomic weapons industry knowingly and recklessly exposed millions of people to dangerous levels of radiation.... Nothing in our past compares to the official deceit and lying that took place in order to protect the nuclear industry. In the name of national security, politicians and bureaucrats ran roughshod over democracy and morality. Ultimately, the Cold Warriors were willing to sacrifice their own people in their zeal to beat the Russians. (D'Antonio 1993)

—Stewart Udall

The day after the explosion it was clear that northeast winds were spreading radioactive materials over population centers and waterways, so we began evacuating the people from their native villages.... It's amazing that the whole evacuation was completed in a relatively short period and without any resistance from the population...very soon the people adapted to their new conditions and new life. (Gladyshev 1990)

—Mikhail Gladyshev, former director of the Mayak plutonium facility

The making of the first atomic bomb was documented in a film called *The Day after Trinity* (1980). Filmmaker Jon Else pointed out that the making of the bomb necessitated pulling scientists out of normal life, away from their families, away from dissent, away from citizen concerns. Los Alamos was the place—isolated, beautiful, and hard to get to in those times. Life at Los Alamos pretty much revolved around physicist J. Robert Oppenheimer and his nominal boss, General Leslie Groves—the man who built the Pentagon before being put in charge of the Manhattan Project. Oppenheimer provided the vision, the ideas, and the leadership, and Groves provided the wherewithal—more resources than scientists had ever before imagined.[1] There was booze, parties, the piano music of Edward Teller, and long days at work. The purpose was to beat the Nazis to the bomb so that Hitler could not use the bomb to defeat the Allies and destroy Western civilization as they knew it. Before the first test on July 16, 1945, scientists were betting on whether the bomb would work, whether the whole state of New Mexico might be incinerated, and even—in a side bet by Enrico Fermi—whether the earth's atmosphere might ignite. In other words, from the outset of the nuclear age, there was a troubling leap-before-you-look mentality.

The filmmaker also interviewed some of the scientists who had been present about their reactions after Hiroshima. For many, "Thank god it worked" came before the realization of the terrible effect the bomb had had on human lives, although a few Los Alamos scientists—over Oppenheimer's objections—sponsored a discussion of the social and political implications of the bomb toward the end of the Manhattan Project, and a group of scientists under the leadership of James Franck signed a petition urging that the bomb not be used on a live population. The audience sees all too clearly the moral blinkers the scientists wore and their obsession with realizing the potential of the technology before all else. "The Gadget," as it was called, had a life of its own. This attitude was inevitable, because social self-knowledge was optional for the Los Alamos team. But Robert Oppenheimer, the charismatic man who made it work, would say many years later, before he died as a broken, regretful man, that "physicists have known sin." Indeed, the first eruption of the bomb adumbrated the nuclear scenario that followed: arrogance, ignorance, limited vision, secrecy, lack of accountability, and lack of compassion in dealing with the victims of nuclear experimentation.

Nor was this tragic pattern confined to the United States. The behavior of the world's handful of nuclear weapons states, no matter what their avowed political system, has been sufficiently uniform that we should see it as belonging to a single category. The British historian and public intellectual E. P. Thompson (1982, 1985) has referred to this behavior and the form of society that produced it as "exterminism." The American psychologist and public intellectual Robert Jay Lifton (Lifton and Falk 1982; Lifton and Markussen 1990) calls it "nuclearism." Whatever label we choose, it has by now become clear that the development of nuclear weapons reshapes and deforms the societies that embrace these weapons in certain consistently patterned ways. Four stand out.

First, in a form of nuclear colonialism, nuclear weapons states have consistently externalized the health and environmental costs associated with nuclear weapons development either to colonies abroad (for example, Australia for the British, the Pacific Islands for the Americans and French) or to victims of internal colonization (the Shoshone Indians of Nevada in the United States, the Kazakhs of the former Soviet Union, the Uighurs of China). In a process of "radioactive nation-building" (Masco 2006), the lands of indigenous peoples within the boundaries of the nuclear state have become what Valerie Kuletz (1998) calls "national sacrifice zones"; the bodies of the people in these sacrifice zones are expendable. In a little-known subplot of the nuclear age, the Atomic Energy Commission (AEC) and nuclear weapons scientists at the Lawrence Livermore National Laboratory were pushing in the late 1950s and early 1960s to use as many as three hundred nuclear weapons to excavate a new trans-isthmian canal through either Panama or Colombia. They anticipated displacing thirty to forty thousand "natives" who had the misfortune of living too close to the planned canal (Kirsch 2005).

Second, new and formidable practices of secrecy that corrode public dialogue have profoundly deformed public debate and citizens' abilities to hold government accountable. This secrecy emerged, in part, in response to an understandable urge to safeguard the technical secrets underlying nuclear weapons design, but it was also a reflex of governments seeking ways to conceal the terrible costs to the environment, public health, and world peace entailed in nuclear weapons development. Under the guise of safeguarding technical secrets, governments used secrecy laws to punish those seeking to alert their fellow citizens to the dangers of the bomb. Celebrity examples of those who have been thus punished include Robert Oppenheimer (stripped of his security clearance for opposing the hydrogen bomb) in the United States, Andrei Sakharov (sent into internal exile for, among other things, speaking out about the health and environmental consequences of nuclear testing) in the former Soviet Union, and Mordechai Vanunu (kidnapped and put in solitary confinement for several years for telling the international press that his country had a nuclear weapons program) in Israel; but nuclear weapons states are also full of lesser-known citizens who have paid a price for speaking truth to nuclear power—scientists who have lost their jobs, activists who have been watched and harassed, intellectuals whose integrity has been impugned by vulgar nationalists. Moreover, as Richard Falk (1982) has pointed out, nuclear weapons are, by their nature, incompatible with democratic control over the decision to go to war: given that the United States could be utterly destroyed by Russian nuclear weapons with only twenty minutes' warning—not enough time to convene Congress —the power to use (or else lose) nuclear weapons must be delegated to the president. Nuclear weapons are toxic to democracy.

The third defining feature of nuclearism is its reliance on mass practices of "othering." It is very hard to prepare the mass destruction of another society if one recognizes its inhabitants as fellow humans, each with his or her own worth. And it is hard to proclaim the moral unfitness of other societies to possess the weapons of mass destruction one possesses oneself, unless one sees these societies as somehow inferior.

Whether states are actually engaging in the genocide of other peoples (as in the Nazi and Armenian holocausts) or merely rehearsing it (as in all those strangely named Pentagon military exercises), dehumanization of the other is essential to getting the task done. And when citizens of designated enemy societies have been othered and dehumanized in this way, nuclearist societies then also designate as other those within their own societies who threaten the massive binary confrontation with the external other: dissident scientists, intellectuals worried about the morality of preparing for genocide, uranium miners dying an inconvenient death. Especially in moments of national hysteria (the archetype being the McCarthyist period in the United States), such people are liable to be incarcerated, isolated, or socially destroyed.

All this adds up psychologically to the fourth defining feature of nuclearism: mass numbing. Living under the shadow of perpetual mass extinction, living a life of pretended normality in a society that is preparing to exterminate millions of people, practicing routinized indifference to people whose bodies are wrecked by the toxic production and testing of the weapons, and trying not to look too closely at the clumsy and shallow propaganda used to justify the whole endeavor—all this takes a psychic toll. In nuclearist societies, citizenship is often enacted in a context marked by rationalized paranoia in public discourse, nationalist excess, and a dull indifference to the humanity of others.

Because this volume represents insights and contributions by anthropologists, it is worth pausing to contextualize this work within the broader history of American anthropology and its historical complicity with nuclearism and the national security state. Anthropologists, like other scientists, have a mixed and troublesome history with regard to their role in Cold War militarism. Along with other social scientists, anthropologists have been complicit with nuclear weapons testing in some cases and more often have simply let nuclearism proceed unhindered, without demanding a public accounting of its costs.

Anthropology as Intelligence

A number of publications since the 1990s have detailed the role of American anthropologists in World War II and the Cold War that followed (e.g., Foerstel and Gilliam 1992; Nader 1997; Price 1998). The Foerstel and Gilliam volume *Confronting the Margaret Mead Legacy* depicted for one geographic area, the Pacific, the role that anthropologists played in providing intelligence for the national security state by retelling the legacy of one singular and world-renowned American anthropologist. Foerstel and Gilliam singled out Margaret Mead for this telling because she was so well known and well respected, not because others were not also complicit.

Interest in the Pacific did not begin with World War II, since it was during the nineteenth century that most Western colonization took place. The United States annexed Hawaii in 1898, and the Philippines came under US control in 1899. The US Navy administered American Samoa from 1899 to 1951, and of course Great Britain, then Australia, the French, and others had their own datelines for colonization. Mead represented a kind of science that was comfortable in speaking about primitives, about their locations as laboratories—good places for testing scientific hypotheses. Mead, like others of the same era, had an underlying belief in modernization and progress involving assimilation of Native peoples, although she gave this modernist view a pluralist edge with her romantic evocation of child rearing and gender roles in the Pacific. She and other anthropologists represented the Pacific area as lightly populated by peoples who, compared to highly technological societies, were deemed backward or at least exotic. Representation in ethnographic fieldwork is powerful. Framing the Pacific peoples as being outside of history, a "Pacific where hardly anybody lives," made these inhabitants of "our" laboratories vulnerable, their land a vacant backdrop against which to dramatize the power of nuclear weapons.

Although you would never know this from the canonical ethnographies of the region, the Pacific was profoundly shaped by nuclear weapons—from the bombing of Hiroshima and Nagasaki to the testing and deployment of nuclear weapons during the Cold War. In the aftermath of World War II, the United States gained twenty-one hundred Micronesian islands as a kind of war booty, and lots of American anthropologists got their PhDs doing fieldwork on peoples whose lives the United States, by consensus it seemed, would permanently administer. Perhaps the silence from anthropology is to be expected, given the number of anthropologists in the Pacific who worked for the US Navy or were supported by the National Research Council to carry out salvage ethnography. Following Operation Crossroads tests in the Marshall Islands in 1946, the Pacific became the premier site for nuclear testing, and large portions of the Marshall Islands trust territory were transformed into a nuclear waste dump. The United States portrayed its waste importation schemes as development, and other nuclear nations also exported their tests and wastes to the region. Few questioned the destruction of the islands and destruction of the health and well-being of their residents; indeed, few seemed informed. Margaret Mead, who had started to consult for the US national security state during World War II, apparently had little knowledge of the dangers of nuclear radiation in the late 1950s, and although her public statements were against nuclear war, she along with countless others had nothing to say about testing in the Pacific. According to Foerstel and Gilliam (1992:128–29), she believed she had a duty to support the national security interests of the United States.

Meanwhile, Pacific peoples were shifted from island to island in the wake of radiation poisoning and contamination—a sad period in human history that anthropologists did little to protest. Gilliam and Foerstel conclude that Mead's intellectual heritage was an outgrowth of empire. She had a deep belief in progress as a good that would be brought about through Westernization.

In its capacity as the Pacific trust territorial government, the United States closed off Micronesia—3 million square miles of oceanic territory, about the size of the continental United States. The area was militarized, and the people of Bikini became "nuclear nomads," dislocated by testing (Kiste 1974). As trust territory residents, and later as independent citizens whose foreign relations were controlled by the United States through a series of treaties establishing "Compacts of Free Association," Pacific Islanders found themselves in a battle "between the representatives of powerful nations who perceive of the Pacific as a nuclear testing ground and those who are increasingly concerned about the damage to their genetic heritage and environment" (Foerstel and Gilliam 1992:268; see also Barker, this volume). Yet over the past fifty-plus years, relatively few American anthropologists or the American Anthropological Association have voiced opposition to this destruction. Luis Kemnitzer and a few others have condemned this silence (Alcalay 1992:195), but even the indigenous move to denuclearize the Pacific region—the Nuclear Free Pacific movement of the 1970s and the Nuclear Free and Independent movement of the 1980s—found little public anthropological support. Today the Marshallese have one of the highest suicide rates in the world and a deteriorated economy. They suffer the long-term consequences of sixty-seven nuclear blasts, and they experience continued contamination from the US Pacific Missile Range Facility at Kwajalein Atoll and related service as the impact site for intercontinental ballistic missiles.[2]

In little bits and pieces, the consequences of nuclearism came to light—first in Japan, then in the Pacific, the United States, the Arctic, Peru, and Amazonia—in places where anthropologists normally do their work. And slowly a few determined anthropologists studied the uses being made of research, the uses of human subjects, and the nuclear weapons scientists themselves. Interestingly, examination of nuclear institutions came even before victims claimed our attention. Probably the earliest anthropologist-activist was physical anthropologist Earle Reynolds (see Price, this volume), who tried to disrupt nuclear testing in the Pacific and even sailed into Vladivostok in protest over Soviet nuclear testing. Years later, Mead's kind of anthropology was in part thrown into crisis by the Vietnam War, a turning point that forced an examination of US colonialism and empire, as well as an examination of the notion of manifest destiny, which had justified the extension of the United States from the Atlantic to Southeast Asia. Anthropologists recently writing on the subject of militarism and nuclear consequence are a relatively small group. For example, Hugh Gusterson (1996, 2004), Joe Masco (2004, 2006), and Laura McNamara (2001) have written about weapons scientists and their neighboring communities; Robert Kiste (1974), Lenora Foerstel and Angela Gilliam (1992), Glen Alcalay (1992), Barbara Rose Johnston (1994), and Holly Barker (1997, 2004) have written on the Pacific; and Angela Gilliam (1988) and Cathy Lutz (2001) have written on the social dynamics of US militarism. And in recent years anthropologists have also been able to study and publish work on the human effects of nuclear militarism in the former Soviet Union (see, e.g., Garb 1997; Petryna 2002) and French Polynesia (Kahn 2000).

One could, incidentally, tell a broadly similar story about historians' writing on the nuclear age. It was only in the 1960s, during the upheaval of the Vietnam War, that revisionist historians emerged to question the official story and ask whether Americans should really have a clean conscience about the atom bombs. In 1965, in his book *Atomic Diplomacy*, Gar Alperovitz argued that the United States used the atomic bomb against Japan as much to intimidate the Soviets in the emerging Cold War struggle as because the bomb was necessary to defeat Japan. Further scholarship revealed that the US government had cracked the Japanese code and knew that Japanese leadership was debating surrender and trying to enlist the Soviets as intermediaries in approaching the United States, and that the United States ruthlessly censored discussion of the health and environmental consequences of the bombings in Japan in the years after 1945 (Bernstein 1986; Dower 1995; Lifton and Mitchell 1995; Sherwin 1973; Walker 1990). The evolution in the thinking of professional historians about US nuclear weapons, from passive inhalation of the official point of view to a more muscular interrogation of received wisdom, broadly mirrors the evolution of thinking in anthropology.

From Complicity to Accountability

In this volume, the contributors reexamine the connections between national security states' nuclear policies and the vulnerable peoples on whom nuclear technology was tested—both in the United States and in the former Soviet Union. Although all nuclear states tested on ethnic peoples or minorities of one sort or another—the United States on the mainland, in the Arctic, and in the Pacific; the Soviets in Siberia and Central Asia; the Chinese on the Uighurs; the French in the Sahara and the Pacific; the British on Australian Aborigines—the focus in this volume is on peoples and places victimized by Soviet and US nuclearism.

The papers in this volume are not speaking about the past; the issues are enduring, and the past is the present. The places where nuclear experiments have taken place are still contaminated, and people are still sick and dying. To have their complaints recognized, victims of nuclear testing have to prove that their health problems did not occur prior to nuclear testing. There was no informed consent; for four decades, the Marshallese, to cite one of the worst examples, were human subjects in a nuclear medical science program that was about body parts—thyroids, eyes, bone marrow, blood, and urine—not whole human beings, without knowing they were experimental subjects. Around Hanford in Washington State (Liebow, this volume), some observed health effects defied adequate causal attribution; so despite very well-funded research to prove or disprove such connections, there was no national health insurance to take care of those in need. Besides, the research industry concluded that "no data are available to suggest adverse impacts to the region's Indian [or white] people."

Yet again, science is saturated with politics. The story told about Earle Reynolds (Price, this volume), who studied survivors and offspring of Hiroshima—people he saw as his equals—is unusual because he saw through science politics. The unspoken goal of his funders was to use the bodies of Hiroshimans to calculate casualties in a future nuclear war. His dissent—like that of a courageous group of ecologists at the University of Alaska who spoke out against Edward Teller's plans to excavate a harbor in Alaska with hydrogen bombs—led to his prompt marginalization in the academy (Kirsch 2005; O'Neill 1994). How free are scientists to dissent? The politicization of science is an issue very much with us today as homeland security programs invade national laboratories and universities with special funding and as government scientists who seek to alert the public to the dangers of global warming find themselves muzzled by the White House.

Human radiation experiments in the 1940s were performed on required human subjects—found in the Marshall Islands, the Arctic, the Andes, the Amazon, and among civilian "volunteers" (soldiers, inmates, students, and minorities). As outlined in Johnston's chapter on human radiation experimentation (this volume), the United States wanted to model the damage that radiation caused; to identify "natural background" radiation, believing that a minimal threshold existed and that amounts below that threshold were not harmful or even beneficial; and to assess the genetic effects of atomic weapons in ways that would alleviate public and scientific fears (and limit potential economic liability) concerning the mutagenic effect of radiation. Meanwhile, in Nye County, Nevada, downwind rural communities—Mormons who supported government nuclear testing—began noticing that their cattle, sheep, children, and wildlife were ill or dying. The AEC knowingly disregarded and covered up evidence correlating the death of sheep to radiation exposure.

As the research in this volume shows, the cover-up continues, and victims and their families have had to work hard to get accurate information about what was done to them and even harder to get any kind of remedy. The difficulty experienced by downwinders and atomic veterans in getting compensation has been compounded by the fact that the US government, claiming a prerogative originally exercised by European monarchs before the United States was founded, claimed "sovereign immunity" from lawsuits by citizens alleging harm from their government. Finally, in 1990 the US Congress enacted the Radiation Exposure Compensation Act (RECA). Throughout the testing and the campaign for compensation, rural downwind communities divided over the question of jobs versus radiation. In Nevada, the preponderance of the population has always supported nuclear testing, although they—along with almost every elected official in Nevada—oppose the federal government's plan for a high-level nuclear-waste storage facility at Yucca Mountain (Macfarlane and Ewing 2006).

The two papers on nuclear testing and contamination in the Soviet Union, one on Chelyabinsk and the other on Kazakhstan (Garb, this volume; Werner and Purvis-Roberts, this volume), indicate that environmental disasters occurred around weapons-grade plutonium facilities. Again there was secrecy: officials denied the truth, and scientists dealt with a technology they did not fully understand. They did not yet know that plutonium would not dissolve in water, thereby losing its lethal power. Although Russians were evacuated after the 1957 Kyshtym explosion, minority Tatars were left behind as human subjects in a grotesque experiment. In Chelyabinsk, twenty-two villages along the river were evacuated, and evacuees had to sign papers swearing themselves to secrecy. The Soviet state, in a prequel to the Chernobyl disaster thirty years later (Petryna 2002), showed a general disregard for the health of all peoples, including plant employees. Not until 1989 did the Soviets acknowledge the Mayak disasters. Yet a government official was quoted as saying, "We've been doing this [producing material for nuclear weapons] for 30 years with no negative effect on the environment." (The same optimism is of course recorded for various AEC directors in the United States.) In Kazakhstan, people were exposed to harm from some 456 nuclear tests between 1949 and 1989. Apparently the Soviet military did not know how fallout would affect this area of nomadic pastoralists and low population density. The same pattern of testing nuclear weapons near or on the land of vulnerable minority populations and exposing them to contamination now seems to be repeating itself in India and Pakistan (Ramana and Reddy 2003).

Several chapters in this volume deal with the abuse of government trust responsibilities. In the Pacific, after all, the territories were under US control under a United Nations trusteeship before the movement for independence was initiated. On the mainland, the public health damages to Navajo uranium miners abused the trust relationship that exists between Indian reservations and the federal government. Damages for the workers and the community have come too little and too late. For the Navajo the land is sacred, life giving, and sustaining (Hiesinger 2002:40); for the nuclear industry it is a wasteland (Kuletz 1998:197). Places the Navajo use for medicine and sacred ritual the nuclear industry classifies as desert wastelands. It is hard to call this behavior by the superpowers anything other than environmental racism. It is revealing that in both the United States and the Soviet Union, one a democracy and the other a totalitarian regime, as Stewart Udall observed, "the Cold Warriors were willing to sacrifice their own people in their zeal." Ironically, the United States and the Soviet Union may have hurt their own citizens and environments more than each other's.

With a few noteworthy exceptions, nuclear scientists distanced themselves from the suffering that resulted from their endeavors. They were socially and physically distant from the uranium miners, nuclear production-line workers, and villagers whose health has been most damaged by nuclear weapons testing and production, and they often dismissed the concerns of ordinary people as nothing more than ignorant "radiophobia." Of course, from the vantage point of current knowledge, it is clear that the scientists and government bureaucrats suffered from a Panglossian radiophilia. Only in recent years have victims begun to receive compensation from the state for the harms they suffered at the hands of the nuclear state, and the compensation, as we shall see below, is often patchy, capricious, and inadequate. Meanwhile, weapons scientists today often exculpate their forebears by resorting to a progress narrative that excuses the sins of the fathers as the result of an ignorance now allegedly erased by scientific progress.

Whose Survival?

Three concepts (Nader 1983) are useful in understanding the environment surrounding the development and testing of weapons of mass destruction: bureaucratic fantasy,[3] organizational survival, and short-term self-interest. In his 1999 book *Mission Improbable: Using Fantasy Documents to Tame Disaster*, sociologist Lee Clarke shows that bureaucracies confronted with potential human disasters often engage in the preparation of hyper-rational "fantasy documents" that may strike others as surreal exercises in bureaucratic denial. Examples include plans developed by the US Post Office under the Reagan administration to make sure people filled out change-of-address cards so their mail could be forwarded after their cities were destroyed in a nuclear war. The Federal Emergency Management Administration developed plans at the same time to evacuate cities under threat of nuclear attack by having all those with license plates ending in odd numbers leave a day before the rest. Institutional bureaucracies are particularly prone to this kind of institutionalized insanity, which has not been adequately recognized as a social problem.

The concept of organizational survival means that no matter what the explicit goals of an organization are, its most central, albeit usually implicit, goal is its own survival. Although both bureaucratic fantasy and organizational survival are ubiquitous, they are of particular importance in the arms race. If institutionalized fantasy thinking operates among military and defense people, behavior in their circles that outsiders might think crazy (such as the idea that someone can win a nuclear war if there are enough shovels) goes undetected and unseated. This situation can persist long enough to ensure that many organizations invest so much in policies arising from this insanity that organizational survival begins to take precedence over national or even personal survival. Ideologies and rationales are developed within groups to defend their plan of action. These defenses are reinforced by actual or perceived outside criticism and become so strong that the insanity is further strengthened even though ideological obsessions among bureaucrats may be more the result of perceived powerlessness than the political persuasion of the government.

The third concept—self-interest—has to do with the defense industry as both self-interested and profit motivated. Although President Dwight D. Eisenhower warned of the perils of the military-industrial complex, it was during the Eisenhower years that the theory developed among liberal politicians, economists, and business that high military spending would stimulate the economy. The economist Seymour Melman first dispelled such theories in his book *Our Depleted Society* (1965), in which he argued that the dominance of a permanent war economy in the United States had led to serious underinvestment in science, engineering, and technology for civilian ends. Nevertheless, the dominant theory was put into practice during the Kennedy administration through an enormous increase in military spending and the training of science and engineering graduates for careers in the armaments industry. Due to government sponsorship, defense industries profit from the benefits of long-term contracts, interest-free loans, payment by government for most plant and capital equipment, and government willingness to pay prices subjected to continuous upward renegotiation. These industries are among the biggest, most powerful, and most technologically advanced units of economic power in the country, and US national security policy is directed by elite groups largely recruited from business. *Why We Fight*, a recent documentary about US military involvements since Eisenhower's famous farewell address, shows that the military-industrial complex has seemingly become normalized, an accepted phenomenon in which lessons not learned predominate. As government contractors spread government wealth among the fifty states, turning the military budget into a surrogate welfare and development budget, it becomes increasingly difficult to cancel military programs. In his book *Wild Blue Yonder* (1988), Nick Kotz tells the story of the Carter administration's failed attempt to cancel the B-1 bomber in the face of an alliance of contractors who had ensured that every state in the Union had been given some piece of the B-1 to build. With so many converging interests, it becomes ever more difficult to arouse indignation against the toxic effects of military programs, even though in many of these same states radiation sicknesses and general environmental contamination—what some call atomic harvest—are there for all to know. There are enormous mental gaps between industrial and business policies and those who suffer the consequences—what economists call externalities.

The Power of Voices

Silence can be addressed only by speaking out. Whether one calls for remedy, redress, reparations, damages, or compensation, it is clear from the outset that no amount of damages or compensation alone can cure nuclear wrongs. From 1951 to 1992, the United States carried out 100 atmospheric and 828 underground nuclear tests at the Nevada Test Site alone, without enough knowledge to evaluate the dangers the tests posed. In an era when dissent was discouraged and the Cold War provided an atmosphere of military emergency, it was easy to ignore harms to human bodies that would be masked by a twenty-year latency period. As the authors in this volume have indicated, there could be long periods between research results and allowed publication: the 1961 Weiss study and the 1963 Knapp study on radioactive iodine in the food chain were not released until 1978. After the Cold War ended, thanks to Secretary of Energy Hazel O'Leary's aggressive declassification policy more materials on testing consequences came to light. In view of what we know today, it is remarkable that there is so little public opposition to the Bush administration's current plans to build a new facility for the production of plutonium pits in nuclear weapons and, possibly, design a new generation of nuclear warheads.

It has often been said that the only thing we learn from history is that we do not learn from history. The principles of organizational survival, profit making, and bureaucratic fantasy contribute to the failure. However, in 2006 people do know what they did not know in the first years of nuclearism, and they are pushing for redress. From the mid-1970s to the 1980s, people began to sue the government. One of the most publicized cases was the work of Stewart Udall on behalf of the uranium miners (see Udall 1994). The Mormon ranchers downwind of the Nevada Test Site were active in pursuit of legal redress, and grassroots support groups from Hanford to the Southwest to the Arctic were critical in testifying before congressional committees, developing registries of victims, and more (see Turner, this volume). Finally, all due to activists, attorneys, legislators, scientists, and radiation victims, RECA was signed into law in 1990. In 2000 RECA amendments were signed into law. As Dawson and Madsen note in chapter 6, the compensation is rather minimal—from $50,000 to $100,000 in most cases. This is less than the annual salary of an average Washington lobbyist and much less than victims of comparable damage would earn from a medical malpractice suit. In the Arctic, award settlements of $7 million included $67,000 to each study participant and another $1.36 million for community damages.

These limited awards are a drop in the bucket given what is still needed, not only to compensate the sick and the families of people who have died but also to clean up former testing and nuclear weapons facilities. And the decisions are difficult to make. At Rocky Flats in Colorado (see Satterfield and Levin, this volume), there was a crisis in confidence in public policy when citizens participated in hearings. They were being asked to sacrifice human health for dollars, and tradeoffs in cleaning up the contamination were not what people wanted. In spite of facilitators at these public meetings, there to ensure free and open debate, citizens lost faith in militarized science. In the Marshall Islands, judgments from the Nuclear Claims Tribunal have little meaning when the US Congress fails to provide the monies to pay awards. To date, no judicial mechanism appears to exist to address abuses and compensate for human radiation experiments in Peru and the Amazon. And what about fallout victims in the US states of Idaho, Colorado, and Wyoming? Still pending.

In addition to monetary remedy, victims seek accountability. They seek apology from their government. They seek "never-again" policies. They seek transparency. They do not need facilitators to cool out public participation and prepare them for "reasonable" negotiations; they need a chance to voice their righteous anger and be heard by their governments.

Does Democracy Matter?

There is democratic form and democratic practice. When people in a democratic society cede too much power to the government, what happens is the sort of activity recorded in this volume: the government becomes authoritarian and unaccountable. When victims demand accountability, as in some cases also recorded here, practice may begin to conform to democratic form. In the stories told in this volume, institutionalized racism compounds the erosion of democracy. The people carrying out nuclear tests and weapons development saw some places as basically "empty," since the few who lived there were for the most part indigenous peoples or other minorities. Meanwhile, for all Americans, the denial, the censoring, and the suffering were apparently justified by the needs of the national security state and the military-industrial complex. Propaganda becomes intermixed with scientific research: "Fallout is safe," "Exposure is external," "We can win a nuclear war." And in the final act of cowardice, the victim assumes the burden of proof.

In the Soviet Union the picture is not much different. The level of secrecy in the Soviet Union was intense, with entire cities off-limits (and off maps) to the general Russian population and an even greater constriction of scientific freedom than in Cold War America. Not until Gorbachev's glasnost policy emerged in the late 1980s were people free to organize political movements that eventually, in the case of Kazakhstan, led to the closure of the Semipalatinsk test site in 1991. For a transitory moment in the mid-1990s, environmental activists around Chelyabinsk, Krasnoyarsk, and Tomsk publicly pressed for greater disclosure and accountability from the traditionally secretive Russian nuclear weapons complex. In the late 1980s, the renowned Kazakhstani poet Olzhas Suleimenov appeared on television to read his poetry, only to throw away his script and appeal to the Kazakhstani people to attend an impromptu meeting to protest continued nuclear testing in Kazakhstan—a meeting attended by thousands of Kazakhstani citizens gingerly learning the practice of democracy. The Kazakhstani protestors reached out to Americans protesting continued US nuclear testing and formed the Nevada-Semipalatinsk Movement. They realized that the nuclear arms race had inextricably linked the fates of Soviets and Americans in a maze of mirrored positions, and that they would prosper or perish together. They imagined not a community of nation-states locked in conflict but a community of the afflicted whose solidarity undermines the military business as usual of generals, politicians, and military contractors. Although scientists defended their positions in the name of national security, political activists struggled to secure medical care and compensation, making their case to the government as well as to international NGOs and other international organizations. Health and mortality statistics are still difficult to obtain and will become more so as the Russian military-industrial complex tries to make a comeback.

When the Soviet Union collapsed, the government became less authoritarian; there were more public discussions about the harmful effects of nuclear testing, culminating in 1991 when Kazakhstan became an independent nation. More recently, scientists are defending their version of the past, and the victims of nuclear testing still await apologies and compensation commensurate with their difficulties. Much the same is reported for Chelyabinsk and the 1957 Kyshtym explosion, known about by Western powers but not made public either here or there, making Western powers complicit with the Soviets, perhaps because similar (if less severe) incidents were occurring in the United States and Britain. Secrecy was beneficial to all parties.

The Soviet practice of controlling health statistics was similar to that in the United States, and the compensation offered to victims is even less adequate in Russia and the former Soviet republics. The Chernobyl law, which allows government allocations to those affected by the Chernobyl accident, was supposed to apply also to the Chelyabinsk region. Some Russian scientists attributed the health problems there to radiophobia, and nothing was done. We are told that doctors who spoke openly about health problems in the 1990s are no longer talking. The environmental activism that began under Gorbachev is now threatened, ever since Russian president Vladimir Putin spoke out in 2003 against overseas funding of political activities in Russia and passed laws to restrict it. Meanwhile the victims wait and suffer—here and there.

Perhaps the most ubiquitous inequity in democratic societies has been the inability of people to participate in decisions about that ultimate equity instance—the likelihood of survival. And people in the United States are in no better position in terms of decision making than people in nondemocratic states. One of the dangers of the contemporary world is that the general public is not fully aware of the risks and uncertainties it faces from the activities of the national security state. And as Bronislaw Malinowski put it for the Trobrianders of the western Pacific, people practice more magic when they find themselves afloat in "unknown and dangerous waters." For this reason, we might conclude that scientists—military scientists—are less competent than is generally believed to be charged with the responsibilities for policies in "unknown and dangerous waters" that lead to the ultimate equity instance—human survival.

Notes

1. On Oppenheimer and Groves, see Bird and Sherwin (2005); McMillan (2005); Norris (2002); Rhodes (1986).

2. The tests are listed at http://nuclearweaponarchive.org/Usa/Tests/index.html.

3. Laura Nader (1983) referred to this behavior as the result of institutionalized insanity.

References

Alcalay, Glen
1992   The Ethnography of Destabilization: Pacific Islanders in the Nuclear Age. Dialectical Anthropology 13:243–51.

Alperovitz, Gar
1965   Atomic Diplomacy: Hiroshima and Potsdam. The Use of the Atomic Bomb and the American Confrontation with Soviet Power. New York: Simon and Schuster.

Barker, Holly
1997   Fighting Back: Justice in the Marshall Islands and Neglected Radiation Communities. *In* Life and Death Matters: Human Rights and the Environment at the End of the Millennium. Barbara Rose Johnston, ed. Pp. 290–306. Walnut Creek, CA: AltaMira.
2004   Bravo for the Marshallese: Regaining Control in a Post-Nuclear, Post-Colonial World. Belmont, CA: Wadsworth/Thomson Learning.

Bernstein, Bart
1986   A Post-War Myth: 500,000 Lives Saved. Bulletin of the Atomic Scientists 42(6):38–40.

Bird, Kai, and Martin Sherwin
2005   American Prometheus: The Triumph and Tragedy of J. Robert Oppenheimer. New York: Knopf.

Clarke, Lee
1999   Mission Improbable: Using Fantasy Documents to Tame Disaster. Chicago: University of Chicago Press.

D'Antonio, Michael
1993   Atomic Harvest: Hanford and the Lethal Toll of America's Nuclear Arsenal. New York: Crown Publishers.

Dower, John
1995   The Bombed: Hiroshimas and Nagasakis in Japanese Memory. Diplomatic History 19(2):275–95.

Else, Jon
1980   The Day after Trinity. San Jose, CA: KTEH Television.

Falk, Richard
1982   Nuclear Weapons and the End of Democracy. Praxis International 2(1):1–22.

Foerstel, Lenora, and Angela Gilliam, eds.
1992   Confronting the Margaret Mead Legacy: Scholarship, Empire, and the South Pacific. Philadelphia: Temple University Press.

Garb, Paula
1997   Complex Problems and No Clear Solutions: Radiation Victimization in Russia. *In* Life and Death Matters: Human Rights and the Environment at the End of the Millennium. Barbara Rose Johnston, ed. Pp. 307–29. Walnut Creek, CA: AltaMira.

Gilliam, Angela
1988   Anthropology, Geopolitics, and Papua New Guinea. Central Issues in Anthropology 8(1)37–51.

Gladyshev, Mikhail
1990   Unpublished memoirs, recorded by Pyotr Tryakin.

Gofman, John W.
1981   Radiation and Human Health: A Comprehensive Investigation of the Evidence Relating Low-Level Radiation to Cancer and Other Diseases. San Francisco: Sierra Club Books.

Gusterson, Hugh
1996   Nuclear Rites: A Weapons Laboratory at the End of the Cold War. Berkeley: University of California Press.
2004   People of the Bomb: Portraits of America's Nuclear Complex. Minneapolis: University of Minnesota Press.

Hiesinger, Margaret A.

2002   The House That Uranium Built: Perspectives on the Effects of Exposure on
Individuals and Community. Kroeber Anthropological Society Papers 87:7–53.

Johnston, Barbara Rose

1994   Experimenting on Human Subjects: Nuclear Weapons Testing and Human Rights
Abuses. *In* Who Pays the Price? The Sociocultural Context of Environmental Crises.
Barbara Rose Johnston, ed. Pp. 131–41. Washington, DC: Island Press.

Kahn, Miriam

2000   Tahiti Intertwined: Ancestral Land, Tourist Postcard, and Nuclear Test Site.
American Anthropologist 102(1):7–26.

Kirsch, Scott

2005   Proving Grounds: Project Plowshare and the Unrealized Dream of Nuclear
Earthmoving. New Brunswick, NJ: Rutgers University Press.

Kiste, Robert

1974   The Bikinians: A Study in Forced Migration. Menlo Park, CA: Cummings
Publishing Company.

Kotz, Nick

1988   Wild Blue Yonder: Money, Politics and the B-1 Bomber. Princeton, NJ: Princeton
University Press.

Kuletz, Valerie

1998   The Tainted Desert: Environmental and Social Ruin in the American West. New
York: Routledge.

Lifton, Robert Jay, and Richard Falk

1982   Indefensible Weapons: The Psychological and Political Case against Nuclearism.
New York: Basic Books.

Lifton, Robert Jay, and Eric Markussen

1990   The Genocidal Mentality: Nazi Holocaust and Nuclear Threat. New York: Basic
Books.

Lifton, Robert Jay, and Greg Mitchell

1995   Hiroshima in America: A Half Century of Denial. Collingdale, PA: Diane
Publishing Company.

Lutz, Catherine

2001   Homefront: A Military City and the American Twentieth Century. Boston: Beacon
Press.

Macfarlane, Allison, and Rodney Ewing

2006   Uncertainty Underground: Yucca Mountain and the Nation's High-Level Nuclear
Waste. Cambridge, MA: MIT Press.

Masco, Joseph

2004   Nuclear Technoaesthetics: Sensory Politics from Trinity to the Virtual Bomb at Los

Alamos. American Ethnologist 31(3):1–25.

2006   The Nuclear Borderlands: The Manhattan Project in Post–Cold War New Mexico. Princeton, NJ: Princeton University Press.

McMillan, Priscilla
2005   The Ruin of J. Robert Oppenheimer: And the Birth of the Modern Arms Race. New York: Viking.

McNamara, Laura
2001   Ways of Knowing: The Cold War's End at the Los Alamos National Laboratory. PhD dissertation, Anthropology Department, University of New Mexico.

Melman, Seymour
1965   Our Depleted Society. New York: Holt, Rinehart and Winston.

Nader, Laura
1983   Two Plus Two Equals Zero—War and Peace Reconsidered. Radcliffe Quarterly, March: 7–8.
1997   The Phantom Factor: Impact of the Cold War on Anthropology. *In* The Cold War and the University. Noam Chomsky, Ira Katznelson, R. C. Lewontin, David Montgomery, Laura Nader, Richarod Ohmann, Ray Siever, Immanuel Wallerstein, and Howard Zinn, eds. Pp. 107–46. New York: New Press.

Norris, Robert S.
2002   Racing for the Bomb: General Leslie R. Groves, the Manhattan Project's Indispensable Man. South Royalton, VT: Steerforth Press.

O'Neill, Dan
1994   The Firecracker Boys. New York: St. Martin's.

Petryna, Adriana
2002   Life Exposed: Biological Citizens after Cherobyl. Princeton, NJ: Princeton University Press.

Price, David H.
1998   Cold War Anthropology: Collaborators and Victims of the National Security State. Identities 4(3–4):389–430.

Ramana, M. V., and C. Rammanohar Reddy, eds.
2003   Prisoners of the Nuclear Dream. New Delhi: Orient Longman.

Rhodes, Richard
1986   The Making of the Atomic Bomb. New York: Simon and Schuster.

Sherwin, Martin
1973   A World Destroyed: The Atomic Bomb and the Grand Alliance. New York: Vintage.

Thompson, E. P.
1982   Beyond the Cold War: A New Approach to the Arms Race and Nuclear Annihilation. New York: Pantheon Books.

1985   The Heavy Dancers: Writings on War, Past and Future. New York: Pantheon.

Udall, Stewart L.
1994   The Myths of August: A Personal Exploration of Our Tragic Cold War Affair with the Atom. New York: Pantheon Books.

Walker, J. S.
1990   The Decision to Use the Bomb. Diplomatic History 14:97–114.

Index

Athabascan Indians, 34
Atom Bomb Museum (Hiroshima), 62
Atomic Bomb Casualty Commission (ABCC), 27–29, 55, 57–58, 62–63, 71
Atomic Diplomacy (Alperovitz 1965), 305
Atomic Energy Commission (AEC): and access to documents, 29; and early biomedical research on radiation exposure, 32; and federally supported genetic research in 1950s and 1960s, 28; and funding of research supporting preconceived conclusions, 8–9; and health assessment of downwind effects from Nevada Test Site, 193, 195, 198; and non-military uses of nuclear devices, 301; and nuclear testing in Marshall Islands, 59; and promotion of nuclear testing, 124–25; and radiation experiments with indigenous peoples, 25–27, 37–38, 39; and reparations for uranium miners and downwinders, 127, 127–28; and uranium mining, 98–99, 122. *See also* Department of Energy; Nuclear Regulatory Commission
Baker atomic bomb test, 30, 214, 219
Bale, William, 120
Ball, Howard, 132–33
Balmukhanov, Saim, 288–90, 294
Barker, Holly, 17, 288, 304
Baron, Jonathan, 177
Bashkirs (Russia), 252–53, 254–55, 258, 259, 269
Battelle Pacific Northwest National Laboratory, 150–51
Beatty, J., 28
Bell, David M., 131
Berger, Thomas, 83
Bikini Atoll (Marshall Islands), 30–31, 39, 41, 59–64, 67, 214, 216, 219, 228, 234, 303
Biological Effects of Ionizing Radiation (BEIR), 9, 228–30
biomedical research: atomic agenda and indigenous population of Marshall Islands, 38–44, 220–24; early atomic detonations and radiation exposure of humans, 29–33; and nuclear testing in Soviet Republic of Kazakhstan, 288–90. *See also* health; human-subjects research
birth defects, and radiation exposure, 10, 158–59, 199–200
"blame-affixing adversarial model," of risk research, 160–61
Board on Radiation Effects Research, 9–10
Bolivia, and high-altitude research with indigenous peoples, 36
Boutros-Ghali, Boutros, 85–86
Boutté, Marie, 16–17, 158
Boxcar nuclear test, 197
Boztayev, Keshirim, 282
Bravo nuclear test, 40, 214, 217, 220, 222, 230, 231, 240
Brookhaven National Laboratory, 41, 42, 243n6, 243n8
Brown, Phil, 129

Brugge, Doug, 133
Bulletin of the Atomic Scientists, 165
Bulloch v. United States, 131
bunker-buster bomb, 118
Bureau of Indian Affairs, 100
Bureau of Mines, 121
Bush administration: and access to documents, 46n2; and government relations with Native tribes, 159; and nuclear weapons policy, 11, 117–18, 309
Bushnell, Dan, 131

Caldicott, Helen, 216
Caliente (Nevada), 203–208
Canada, and uranium production, 98
cancer: and Chelyabinsk nuclear accidents, 258, 260, 270; death rate from in US, 94n11; and downwind effects from nuclear testing, 200–201, 202; and nuclear dumping in Arctic, 80, 81, 83, 89, 90; and Radiation Exposure Compensation Act, 202; and uranium mining, 101, 103, 104, 119–20, 122–23. *See also* health
Carter administration: and controversy on military spending, 309; and Nuclear Nonproliferation Act, 148
case-control studies, 127, 153
Castle series of nuclear tests, 230. *See also* Bravo nuclear test
Caufield, Catherine, 99, 103
censorship and suppression: and access to documents, 29, 46n2; and nuclear testing in Soviet Republic of Kazakhstan, 289; of reports by Earle Reynolds, 62– 63; of reports on livestock deaths from radiation released by nuclear tests, 198; of scientific studies on health of uranium miners and downwinders, 127. *See also* Freedom of Information Act; information
Centers for Disease Control and Prevention (CDC), 151, 152, 155, 157, 158, 202
Central Intelligence Agency (CIA), 59, 67
cesium-137, 6, 250, 251
Charley, Perry H., 135
Chelyabinsk nuclear accidents (Soviet Union), 249–73
chemical weapons, and reconceptualization of atomic bomb, 31
Chernobyl accident (Soviet Union 1986), 161n1, 249–50, 256, 261, 262, 271, 311
children: and differential health risks from radiation exposure, 10, 229–30; and research on radiation exposure in Soviet Republic of Kazakhstan, 287, 288. *See also* birth defects
China: and nuclear weapons testing, 4; and political activism of Earle Reynolds, 68–69
chromium (Cr-51) tagging, 42
Church rock disaster (1979), 104–105
Citizen's Advisory Board (CAB), on Rocky Flats site, 168, *169t*, 171, 172, 178, 179–80, 181, 182–83, 189n5
Clark County Board of Commissioners (Nevada), 209

Murata, Takeo, 67
Murkowski, Frank, 34, 88–89
Muslims, and lifestyle adaptation in regions of Chelyabinsk nuclear accidents, 259
Muslyumovo village (Siberia), 253, 256–57, 266, 271

Nader, Laura, 18, 71, 72, 312n3
Nagasaki atomic bomb, 3, 29, 147, 214, 219, 243n2. *See also* Hiroshima
narrative, and anthropological methodology, 78
Nation, The (magazine), 63
National Academy of Sciences, 9–10, 44–45, 134, 148, 228–30
National Association of Atomic Veterans, 243n5
National Cancer Institute (NCI), 120, 125, 201, 215, 231–32
National Geographic (magazine), 295
National Institute of Environmental Health Sciences, 109, 123
National Nuclear Center (Kazakhstan), 285, 288, 295
National Research Council (NRC), 34–35, 46n4
national security: and nuclear weapons policy, 117–18; and release of government documents, 219. *See also* Homeland Security Agency
National Security Archives, 29, 46n2
Native Americans: and exposure to radiation from Nevada Test Site, 284; and location of uranium sources in Southwest, 99. *See also* American Indians; indigenous peoples; Mescalero Apache; Navajo; Pueblo Indians
Navajo: and health effects of uranium mining and processing, 97–111, 118–19, 307; and Radiation Exposure Compensation Act, 135
Navajo Environmental Protection Agency, 110
Navajo Office of Uranium Workers, 109
Navajo Tribal Council, 100, 110–11
Naval Arctic Research Laboratory, 34.
Navy, US, and nuclear tests in Marshall Islands, 30, 214, 219, 304. *See also* military
Nazarbaev, Nursultan, 282, 294
Neel, James V., 27–28, 37–38, 39, 46n5, 57–58
Nehemias, John V., 63
Nelkin, Dorothy, 185
Nevada. *See* Nevada Test Site; Yucca Mountain nuclear waste dump site
Nevada Protection Fund, 209
Nevada-Semipalatinsk Antinuclear Movement, 282–83, 290, 293, 294, 295, 311
Nevada Test Site: and current nuclear policy, 118; downwinders and Radiation Exposure Compensation Act, 123–26, 236, 240–41; health assessment of downwind effects of radiation exposure from, 193–210, *237m*; and military personnel, 283–84
Nevada Test Site Workers Victims' Association, 130
New Mexico, and workers' compensation for uranium miners, 131
Newsday (magazine), 71–72
New York Times, 295

Nez Percé (Idaho), 150, 161n4, 161n6
North Korea, and nuclear weapons testing, 4, 117
North Vietnam, and political activism of Earle Reynolds, 67–68
Northwest Area Portland (Oregon) Indian Health Board, 154
Note, Kessai, 239
Novaya Zemlya test site (Soviet Union), 33, 296n3
Nuclear Claims Tribunal (Marshall Islands), 26, 29, 43–44, 46n2, 227–28, 233, 236, 241, 242, 244n9, 310
Nuclear Claims Trust Fund (Marshall Islands), 235, 239
Nuclear Free Pacific movement, 304
Nuclear Nonproliferation Act (1978), 148
Nuclear Regulatory Commission (NRC), 108, 117, 209. *See also* Atomic Energy Commission
nuclear waste: health effects of and search for redress by Iñupiat of northern Alaska, 77–93; and Marshall Islands, 303; proposed storage of at Hanford site, 150; Russia and importation of, 271; Yucca Mountain as proposed repository for, 193–94, 203, 204, 208–10, 306. *See also* cleanup; Superfund sites
Nuclear Wastelands (Makhijani et al. 1995), 125
Nuclear Waste Policy Act (1982), 148, 150
Nuclear Waste Projects Office (NWPO), 194, 202–208
nuclear weapons policy: and Bush administration, 11, 117–18, 309; and Kennedy administration, 308
nuclear weapons production, and health results of Chelyabinsk accidents in 1950s and 1960s, 249–73
nuclear weapons testing: activism and legacy of in Marshall Islands, 213–43; downwinders in US and health assessment studies, 193–210; downwinders in US and Radiation Exposure Compensation Act, 123–26; and human-subjects research in Marshall Islands, 26–27, 38–44; and legacy of Cold War, 1–18, 299–312; national security and development policy, 117–18; and proving grounds for US, 3–4; and secrecy in Soviet Republic of Kazakhstan, 277–96. *See also* downwinders; fallout; Nevada Test Site; radiation

Oakridge National Laboratory (Tennessee), 32, 147
Okinawa, US occupation of, 66–67
O'Leary, Hazel, 129, 309
O'Neill, Dan, 82
Operation Body Snatch, 32
Operation Crossroads, 29–30, 219, 303
Operation Dominic II, *196f*
Operation Hardtack, 40, 59
Operation Sunshine, 32, 36
Operation Teapot, 32
Operation Upshot-Knothole, 197–98
Oppenheimer, J. Robert, 300, 301

Oregon, and Hanford Health Information Network, 154. *See also* Columbia River
others and othering, and nuclear legacy of Cold War, 301–302
Our Depleted Society (Melman 1965), 308
Owens, Wayne, 132

Pacific Health Research Institute (PHRI), 41, 243n8
Pakistan, and nuclear weapons testing, 4, 307
Patriot Act, 117
Paul, D. B., 28
Pauling, Linus, 61, 70
Peace Corps, 216, 217
peace dividend, 160
Péna, Federico, 165
Peru, and human-subjects research, 35–36
Peters, F. Whitten, 35
Phoenix of Hiroshima (ship), 58, 59–60, 64, 67–69
Physicians for Social Responsibility, 70
pitchblende, 101
Plutonium Files (Welsome), 283–84
Point Barrow (Alaska), 34
Point Hope (Alaska), 79–93
politics, and Cold War influences on science, 305–307. *See also* activism
Porter, Jon, 209–10
posttraumatic stress disorder, and radiation exposure, 255–56
Powers, Francis Gary, 251
Preston, Diana, 111n1
Price, David, 14, 188n1
Private Ownership of Special Nuclear Materials Act (1964), 119
Project Chariot, 79, 81, 82, 89
Project 4.1, 39–40, 214, 215, 220–21, 223
Project 48, 31
Project Gabriel, 8, 31–32, 39
Project Gnome, 5
Prospecting for Uranium (AEC 1951), 100
"protected peoples," and indigenous groups, 45
psychological trauma, and radiation exposure, 255–56
publication, differences in scientific venues for, 129–30
Public Health Practice Training Program, 151–52
Public Law 97–414, 125
Public Law 99–239, 215, 245
public participation, in cleanup plan for Rocky Flats site, 167, 179–88
Pueblo Indians, 103
Purvis-Roberts, Kathleen, 17–18
Putin, Vladimir, 271, 311–12

radiation: early atomic detonations and human-subjects research, 29–33; health effects of different forms of, 5–6, 229; latency period for health outcome of exposure to, 9; linear hypothesis for health effects of, 168. *See also* downwinders; fallout; health; uranium

Radiation Exposure Compensation Act of 1990 (RECA), 109, 110, 117–36, 201–202, 236, 244n11, 306
radiogenic community, 2, 6–7
radionuclide soil action level (RSAL), and Rocky Flats site, 173, 174, 175, 176–78, 184
Radionuclide Soil Action Level (RSAL) Working Group, 168, *169t*, 181–82, 184
radiophobia, use of term in Russia, 261, 287, 307
radon, and uranium mining, 120, 121, 122, 123
radium, 98, 119
Rand Corporation, 8
Reagan administration, and government relations with Native tribes, 159
Red Valley Uranium Radiation Victims Committee, 130
reflexivity, and anthropological fieldwork, 90
Reistrup, J. V., 130
religion. *See* Mormon Church; Muslims; shamanism
Republic of Kazakhstan Institute of Nonproliferation, 284–88
resistance, and tradeoffs in cleanup plan for Rocky Flats site, 178
Reynolds, Akie, 68, 69
Reynolds, Earle, 14, 55–72, 304, 305
Río Puerco, and radioactive contamination, 104
risk research, and "blame-affixing adversarial model," 160–61
Rita village (Marshall Islands), 41
river-borne release, of radiation, 147, 148, 157–58. *See also* Columbia River; Savannah River; T River
Robust Nuclear Earth Penetrator (RNEP), 117–18
Roche, Marcel, 37, 38
Rocky Flats Cleanup Agreement Focus Group (RFCA) Focus Group, 168, *169t*, 183–84
Rocky Flats Council of Local Governments (RFCLOG), 168, *169t*, 183
Rocky Flats Environmental Technology Site (Colorado), 165–88, 310
Rocky Flats History Project, 168, *169t*
Rocky Mountain News, *169t*, 250
ROMIR Monitoring, 271
Rongelap Atoll (Marshall Islands), 26, 27, 39–44, 220, 225, 229, 230, 235, 284
Rongerik Atoll (Marshall Islands), 39, 217
Roscoe, Robert J., 123
rubidium-90, 5–6
Rumyantsev, Alexander, 271
Russia: and defense industry, 263–65; and environmental movement, 252, 267–68, 271, 311–12; and legacy of Chelyabinsk nuclear accidents, 265–73; and Ministry of Atomic Ener 262–63. *See also* Soviet Union
Rylko-Bauer, Barbara, 111n1
Ryzhkov, Yevgeny, 260–61, 270–72

Sadovnikov, Vitaly, 273
Sakharov, Andrei, 301

sample size, and epidemiological studies, 128–29
Sandia National Laboratories, 284–88
San Francisco Chronicle (newspaper), 69
San Juan River, and uranium mining, 104
Satterfield, Theresa, 16
Savannah River (South Carolina), 155
Scandinavia, and research in arctic regions, 34
Schaefer, Jack, 83, 84, 85, 86, 87, 88, 89, 94n10
science: Cold War and influence of politics on, 305–307; and nuclear testing in Soviet Republic of Kazakhstan, 284–88, 295; and political activism of Earle Reynolds, 69–72; and public participation in cleanup plans for Rocky Flats site, 168–78, 187, 189n2; and reparations for uranium miners and downwinders, 126–30; security state and control over, 7–9
Seattle Times (newspaper), 268–69
secrecy: and Chelyabinsk nuclear weapons facility, 250–51, 272–73, 311; and nuclear legacy of Cold War, 301; and nuclear testing in Soviet Republic of Kazakhstan, 277–96, 311; and political activism by scientists, 71; and reparations for uranium miners and downwinders, 127
security. *See* Homeland Security Agency; national security
Sedan nuclear test, 197
Semipalatinsk Nuclear Test Site (SNTS Kazakhstan), 277–96
Semipalatinsk Test Site: Creation, Operation, and Conversion, The (Shkolnik et al. 2002), 284–88, 290
Senate Energy and Natural Resources Committee, 231
Seth, Oliver, 198–99
Sever, Lowell, 158–59
shamanism, and Iñupiat, 92
Sharp, Harry Stephen, 85, 95n7
Shkolnik, Vladimir, 284–88
shock waves, and nuclear testing in Soviet Republic of Kazakhstan, 281–82, 286
Sibley, Margaret, 203–204
Silard, John, 61
Simon nuclear test, 195
Siri, William, 36
Slivyak, Vladimir, 271
Small Boy nuclear test, *196f*
Small Business Administration, 99
social movements, and antinuclear activism in Kazakhstan, 282–83
Social Security, 106
social services, Navajo uranium workers and lack of access to, 106–107
social status, and radiogenic communities, 2, 7
Society for Latin American Anthropology, 28
Solovyova, Nina, 260
songs, and nuclear legacy in Marshall Islands, 224–27
South Africa: and nuclear weapons testing, 4; and uranium mining, 98
South America, atomic agenda and indigenous popu-

lation research in, 35–38
Soviet Union: and Chelyabinsk nuclear disasters, 249–73; Cold War and secrecy in, 250–51, 272–73, 277–96, 306–307, 311; and nuclear proving grounds, 4; and nuclear testing in Arctic, 33, 296n3; and nuclear testing in Kazakhstan, 277–96; and political activism of Earle Reynolds, 64–66; and uranium mining, 112n1. *See also* Cold War; Russia
Speer, Albert, 3
Spokane Tribe (Washington), 156, 157, 161n6
Spranca, Mark, 177
Spykerman, Bryan, 107–108
staphylococcal enterotoxin B (PG), 40–41
state, and fundamental transformations in social meaning of government, 11–12
statistical significance, in epidemiological studies, 128–29
Stevens, Ted, 88–89
Stewardship Working Group (Rocky Flats site), 168, *169t*
Strassmann, Fritz, 98
stratospheric fallout, 5
strontium-90, 6, 8, 250–51
Suleimenov, Olzhas, 282, 295, 311
Superfund sites, 105, 155. *See also* cleanup; nuclear waste
support groups, and model for environmental justice, 109
suppression. *See* censorship and suppression
Supreme Court (US), 131
survival, and nuclear legacy of Cold War, 307–309, 311
Sylvia Barnson et al. v. Foote Mineral Col, Vanadium Corporation, and the United States, 131

taboo tradeoffs, and values, 177
Tatars (Russia), 252, 253, 254, 258, 259, 269, 272
Taylor, Grant, 57
Techa River (Soviet Union), 251, 253–54, 256–57, 259, 260, 269, 270, 271, 273, 283
Teller, Edward, 81, 88, 305–306
Tetlock, Philip E., 177, 178
Thompson, E. P., 300
Three Mile Island accident (1979), 161n1
thyroid disease, and radiation exposure, 147, 150, 152–54, 201
Tierney, Patrick, 27, 28, 38
Tikigaq Native Corporation, 83–84
toxic tracer chemicals, in nuclear weapons, 231
tradeoffs, and Rocky Flats cleanup plan, 171–78, 182, 186–87, 188
Trinity nuclear test, 219, 278–79
tropospheric fallout, 5
Truman, Preston Jay, 130, 134
trust territories, and United Nations covenants, 45. *See also* Marshall Islands
Turapin, Col. S. L., 289
Turner, Edith, 14